# Gourmet Gallery

Presented By

## The Stuart Society

D1607206

*MUSEUM of FINE ARTS*

255 BEACH DRIVE NORTH    ST PETERSBURG, FLORIDA

*First Printing*     10,000
*Second Printing*   10,000
*Third Printing*     10,000
*Fourth Printing*    12,000

International Standard Book Number—0-918544-88-2

For additional copies, use order blanks in back of book or write:
Gourmet Gallery Cookbook
255 Beach Drive North
St. Petersburg, Florida 33701
**Checks should be made payable to Gourmet Gallery Cookbook for the amount of $9.95 plus $1.55 postage and handling per book. For Florida delivery add 4% sales tax per book.**

**Printed in the United States of America**
**WIMMER BROTHERS FINE PRINTING & LITHOGRAPHY**
**Memphis, TN 38118**
*"Cookbooks of Distinction"*™

# ORIGINAL COOKBOOK COMMITTEE

| | |
|---|---|
| Chairman | Mrs. J. Milton Newton |
| | |
| Indexing and Editing | Mrs. James P. Bennett |
| Co-chairman | Mrs. John W. Barger |
| Promotion | Mrs. Edgar Andruss |
| | Mrs. Richard W. Buckingham |
| Recipe Commentary | Mrs. Thomas S. Miller |
| Advisors | Mrs. Malcolm Gray |
| | Mr. William W. W. Knight |
| | Mrs. Homer Moyer |
| Restaurants | Mrs. Richard Hilburn |
| | Mr. Peter Kersker |
| History | Mrs. Edmund Read |
| | Mrs. Harman Wheeler |
| | |
| Illustrations by | Diane Tonelli |

## Recipe Chairmen

| | |
|---|---|
| Mrs. Vance Bishop | Mrs. John D. Harris, Jr. |
| Mrs. William Brown | Mrs. John B. Lake |
| Mrs. Cecil H. Deighton | Miss Charlotte Lake |
| Mrs. Charles K. Donegan | Mrs. Angel P. Perez |
| Mrs. Thomas Dreier | Mrs. Robert V. Workman |

The Gourmet Gallery Committee expresses sincere appreciation to the members of the Museum of Fine Arts and friends who contributed recipes, time and their efforts so generously, all of which have made this book possible.

# Museum of Fine Arts

There is a taste for the old and a taste for the new, and there is always a taste for taste. Museums are usually regarded as leaders of taste; by their thoughtful study and selectivity they introduce to us those enduring standards of quality in the visual arts that have appealed to many generations. We know, too, that artists by the cultivation of their sensitivities are always opening up new awareness of life's many varieties of experience. The painter Ingres brought new understanding of the violin to his contemporaries, and it is well known that Rossini's banquets were as impressive as his operas.

This cookbook has been prepared by the Stuart Society for our Museum of Fine Arts. This Society, named in honor of Mrs. Margaret Acheson Stuart, the Museum's founder, was instituted in 1963 "to promote the welfare of the Museum, to stimulate public interest and participation in its activities . . ."

In 1961, with the assistance of leading local citizens and the encouragement of the City Council, Mrs. Stuart formed a non-profit corporation to provide an art museum for St. Petersburg. She also established an endowment fund for operations and made a substantial initial contribution towards construction of the building which was opened in February, 1965, under the guidance of Rexford Stead, its first Director.

Today the Museum is an important cultural center for the Southeastern states. In its galleries the art of many ages and periods is represented. It houses an outstanding art reference library, and its handsomely equipped theatre, the Marly room, adds another dimension for lectures and the performing arts.

Since 1963 the Stuart Society has been the Museum's invaluable auxiliary, attracting a group of dedicated and talented women to its service. It has not only accompanied the Museum's first steps, but has consistently fulfilled its purpose by undertaking projects such as the publication of this most welcome cookbook.

Lee Malone
**Director**

# ST. PETERSBURG — THE SUNSHINE CITY

"It'll never amount to much anyway, so its name won't make much difference," snapped Josef Henschen when the post office people were pressing for a name for the new community on Pinellas Point in 1888. "Why not call it St. Petersburg?"

So it became St. Petersburg, and namesake for the home town of Henschen's partner in bringing the narrow guage railroad to the Gulf of Mexico, Peter A. Demens. St. Petersburg in Russia is now known as Leningrad. The first train chugged in here on April 30, 1888.

Until the comical Orange Belt Railroad came to the Point, there had been little settlement here. Oh, there has been habitation for centuries, first came the colorful Mound Builders tribes of Indians. The Spanish Conquistadors flirted with the area, Ponce de Leon scraped barnacles off his ships here; Panfilo de Narvaez got into a scrape with the Indian chief here; Hernando de Soto was in the area.

The "father" of St. Petersburg was Gen. John C. Williams, formerly of Detroit, who came in 1875, laid out the city's wide streets here and spurred development.

The city's healthful clime gained worldwide publicity in 1885 when Dr. W. C. VanBibber of Baltimore read a paper at the American Medical Association convention in New Orleans proclaiming St. Petersburg as the "Health City" the A.M.A. had sought for a decade.

On Leap Day — February 29 — in 1892, St. Petersburg's few residents voted by a narrow margin of 15 to 11 to incorporate.

Famed developer Henry B. Plant got interested in the Pinellas area and in 1893 acquired the old Orange Belt Railroad and replaced its narrow gauge with standard tracks. He built the Belleview Biltmore Hotel at Belleair and the entire peninsula blossomed.

Tired of being the "stepchild" of Hillsborough County, the western portion agitated for secession. In 1907, W. L. Straub, editor of the **St. Petersburg Times** issued a "Declaration of Independence" for his neighbors. Finally, the 1911 Legislature created Pinellas County.

The community began to capitalize on its enviable sunshine in 1910 when Maj. Lew B. Brown, publisher of the evening newspaper, **The Independent,** promised to give away all copies of his newspaper every day the sun didn't shine on St. Petersburg! The newspaper continues a similar offer to this very day.

The year 1914 was exciting and significant. On New Year's Day, the intrepid pilot Tony Jannus flew the first commercial airline in his airboat from St. Petersburg to Tampa. And in the Spring of the year, Mayor Al Lang had persuaded the St. Louis Browns to train in the city, thus beginning the annual trek to Florida by pro teams.

The Florida real estate boom of the mid-20s was active in St. Petersburg. Developments developed, 10 big hotels were erected downtown, new streets were laid. Gandy Bridge was constructed to connect St. Petersburg with Tampa in 1924. The "Million Dollar Pier" was erected. Tourists flocked here.

In the Spring of 1973 it was announced that St. Petersburg had been named the All-American City, a much sought after award of the National Municipal League and the **Saturday Evening Post.**

"Yesterday's St. Petersburg," by Hampton Dunn

# ABBREVIATIONS USED IN THIS BOOK

Cup _____ c.
Tablespoon _____ T.
Teaspoon _____ t.
Pound _____ lb.
Ounce _____ oz.
Gallon _____ gal.

Medium _____ med.
Package _____ pkg.
Quart _____ qt.
Dozen _____ doz.
Pint _____ pt.

Our "Easy Gourmet" symbol will be found by
the recipes we consider quick and easy
and yet strictly gourmet fare.

# TABLE OF CONTENTS

BEVERAGES

FIRST COURSE

APPETIZERS

SOUPS

# HELPFUL HINTS FOR PARTIES

Here are a few quick and easy party food ideas for that day in your life when time is of the essence and yet the show (or party) must go on. Many of the ingredients are not unusual and you may have them on hand.

Cut the crusts from white bread, roll flat, spread with mayonnaise mixed with blue cheese. Add a little Worcestershire and dill. Lay an asparagus spear in the middle and roll as a jelly roll. Brush with melted butter and brown in the oven.

Wrap half strip raw bacon around a Waverly cracker, overlapping seam. Place on rack in a shallow pan and bake at 200 degrees 1 hour.

Split dates; remove the pits and stuff with a cube of cheddar cheese. Wrap half slice raw bacon around date; fasten with toothpick and broil until bacon is crisp.

Wrap a 2 lb. block of Brie cheese in your favorite pie crust recipe. Mix an egg and water and brush the top. Bake at 400 degrees until crust is brown. Serve warm; cut into thin wedges.

Work a cup of cheese into your pie crust recipe and wrap small bits around stuffed olives, pitted dates, cocktail sausages . . . bake 10-15 minutes.

Marinate canned mushrooms in French garlic or Italian dressing. Let stand in refrigerator overnight. Serve with toothpicks.

Add 1 cup Parmesan cheese, ¼ teaspoon nutmeg, ⅛ teaspoon pepper to our cream puff recipe. Drop by scant teaspoon on ungreased cookie sheet. Bake 20 minutes. Fill with chicken salad or serve as is.

# APPETIZERS

## ANGELS ON HORSEBACK

1-12 oz. jar oysters
2 T. chopped parsley
½ t. salt
Paprika
Pepper
8 slices bacon, cut

Yields 20 to 25

Drain oysters. Cut each slice bacon into thirds. Place oyster on each piece bacon. Sprinkle with parsley and seasonings, roll up and secure with toothpicks. Place in pan on broiler rack and broil 15 minutes turning until bacon is crisp and oysters curl.

## ARTICHOKE APPETIZER

1-8½ oz. can artichokes
French dressing
6 oz. cream cheese
¼ c. cream
2 T. grated onion
Dash Tabasco
1 oz. caviar

Serves 10

Marinate artichokes in French dressing over night. Drain and pour dressing back into bottle. Cream the cheese and cream. Add onion and Tabasco. Cut artichokes into quarters, making 32 or halves making 16. Put cheese mixture on artichokes and top each with small amount caviar.

## BENNE (SESAME) SEED COCKTAILERS

2 c. flour
1 t. salt
¼ t. cayenne pepper
¾ c. margarine
Ice water
1 c. roasted benne seed
  (sesame seeds)

Yields several dozen

Mix dry ingredients; cut in shortening; add enough ice water to make a dough the consistency of pie crust, add seed. Roll dough into rolls about 1½ inches across. Wrap in waxed paper; chill thoroughly. Cut into thin wafers, place on cookie sheet and bake at 300 degrees 15 to 20 minutes. Before removing from pan and while hot, sprinkle with salt. These may be kept in covered tin or cracker jar, and before serving run into a slow oven to crisp.

## BLACK OLIVE AND CHEESE DIP

**1 roll smoked hickory
  cheese (squeeze type pkg.)**
**Few drops liquid smoke**
**1 small can chopped black
  olives (about ¼ cup)**
**¼ c. finely chopped onion**

Combine all ingredients in pan, and heat until cheese melts. Serve as dip or spread with crackers or chips.

## BOURBON HOT DOGS

**1 pkg. all beef hot dogs**
**¾ c. bourbon**
**¾ c. brown sugar**
**½ c. catsup**

**Serves 12**

Slice hot dogs into bite-size pieces. Mix the bourbon, catsup and brown sugar together and simmer until sugar is dissolved. Add the hot dogs and pour into a chafing dish and serve.

*Use 1 cup each bourbon, brown sugar and chili sauce. Add Polish sausage cut into bite-size pieces.*

## RUM HOT DOGS

**1 lb. wieners or sausage**
**½ c. brown sugar**
**1 c. soy sauce**
**1 c. golden Rum**
**2 t. onion, grated**

**Serves 10**

Cut sausage into bite size slices and heat in soy sauce and brown sugar. Add onion and simmer 20 minutes. Put in chafing dish. Add rum and ignite. Serve with toothpicks.

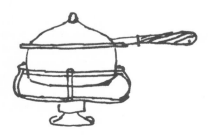

# BROCCOLI DIP

½ c. butter
1 c. chopped onion
2 pkgs. frozen chopped
 broccoli
1-4 oz. can mushrooms
1½ rolls garlic cheese
1 t. Accent
1½ cups slivered almonds
2 cans mushroom soup
Tabasco to taste
Worcestershire to taste
Beau Monde to taste

Serves 25

Saute onions in butter until soft. Add broccoli and simmer until tender. Add remainder of ingredients. Serve in chafing dish with corn chips.

# CAPONATO

4 to 6 c. peeled, cubed
 eggplant
⅓ c. olive oil
1 large onion, sliced and
 separated into rings
1 clove garlic, crushed
2 tomatoes, quartered
2 T. capers
⅓ c. wine vinegar
1 T. sugar, heaping
½ c. sliced green olives

Heat oil in heavy skillet; add eggplant cubes, onions, and garlic. Saute until eggplant is tender. Cool. Add tomatoes, capers, vinegar, sugar and olives. Marinate for at least an hour. Serve as antipasto.

# CAVIAR MOLD

3 envelopes unflavored
 gelatin
2 c. chicken broth
1-2 oz. jar black caviar
2 hard cooked eggs,
 chopped
¼ c. chopped scallion tops
Mayonnaise
1-2 oz. jar red caviar

Soften gelatin in broth; stir over medium heat until gelatin is dissolved. Chill until just slightly thickened. Divide into three portions of ⅔ cup each. Fold red caviar into one portion. Fold chopped eggs, scallions and little mayonnaise into another. Fold black caviar into last. Pour red caviar mixture into lightly oiled 3 cup mold. Chill until set, but not firm. Pour egg mixture over; chill until set. Add black caviar portion last; chill until firm. Unmold; Garnish with parsley and sliced lemons.

15

# CELERY CHEESE BALLS

2-3 oz. pkgs. cream cheese
2 T. roquefort cheese,
  mashed
3 T. celery, finely chopped
1 T. onion, chopped
⅛ t. cayenne pepper
Mayonnaise
1½ c. pecans, finely
  chopped
16 thin pretzel sticks

**Yields 16**

Mash cheeses together; combine with other ingredients, reserving nuts. Add just enough mayonnaise to soften. Shape into balls about 1-inch in diameter. Roll in nuts, coating thick. Put pretzel stick in top of each ball.

# CHEDDAR-ALE CHEESE SPREAD

6 c. shredded cheddar
  cheese (about 1½ lbs.)
1 pkg. (3 oz.) cream cheese
4 T. soft butter or margarine
¾ c. ale or beer
1 t. dry mustard
¼ t. crushed red pepper
½ c. finely chopped walnuts
½ c. chopped parsley

**Yields 2 balls**

Blend cheddar, cream cheese and butter or margarine in a large bowl with electric mixer until smooth. Gradually add ale or beer, mustard and crushed red pepper. If mixture is very soft, refrigerate until firm enough to hold its shape.

Divide mixture in half and shape into 2 balls. Combine walnuts and parsley on a sheet of wax paper. Roll cheese balls in nut/parsley mixture to cover completely. Place on serving plates or boards and serve with crackers.

# CHEESE DREAMS

½ c. butter or margarine
1 c. sharp cheese, grated
½ pkg. crushed onion
  soup mix
1 c. flour, sifted
½ t. seasoned salt

**Yields 50**

"Flat Rock" version of
  Cheese Dreams:
Add 1 cup rice crispies
Increase seasoned salt to
  1 tablespoon
Decrease onion soup mix to
  1 tablespoon

Cream butter and cheese. While onion soup is still in its sealed envelope, roll it with rolling pin until well crushed. Measure half of contents (about 2½ tablespoons), and blend this into cheese and butter. Stir sifted flour and seasoned salt into mixture. Chill until easily handled, about one hour. Press dough through star form of cookie press onto ungreased cookie sheet; put knife mark every 1½ inches. Bake at 375 degrees 10-14 minutes. They should be light brown and crisp when done. WATCH CAREFULLY throughout baking time.

Baking time will be a little longer (14 to 18 minutes).

Cheese Press

# CHEESE STRAWS

1½ c. grated sharp cheese
1½ c. flour
1 t. baking powder
1 t. sugar
½ t. salt
½ c. butter
1 t. red pepper
  (or less, to taste)

**Yields 6 dozen**

Blend grated cheese and butter until smooth. Sift together flour, baking powder, sugar, salt and red pepper. Gradually blend the two mixtures together. Mix well. Put into cookie press and press out into long strips. Bake at 350 degrees for 18 minutes or until just lightly brown.

# CHICKEN LIVER PATE

**Topping:**
**1½ t. gelatin**
**1 can consomme**
**1 T. Cognac**
**Olives, pimientos.**

Soften gelatin in small amount consomme. Stir over heat until gelatin melts; pour in rest of consomme and cool. Add Cognac. Decorate bottom of 1 quart mold with olives and pimientos. Pour in consomme and chill until set.

**Pate:**
**1½ lb. chicken livers**
**2 t. salt**
**1½ c. soft butter**
**Pinch cayenne, cloves**
**½ t. nutmeg**
**6 T. onion, grated**
**Cognac to taste**

Saute livers for 15-20 minutes until done. Put through finest blade of food chopper while hot. Blend well with rest of ingredients; put into mold over gelatin. Chill till set.

**Serves 15**

# CHIPPED BEEF DIP

**8 oz. cream cheese**
**2 T. milk**
**1 jar (2½ oz.) dried beef**
**¼ c. chopped green pepper**
**½ t. garlic salt**
**¼ t. pepper**
**2 T. dry onion flakes**
**½ c. sour cream**
**½ c. chopped nuts**
**2 T. melted margarine**
**½ t. salt**

Combine first seven ingredients; mix thoroughly. Fold in sour cream. Saute nuts in melted margarine; add salt. Sprinkle over above mixture; bake in a small pyrex dish 20 minutes in a 350 degree oven. Let stand 10 minutes before serving. Serve hot with large corn chips or assorted crackers.

**Serves 8 to 10**

*To make a similar hot crabmeat appetizer, substitute 1 1/2 cups flaked crabmeat for the chipped beef; add 1/2 teaspoon cream style horseradish. Spread 1/3 cup sliced, toasted almonds on top.*

# CHUTNEY CHEESE LOG

**8 oz. pkg. cream cheese**
**½ jar Major Grey's Chutney**
**(chopped fine)**
**½ c. slivered almonds,**
**sauteed**
**1 to 2 T. curry powder**
**(according to taste)**

Soften cheese; add other ingredients. Shape into log and roll in almonds. Refrigerate.

Serve with crackers.

# CORN APPETIZERS

**1½ c. flour**
**2½ t. baking powder**
**1 t. salt**
**¼ t. pepper**
**2 eggs, slightly beaten**
**⅓ c. milk**
**1–12 oz. can whole kernel**
**corn**
**1-8½ oz. can cream style**
**corn**
**⅔ c. bacon, fried and**
**crumbled**

**Yields 45 to 50**

Sift dry ingredients. Combine egg, milk, corn and bacon. Add to dry ingredients. Mix until well moistened. Drop by teaspoonsful into hot oil. Fry until golden brown.

# CRABMEAT DIP

**1-3 oz. pkg. cream cheese**
**½ c. mayonnaise**
**½ c. tomato soup**
**1 can (6½ oz.) crab meat**
**1 clove garlic, minced**
**1 t. Worcestershire sauce**
**Salt and pepper to taste**

Blend the ingredients together and serve warm in a chafing dish with favorite chips for dipping.

# CREAMY CRAB COMBO

**1 can of cream of shrimp**
**soup, undiluted**
**1 can of flaked king crab**
**(or frozen)**
**⅓ c. mayonnaise**

Heat all together very slowly, stirring often. Keep hot in a chafing dish. Serve with Triscuits.

# FASOLA DIP

4 c. great northern beans
½ c. olive oil
1 cucumber, chopped
3 green onions, chopped
2 cloves of garlic, minced
½ c. feta cheese crumbled
¼ c. lemon juice
1 t. salt

Cook beans according to directions on package (cook with ham hock or bacon). Drain. Mash and add other ingredients, chill overnight. Good served with cracker or rye round.

# DEVILED HAM AND CHEESE APPETIZERS

2 c. self-rising flour
½ t. dill
¼ c. shortening
½ t. dry mustard
1-4½ oz. can deviled ham
½-¾ c. milk
2-5 oz. jars pastuerized
   process cheese spread

Yields 60

Sift flour and seasonings; cut in shortening until mixture resembles coarse crumbs. Mix in ham. Blend in enough milk to make soft dough. Turn out onto lightly floured surface; knead gently 30 seconds. Roll out ¼ inch thick; cut with floured ⅝ inch cutter. Place on ungreased baking sheet. Bake at 450 degrees 10-12 minutes or until lightly browned. Pipe 1 teaspoon cheese through pastry tube atop each.

# GUACAMOLE DIP

3 large avocados
1 t. lemon juice
1 clove garlic, crushed
1 can (4 oz.) peeled green
   chilies, chopped
1 t. salt
Cayenne pepper to taste

Mash ripe avocados until almost smooth, but with a few chunks showing. Mix well with lemon juice, garlic and peeled peppers. Add salt and cayenne.
Serve with raw vegetables or chips.

# HAM BALLS IN CRANBERRY-ORANGE SAUCE

1½ lbs. ground fully-cooked
  or canned ham
1½ c. soft torn bread
  crumbs
½ c. milk
¼ c. finely chopped onion
1 egg
½ c. sugar
2 T. cornstarch
1 c. orange juice
¼ c. vinegar
1 c. whole cranberry sauce
1 c. diced orange

Yields 5 dozen

Combine ham, bread crumbs, milk, onion and egg; mix well. Shape into balls using 1 level tablespoonful of meat for each. Arrange in greased shallow baking pan. Bake 375 degree oven until meat is lightly browned, 20 to 25 minutes. It is not necessary to turn ham balls during cooking.

To prepare sauce while balls are baking, combine sugar and cornstarch in saucepan; mix. Stir in orange juice and vinegar. Cook, stirring constantly until clear and thickened. Add cranberry sauce and orange; mix and heat. Arrange hot ham balls in heated chafing dish. Pour sauce over them; keep hot.

# HOLIDAY HAM BALL

1 lb. ground ham
1 c. raisins
1 onion, grated
1 t. curry powder
¾ c. mayonnaise
8 oz. pkg. cream cheese
1 T. milk
Dash Tabasco

Combine first five ingredients; mound into nice shape. Blend milk with cream cheese; add Tabasco. Frost mounded ham with cream cheese mixture; chill. Serve with bland-flavored crackers like toast rounds.

# MEATBALLS PIQUANT

1 lb. lean ground beef
1 med. size minced onion
1 egg, beaten
1 t. garlic powder
1 t. parsley
Dash Worcestershire sauce
¼ c. milk
Bread crumbs

Sauce:
12 oz. jar chili sauce
10 oz. jar grape jelly

Yields 24 balls

Mix the first seven ingredients together and add enough bread crumbs to hold together. Form into small balls and brown in cooking oil. While meatballs are browning, mix in another pan the chili sauce and grape jelly. Remove meatballs from skillet and add to jelly mixture. Simmer 30 minutes. Serve in chafing dish.

# MEATBALLS WITH MARMALADE SOY SAUCE

2 egg yolks or 1 whole egg
½ c. water
½ c. packaged bread
  crumbs
2 T. prepared horseradish
1 c. finely chopped water
  chestnuts
1 lb. ground chuck beef

Preheat oven to 350 degrees. In bowl beat egg with water; stir in bread crumbs, horseradish, water chestnuts and ground beef. Mix gently with hands and shape into one-inch balls. Place in greased shallow pan and bake 12 minutes.

⅓ c. orange marmalade
1 clove garlic, minced
2 T. fresh lemon juice
⅓ c. cold water
¼ c. soy sauce

Yields 44 balls

Mix all ingredients in pan, and cook to boiling point. Place in chafing dish and add meat balls as they are needed. Makes 1 cup. Use toothpicks for meatballs. Sauce and balls can be served in separate dishes. Keep warm.

*Good as a main dish also; make meatballs larger and pour the sauce over them; add garnish.*

# MEXICAN EMPANADITAS

1 recipe 2 crust pie shell
½ lb. ground beef
1 c. choppd onion
1 c. chopped green pepper
1 c. chopped ripe tomato
1 clove garlic, finely
  chopped
¼ c. raisins
1½ t. cornstarch
1 t. salt
1 t. sugar
½ t. pepper
½ t. Tabasco
¼ c. Sherry (dry)

**Yields 24**

Brown beef; add onion, pepper, tomato and garlic. Simmer 10 minutes. Stir in remaining ingredients; simmer 5 minutes. Divide pastry into 24 balls. Roll each ball into a 2½ inch circle. Place 1 large table-spoon beef mixture in center. Fold in half; seal edges with fork. Place on ungreased cookie sheet; bake at 425 degrees 12-15 minutes, or until lightly browned.

# ITALIAN STUFFED MUSHROOMS

12 large mushrooms
2 T. butter or margarine
1 med. onion, finely chopped
2 oz. pepperoni, diced
  (about ½ c.)
¼ c. finely chopped green
  pepper
1 clove garlic, minced
½ c. finely crushed rich
  round crackers (about 12)
3 T. grated parmesan cheese
1 T. snipped parsley
½ t. seasoned salt
¼ t. dried oregano, crushed
Dash pepper
⅓ c. chicken broth

**Yields 12**

Wash mushrooms. Remove stems; finely chop stems and reserve. Drain caps on paper toweling. Melt butter or margarine in skillet; add onion, pepperoni, green pepper, garlic and chopped mushroom stems. Cook until vegetables are tender but not brown. Add cracker crumbs, cheese, parsley, seasoned salt, oregano and pepper; mix well. Stir in chicken broth. Spoon stuffing into mushroom caps, rounding tops. Place in shallow baking pan with about ¼ inch of water covering bottom of pan. Bake, uncovered, in 325 degree oven 25 minutes, or until heated through.

*These may also be used as a first course (with 2 mushrooms per serving), or as a main course (with 6 mushrooms per serving).*

# HEAVENLY NUTS

8 oz. whole walnuts
8 oz. whole almonds
2 egg whites, stiffly beaten
⅛ t. salt
1 c. sugar
½ c. butter, melted

Beat egg whites until soft peaks form. Fold in salt and add sugar gradually, beating constantly, until stiff peaks form. Mix in nuts until evenly coated. Pour melted butter on cookie sheet; add nuts. Bake at 325 degrees 30 minutes, stirring at 10-minute intervals.

# HERBED PECANS

3 T. butter or margarine
3 T. Worcestershire sauce
1 t. salt
½ t. ground cinnamon
¼ t. garlic powder
¼ t. cayenne
Dash bottled hot pepper
  sauce
1 lb. pecan halves

Yields 4 cups

In heavy skillet, melt butter or margarine. Stir in Worcestershire sauce, salt, cinnamon, garlic powder, cayenne, and hot pepper sauce. Add pecans; toss till nuts are well coated. Place in single layer in 15½x10½x1 inch baking pan. Bake in 300 degree oven 20 to 25 minutes, stirring often until nuts are brown and crisp.

# ONION CANAPES

2 bunches green onions,
  tops and bottoms, chopped
1 small onion, chopped
2 c. mayonnaise
1 lb. bacon, fried and
  crumbled
1 lb. sharp cheddar cheese,
  grated
2 loaves thin sliced bread

Combine onions, mayonnaise, bacon and cheese. Put through food grinder or put in blender and mix thoroughly. Cut bread into desired shapes. Spread mixture on bread and brown under broiler. Toast rounds can be used instead of bread.

## SMOKED OYSTER DIP

1-8 oz. pkg. cream cheese
¼ t. lemon juice
1 t. Worcestershire
½ t. soy sauce
1 clove garlic, halved
1 can smoked oysters

Blend first four ingredients; add garlic. Chop oysters; add. Remove garlic. Serve with small crackers. To thin dip, add sour cream.

## PANAMANIAN CEVICHE

5 lbs. any white fish, boned
3 onions, minced
2 c. lime juice
Salt to taste
1-2 small hot red peppers, minced
1 T. olive oil

Serves a crowd

Chop raw fish in very small pieces. Put in glass or china dish as you chop and keep coverd with lime juice at all times. Add other ingredients and mix with wooden spoon (no metal, please!) Store covered in the refrigerator overnight, or for 2 or 3 days. Serve on tiny pastry shells; or let each guest place a teaspoonful on a saltine cracker. If this is too hot for American palates, chop part of the peppers in large chunks and remove after marinating.

*This recipe comes from a friend living in Panama. Be brave and try it at your next cocktail party.*

## PICKLED BLACKEYED PEAS

4 c. cooked blackeyed peas
1 c. oil
½ c. vinegar
¼ c. thinly sliced onions
½ t. salt
Dash of black pepper
6 cloves garlic

Serves 12

Combine all ingredients. Place in bowl and refrigerate a week or two.

# PICKLED OYSTERS

½ gallon oysters
3 sticks cinnamon
4 blades of mace (1 t.
  ground mace may be
  substituted)
1 T. grain pepper
1 T. allspice
1 T. salt
1 t. whole cloves
1 pt. vinegar
1 pod red pepper

Drain all liquor off oysters and put them in skillet. Add cinnamon, mace, grain pepper, allspice, salt and cloves. Steam until gills turn (they will be dark and ruffled around edges; cook not more than 10 minutes). Chill thoroughly; add vinegar and red pepper.

*May be served as Hors d'oeuvres or as a sideboard snack during the holidays.*

# PSARI PSOMI

1 loaf Greek bread (large)
Butter
2 c. grated cheddar cheese
½ c. ripe olives
2 T. chopped pimiento
½ c. mayonnaise
3-8 oz. pkgs. cream cheese
1 lb. 4½ oz. can crushed
  pineapple

Serves 20 to 24

Thinly slice bread, cutting to within ½ inch of bottom. Butter both sides of each slice. Mix cheddar cheese, ripe olives, pimiento and mayonnaise together. Fill each slice with cheese mixture; wrap bread in foil; refrigerate. Mix cream cheese with enough pineapple juice until of spreading consistency. Add crushed drained pinapple. Before serving, spread pineapple-cheese mixture over sides and top of loaf. Garnish with olives, tomatoes and pineapple.

# BABY PIZZAS

1½ c. sharp cheese, grated
½ c. butter
1½ c. flour
Dash salt
Filling:
1-6 oz. can tomato paste
1 t. oregano
1 t. garlic juice
½ onion, finely minced
Parmesan cheese

Yields 45

Blend ingredients well and roll into tiny balls (size of walnuts). Press in the top of each with your thumb to make somewhat of a wide hole. Refrigerate overnite.

Mix the tomato paste, onion and seasonings. Fill holes with the mixture and sprinkle each top with generous amount parmesan cheese.

Bake at 350 degrees for 15 minutes or until crust has baked.

## ROQUEFORT MOLD

1 envelope unflavored
  gelatin
¼ c. water
6 oz. Roquefort cheese
6 oz. cream cheese
½ c. heavy cream
½ onion, grated
10 black olives, minced
Dash salt and cayenne
  pepper

**Serves 10 to 15**

Soften gelatin in water over heat until dissolved. Cool. Blend the cheeses together, mixing well. Stir in cream, gelatin, olives, onion and seasonings. Pour into 3 cup mold and chill. Stir occasionally until set.

## SALMON MOLD

1 lb. can pink salmon, well
  drained, boned and skin
  removed
8 oz. cream cheese
1½ T. liquid smoke
1 T. finely chopped onion
Lemon juice to taste
1 c. chopped pecans
1 t. salt

Divide pecans. Blend ½ cup nuts with remaining ingredients. Mold into ball and cover with remaining nuts. This will freeze well.

# SAUERKRAUT BALLS

3 T. butter
1 onion, minced
1 clove garlic, crushed
1 c. minced cooked ham
1 c. minced cooked corned
  beef
6 T. flour
1 egg
Dash salt, M.S.G.,
  Worcestershire
1 T. parsley
2 c. drained, rinsed
  sauerkraut
½ c. bouillon
2 c. milk
2½ c. flour
2 c. dry bread crumbs
Deep fat

**Yields 4 dozen**

Saute onion and garlic until tender; stir in ham and corned beef. Simmer a few minutes. Blend in flour, egg and seasonings. Add sauerkraut and bouillon. Cook until thick. Chill. Shape into small walnut shaped balls. Mix milk with flour. Coat each ball evenly. Roll in bread crumbs and fry at 375 degrees until brown. Drain and serve warm with tooth picks.

# SEA FOOD DIP

4½ oz. can lobster, shrimp
  or crabmeat
8 oz. pkg. cream cheese
2 t. chili sauce
2 t. horseradish
⅓ c. mayonnaise
1 t. lemon juice
Salt to taste

**Yields 2 cups**

Soften cream cheese; add all other ingredients. Beat well with electric beater, and chill 2 hours.

## SHRIMP DIP

1 can shrimp soup
1-8 oz. pkg. cream cheese
1-7 oz. can crabmeat
1 c. shrimp, chopped
1-3 oz. jar cocktail onions
1 T. Worcestershire

**Serves 15 to 20**

Combine all ingredients and heat together before pouring into chafing dish. Serve with Melba rounds or Doritos.

## SHRIMP MARINADE

5 lbs. shrimp, cooked in
  pickling spices
2 c. onion, finely chopped
2½ c. vegetable oil
1 c. white vinegar
Juice of two lemons
5 T. celery seed
3 t. salt
⅛ t. Worcestershire sauce
Dash of Tabasco

**Serves 15 to 20**

Mix all ingredients together. Best results are obtained when shrimp are placed in marinade at least 24 hours before serving. When ready to serve, lift shrimp with slotted spoon into deep bowl. Spoon a small amount of marinade over them.

## MUSHROOM SANDWICHES

1 lb. fresh mushrooms, or
  8 oz. can
4 T. butter
3 T. Sherry
½ c. cream
2 T. cornstarch
Salt and pepper
Dash cayenne
1 loaf thin sliced bread

**Yields about 5 dozen**

Put mushrooms through fine blade of food grinder. Saute in butter; simmer until almost dry. Stir in Sherry, cream and cornstarch. Season to taste. Cook until thickened; cool. Spread between thin sliced bread. Stack 6 high; wrap and freeze. To serve, thaw and butter both sides; cut into 4 pieces. Put on cookie sheet; bake at 450 degrees, turning when brown. Serve hot.

# STEAK TARTARE
## (as an appetizer for two people)

2 eggs, separated
½ lb. sirloin steak (ground once)
1 t. chopped capers
¼ med. onion, minced (use any amount of onion to taste)
Chopped Anchovy filets to taste
Ground pepper to taste
Salt to taste
Dash of Worcestershire sauce
Dash of dry English mustard
Dry red wine to taste (facsimile of a Bordeaux is fine)
½ t. brandy or cognac

Mix ONLY 1 egg white with the ground meat. Mix in ALL other ingredients except egg yolk. Form into balls, making a well in each in which to place egg yolk. Please ask your guests to mix the egg yolk into the mixture before eating.

Serve with party rye or similar dark bread.

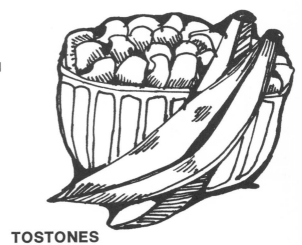

## TOSTONES

3 green plantains
8 c. water
2 cloves garlic, peeled and crushed
2 T. salt
2 c. vegetable oil or lard, for frying

Peel the plantains and cut into diagonal slices ½ inch thick. Add the garlic to 4 cups of water and soak the plantain slices for 15 minutes. Drain well and fry in the oil or lard to 350 degrees for around 7 minutes. Remove from the pan and place on absorbent paper. Mash the slices flat and soak in 4 cups water that has been salted, and remove immediately. Drain thoroughly on absorbent paper. Heat oil or lard to 375 degrees and fry plantain slices until golden. Drain on absorbent paper and sprinkle lightly with salt. Use as an hors d'oeuvre with your favorite sauce.

Serves 12

# BEVERAGES

## COCKTAILS

### AGGRAVATION

1½ oz. Scotch
1 oz. Kahlua
Milk
Ice

Yields 1

Fill a milk punch glass with ice. Pour Scotch and Kahula in glass. Fill with milk and blend well. May be put into a blender.

*This is a very good milk punch. Serve it instead of the usual Bloody Mary. A great way for the ulcer prone to start the day!*

### BORDER BUTTERMILK

1-6 oz. can frozen lemonade
  concentrate
1 lemonade can tequila

Serves 4 to 6

Put into blender fill with crushed ice and blend at high speed until smooth, frothy and milky looking.

### COFFEE ALEXANDER

1 oz. coffee flavored brandy
1 oz. brandy
1 oz. cream

Serves 1

Shake with ice and strain into champagne glass. Dust with powdered coffee.

# MARGARITA

1½ oz. tequila
½ oz. triple sec
½ lime, juiced

Serves 1

Blend in blender with crushed ice. Rub rim of cocktail glass with rind of lemon (or lime). Dip rim in salt and pour liquid in glass.


# MR. AND MRS. BILL SAMUELS, JR.'S
# PARTY MINT JULEP

Simple Syrup=
  2 parts sugar
  1 part water
Tender mint leaves
Maker's Mark Bourbon
Powdered sugar

Select tender spearmint leaves; crush in the quantity of Maker's Mark that you wish to prepare until you have the mint flavor most pleasing to you. Strain out mint leaves. Prepare simple syrup (make sure sugar is dissolved). Mix 1 part simple syrup to 4 parts mint-flavored bourbon. Can be prepared in advance and refrigerated in bottles. To serve: crush ice until pulverized; pack julep glass full. Pour in 2 ounces mix, sprinkle on ½ teaspoon powdered sugar and lay few mint leaves on top. Drink through a straw close to cup's rim so that aroma is inhaled while sipping.

*The Samuels family owns the distillery which makes Maker's Mark. They have an annual Derby Country Brunch at the distillery in Loretto, Ky. in the restored original farm house on the grounds. These juleps are served and they are fabulous.*


# ORANGE BLOSSOM

1½ oz. gin
1 oz. orange juice
1 t. sugar

Serves 1

Shake well with cracked ice. Strain into chilled 4½ ounce cocktail glass.

# PIÑA COLADA

**1 oz. coconut cream**
**1 oz. pineapple juice**
**4 pineapple chunks**
**1½ oz. light rum**

**Serves 1**

Blend coconut cream, pineapple juice and rum in a blender. Put pineapple chunks in a glass and pour mixture over.

# ELSIE WALLBANGER

**1 oz. vodka**
**½ oz. Galliano**
**1 oz. cream**
**Orange juice**

**Serves 1**

Blend the vodka, Galliano and cream. Pour over ice and fill glass with orange juice.

# HARVEY WALLBANGER

**1 oz. vodka**
**½ oz. Galliano**
**Ice**
**Orange juice**

**Serves 1**

Fill cocktail glass with ice; fill three fourths full with orange juice. Add vodka and stir. Top with Galliano.

# PUNCHES

## BANANA PUNCH

6 c. water
4 c. sugar
1-6 oz. can frozen orange
  juice
1-18 óz. can pineapple juice
6 bananas
4 lemons, juiced
1 gal. chilled ginger ale
2 c. rum (optional)

**Yields 2 gallons**

Boil water and sugar 4 minutes; cool. Blend bananas and lemon juice in blender. Add juices and banana mixture to sugar and water. Pour into containers (½ gallon milk cartons) and freeze. Can be kept up to 1 month. When ready to use, defrost until slushy and add equal amount chilled ginger ale. Stir in rum.

## CHAMPAGNE MELBA

1 bottle white wine (25 oz.)
1 bottle champagne
1 large bottle club soda
1-16 oz. can peach halves
Cloves

**Serves 14**

Pour chilled wine, champagne, and club soda into large punch bowl. Decorate peach halves with cloves (one for each guest). Float peach halves in punch round side up. Chill champagne glasses and place a peach half in each. Pour punch over peach.

*The longer the peaches stay in the punch the better thay become. If it's dessert time, give each guest a spoon so they can have the peach for dessert. Bourbon meat balls and small cream puffs filled with salmon salad makes a great party.*

# GEORGETOWN (KY) EGGNOG

6 eggs, separated
1 c. sugar
1 pt. whiskey
1 qt. whipping cream
Nutmeg

Serves 16 to 20

Beat yolks, add 2/3 cup sugar and beat until thick and lemon colored. Slowly pour whiskey over yolks, beating constantly. Set aside. Beat whites until stiff; add remaining sugar gradually. Fold whiskey mixture into whites. Beat cream and fold into mixture. Pour into punch bowl and sprinkle with nutmeg.

*If you wish to double the recipe, we suggest you follow the above ingredients for the first allotment but for the second, reduce the sugar to 2/3 cup and whiskey to 2/3 of a pint.*

# GLUWEIN

2 bottles red wine
Juice of 2 lemons
Juice of 2 oranges
2½ c. lump sugar*
½ bottle 151 proof rum
   (1¼ c.)

*In Germany they have a
   special sugar loaf made
   for this.

Serves 8 to 10

Heat wine in chafing dish; **do not boil.** Add orange and lemon juice. In the meantime slightly warm the rum. Put sugar on special flaming tongs and put them across top of chafing dish. Ladle rum over sugar and ignite. Turn lights out and watch blue flames of sugar melt down into the wine. Serve in heat-resistant glasses or cups. For a lighter party punch it may be made ahead without flaming; only use ½ to 1 cup of a lower proof rum and heat all ingredients together.

35

# SOUTHERN EGGNOG

**12 eggs, separated**
**3 c. sugar**
**1 qt. bourbon**
**1 pt. rum**
**1 pt. Cognac**
**1½ pt. milk**
**3½ pt. heavy cream**

**Serves 25**

Beat yolks well. Beat in sugar. Slowly stir in the rum and bourbon. Add milk. Beat cream until slightly thick. Add with Cognac to the milk and egg mix. Whip the whites until stiff. Fold in. Pour into punch bowl and sprinkle with nutmeg.

# GIN PUNCH

**12 lemons, juiced**
**20 oranges, juiced**
**6 oz. Grenadine**
**2 qts. gin**
**2 qts. Club Soda**

**Serves 20**

Combine all ingredients. Serve in a punch bowl with ice.

# HOT SPICED PUNCH

**1½ qt. cranberry juice**
**1-46 oz. pineapple juice**
**1 c. brown sugar**
**4½ t. ground cloves**
**4 sticks cinnamon, broken**
**¼ t. salt**

**Serves 30**

Put cranberry and pineapple juice in a 30 cup coffee maker; fill to 30 cup marker with water. Put sugar, cloves, cinnamon and salt in coffee basket. Perk thru cycle. Serve hot or cold.

# LEMONADE PUNCH

**3-6 oz. cans frozen pink
lemonade mix
1-6 oz. can water
1 c. pineapple juice
1 qt. lemon-lime soda**

**Serves 16**

Blend all ingredients together and serve cold.

# ORANGE VODKA PUNCH

**2 qts. orange sherbert
1 fifth vodka
2 cans frozen orange juice
Club soda**

**Serves 12-15**

Combine all ingredients and let stand one hour. Add 2 trays ice cubes and a little soda before serving.

*This is served every year at the St. Petersburg Beach Garden Club Christmas party.*

# POOR MAN'S PUNCH

**4 c. sugar
2 c. water
2 grated lemon rinds
1-8 oz. bottle Real lemon
juice
2 c. very strong tea
1 t. salt
1 t. vanilla
3 t. almond extract**

**Serves 20**

Mix sugar, water, lemon rind and bring to boil. Boil gently 2 minutes. Cool. Add lemon juice, tea, salt and extracts. Let blend for 3 hours or more. Keep chilled. Serve in punch bowl with large amount crushed ice. Let stand 10-15 minutes, before serving. Delicious!

## WHITE WINE PUNCH

2 fifths any good white rhine
   wine
2-28 oz. bottles soda
14 ounces quinine water
2-6 oz. cans frozen limeade,
   thawed

**Serves 25 to 30**

Chill wine, soda and quinine water. Mix all ingredients together in large punch bowl. Serve with ice ring.

# MISCELLANEOUS

## CAPPUCCINO

8 c. strong coffee
8 oz. hot chocolate mix
8 oz. brandy

**Serves 16**

Mix together coffee, hot chocolate mix and brandy. Serve piping hot in demitasse cups. Delicious!

## CREAMED BRANDY ICE

Vanilla ice cream (2 scoops
   per guest)
Brandy (1 oz. per guest)

Put ice cream and brandy in a blender. Blend 30 seconds. Pour into champagne glasses; serve immediately.

*This is a good way to have dessert and an after dinner drink all in one. You may vary this by adding 1/2 ounce Creme de Cocoa.*

# FRUIT VODKA
## HOTEL IMPERIAL VIENNA

BEVERAGES

2 pineapple rings
Peeled orange, sliced
Peeled grapefruit, sliced
Halves of pears, apples,
  apricots and peaches
10 red cherries
Few grapes
1 liter 60 proof vodka
4 oz. Kirsch
4 oz. gin
4 oz. Benedictine
Grated nutmeg

Serves 20

In a glass pitcher of about 2 litres, place fruit of the season in an appetizingly looking manner. Put spirally cut orange peel on top. Mix the liter vodka, Kirsch, gin and Benedictine. Pour over the fruit. Season with little nutmeg. Put pitcher into refrigerator for 8 hours. The fruit vodka can be served ice cold right from this pitcher. Serve in cordial glasses.

*A great replacement for after dinner brandy.*

## KAHLUA

1-2 oz. jar expresso coffee
  mix (instant)
4 c. sugar
2 c. boiling water
1 whole vanilla bean
1 pt. inexpensive brandy

Yields 2 quarts

Combine coffee, sugar and boiling water. Stir until sugar and instant coffee are dissolved. Cool. Add brandy. Pour into quart bottles. Cut vanilla bean in half and split each half lengthwise. Put vanilla beans in each bottle. Age for one month.

## KAHLUA

1 fifth 100 proof bourbon
3 c. sugar
4 c. hot water
1 small jar instant coffee
1 vanilla bean
(vodka may be substituted
  for bourbon)

Yields 2 quarts

Mix sugar, coffee and water together. Stir until sugar is dissolved. Add bourbon and vanilla bean. Store in two 1 quart bottles in a dark place for 3-4 weeks. Vanilla bean may be used again.

39

## JAMAICAN AFTERNOON TEA

**Lemon slices**
**Sugar**
**Tea**
**Rum**

In each cup of tea put a teaspoon sugar and rum. Garnish with a lemon slice. Add little more rum on top and ignite it.

## INSTANT SPICED TEA MIX

**1 jar Tang (1 lb. 2 oz.)**
**½ c. instant tea**
**1 c. sugar**
**1 t. cloves, ground**
**1 t. cinnamon**

**Serves 30**

Mix all ingredients together and store. To serve, place 2 teaspoons of mix in cup and fill with boiling water.

## TEA

**2 or 3 tea bags**
**qt. cold water**

**Yields 1 quart**

Put tea bags into quart jar filled with water. Put outside in the sun for several hours. Very good.

# SOUPS

## SOUP A LA ALICE

2¼ lbs. carrots
2 large leeks, white part only
2 cans chicken broth
2 c. half and half cream
1 t. sugar

**Serves 6**

Peel and cut carrots and leeks. Cook in pressure cooker 4 to 5 minutes with broth. Cool; then put thru blender until puree is thick. Add cream and sugar. Delicious hot or cold.

## BLOODY MARY SOUP

3 stalks celery, diced
1 med. onion, diced
2 T. butter
2 T. tomato puree
1 T. sugar
5 c. tomato juice
2 t. Worcestershire sauce
1 t. salt
¼ t. pepper
1 T. lemon juice
½ c. vodka

**Serves 6**

Saute celery and onion in butter until soft and golden; add tomato puree and sugar. Cook 1 minute. Add tomato juice; simmer 8 to 10 minutes. Add remaining ingredients and strain. Return soup to heat; bring to a boil. Remove and cool. Refrigerate at least 4 hours. Serve in chilled, salt rimmed, low highball glasses.

*Excellent recipe for a brunch.*

*EasyGourmet*

## EASY BROCCOLI SOUP

1 pkg. frozen chopped broccoli
1 c. chicken broth
1 onion, minced
1 t. nutmeg
1 c. cream of onion soup
1 T. butter, melted
1 c. sour cream

**Serves 4**

Combine broccoli, chicken broth, onion and nutmeg; bring to boil over moderate heat. Simmer 5 minutes. Pour into blender, adding onion soup and butter; blend on high speed until smooth. Add sour cream and blend a few more seconds. Serve hot or cold.

41

# CALDO GALLEGO

2-15 oz. cans Great Northern beans
1 med. ham bone
1 lb. cured ham, cut in 1 inch pieces
¼ c. green pepper, chopped
2 c. onion, chopped
3 large garlic cloves
4 oz. tomato paste
2 qts. water
1-10 oz. pkg. frozen chopped turnip greens
3 med. turnips, peeled and cubed
Salt and pepper to taste

Serves 6 when used as main course, 10 as a first course

Place first eight ingredients in a large saucepan or dutch oven; simmer for 2 hours. Add remaining ingredients and cook ½ hour. If a thicker soup is desired, measure about one cup of ingredients, without the ham, and puree in the blender a few minutes. Return mixture to saucepan; cook 10 minutes more.

# CAVIAR SOUP

1 can Madrilene soup
2 ozs. caviar
Salt and pepper to taste
½ t. lemon juice (or to taste)
Pinch of parsley, chives or dill (to taste)
Sour cream

Serves 4

Pour Madrilene soup into a large bowl; cool in refrigerator until slightly thick. Comb caviar with a fork through Madrilene to distribute evenly. The consistency will prevent caviar from settling to the bottom. Put the soup in bowls for serving; place them in the refrigerator to completely thicken. When ready to serve, season with salt, pepper, lemon juice and your favorite herb to taste. Cover with a layer of sour cream. Serve cold.

# CHEESE SOUP

**2 cans cream of mushroom soup**
**1 c. beer**
**¾ c. cheddar cheese, shredded**
**1 t. Worcestershire**

**Serves 2 to 4**

Mix together all ingredients. Simmer for one half hour.

## SENEGALESE CREAM OF CHICKEN SOUP

**1 can cream of chicken soup**
**1 soup can of milk**
**2 t. curry powder**
**3 T. lemon juice**

**Serves 3 to 4**

Blend chicken soup, milk, curry powder and lemon juice. Serve either ice cold or hot, and pass a variety of curry accompaniments; chopped peanuts, pistachio nuts, thinly sliced scallions, thinly sliced apples, chopped green pepper, fluffy rice or chutney.

## EASY CORN CHOWDER

**1-16½ oz. can cream style corn**
**1 can mushroom soup**
**1 c. milk**
**½ c. diced green pepper**
**½ c. diced onion**
**2 T. butter**
**2 t. curry powder**
**3 slices bacon, fried and diced**

**Serves 4**

Mix corn, mushroom soup and milk together. Saute onion and green pepper in butter; add to mixture. Add curry powder and heat thoroughly. When ready to serve add diced bacon.

# BOCA CIEGA FISH CHOWDER

½ lb. bacon, cut in 1 inch
 pieces
6 lbs. fish fillets,* cut in
 1½ inch pieces
1 lb. onions, thinly sliced
3 med. potatoes, thinly
 sliced
½ c. celery, chopped
½ c. green pepper, sliced
1 pkg. (3½ oz.) unsalted
 crackers
3 T. butter
Salt and pepper to taste
1 c. white wine
Hot water
½ c. half and half cream

Serves 10

In dutch oven or large baking dish place a layer of bacon; add fish, onions, potatoes, celery and green pepper, then a layer of crackers. Dot with butter; add salt and pepper. Repeat layers until all ingredients are used. Pour in wine with enough hot water just to cover. Cook over low heat or in low oven until tender and the water is gone, about 45 minutes. Pour cream over chowder before serving; sprinkle with chopped parsley. Garnish with lemon slices.

* Choice of any firm meat fish such as snapper, grouper, snook.

# MARION'S FISH CHOWDER

2 med. carrots, diced
2 small potatoes, diced
1 onion, chopped
½ green pepper, chopped
Salt and pepper
4 T. butter
3 c. fresh fish, cut into 1 inch
 pieces (mullet, trout,
 redfish)
3 c. milk
1 c. cream

Serves 4 to 6

In large pot, place carrots, potatoes, onions and pepper. Barely cover with water. Season to taste. Simmer 20 minutes. Add fish, under vegetables, and cook 10 minutes. Stir in milk and cream. Heat slowly. Do not boil.

# OVEN FISH CHOWDER

2 lbs. haddock, cut up, skin
   removed
4 potatoes, cubed
3 small onions, sliced
½ c. celery leaves
1 bay leaf
2½ t. salt
4 whole cloves
1 clove garlic
½ c. butter
1 t. dill weed
½ t. pepper
½ c. dry vermouth
2 c. boiling water
2 c. half and half cream

**Serves 6**

Place all ingredients in a large pyrex bowl. Bake at 375 degrees one hour. Just before serving, add **scalded** cream.

# CRAB BISQUE

1 can pea soup
½ can tomato soup
2 c. milk or chicken broth
1 c. crab meat or cooked
   shrimp, cut up
Rum, Sherry or
   Worcestershire to taste

**Serves 4**

Mix first four ingredients and slowly heat to almost boiling; add rum, Sherry or Worcestershire to taste.

*To vary: Use one can of tomato soup and 1 cup of cream in place of milk or broth.*

## COOL-AS-A-CUCUMBER SOUP

1 qt. chicken broth or 3
 (10½ oz.) cans of broth
1½ envelopes unflavored
 gelatin
½ c. minced onion
½ t. salt
1 t. finely chopped fresh dill
 or ¼ t. dried dill, crushed
3 T. fresh lemon juice
½ t. Worcestershire sauce
Dash Tabasco
⅛ t. white pepper
2 med. cucumbers, peeled,
 seeded and coarsely grated
¼ c. pimiento, chopped
2 T. finely chopped parsley
Lemon, sliced in thin
 wedges

**Serves 6**

Soften gelatin in ½ cup cold broth. Simmer rest of broth 10 minutes with onion, salt and dill; remove from heat. Stir in gelatin, lemon juice, Worcestershire sauce, Tabasco and white pepper. Cool; chill until syrupy thick. Stir in grated cucumbers, pimiento and parsley. Refrigerate at least 4 hours, either in individual cups or large bowl. Garnish with lemon wedge when served.

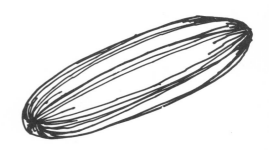

## COLD CUCUMBER SPINACH SOUP

1 bunch scallions, sliced
2 T. butter
4 c. cucumber, diced
1 c. spinach, chopped or
 chopped frozen spinach
3 c. chicken broth
½ c. potatoes, sliced
½ t. salt
Pepper to taste
Dash of lemon juice
1 c. half and half cream
Thin slices of cucumber

**Serves 8**

Saute scallions in butter until soft; add cucumbers, spinach, chicken broth, potatoes, salt, pepper and lemon juice. Simmer until potatoes are tender. Put mixture into blender and puree. Transfer to bowl and add cream; cool and chill several hours or overnight. Serve in chilled bowls with thin slices of cucumber floating on top.

## CREME VICHYSSOISE CUCUMBER

4 med. cucumbers, peeled
  and sliced  *
2 c. mashed potatoes
1 qt. chicken stock
1 c. heavy cream
1 small onion, grated
Salt and pepper
Fresh tarragon

*Leave a little of the peel
  on cucumbers.

Serves 10

Puree sliced cucumbers in blender; add mashed potatoes. Blend a little of the chicken stock into mixture. Add heavy cream and remainder of stock; mix well. Add onion, salt and pepper to taste. Chill in serving bowls. Top with fresh tarragon before serving.

## CURRY SOUP

1 c. fresh or frozen peas
1 med. onion, sliced
1 carrot, sliced
1 stalk celery, diced
1 med. potato, sliced
1 clove garlic, mashed
1 t. salt
1 t. curry powder
2 c. chicken broth
½ pt. heavy cream
Whipped cream for garnish

Serves 4

Can be made a day ahead.

Simmer all vegetables and seasonings in 1 cup of chicken broth for 15 minutes. Add second cup of broth and blend in blender. When cool mix in cream. Serve chilled with a dollop of whipped cream on top.

# EMERALD SOUP

1 pkg. frozen chopped
  spinach
2 cans cream of chicken
  soup
1 soup can milk
Dash Tabasco
⅛ t. garlic salt, optional
Sour cream (only if served
  hot)
Freshly ground pepper (only
  if served hot)

**Serves 8**

Defrost spinach; place in blender with cream of chicken soup and milk. Add Tabasco and garlic salt; blend thoroughly. Chill. To serve hot, simmer at 200 degrees about 15 minutes. Serve with sour cream and freshly ground black pepper.

# FRIJOLES NEGROS
## BLACK BEANS AND RICE

¾ lb. black beans
1½ qts. cold water
2 oz. salt pork, optional
¾ lb. ham hock, or bone left
  from smoked ham
1 large onion, finely
  chopped
1 clove garlic, minced
2 green peppers, chopped
½ c. bacon drippings or
  olive oil
1 bay leaf
⅛ t. oregano
1 T. salt
¼ c. vinegar

**Serves 6**

Wash beans thoroughly; put in large pot and soak overnight. Add salt pork and ham hock; simmer over low heat. Saute onion, garlic and green peppers in bacon drippings until tender. Add to beans. Season with bay leaf, salt and oregano; simmer until beans are tender and liquid is thick (about 3 hours). Add vinegar just before serving. Serve over rice with finely chopped onion on top.

*Serve with hot Cuban bread, a green salad and your favorite red wine.*

## LOUIS PAPPAS' FAMOUS GARBANZO SOUP
## (GREEK STYLE)

2 No. 2 cans Garbanzo
  beans
½ cup olive oil
2 med. onions, cut fine
1 clove garlic, minced
1 or 2 carrots, sliced
2 stalks celery, cut into
  small pieces
1 large potato, peeled and
  diced
1 sprig parsley, chopped
  fine
2 T. tomato paste
1-8 oz. can tomato sauce
1 T. salt - dash of pepper
5 c. water or meat stock (if
  using water, add 2 bouillon
  cubes)
1 small green pepper,
  cut fine

**Serves 10-12**

Heat oil in skillet and cook the onions, celery and garlic about 5 minutes. Add remaining cut up vegetables, tomato paste and tomato sauce. Stir in salt and pepper and boil gently about 30 minutes. Add the two cans of well-drained beans, and 5 cups of stock. Bring back to boil and simmer for 10 minutes. Stir well before serving.

# GAZPACHO

⅔ c. green pepper, finely
  chopped
⅔ c. onion, finely chopped
3 hard boiled eggs, chopped
⅔ c. fresh tomatoes,
  chopped
⅔ c. cucumber, finely
  chopped
1 c. croutons, plain or
  seasoned
2½ c. tomato juice
1 can chicken broth
  (10½ ozs.)
¼ c. wine vinegar
¼ c. olive oil (optional)
1 T. sugar
1 t. seasoned salt
⅛ t. white pepper

**Serves 4 to 6**

Keep green pepper, onion, eggs, tomatoes and cucumber in separate bowls or containers; chill. Pour the liquid ingredients and seasonings into a refrigerator container; chill for 3 hours. Serve the liquid in a tureen with a few ice cubes. Serve chopped ingredients and croutons in small bowls to be passed when soup is served. For luncheon, serve with crusty Cuban or French bread.

# KENTUCKY SOUP

1 can She-Crab soup
1 can cream of mushroom
  soup
1 can cream of shrimp soup
½ soup can milk
Dash Worcestershire sauce
¼ c. Sherry
Salt and seasoned pepper
  to taste

**Serves 6**

*Men love this soup.*

Combine all ingredients as listed. Stir and heat.

## LOBSTER SOUP

1 can cream of mushroom
  soup
2 can evaporated milk
1-4½ oz. can lobster meat
  (save liquid)
1 small jar pimiento, diced
1 green pepper, diced
2 doz. small stuffed olives,
  diced
½ t. thyme
3 T. butter
Sherry to taste

Serves 4

Heat mushroom soup and milk together; whisk until smooth. Add lobster meat, cut in bite size pieces, and lobster liquid, pimiento, green pepper, olives, thyme and butter. Just before serving add Sherry to taste. Do not allow to boil.

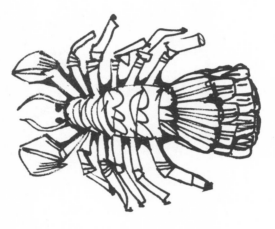

## MULLIGATAWNY SOUP

1 whole chicken breast
3 c. chicken broth, skimmed
  free of fat
1 med. onion, minced
1 stalk celery, minced
½ green pepper, minced
2 T. vegetable oil
1 T. curry powder
½ t. powdered cardamon
1 large tomato, peeled and
  chopped
1 t. salt
1 c. cooked rice

Serves 4 to 6

Poach the chicken breast in broth 8 to 10 minutes; drain, reserving broth. Cut chicken meat into small pieces. Saute onion, celery and green pepper in oil until slightly brown; add curry powder, cardamon, tomato, salt and chicken broth. Reduce heat; cover and simmer 1 hour. Add chicken pieces and boiled rice. Serve piping hot in warm bowls. If desired, spoon rice into each bowl before adding soup.

# CREAM OF MUSHROOM SOUP

**1 small slice of onion,
  minced**
**¼ lb. fresh mushrooms,
  finely chopped**
**4 T. butter**
**2 T. flour**
**2 c. chicken stock**
**Dash of lemon juice**
**½ t. salt**
**⅛ t. pepper**
**½ c. cream**

**Serves 6**

Saute onion and mushrooms in butter; cook over low heat 15 minutes, stirring occasionally. Stir in flour. Add stock slowly and bring to boiling point; remove from pan and place in double boiler. Cook 20 minutes. Season with lemon, salt and pepper to taste. Just before serving, add cream and reheat.

# ONION SOUP

**12 onions, thinly sliced**
**¼ c. olive oil**
**4 T. butter**
**Salt and pepper to taste**
**5 T. sugar**
**6 c. beef broth**
**4 T. brandy**
**French Bread \***
**Fresh grated Parmesan
  cheese**

**Serves 6**

In a heavy pan place onions, olive oil, butter, salt, pepper and sugar. When onions are limp add beef broth and let simmer 15 minutes. Prepare French Bread* and sprinkle with Parmesan cheese; place under broiler to melt. Add brandy to soup. Fill soup bowls; put bread on top and serve immediately.

* Cut bread ½ to 1 inch thick; place on cookie sheet. Bake at 325 degrees about 30 minutes or until thoroughly dried out and golden brown.

*Good for Sunday breakfast when Saturday night has been long and busy.*

## "GRAND CENTRAL OYSTER BAR" STEW

**1 pt. oysters**
**3 T. butter, divided**
**½ t. Worcestershire sauce**
**½ t. celery salt**
**½ c. liquor from oysters**
**½ c. clam juice**
**2 c. milk**
**Dash of paprika**

**Serves 2**

Drain oysters, reserving liquor. Heat together 1½ tablespoons butter, Worcestershire sauce and celery salt; bring to boil. Add oysters and mixed oyster and clam liquors; heat until edges of oysters curl. Pour in milk and heat just to boiling. When serving, add ¾ tablespoon butter and a dash of paprika to each bowl.

## PARADISE SOUP

**5 c. tomato juice**
**1 c. sour cream**
**¼ c. grated onion**
**2 T. lemon juice, or to taste**
**1 t. grated lemon rind**
**Salt and white pepper to taste**
**¾ c. cooked diced ham**
**1 cucumber\***
**1 small cantaloupe\***
**Fresh minced basil**

**Serves 6 to 8**

In a large bowl whisk tomato juice with sour cream, grated onion, lemon juice, lemon rind, salt and white pepper; stir in diced ham. Cover; chill 4 hours or overnight. Cut cucumber and cantaloupe into balls with a melon ball cutter; sprinkle the balls with basil and chill 4 hours. To serve, pour soup into iced servers; garnish each with cucumber and melon balls.

\* You may garnish with minced basil only, excluding cucumber and cantaloupe balls.

# PEANUT SOUP

1 stalk celery, chopped
1 onion, minced
¼ c. butter
2 T. flour
8 c. chicken broth (size
   10½ oz. cans)
1-12 oz. jar crunchy peanut
   butter
1 c. light cream
Sour cream
Chopped peanuts

**Serves 10**

Saute celery and onion in butter until tender; add flour and blend. Pour in broth and bring to a boil. Add peanut butter; cook 15 minutes. Remove from heat; stir in cream. Serve hot topped with chopped peanuts, or chill in refrigerator and serve with a dollop of sour cream.

# QUEEN VICTORIA SOUP

1 T. butter
1 t. finely chopped onion
½ c. finely chopped
   mushrooms
1 c. diced celery
4 c. chicken stock or canned
   chicken broth
1 T. quick tapioca
½ c. diced cooked chicken
½ c. diced cooked ham
Sage, nutmeg and onion salt
   to taste
2 hard boiled eggs, chopped
2 c. cream
Chopped parsley

**Serves 7 to 8**

Saute onion in butter until tender. Add mushrooms and celery; cook 10 minutes. Stir in chicken broth, tapioca, chicken, ham and seasonings to taste; cook 20 minutes. Add chopped eggs and cream. Serve in large bowls garnished with parsley.

*This soup is a modern adaptation of a famous English recipe. It is rich and hearty enough for the main dish at lunch or supper.*

## SHRIMP GUMBO

2 lbs. shrimp
3 T. flour
3 T. bacon drippings
2 onions, chopped
1 green pepper, chopped
3 cloves garlic, minced
1 c. cooked ham, chopped
 (optional)
2½ c. chopped okra
1-16 oz. can tomatoes
2 qts. water
1 t. salt
1 bay leaf
Red pepper to taste

Serves 8

Peel uncooked shrimp and devein. Make a roux* of the flour and drippings. Add chopped onion, green pepper and garlic; saute until tender. Stir in ham and okra; cook until okra is tender. Add tomatoes and cook a few minutes. In a large pot put the water and seasonings; stir in all other ingredients except shrimp. Cook for 1 hour. Add shrimp and cook slowly 30 minutes. Serve over rice.

* A roux is the base for gumbos, stews, soups and gravies. To make a proper roux it is important to have a heavy pot or skillet. Mix the flour and drippings thoroughly in the pot. Brown the roux over slow heat until it is a **rich dark brown**: take off fire immediately, stirring all the time (do not burn or scorch; it will ruin the taste). Stop the browning of the roux by adding a little hot water or onions, peppers, etc. as in above.

## ITALIAN VEGETABLE SOUP

1 c. sliced carrots
1 c. sliced squash
1 c. shredded cabbage
1 c. chopped celery
2 T. butter
2 T. salad oil
2 t. salt
2 beef bouillon cubes
8 c. water
1 c. chopped tomatoes
1 c. spaghetti, broken
½ t. thyme
Grated Parmesan cheese

Serves 4

*A good luncheon soup.*

Saute vegetables, excepting tomatoes, in butter and salad oil until limp. Add salt, bouillon cubes and water; cook 30 minutes. Stir in tomatoes, spaghetti and thyme; cook 20 minutes longer. Serve hot with Parmesan cheese sprinkled over top.

# ROSA'S VEGETABLE SOUP

**1 large meaty soup bone**
**1 lb. beef, cubed**
**1 c. each chopped**
 **vegetables such as:**
 **green beans, carrots,**
 **celery, corn, onions and**
 **peas**
**3 young okra pods**
**1-29 oz. can whole tomatoes**
**¾ c. pearl barley**
**Salt and pepper to taste**

**Serves 6**

First day: Place the soup bone and beef cubes in a large pot with water to cover; bring to boil. Lower heat; cook until meat is very tender. Let stock cool. Remove meat from bone and discard bone. Put stock in refrigerator overnight.

Second day: Remove most of the fat from the stock, leaving only enough to flavor. Add chopped vegetables, tomatoes, okra and barley. Cook until vegetables are nearly done; salt and pepper to taste.

*This soup improves with age, and makes a really delicious hearty lunch or supper.*

# VICHYSQUASH

**1 med. Spanish onion,**
 **thinly sliced**
**1 T. butter**
**6 med. summer squash**
 **(yellow), sliced**
**½ c. chicken broth**
**Salt and med. ground black**
 **pepper**
**1 c. milk**
**Chopped chives**

**Serves 4-6**

In an electric frying pan saute onion in butter until limp, but not brown; slice in the squash. Add chicken broth and cover; cook until tender, about 15 minutes. Season with salt and pepper to taste; cool. Puree the mixture in blender. Serve cold with milk added to taste; top with chives.

*This is a lovely pale, delicate summer soup. Freeze the puree and it will be delicious anytime.*

## VICHYSSOISE

4 leeks, or 2 large onions,
  chopped
½ c. butter
1 qt. chicken broth
4 med. potatoes, thinly
  sliced
1 stalk celery
1 sprig parsley
¼ t. salt
Pinch nutmeg
4 drops Worcestershire
1 pt. heavy cream
Chopped chives for garnish

Serves 6

Saute onion in butter over very low heat 10 minutes; add chicken broth and potatoes. Tie celery and parsley together and add; boil for 30 minutes or until potatoes are soft. Remove celery and parsley; blend ingredients in blender, or put through strainer. Add seasonings. When cold, add cream and chill in china bowl; the colder the better. Serve garnished with chopped chives. Can be made a day ahead.

## CREAM OF WATERCRESS SOUP

1 envelope (2 oz.) Wyler's
  Potato with Leek soup mix
⅛ t. nutmeg
1 qt. clear chicken broth
  (3 cans)
2 c. light cream
1 large bunch watercress,
  stems removed

Serves 8 to 10

Place soup mix and nutmeg in large kettle; gradually add chicken broth. Bring to a boil, stirring occasionally; cover, simmer 10 minutes. In blender, at high speed, blend ½ cup cream and ½ of the watercress; gradually add rest of watercress and ½ cup cream. Blend mixture and remaining 1 cup cream into soup; simmer 5 minutes. Serve in warm bowls.

## WATERCRESS FRAPPE

1 bunch watercress
1 cucumber, peeled
1 can cream of celery soup
½ c. half and half cream
1 c. milk
Salt and white ground
pepper to taste

Serves 6

Place everything in blender. Chill when blended. Chill bowls before serving.

# WATERCRESS SOUP

3 large leeks,chopped
2 onions, thinly sliced
1 garlic clove, crushed
¼ c. butter
4 potatoes, thinly sliced
6 c. chicken stock or broth
2 bunches watercress,
  stems removed
  and coarsely chopped
1 c. milk
½ c. heavy cream
Salt and pepper to taste
2 T. butter

Serves 8

In a kettle saute leeks, onions and garlic in butter. Cover with a round of wax paper and lid; steam over moderate heat 20 minutes. Add potatoes and 4 cups of chicken stock; simmer 15 minutes. Blend in watercress, reserving ½ cup; simmer 20 minutes. Puree soup through medium disk of food mill or in blender. Add 2 cups chicken stock or broth to puree; stir in milk, heavy cream, and reserved watercress. Simmer until heated through. Season with salt and pepper to taste; swirl in butter. Serve in heated bowls.

# SANDWICHES

## AMERICAN TACO

1 lb. ground round
1 small onion, chopped
1 green pepper, chopped
3 T. oil
1-1¼ oz. pkg. Taco
  seasoning mix
1 can stewed tomatoes
1 can Mexicorn
½ c. chopped black olives
Cornbread

Serves 6

Brown meat with onions and green pepper. Stir in Taco mix, tomatoes, corn and black olives. Simmer 20 minutes, or until sauce has thickened. Bake cornbread in an 8x8 inch square pan. Cut into 6 large squares. Cut each square in half and serve with meat sauce poured over cornbread.

## CHEESE CHIPPED BEEF SANDWICH

½ c. cut chipped beef,
  rinsed in hot water and
  drained
1-3 oz. pkg. cream cheese
1 T. horseradish
1 T. minced onion
1 T. mayonnaise

Mix ingredients together thoroughly. Spread on bread cut into desired shapes. May be topped with another slice of bread or open face sprinkled with dill or parsley. These freeze well.

## HOT CHICKEN SANDWICH

1 can cream of chicken soup
3 c. cooked chicken
1 T. flour
¾ c. milk
4 eggs, beaten
Large bag potato chips,
  crushed

**Yields 16 sandwiches**

Blend first four ingredients well. Cook until thick. Cool. Cut crusts off bread; butter. Spread on chicken mixture. Cut sandwich in half; freeze. While still frozen, dip in eggs and roll in crushed potato chips. Bake at 325 degrees for 30 minutes or until brown.

*For appetizers cut each sandwich into 4 pieces.*

# CRABMEAT OR SHRIMP SANDWICH

Easy Gourmet

1-7½ oz. can crabmeat or
  shrimp
½ lb. Velveeta cheese
4 T. butter or oleo

Serves 4

Mix together in top of double boiler, stirring until cheese melts. Cool. Spread on halved buns and brown under broiler.

# GRILLED MEXICAN BEEF SANDWICHES

½ lb. bacon
½ lb. dried beef, torn in
  small pieces
½ lb. American cheese,
  grated
¼ c. pimientos, drained and
  diced
½ c. salad dressing
½ c. canned tomatoes

Yields 9 sandwiches

Dice bacon and fry crisp; drain well. Reserve. Combine remaining ingredients. Heat in pan in 400 degree oven until cheese melts. Blend in bacon thoroughly. Spread on cheese bread, or any white or wheat bread. Butter each side and grill. Delicious!

# BARBECUED HAM IN PITA BREAD (SYRIAN BREAD)

1 T. oil
2½ c. cooked smoked ham,
  shredded
1 onion, chopped
1 green pepper, chopped
1-8 oz. can tomato sauce
2 T. brown sugar
2 T. vinegar
1 T. chili powder
1 t. dry mustard
⅛ t. pepper
3 pita breads
Yields 6 sandwiches

Saute ham, pepper and onion in oil until lightly browned. Stir in tomato sauce, sugar, vinegar, chili powder, mustard and pepper. Simmer 10 minutes. Warm pita. Cut in half and with fingers spread pocket open in each half. Spoon in ham mixture.

# HAM AND EGG SANDWICH PUFFS

2 T. butter
½ c. chopped onion
¾ c. chopped green pepper
2 c. chopped fresh tomatoes
2 c. minced cooked ham
1 c. grated Cheddar cheese
12 slices white bread
Mayonnaise
8 eggs
½ c. evaporated milk
¼ c. water
¼ t. pepper
½ t. salt
⅓ c. grated Parmesan
cheese

**Yields 6 sandwiches**

Preheat oven to 350 degrees. Saute onion, green pepper, tomatoes and ham in butter. Stir over low heat until moisture is reduced. Add cheese and stir until melted. Spread bread slices with mayonnaise. Arrange 6 slices in 13x9 buttered baking dish. Top each slice with ham filling and then another slice of bread. Beat eggs with milk, water and seasonings; pour over sandwiches. Sprinkle grated cheese over sandwiches. Bake 35 to 40 minutes, or until sandwiches are puffed and browned. To serve, cut around sandwiches with a spatula and lift out with surrounding egg custard.

# HOT TUNA SANDWICH

2 cans white tuna
½ c. chopped ripe olives
3 oz. can mushrooms, chopped
3 green onions, chopped
4 hard cooked eggs, chopped
Mayonnaise
24 slices bread, trimmed
1 can cream of chicken soup
1½ c. sour cream
¼ c. dry Sherry
Paprika

**Yields 12**

Mix first five ingredients with just enough mayonnaise to hold together well. Spread thick coating mayonnaise on 12 slices bread. Place on baking sheet mayonnaise side down. Top each with generous amount tuna mixture then other slice of bread. Cover top with thick coating mayonnaise and brown each side slightly under broiler. Blend soup, sour cream and Sherry; heat until hot and smooth. Place sandwich on serving plate; top with soup mixture. Sprinkle with paprika.

*Vary recipe by omitting mayonnaise coating. Instead spread tops and sides (only) with ½ cup margarine mixed with one 5 oz. jar sharp cheese spread. Bake at 400 degrees 10 minutes or until heated through. Use soup topping if desired.*

61

## OPEN FACE CUCUMBER SANDWICHES

2 cucumbers
French dressing
Garlic powder
3 oz. cream cheese
Homemade mayonnaise
Fresh dill
2 loaves Pepperidge Farm
  whole wheat bread

Yields 90

Peel cucumbers, leaving small strip of peel on. Run fork down sides; slice. Marinate all night in French dressing and sprinkling of garlic powder. Make rounds of bread the size of cucumber slices Mash cream cheese and add enough mayonnaise to spreading consistency. Spread bread with the above. Put a slice of cucumber on top. Sprinkle with finely cut dill. Delicious.

## HOT OPEN-FACED SANDWICH

6 Holland Rusks
1-8 oz. pkg. cream cheese
1 T. mayonnaise
1 T. catsup
1 t. Worcestershire
Dash garlic or onion powder
1-7½ oz. can crabmeat
4 tomatoes, sliced
6 slices sharp cheddar
  cheese
Olives or parsley

Yields 6

Blend cream cheese, mayonnaise, catsup, Worcestershire, seasonings and crabmeat. Butter rusks and spread with crabmeat mixture. Top with slice of tomato then cheese. Bake at 325 degrees 30 minutes. Garnish with an olive or parsley.

## HOMEMADE PIMIENTO CHEESE

4 c. grated sharp cheese
1 large jar pimientos,
  chopped
1 T. grated onion
Tabasco to taste
Mayonnaise
Hot water

Grate the cheese and stir in the cut pimientos. Add the onion and enough hot, hot water to mix everything. Stir in mayonnaise to the spreading consistency and add Tabasco to taste.

*Delicious as pimento sandwishes or to fill celery stalks.*

ENTREÉS

CHEF

- CASSEROLES
  - MEATS
  - Poultry
  - Seafood
  - EGGS, RICE, CHEESE AND PASTA

## CASSOULET

1 small shoulder of fresh
  pork
1 pt. cooked black-eyed
  peas
1 c. beef bouillon
1 c. red wine
2 T. soy sauce
2 c. canned white grapes
Pepper

Serves 6

Bake pork at 450 degrees 20 minutes. Place in 13 x 9 inch baking dish. Add peas, bouillon, wine, soy sauce and pepper. Cover and bake at 350 degrees 3 hours. Before serving, stir in white grapes.

## CHICKEN CASSEROLE

2 c. diced cooked chicken
1 can cream of chicken soup
1 can cream of celery soup
1 can cream of mushroom
  soup
1-13 oz. can evaporated milk
½ c. Sherry
1-5½ oz. can chow mein
  noodles
1 pkg. corn bread stuffing
  mix
4 T. butter or margarine

Serves 8

In large bowl combine all ingredients except stuffing and butter. Place in 13 x 9 inch pyrex baking dish. Cover with stuffing. Melt butter; pour over top. Leave out 1 hour before baking. Bake at 350 degrees 30 minutes. May be frozen.

## CHICKEN CASSEROLE WITH RICE

1 c. cooked chicken breast,
  chopped
1 c. cooked rice
1 c. celery, partially cooked
2 T. chopped onion
1 c. cream of chicken soup
⅓ c. mayonnaise
1 c. crushed potato chips
¼ c. slivered almonds
2 T. butter

**Serves 2 to 4**

Mix celery, onion, soup and mayonnaise. Layer rice, chopped chicken and soup mixture in a 2 quart casserole. Top with potato chips, slivered almonds and butter. Bake at 350 degrees 45 minutes.

## CHICKEN, RICE AND SHRIMP CASSEROLE

1-5 lb. roasting chicken,
  cut up
1 med. onion, sliced
1 med. carrot, sliced
4½ c. salted water
1½ lbs. shrimp, peeled,
  cooked
Salt and pepper
½ t. dried or 1½ t. fresh dill
1 c. raw rice
12 small white onions
1 lemon, sliced thin

**Serves 6**

Simmer chicken, onion and carrot in water 30 minutes. Remove meat; strain and save broth. Skin chicken, arrange in casserole with shrimp, seasonings, rice, onions and lemon slices. Boil broth to 2 cups; pour over mixture. Cover, bake in 325 degree oven 40 minutes or until chicken is tender and rice has absorbed broth. Stir with fork to release steam.

# FANCY FREE CASSEROLE

3 cans macaroni with cheese
4 large chicken breasts,
  cooked
1-8 oz. can mushrooms
  (optional)
8 ozs. sharp cheddar
  cheese, shredded
1 T. Worcestershire sauce
2 large onions diced to
  equal 1½ cups
3 crumbled hamburger buns
3 T. butter
Salt and pepper to taste

Serves 8

Mix macaroni with cooked chicken, boned and cut in large chunks. Saute onions until tender in 2 tablespoons butter and add to the above mixture along with 6 ounces shredded cheese and Worcestershire sauce. Stir crumbs with 1 tablespoon melted butter in the pan used for onions until well buttered. Put macaroni mixture in 2 quart casserole. Top with buttered crumbs and remaining shredded cheese. Bake at 350 degrees until heated through and the crumbs and cheese are nicely browned.

# ENCHILADAS

1 lb. ground beef
1 large onion, chopped
2 t. salt
1 T. chili powder
½ c. enchilada sauce

Enchilada Sauce:
4 T. flour
4 T. vegetable oil
3 c. water
1 (6 oz.) can tomato paste
1 can tomato paste
4 T. chili powder
1 T. ground cumin
Salt
1 T. Tequila
24 frozen tortillas
Vegetable oil
1 large onion, chopped
1 lb. Longhorn cheese,
  grated

Serves 10 to 12

Brown meat and onion; add salt, chili powder; mix together thoroughly. Set aside.

In skillet, heat oil; add flour; blend well. Stir in tomato paste, water, chili powder, cumin and salt. Simmer 30 minutes. Take ½ cup and add to meat mixture; add Tequila to remaining sauce.

Separate tortillas. Using tongs, fry each one in hot shortening until limp. Dip each into enchilada sauce, remove to plate and put about 2-3 tablespoons meat mixture in center of each tortilla.

Place seam side down in 13 x 9 inch baking dish. Pour remaining sauce over the enchiladas. Sprinkle with the onions and cheese; bake at 375 degrees until bubbly and cheese browns (about 25 minutes).

*Takes time to make, but freezes beautifully. A must for any Mexican dinner party. Serve with salad and toasted tortillas.*

## HAM AND SPAGHETTI MOLD

**1 recipe medium white
  sauce (see index)
1 c. cooked diced ham
½ t. prepared mustard
1 T. wine vinegar
1 egg yolk, beaten
⅔ c. cooked spaghetti**

**Serves 4**

Combine all ingredients. Put in 1½ quart well greased ring mold. Cook at 350 degrees 20 minutes. Fill center with green peas and serve.

*Good way to use left over ham that looks like party fare.*

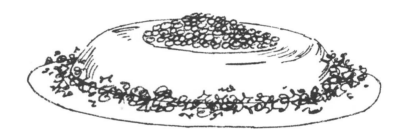

## HAMBURGER CRUNCH CASSEROLE

**1 lb. ground beef
1 med. onion
4 T. soy sauce
Pepper and salt
1 can cream of mushroom
  soup
1 can cream of chicken soup
1 can (small) sliced
  mushrooms
2½ c. water
½ c. regular rice
1 (5 oz.) can chow mein
  noodles**

**Serves 6**

Grease 13 x 9 inch pyrex baking dish. Put rice over bottom. Mix other ingredients (except noodles). Pour over rice. Bake 325 degrees uncovered for one hour. Add noodles and bake 10 minutes longer.

# LASAGNA

1 lb. ground beef
1 clove garlic, minced
1 T. chopped parsley
1 T. basil
1 large onion, diced
1½ t. salt
1-16 oz. can tomatoes
2-6 oz. cans tomato paste
1-10 oz. pkg. lasagna
  noodles

Brown meat; add garlic, parsley, basil, onion, salt. Cook 10 minutes; add tomatoes and paste; simmer uncovered 1 hour. Cook noodles in salted water until done.

Cheese Filling:
2-12 oz. cartons cream-style
  cottage cheese
2 eggs, beaten
2 t. salt
½ t. red pepper
2 T. parsley flakes
½ c. Parmesan cheese
2 lbs. Mozzarella cheese

Serves 8 to 10

Combine cottage cheese, eggs, salt, pepper, parsley flakes and Parmesan cheese. Blend thoroughly. Place ½ the noodles in 13 x 9 inch baking dish; spread with ½ the cheese mixture, add Mozzarella cheese to cover; add ½ meat mixture. Repeat layers, ending with meat. Put more Mozzarella on top; bake at 375 degrees 40 minutes. Let stand 10 minutes before cutting into squares.

*This is one of the best Lasagna recipes ever! Freezes beautifully.*

## MEATBALL LASAGNA

1-10 oz. pkg. lasagne
  noodles
2-1 lb. cans Italian tomatoes
2-6 oz. cans tomato paste
1 t. salt
2 T. oregano
1½ lbs. hot Italian sausage,
  sliced
3 lbs. ground chuck
6 slices bread, soaked in
  water
3 eggs
½ t. salt, pepper, garlic salt
2 lbs. Ricotta cheese
1 lb. Mozzarella cheese
Parmesan cheese

Serves 12 to 14

Cook noodles according to package directions; drain. Combine tomatoes, tomato paste, oregano and salt. Simmer. Fry hot sausage; remove and save fat. Blend ground chuck, bread, eggs and seasonings together; form into 3 x 3 incn balls. Brown in sausage fat. In a 13 x 9 inch baking dish, place half of noodles, spread with half of Ricotta cheese, sprinkle with Parmesan cheese, add half of Mozzarella cheese then sausage and meat balls. Repeat layers. Sprinkle with Parmesan cheese on top and more slices of Mozzarella. Bake at 375 degrees 40 minutes. Let stand 10 minutes before cutting.

# MOUSSAKA

1 large eggplant, peeled
  and sliced
Vegetable oil
Salt
1½ lbs. ground beef
1 large onion, finely chopped
2 cloves garlic, pressed
1½ t. salt
1 t. sugar
1 t. thyme or oregano
1-16 oz. can tomato sauce
1 c. water
⅓ c. butter or margarine
⅓ c. flour
1 t. salt
2 c. milk
3 eggs

Serves 6

Season eggplant slices with salt. Fry in large skillet until brown on both sides. Drain on paper towels.

Cook ground beef, onions and garlic. Add salt, sugar, thyme, tomato sauce and water. Simmer slowly 30 minutes.

Melt butter in saucepan, stir in flour and salt. Gradually add milk and cook over medium heat until thickened. Remove from heat. Stir a few tablespoons of sauce into beaten eggs in a small bowl. Gradually stir the eggs into sauce.

To assemble casserole: layer eggplant slices in a 9 inch square baking pan, or shallow casserole. Spoon layer of meat sauce over eggplant. Repeat layers of eggplant and meat sauce until all are used. Cover evenly with cream sauce and bake in 350 degree oven 40 minutes or until nicely browned.

*Serve with Pappas Greek Salad (see index) for a truly delicious Greek dinner.*

# LOW FAT MOUSSAKA

1½ lbs. ground beef
½ pkg. hamburger
  seasonings
¼ c. catsup
1 c. dry bread crumbs
  (flavored, o.k.)
1 large or two small
  eggplants
1 lb. can tomatoes
1 onion, minced
½ c. dry wine or vermouth
2-3 cloves garlic, pressed
  (optional)

Serves 8

Mix beef, seasonings, catsup and bread crumbs together well. Shape into loaf. Place loaf on rack in baking pan. Bake at 325 degrees for 1 hour. Discard drained fat.

Peel and cube eggplant. Mix all next ingredients together and cook in large skillet over medium heat. Stir to prevent sticking. Cook until eggplant is tender. Grease a 2 quart casserole. Slice the meat loaf and pack into bottom of casserole; add the eggplant mixture. Sprinkle top lightly with crumbs or grated cheese. Cover with foil or tight lid. Bake at 300 degrees 1 hour. This can be frozen.

*Serve with a mixed green salad and rice for buffet. Doubles well. This is an American version of a favorite Greek dish. This recipe omits the egg, olive oil, beef fat and usual bechamel sauce topping.*

## ORIENTAL GOULASH

1 green pepper, chopped
1 med. onion, chopped
2 stalks celery, chopped
2 T. shortening
1 lb. ground beef
Dash pepper
1 can beef consomme
2-3 T. soy sauce
½ c. raw rice
1-4 oz. can chopped
   mushrooms and liquid
1-8½ oz. can water
   chestnuts, sliced
1-8½ oz. can bamboo
   shoots
1-16 oz. can bean sprouts

Serves 6 to 8

Saute green pepper, onion and celery in shortening. Add ground beef. Brown; season. Drain water chestnuts, bamboo shoots and bean sprouts. Combine all ingredients; simmer covered 20 minutes or until rice is tender.

## PAM'S CASSEROLE

1 onion, chopped
2 green peppers, chopped
1 lb. ground beef
1-8 oz. can tomato sauce
1-16 oz. can stewed
   tomatoes
1-16 oz. can whole kernel
   corn
1 t. onion salt, garlic salt
1 T. chili powder
1 lb. cheddar cheese,
   grated
1 large pkg. Frito corn chips

Serves 6

Saute onions and pepper until limp; add ground meat and cook until no longer pink. Stir in tomato sauce, stewed tomatoes, corn and seasonings. Simmer 30 minutes. In a 2 quart casserole, layer first Fritos, meat sauce then cheese; repeat. Top with additional cheese. Bake at 350 degrees 40-45 minutes.

*The teenagers will love this (and so will the grown-ups). Serve with a tossed salad to complete an easy menu.*

# PAELLA

1-3 lb. chicken
1 qt. salted water
1 lb. mussels or clams
1 lb. raw shrimp, cleaned
6 T. olive oil
2 green peppers
4 med. tomatoes, chopped
1-2 cloves garlic, minced
1 t. salt
½ t. pepper
Pinch saffron
1½ c. raw long grain rice
3-4 c. chicken broth
1-10 oz. box frozen peas,
  cooked

**Serves 6 to 8**

Cook chicken in salted water 1 hour. Remove; strain and reserve broth. Remove meat from chicken bones in large pieces. Scrub mussels; cook with shrimp in salted water 3 minutes. Drain. Saute peppers, that have been cut in strips, tomatoes and garlic in olive oil until tender. Blend in spices. Add rice and stir fry 2 or 3 minutes. Pour in 4 cups broth and simmer 20 minutes. Add chicken, ½ the shrimp and mussels. Cook 15 minutes. Stir once or twice to be sure liquid has been absorbed by rice. Place remaining shrimp and mussels on top and cover with cooked peas.

# PORK CHOP AND CHILI BEAN CASSEROLE

4 pork chops
1 T. oil
½ c. water
1-16 oz. can kidney beans
2 T. onions, minced
2 t. chili powder

**Serves 4**

Flour and season chops. Brown in oil in hot skillet. Add water; simmer 20 minutes. Add onion and chili powder to beans and pour into shallow 8 x 8 inch baking dish. Arrange chops over beans and pour pan juices over all. Bake at 375 degrees 20-30 minutes.

*Doesn't sound very glamorous but try it, you will find it very good.*

## INSIDE-OUT RAVIOLI CASSEROLE

1 lb. ground beef
1 med. onion, chopped
1 clove garlic, minced
1 T. vegetable oil
1-10 oz. package frozen
chopped spinach
1-1 lb. can spaghetti sauce
with mushrooms
1-8 oz. can tomato sauce
1-6 oz. can tomato paste
½ t. salt
Dash pepper
1-7 oz. package shell or
elbow macaroni, cooked
1 c. shredded sharp
processed American
cheese
½ c. soft bread crumbs
2 eggs, beaten
¼ c. vegetable oil
1½ t. salt

Serves 8 to 10

Brown first 3 ingredients in the table-spoon salad oil. Cook spinach according to directions on package. Drain, reserve liquid; add water to make 1 cup. Stir spinach liquid and next 5 ingredients into meat mixture and simmer 10 minutes. Combine spinach with remaining ingredients.

Spread spinach mixture in 13 x 9 inch baking dish. Top with meat sauce. Bake at 350 degrees 30 minutes. Let stand 10 minutes before serving.

## ROMAN HOLIDAY BAKE

1 lb. ground beef
½ lb. hot Italian sausage cut
in ½ inch slices
1 c. chopped onion
2 t. oregano leaves, crushed
1 can cheddar cheese soup
1 can tomato soup
1 c. water
4 c. cooked, wide noodles
4 slices (about 4 ozs.
cheddar cheese cut in half
diagonally)

Serves 6

Brown beef, cook sausage and onion with oregano until done. Pour off fat. Add soups and water and chill overnight. Chill noodles overnight. Combine meat mixture and noodles; pour into 2 quart shallow baking dish (12 x 8 inch). Cover; place in cold oven. Bake at 400 degrees 40 minutes or until hot. Stir; top with cheese. Bake until cheese melts.

# FIESTA TAMALE CASSEROLE

½ lb. bulk pork sausage
1 c. minced onion
¾ c. minced green pepper
½ lb. ground beef
1 c. whole kernel corn
1 c. ripe olives, sliced
2 T. water from olives
1½ t. salt
1 t. chili powder
½ t. garlic salt
1½ c. tomato sauce
2-15 oz. cans tamales
¾ c. sharp cheese, grated

**Serves 6**

Brown sausage; remove to drain. In 3 tablespoons sausage drippings, saute onion and green pepper until tender. Stir in ground beef; brown. Add sausage, corn, olives, liquid and seasonings; stir in tomato sauce. Simmer 15 minutes. Pour into 13 x 9 inch baking dish and arrange tamales on top. Bake uncovered at 350 degrees 15 minutes. Sprinkle with cheese and bake until cheese melts and casserole is bubbly, (about 20 minutes).

# TAMALE CASSEROLE

½ lb. chuck or other lean beef (may use left-over meat)
1 onion, chopped
1 clove garlic, minced
⅓ c. salad oil
1 T. margarine
1 egg
1 t. chili powder
⅓ c. milk
½ c. corn meal
1 c. stewed tomatoes, broken up
1 c. niblet style canned corn
½ c. pitted ripe olives (if very large, cut in half)
1 t. salt

**Serves 5 to 6**

Brown meat. Add oil and margarine, then onion and garlic, simmer about 15 minutes, stirring occasionally. Beat egg, chili powder, salt and milk together. Stir in cornmeal, tomatoes and corn, adding the olives last. Mix and then stir all into the frying pan and cook together 15 minutes longer. Put in 2 quart casserole and bake at 350 degrees 30-45 minutes longer. If the meal is delayed, the casserole will be just as good if left for an hour with the oven turned low.

*For a complete meal, serve with Baked Chiles Rellenos. Ole!*

## TURKEY DISASTER

2 c. cooked turkey, cubed
1 c. cooked rice
½ c. celery, chopped
Salt and pepper to taste
1 can cream of chicken soup
1 can cream of mushroom
  soup
20 chicken flavored
  crackers, crushed
½ c. margarine, melted

Serves 6

Place rice in well-greased 2 quart casserole. Layer with turkey and celery; season with salt and pepper to taste. Pour undiluted soups over all. Combine crackers with margarine; sprinkle over top. Bake in 350 degree oven 30 minutes, or until brown and bubbly.

## WILD RICE CASSEROLE

⅔ c. wild rice
2 c. boiling water
1 lb. ground beef
1 lb. hot sausage
3 T. onion, chopped
Olive oil
1 can chicken and rice soup
1 small can mushrooms
½ c. water
1 t. salt
½ t. celery salt, onion
  powder, garlic powder
½ t. paprika
1 bay leaf, crushed

Serves 4 to 6

Soak rice in boiling water 15 minutes. Brown meats and onion in small amount of olive oil. Mix all ingredients together; pour into 3 quart baking dish. Bake at 325 degrees 1½ hours.

*Delicious as a main dish with tossed salad.*

# MEAT

## BUDGET BEEF BURGUNDY

2 lb. beef, cubed
1 can golden mushroom
  soup
1 pkg. dry onion soup
1 c. red wine

**Serves 2 to 4**

Combine all ingredients; bake at 350 degrees 1½ hours. Serve over rice or noodles sprinkled with poppy seeds.

*To extend recipe, add mushrooms, small onions, or carrots. Serve with tossed salad and herbed bread. Can be prepared the day before. It actually tastes better the second day.*

## BEEF STROGANOFF

3 T. shortening
3½ lb. round steak
2 large onions, thinly sliced
3 T. flour
Salt and pepper
1 small can mushrooms
1½ c. milk
½ c. water
2 pkg. dry onion soup mix
3 t. grated sharp cheddar
  cheese
2 c. sour cream
¼ c. brandy

**Serves 6 to 8**

Trim all fat away from steak and slice into narrow strips. Salt and pepper and sprinkle with flour. Heat shortening in a large skillet; add meat and sliced onions. Brown lightly, stirring often. Stir in grated cheese, mushrooms, soup mix, milk and water. Simmer covered, stirring occasionally until meat is tender. Add sour cream and brandy; heat thoroughly, but do not boil. Serve over rice or noodles.

Variation: Stir in 3 tablespoons tomato paste and a dash of Worcestershire.

## MEAT ROLLS WITH SAUSAGE

4 cube steaks
4-4 inch Italian sausage links
8 Mozzarella cheese slices
3 T. oil
1-32 oz. jar spaghetti sauce

Serves 4

Pound cube steaks into 6 inch circles. On each steak place one Italian sausage link. On each side of the sausage, place a strip of Mozzarella cheese. Roll cube steak around sausage and tie up with string. Brown in hot oil. Add spaghetti sauce and simmer covered one hour.

## RAGOUT ALLA MARCHES

4 lb. chuck roast
6 cloves garlic
½ lb. ground round
¼ lb. bulk sausage
5 chicken livers
1 onion, chopped
1 stalk celery, chopped
  with tops
2 c. sliced mushrooms
5 cloves garlic, crushed
1 c. chicken stock
1 can tomato puree
1 T. sugar
½ c. vegetable juice
½ c. red wine
1 carrot, chopped
½ t. cinnamon, nutmeg
¼ t. ground cloves
Pinch basil
1 bay leaf
3 sage leaves
Fresh grated Parmesan
  cheese
Fresh grated Romano
  cheese
Salt and pepper
Fresh chopped parsley

Serves 6 to 8

Pierce roast and insert the 6 cloves garlic. Braise in deep pan. Add next three ingredients; brown. Stir in onions, mushrooms, celery and garlic; cook until tender. Add remaining ingredients (except cheeses and parsley). Simmer 3 hours or more, adding more vegetable juice if necessary. Stir several (6 at least) times and each time you stir add a dash of the grated cheeses; mix well. Remove roast when tender; slice. Ladle on a little of the sauce, cheese and parsley. Serve remaining sauce over noodles. Top with parsley.

## SCHWIBRACHES (BOHEMIAN)

2 lb. boneless steak, cut into
  thin strips
½ c. shortening
1 med. onion, minced
2 cloves garlic, minced
Dash caraway seeds,
  marjoram
1 T. parsley
2 T. flour
2 c. red wine
2 med. pickles
1 small can anchovies in oil
  with capers, minced
1 T. mustard
Salt and pepper to taste
Dash paprika
3 slices bacon, diced
1 c. sour cream

**Serves 4**

Saute onion and garlic in shortening. Add caraway seeds, parsley and marjoram. Fry meat lightly on both sides, add flour then red wine. Reduce heat. Stir and cover pan. Simmer. Slowly add pickles, anchovies, mustard and diced bacon; stir occasionally. Allow to simmer 10 minutes. Increase heat; add salt, pepper and paprika. Bring to boil, stirring constantly. Remove from heat when sauce reaches desired consistency and meat is tender. Add sour cream; heat but do not boil. Serve with dumplings, rice or noodles.

## TERIYAKI

½ c. soy sauce
2 T. brown sugar
2 T. Worcestershire
1 T. white vinegar
¾ t. ground ginger
1 clove garlic, minced
        or
⅛ t. garlic powder
1-2 lb. flank steak or round
  steak ¾ inch thick

**Serves 4**

Blend all ingredients. Place meat in flat dish and pour mixture over meat. Turn frequently. Marinate at least 6 hours. Broil 5-8 minutes on each side, basting with sauce. Slice thin.

# CHILI

2 large onions, chopped fine
2 lb. ground beef
½ c. shortening
1 t. salt
½ t. black pepper
½ t. red pepper
½ t. ground cumin seed
3 t. chili powder (more if
 desired)
2 garlic cloves, chopped fine
1 No. 2 or 2½ can tomatoes,
 mashed
1 can tomato puree (small)
2 c. water
2 green peppers, chopped
 fine
1 T. sugar
6 c. chili beans (4 cans)

**Serves 10**

Melt shortening in large pot, fry onion until half done. Add meat and cook until done. Drain off fat. Add salt, black pepper, red pepper, chili powder, garlic, cumin seed; mix well. Add tomatoes, puree, beans, water, sugar and green pepper. Cook slowly over low fire until the flavors are well blended (about 1½ hours) stirring frequently.

# NEIMAN-MARCUS CHILI

¼ c. shortening
2 lb. beef round, shaved or
 ground
1 lb. pork, cut into small
 cubes
1 onion, diced fine
2 cloves garlic, chopped
 fine
3 T. chili powder
1 T. flour
1-29 oz. can tomatoes
1 t. oregano
1 t. salt
2 bay leaves, crumbled
2 t. cumin seeds
½ t. coriander
1 square (1 oz.)
 unsweetened chocolate

**Serves 4**

Melt shortening in a large skillet. Brown beef, pork, onion and garlic until onion is soft. Combine chili powder and flour; add to meat mixture. Press the tomatoes through a fine sieve twice; add to mixture. Add oregano, salt, bay leaves, cumin seed and coriander. Simmer slowly about 2 hours. Add chocolate during the last hour. Serve with Spanish rice or tamales. Garnish with olives. Makes about 1 quart.

*Served in Dallas in the Zodiac Room.*

# SUPER HAMBURGERS

2 lb. ground round
¼ c. chili sauce
¼ c. chopped onion
¼ c. chopped green pepper
1 t. salt
½ t. pepper
1 t. Worcestershire
1 t. soy sauce

Combine all ingredients. Shape into patties, depending on the size you prefer. Broil or fry to doneness desired.

# CHILI MANICOTTI

½ c. chopped onion
1 clove garlic
1 T. oil
2 cans condensed chili
  beef soup
½ c. water
12 manicotti shells
2 eggs, beaten
2½ c. creamed style cottage
  cheese
1½ c. shredded sharp
  cheddar cheese
1 or 2 Jalapeno peppers,
  seeded and chopped

Serves 6

Saute onion and garlic in oil until tender. Stir in soup and water. Heat thoroughly. Cook manicotti shells in boiling salted water 8-10 minutes. Drain. Combine eggs, cottage cheese, 1 cup cheddar cheese and peppers. Spoon ¼ cup cheese mixture into each shell. Pour half of soup mixture in 12x7 inch baking dish. Top with manicotti. Pour remaining soup mixture over all, being sure shells are covered. Cover; bake at 350 degrees 40-45 minutes. Uncover; sprinkle with remaining cheese. Bake a few minutes longer until cheese melts. Let stand 5 minutes before serving.

# GERMAN CARAWAY MEAT BALLS

1 lb. ground beef
¼ c. dry bread crumbs
1 t. salt
Dash pepper
¼ t. poultry seasoning
1 T. parsley, chopped
¼ c. milk
1 egg
2 T. cooking oil
1-10 oz. can beef broth
1-3 oz. can chopped
  mushrooms, drained
½ c. onion, chopped
1 c. sour cream
1 T. flour
½ to 1 t. caraway seeds

Combine beef, bread crumbs, seasonings, milk and egg; mix lightly. Shape into 24 - 1½-inch balls. Brown slowly on all sides in hot oil, shaking frequently. Add broth, mushrooms, onions; simmer covered 30 minutes. Blend sour cream, flour and caraway seeds; stir into broth. Cook and stir until mixture thickens. Serve with Spaetzles. (see index)

## CHEESEBURGER MEATLOAF

½ c. evaporated milk
1 egg
1 c. cracker crumbs
1½ lb. lean ground beef
2 T. chopped onion
1½ t. salt
1 t. dry mustard
2 T. catsup
1 c. grated American cheese

Serves 6

Mix all ingredients except cheese into meat. Line a loaf pan with heavy waxed paper. Place half of meat mixture in pan; put cheese on top. Add remaining meat. Bake at 350 degrees 1 hour. Let stand 10 minutes; turn out on platter. Remove paper and serve.

## INDIVIDUAL CRANBERRY MEAT LOAVES

1 lb. ground beef
1 c. cooked rice
½ c. tomato juice
1 egg, slightly beaten
¼ c. minced onion
1 T. Kitchen Bouquet
1½ t. salt
2 c. whole cranberry sauce
⅓ c. brown sugar
1 T. lemon juice

Serves 5

Combine meat with rice, tomato juice, egg, minced onion, Kitchen Bouquet and salt; mix thoroughly. Shape into 5 individual loaves; place in 13x9 inch baking dish. Combine cranberry sauce, brown sugar and lemon juice; spoon over loaves. Bake at 350 degrees 40 minutes. Remove meat loaves to warm serving platter. Pour cranberry sauce into gravy boat and pass with meat loaves.

## HILLSPEAK MEAT LOAF

2 slices white bread
2 slices rye bread
1 lb. ground beef
1 med. onion, finely chopped
4 sprigs parsley, finely
  chopped
3 T. Parmesan cheese
1 egg
1 t. salt
¼ t. pepper
2 T. butter or margarine
1-8 oz. can tomato sauce
1 t. oregano

Serves 4 to 6

Put bread in large mixing bowl. Pour 1 cup water over bread and let soak several minutes. Mash bread very fine with a fork. Add meat, onion, parsley, cheese, slightly beaten egg, salt, pepper. Mix together. Put mixture in baking pan and shape into a loaf. Put dots of butter or margarine over top. Bake at 325 degrees 30 minutes. Pour tomato sauce over meat, sprinkle with oregano, and continue baking 20 minutes longer.

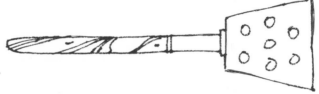

## PATE DE BOEUF (RENVERSE)

5 T. shortening
¼ c. minced onions
1 t. salt
¼ t. pepper
1½ c. flour
½ lb. ground steak
2 c. tomato soup
1 t. celery salt
¼ t. paprika
3 t. baking powder
¾ c. milk

Serves 6 to 8

Sift together flour, baking powder, ½ teaspoon salt, paprika and celery salt. Add 3 tablespoons shortening. Mix together until mealy; add milk to make nice dough. Roll it out to fit the top of a 9 inch square pan.

Saute onions in remaining shortening. When onions are soft, add tomato soup, remaining salt and meat. Let simmer, then come to a boil. Pour into 9 inch baking dish. Put dough over it. Slit for steam. Bake at 475 degrees 20 minutes.

## ITALIAN MEAT ROLL

2 eggs, beaten
¾ c. soft bread crumbs
½ c. tomato juice
2 T. snipped parsley
½ t. orgeano
¼ t. salt
¼ t. pepper
1 small clove garlic, minced
2 lb. lean ground beef
8 thin slices boiled ham
6 oz. shredded Mozzarella
 cheese
3 slices Mozzarella cheese,
 halved diagonally

Serves 8

Combine eggs, bread crumbs, tomato juice, parsley, oregano, salt, pepper and garlic. Stir in ground beef; mix well. On foil or waxed paper pat meat mixture to a 12 x 10 inch rectangle. Arrange ham slices atop meat leaving small margin around edges. Sprinkle shredded cheese over ham. Starting from short end carefully roll up meat, using foil to lift. Seal edges and ends. Place roll seam side down in 13 x 9 inch baking pan. Bake in 350 degree oven 1 hour and 15 minutes. Place cheese wedges over top. Return to oven 5 minutes to melt cheese.

## CHICKEN LIVER SPAGHETTI SAUCE

1 qt. chicken livers
2 cans mushroom buttons
1½ lb. bell peppers
3 lb. fresh tomatoes
3 bunches green onions
2 T. finely cut garlic
3 T. chopped parsley
1 c. margarine
1 t. sugar
1 t. salt
1 t. red pepper
1 8 oz. cup dry Sauterne

Serves 6

Cut livers into 4 pieces. Scald, peel and chop tomatoes. Chop rest of vegetables. In heavy six quart pot, melt ½ cup margarine. Slowly saute mushrooms, stirring constantly. Remove from pot; put aside. In same pot add chopped vegetables. Saute until tender, but not browned. In separate pan melt remaining margarine; add chicken livers and cook gently until done. In large pot add vegetables, chopped tomatoes, livers, mushrooms, juice and chopped parsley. Season to taste. Simmer gently, stirring occasionally. Ten minutes before serving stir in dry Sauterne. Serve on cooked vermicelli with Italian cheese.

*This sauce is the Piece de Resistance for stag suppers.*

MEAT

# MADAME BENOIT'S BROWN STEW

2 lbs. stewing beef
  (1 inch cubes)
½ c. browned flour
1 large onion, minced
1 clove garlic, minced
1 large dill pickle, minced
1 can consomme
½ c. Sherry

Serves 6

To prepare flour, spread on cookie sheet and place in 300 degree oven until brown. Place in paper bag and shake small pieces of beef until well covered. Brown meat in heavy skillet. Add chopped onion, garlic, pickles and consumme. Simmer until meat is tender. Before serving add Sherry. Serve on rice.

# DAUBE PROVENCAL

3 lbs. stew beef (1 inch
  pieces)
1 t. salt
¼ t. freshly ground pepper
4 whole allspice
¼ c. wine vinegar
1 clove garlic, chopped
4 c. dry red wine
12 small (pearl) onions
½ lb. diced salt pork
2 carrots
2 stalks celery, diced
1 bay leaf
⅛ t. thyme

Serves 4

Combine beef, salt, pepper, allspice, vinegar, garlic and 2 cups wine. Let stand overnight in refrigerator. Remove meat; strain marinade; reserve. Dry meat. In a Dutch oven, brown salt pork; add carrots, cut lengthwise into ¾ inch strips, celery, and onions. Simmer until vegetables are tender and golden; remove. Brown meat on all sides. Add bay leaf, thyme, reserved marinade, remaining wine and vegetables. Bring to boil. Cover and bake at 375 degrees 2 hours, or until meat is tender.

# 30-MINUTE SPAGHETTI SAUCE

1 lb. lean ground beef
2 T. shortening
2 T. sugar
1 t. salt
1 t. garlic powder
Pepper to taste (about ¼ t.)
2-6 oz. cans tomato paste
  (rinse cans with ½ can
  hot water each)
1-8 oz. can tomato sauce
Small can mushrooms,
  stems and pieces and
  liquid
Vermicelli or thin spaghetti

Serves 4

Saute beef in shortening until just done. Add remaining ingredients; simmer slowly about 30 minutes, stirring occasionally. Put water on to boil; add vermicelli or spaghetti and cook until just tender. All should be ready at the same time.

# LAMB

## BAKED KIBBEE

**2 lb. lean ground lamb**
**1 onion, chopped**
**1 c. medium cracked wheat**
**1 T. salt**
**1 t. pepper**
**½ t. allspice**
**¼ t. cinnamon**
**3-4 c. cold water**
**½ c. oil**

**Filling:**
**1 c. pine nuts**
**1 lb. ground lamb or beef**
**4 T. butter**
**1 onion, chopped**

**Serves 6 to 8**

Soak cracked wheat in water until soft, but not mushy. Knead lamb, spices and onion together. Squeeze wheat by hand, removing water, and add to meat mixture. Knead well, using small amounts cold water to blend all together. In buttered baking dish, 13x9 inch, put half the mixture, patting until flat.

Melt butter and brown pine nuts, remove and brown meat and onion; add pine nuts and butter. Add the pine nut filling over the first layer. Use the other half of the raw meat and wheat mixture to form a layer on top. Cut into diamond shapes. Pour oil over top and dot with butter. Bake at 350 degrees 1 hour or until brown.

*This is great served with tossed salad, rice pilaf and Syrian bread.*

## STUFFED GRAPE LEAVES

3 c. rice
1 lb. coarsely ground lamb
  or beef or a mixture of both
¼ t. cinnamon
1 t. salt
Pepper to taste
2 T. melted butter
¼ c. lemon juice
20 grape leaves (or enough
  to hold all meat and rice
  mixture).

Serves 3 to 4

Soak rice 10 minutes. Line bottom of cooking utensil with rib bones of lamb and a few grape leaves. Drain rice, mix with meat, melted butter and seasoning. Roll about one tablespoon, or more if needed, in one grape leaf, using back of grape leaf. Turn in corners and form neat roll. Place evenly in pan in layers; add water to cover about ¼ inch above leaves. Cover. (Use a plate to hold down leaves when immersed in water). Put on low fire until rice is cooked (approximately 20-30 minutes). Add ¼ cup of lemon juice and simmer 5 minutes more.

*Serve with yogurt, salad and Syrian bread.*

## SWEDISH LAMB

5 lb. leg of lamb
1 T. salt
1 T. pepper
3 onions, sliced
3 carrots, sliced
1 c. hot beef broth
1½ c. hot strong coffee
½ c. heavy cream
1 T. sugar

Serves 6

Rub salt and pepper into lamb. Place meat on a rack in roasting pan. Surround with onions and carrots. Roast in preheated oven at 425 degrees for 30 minutes. Skim off fat. Reduce oven temperature to 350 degrees. Add beef broth, coffee, cream and sugar. Continue roasting; basting frequently for 1 hour or more. Place meat on serving platter. Puree all vegetables and meat juices in blender to serve as a gravy.

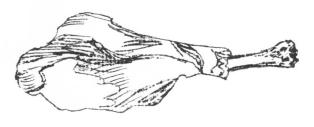

# PORK

## GEORGIA BACON

**Regular breakfast bacon**
**Flour**
**Water**
**Vegetable oil**

Make a batter with the flour and water, about as thick as good cream gravy. Dip bacon in, piece by piece until coated completely. Heat oil in skillet just as if you were going to fry chicken. Drop bacon in slice by slice and brown well (so that the bacon is really cooked).

*This resembles fried chicken, but is crisp and delicious Georgia bacon (named for a cook not the state). With the drippings you can make cream gravy and serve hot biscuits for a good southern breakfast.*

## BAKED HAM

**Ham, cooked or half cooked**
**Powdered cloves**
**Glaze:**
**1-2 c. brown sugar**
**1-2 t. dry mustard**
**Burgundy wine**
**Sauce:**
**1 c. Burgundy wine**
**¼ c. vinegar**
**1 c. pineapple juice**
**Raisins (optional)**

Choose ham size according to number of people to be entertained. Place in heavy brown paper sack; tie end. Place in shallow roasting pan. Bake at 325 degrees, 20 minutes to the pound. Remove ham from sack; cut off skin and most of fat. Sprinkle all over with powdered cloves. Blend brown sugar and mustard. Add enough wine to make thick paste. Spread on ham. Place in shallow roasting pan. Combine wine, vinegar, pineapple juice; pour into pan. Continue baking at 300 degrees 1 hour, basting carefully to avoid breaking sugar crust. Serve with sauce.

## BAKED HAM WITH ORANGE WINE SAUCE

1-8 to 9 lb. canned ham
¾ c. pineapple, apricot or
  other fruit juice
¾ c. port wine
2 t. orange peel
1½ c. light brown sugar
1 t. hot mustard
¼ t. cloves

Serves 12

Scrape off jellied coating. Score and pierce entire surface deeply with kitchen fork. Combine remaining ingredients (except ½ cup brown sugar). Pour over ham; marinate 24 hours, turning several times. Heavy plastic bag is ideal. Bake uncovered at 350 degrees for 2 hours, basting frequently. Thirty minutes before ham is done cover with remaining sugar. Pour marinade around ham. Serve with sauce.

## HAM TIMBALES

4 T. butter
1¾ c. bread crumbs
1¾ c. milk
2 c. cooked ham, chopped
1 T. onion juice
1 T. chopped parsley
3 eggs, beaten

Melt butter; add bread crumbs and milk; cook 5 minutes. Cool. Stir in ham, onion juice, parsley and eggs. Pour into 6 individual custard cups and bake at 350 degrees 35 minutes or until light brown.

## SUPER SIZZLE MARINATED HAM

2 ¾ inch slices ham
1½ c. orange juice
½ c. vinegar
½ c. brown sugar
2 T. ground cloves
1 T. dry mustard
1 T. powdered ginger
1 T. molasses
2 T. brandy or 1 T. brandy
  flavoring

Put ham slices in long flat dish. Combine all other ingredients, mixing well with rotary beater. Pour over ham slices. Marinate 2 hours if ham is pre-cooked and much longer if it is not. Grill, basting with sauce, only long enough to heat through or longer if ham needs to be cooked.

## TOURTIERE (MEAT PIE)

1 recipe 2 crust pie dough
3 lb. ground pork or
 1 lb. pork, 1 lb. beef,
 1 lb. veal
1 large onion, chopped
1 clove garlic, minced
¼ c. boiling water
2 T. parsley
2½ t. salt
Dash freshly ground pepper

Saute onion and garlic; add meat and brown. Stir in other ingredients and simmer 30 to 40 minutes. Cool. Roll out half of dough and place in a 9 inch pie plate. Pour meat mixture in. Roll out other half pie dough and place over top. Slit top and bake at 450 degrees 20 minutes or until golden brown.

*Tourtieres are French Canadian and are traditionally served during the Christmas holidays and on New Year's Day.*

## PORK AND SAUERKRAUT

5 lb. loin of pork
2 bay leaves
8 whole allspice
6 whole black peppers
6 slices bacon, cut
1½ c. chopped onion
1½ c. sliced apple
¼ c. light brown sugar
1 bay leaf, crushed
2-16 oz. cans drained
 sauerkraut
1 c. dry white wine
2 qts. water

Serves 8

In large kettle place pork, water, bay leaves, allspice and pepper. Bring to boil; simmer 1 hour. Cut bacon into ½ inch squares; fry. Add onion and apple; saute. Stir in sugar, bay leaf, sauerkraut, wine and 1 cup liquid from pork. Mix well. Pour into large roasting pan. Place pork in center of pan on top of sauerkraut. Bake uncovered at 375 degrees 30 minutes. Cover and bake until pork is tender.

# LEMON PORK CHOPS

4 loin pork chops
½ t. paprika
½ t. salt
⅛ t. pepper
½ c. raw rice, cooked
1 med. onion
4 lemon slices, thinly cut
1 large green pepper
¼ c. tomato juice
2 t. sugar
½ t. chili powder
1 bay leaf, crushed
1 t. salt

Serves 4

Sprinkle chops with paprika and ½ teaspoon salt; brown. Cut two quarter inch slices from center of onion; separate into rings; chop remaining. Combine chopped onion and rice. Cut pepper into 4 rings. Arrange chops in skillet; place lemon slice and onion slice on each chop. Arrange pepper rings around chops and fill with rice-onion mixture. Combine tomato juice, sugar, chili powder, bay leaf and salt. Pour over chops and top with remaining onion rings. Simmer until chops are tender. Place chops on warm plates; garnish with rice-stuffed pepper rings; spoon sauce over all.

# BARBECUED SPARERIBS

6 lbs. spareribs
2 c. sliced onions
1 jar chili sauce
1 t. salt
¼ t. pepper
2 T. Worcestershire sauce
¼ c. cider vinegar
¼ c. brown sugar
2 t. mustard
1 t. paprika

Serves 6 to 8

Cut spareribs into serving pieces; trim excess fat. Combine all ingredients and pour over ribs, adding one chili jar of water. Cover and bake 2 hours. Spoon sauce over ribs 3 times during baking. Remove cover and bake additional 15 minutes to brown and thicken sauce. Drain off excess fat.

# VEAL

## EXCELLENT VEAL DEAL

4-6 veal chops
½ can beef bouillon
¼ c. dry Sherry
Generous dash thyme
Juice and grated rind of
  1 lemon
½ c. sour cream
Fresh or canned
  mushrooms, optional

Serves 4

Brown meat on both sides in heavy fry pan. Remove meat; pour off excess fat saving crispy part of drippings. Add bouillon, Sherry, thyme, lemon juice, rind and sour cream. Stir over low heat until thick and smooth. Return meat to sauce, cover and cook slowly ½ hour or until meat is tender. If using mushrooms, saute and add to sauce at this point.

*This is delicious substituting either pork chops or chicken breasts, following the same directions. Serve with wild rice to complete an excellent meal.*

## SWISS VEAL

1½ lb. veal round steak, cut
  in 6 pieces
2 beaten eggs
1 c. fine dry bread crumbs
2 T. oil
1 15 oz. can stroganoff
  sauce
1 large avocado, cut in
  6 wedges
1 large tomato, cut in
  6 wedges
¾ c. shredded or six slices
  Swiss cheese

Serves 6

Pound veal very thin with meat mallet. Dip in beaten egg, then in crumbs. Brown on both sides in hot oil. Heat stroganoff sauce. Place veal in 13 x 9 inch baking dish. Pour sauce over meat. Place one avocado and one tomato wedge atop each piece of veal. Cover with Swiss cheese. Bake in 350 degree oven until cheese melts and sauce bubbles.

# VEAL BIRDS

2 lbs. veal
2 c. soft bread crumbs
2 T. butter
2 T. chopped parsley
½ t. onion juice
2 T. chopped celery
½ t. salt
⅛ t. pepper
½ c. hot water

Serves 6

Wipe thin slices of veal (cut from the leg or shoulder) and cut into 3 x 3½ inch pieces. Prepare stuffing with crumbs parsley, onion juice, celery, hot water and butter. Spread pieces with stuffing, roll and tie. Sprinkle with salt and pepper; dredge with flour and brown in hot butter. Put in stew pan, cover with butter and cook slowly until tender. Serve on small circular or square pieces of toast; cover with the sauce and garnish with parsley.

# VENISON

## HUNTER'S STEW

2 lbs. venison, cut in bite
    size pieces
2 T. flour
1 t. salt
1 t. sugar
2 tomatoes, quartered
2 green peppers, quartered
1 c. chopped onions
½ t. oregano
¼ t. thyme
1 t. chili powder
¼ c. catsup
½ c. Burgundy

Serves 4

Brown meat in hot fat; sprinkle with flour, salt and sugar. Add onions and spices; stir in catsup. Cook 15 minutes. Add tomatoes, peppers and wine. Simmer 45 minutes, or until meat is tender.

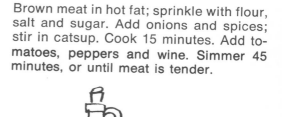

## CHICKEN AND ALMONDS

8 chicken breast halves
½ c. raisins
¼ c. vodka
½ c. slivered almonds
½ c. butter
1 t. salt
½ t. red pepper
1 can mushroom soup
1 can cheese soup
1 large onion, sliced

**Serves 6 to 8**

Soak raisins in vodka. Saute almonds in butter until lightly brown; remove. Put chicken in skillet; season with salt and pepper and brown. Arrange chicken in 13x9 baking dish. Blend soups and pour over chicken. Put onion slices and raisins on top. Cover and bake at 375 degrees 30 minutes; uncover, add almonds and bake 20 minutes longer.

## CHICKEN BREASTS DELUXE

4 whole chicken breasts,
  split and skinned
1-6 oz. can sliced
mushrooms
1 can mushroom soup
½ c. Sherry
1 c. sour cream
Paprika or finely chopped
  parsley

**Serves 6 to 8**

Arrange breasts in a shallow greased casserole so that meat side is up. Cover with mushrooms which have been well drained. Combine soup, sour cream and Sherry. Blend well with a rotary beater. Pour over chicken and be sure that chicken is covered completely.

Bake at 350 degrees about 1¼ hours. When ready to serve either shake paprika over top or sprinkle with chopped parsley.

## CHICKEN BREASTS IN CREAM

**6 chicken breast halves,
  boned**
**¼ c. butter**
**1 envelope onion gravy mix**
**1 c. chicken broth**
**2 T. tomato paste**
**2 T. Sherry**
**½ c. sliced fresh
  mushrooms**
**½ c. half and half cream**

**Serves 4 to 6**

Remove skin and brown chicken in butter. Place in 11x7 baking dish. Combine gravy mix, broth, tomato paste and Sherry in skillet; stir until hot. Remove from heat; add mushrooms and cream. Pour over chicken making sure mushrooms are covered with sauce. Bake at 325 degrees 1 hour or until chicken is tender. May be made ahead.

## CHICKEN BREASTS SUPREME

**8 chicken breast halves,
  boned**
**1 c. sour cream**
**2 T. lemon juice**
**2 t. Worcestershire**
**1 t. celery salt**
**1 t. paprika**
**2 cloves garlic, minced**
**2 t. salt**
**¼ t. pepper**
**1¾ c. bread crumbs, corn
  flakes or potato chips,
  crushed**
**¼ c. butter, melted**

**Serves 6 to 8**

Place chicken in large bowl. Combine next 8 ingredients; pour over chicken coating each piece. Let stand in refrigerator overnight. Remove chicken; roll in crumbs. Place in baking pan; bake uncovered at 350 degrees 50 minutes. Spoon melted butter over chicken; bake 10-15 minutes longer.

## CHICKEN BREASTS WITH CHEESE

6 chicken breast halves,
  boned
Salt and pepper
½ c. butter or margarine,
  softened
¼ lb. Mozzarella cheese
½ c. flour
2 eggs, beaten
½ c. bread crumbs
2 T. parsley, chopped
1 t. marjoram
½ t. thyme
½ c. dry white wine

Pound chicken breasts to ⅛ inch thick. Salt and pepper; spread with half of butter. Cut cheese into 6 pieces; place 1 piece on each breast. Roll jelly roll fashion, tucking in ends to seal. Dip in flour, then egg; roll in bread crumbs. Place in buttered baking dish. Melt remaining butter; mix in parsley, marjoram and thyme. Pour over chicken. Cover tightly; bake at 350 degrees 20 minutes. Remove from oven; pour wine over chicken and return to oven 15 minutes, basting frequently.

## CHICKEN CACCIATORE

3 lb. fryer, cut up
¼ c. olive oil
1 large onion, sliced
1 clove garlic, minced
1 can tomatoes
1-8 oz. can tomato paste
1 c. water
1 t. salt
½ t. pepper
1 t. oregano
1 t. garlic powder
1 4 oz. can mushrooms
½ c. dry red wine

Serves 6

In a large skillet saute onion and garlic in olive oil until tender. Add chicken and brown. Stir in tomatoes, tomato paste, water and seasonings. Cover and cook over low heat 45 minutes or until chicken is tender. Stir in mushrooms and wine; simmer uncovered 15 minutes. (Can be served over spaghetti or noodles).

# CHICKEN CURRY

1 4 lb. roasting chicken
1 onion
4 whole cloves
1 carrot
2 stalks celery
2 T. parsley
8 peppercorns
1 bay leaf
1 t. salt
½ c. margarine
1 clove garlic, minced
2 green apples, peeled
  and sliced
2 onions, chopped
1-14 oz. can tomatoes,
  drained
4 T. instant flour
2 T. curry
½ t. ground ginger
½ t. salt
½ t. freshly ground pepper
4 c. chicken stock
Juice of 1 lime or lemon
½ c. dry white wine
½ c. half and half cream

**Serves 6 to 8**

In deep kettle place chicken with next 8 ingredients. Add just enough water to reach ⅓ way up. Cover; simmer until tender. Remove chicken; strain stock and reserve. Bone and skin chicken; cut into 1 inch pieces. Saute garlic in margarine. Add apples, onions and tomatoes; cover, cook 10 minutes. Sprinkle flour and seasonings over mixture. Add stock, juice and wine; cook 15 minutes more, until smooth and fairly thick. Divide into 2 or 3 batches; put in blender. Add enough cream to reach desired consistency. Remove; add chicken; heat. In separate bowls pass: crumbled bacon, toasted coconut, grated hard cooked eggs, chopped peanuts, oven-heated raisins, crystallized rose petals and chutney.

## BAKED CHICKEN CURRY

4½ lbs. chicken breasts
2 t. salt
¼ t. pepper
2 carrots, diced
1 med. onion, quartered
1-2 stalks celery with leaves
½ c. butter or margarine
1 t. curry powder
½ c. flour
1 t. salt
¼ t. pepper
2-6 oz. cans sliced
  mushrooms
2 pkgs. frozen peas, thawed
2 c. crumbled potato chips
Pimiento

**Serves 10 to 12**

Place chicken in large kettle with water to cover. Add next five ingredients; cook covered until tender. Strain broth and chill. Skin and bone chicken; dice. Skim chicken fat off broth and use it with butter or margarine. Depending upon quantity of chicken fat, you may reduce butter or margarine. Melt butter; blend in curry, flour, salt and pepper. Stir and cook two minutes. Remove from heat; slowly stir in four cups reserved broth. Return to heat; cook, stirring constantly, until sauce thickens. Combine chicken, mushrooms, peas and sauce. Pour into shallow 2 quart baking dish; sprinkle with potato chips and bake at 400 degrees 20 minutes. Decorate top with pimiento.

*This doubles successfully. It may be made ahead of time.*

## CHICKEN DELGADO

3 c. chicken, cooked and
  diced
2 c. thick white sauce
  (see index)
¼ t. salad herbs
Salt
6 ozs. Swiss cheese, grated
½ c. slivered almonds
1-6 oz. can mushrooms,
  drained
2 T. Sherry
2-8 oz. cans artichoke
  hearts, drained
Seasoned bread crumbs
Crushed potato chips
12 black olives, sliced
Pimiento strips

**Serves 6**

Season white sauce with salad herbs and salt; add cheese; stir until melted and smooth. Add chicken, almonds, mushrooms and Sherry. Arrange artichoke hearts in bottom of shallow baking dish; top with chicken mixture. Sprinkle with seasoned bread crumbs and crushed potato chips. Bake at 350 degrees 40 minutes or until lightly browned and bubbly. Garnish with olives and pimiento before serving.

# CHICKEN ENCHILADAS

4 whole chicken breasts
  (8 halves)
1 large onion, chopped
8 ozs. grated cheddar cheese
12 tortillas
2 c. chicken broth

Sauce:
1-8 oz. carton sour cream
1 can cream of chicken soup
1-4 oz. can Taco sauce
1-4 oz. can green chilies
Salt and pepper
8 ozs. Monterrey Jack
  cheese, sliced

Serves 4 to 6

Simmer chicken until tender. Remove meat from bones; dice. Mix chicken, onion and cheese. Soften tortillas in warm chicken broth; fill with chicken mixture and roll up. Place seam side down in greased baking dish. Cover with sauce. Bake at 375 degrees 30-45 minutes or until bubbly and cheese is browned.

Blend all ingredients (except cheese). Pour over casserole and top with Monterrey Jack cheese.

# CHICKEN GLORIA

4 chicken breast halves,
  boned
4 chicken bouillon cubes
4 T. bread crumbs
4 T. Parmesan cheese
1 egg, beaten
4 T. butter
4 T. chicken stock
4 T. Scotch whiskey

Serves 4

Remove skin, trim and flatten chicken. Simmer in 1 quart water with 4 chicken bouillon cubes 1 hour. Reserve stock. Combine bread crumbs and Parmesan cheese. Dip each piece of chicken into beaten egg, then bread crumb mixture. Fry in butter over medium heat until golden brown. Add 1 tablespoon chicken stock per breast; cook 3 minutes. Add 1 tablespoon Scotch per breast. Serve hot or cold.

# CHICKEN IN A POT

2-3 lb. chicken, cut up
¼ c. butter
12 small onions or 3 large
  ones, cut up
2-3 oz. can mushrooms,
  drained
½ c. canned tomatoes,
  drained
½ c. dry white wine
1 t. salt
Pepper to taste
½ t. paprika
½ c. sour cream or plain
  yogurt

Serves 4

Melt butter in skillet; brown chicken on both sides. Add next seven ingredients; simmer 1 hour. Remove chicken to serving dish; keep hot. Add sour cream to pan; stir and heat. Pour over chicken. Serve with noodles or rice.

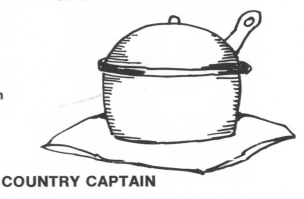

# COUNTRY CAPTAIN

3½ lb. fryer or 8 chicken
  breast halves, skinned
½ c. flour
Salt and pepper
Vegetable oil
1 onion, chopped
1 large green pepper,
  chopped
1 clove garlic, minced
1 t. salt
½ t. pepper
2 t. curry powder
2-16 oz. cans tomatoes
1 t. chopped parsley
½ t. thyme
½ c. currants
1 c. toasted almonds

Serves 6 to 8

Combine flour, salt and pepper; roll chicken in mixture, coating well. Fry in hot oil until brown. Remove to 13x9 inch baking dish. In same pan, saute onion, green pepper and garlic until tender; add seasonings, tomatoes, parsley and thyme. Pour over chicken; cover and bake at 350 degrees 40 minutes. Add currants; cook 5 minutes more. Sprinkle with toasted almonds and serve over rice.

## DRUNKEN CHICKEN

3 lb. chicken, quartered
¼ c. butter
¼ c. flour
Salt and pepper
1 t. paprika
1 can cream of chicken soup
1-6 oz. can sliced
  mushrooms, drained
¾ c. Sherry

**Serves 4**

Melt butter in baking pan. Coat chicken with flour and seasonings. Place skin side down in butter. Bake in 350 degree oven ½ hour. Mix remaining ingredients; turn chicken, cover with sauce. Bake ½ hour more. Serve with rice.

## DUTCH "RIJSTAFEL" AMERICAN STYLE

4 c. cooked chicken, diced
1 large onion, chopped
1 green pepper, chopped
2 T. butter
3 c. med. white sauce
1 T. curry powder
1 c. mushroom caps, broiled
5 c. cooked rice
Avocado slices

**Serves 6**

Saute onion and green pepper in butter until tender; blend into white sauce with curry powder. Add chicken and mushrooms. Heap rice in middle of large serving platter; garnish with avocado slices. Surround with creamed chicken mixture. Serve bowls of almonds, chutney (peach or mango) and raisins around platter.

*Rijstafel means "rice table". This dish originated in the former Dutch East Indies.*

# HOT CHICKEN SALAD

4 c. cooked chicken, diced
2 T. lemon juice
¾ c. mayonnaise
1 t. salt
½ t. monosodium glutamate
2 c. chopped celery
4 hard-cooked eggs, sliced
¾ c. cream of chicken soup
1 t. onion, finely minced
2 pimientos, cut fine
⅔ c. finely chopped toasted
  almonds
1 c. cheese, grated
1½ c. crushed potato chips

Serves 8

Combine first 10 ingredients; place in large rectangular dish. Top with cheese, potato chips and almonds. Let stand overnight in refrigerator. Bake at 400 degrees 20 to 25 minutes.

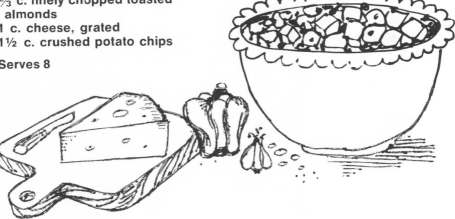

# LEBANESE CHICKEN PILAF

1 stewing chicken
Salt and pepper
1 cinnamon stick
Rice
Butter
½ c. blanched almonds
¼ c. pine nuts

Serves 8 to 12

Place chicken in a pot with enough water to cover. Season with salt, pepper and cinnamon stick. Simmer until meat is tender. Remove meat from bones in large pieces. Reserve stock. For every 2 cups stock measure 1 cup rice. Fry rice in butter a few minutes; blend with stock and cook until broth is absorbed. Saute almonds and pine nuts in butter. Arrange nuts in bottom of 3 quart casserole. Cover with rice; press down gently. Unmold onto serving platter. Garnish with chicken pieces. Serve hot with chicken gravy.

## MEXICAN MOLE POBLANO

4 large chicken breast
halves
¼ c. vegetable oil
1½ t. salt
1 clove garlic, minced
1 small onion, chopped
1 small green pepper,
chopped
2 tomatoes, peeled and
chopped
1½ t. chili powder
⅛ t. cinnamon, nutmeg,
cloves, cumin
½ oz. unsweetened
chocolate
Grated rind of 1 orange
¼ c. pine nuts or almonds
2 T. currants
1½ T. cornstarch
1½ c. chicken broth

Serves 4

Brown chicken in oil; transfer to deep pan; season with salt. Add 2 tablespoons more oil to skillet; saute garlic, onions and peppers. Add tomatoes, seasonings, chocolate, orange rind, nuts, currants and pinch salt. Mix well. Dissolve cornstarch in a little chicken broth, blend into remainder of broth; add to sauce. Pour sauce over chicken. Bake at 350 degrees 45 minutes, or until chicken is tender. Baste frequently.

*To complete the meal in Mexican style serve frijoles refritos (cooked and refried beans) a fresh green vegetable and a salad of lettuce, onions and tomatoes.*

## MIRIAM'S BROWN CHICKEN

2 frying chickens, cut up
Salt and pepper
¼ c. flour
1 onion, sliced thin
1 lemon, sliced thin
2 c. water
¼ c. sugar
2 t. Worcestershire
Juice of 1 lemon
½ c. butter or margarine
Dash red pepper
1 t. dried parsley
½ t. thyme or oregano
(optional)

Serves 6 to 8

Place chicken in 13x9 inch baking dish; season with salt and pepper. Dust with flour. Arrange onion and lemon slices over chicken pieces. Mix together remaining ingredients in small pan, heating until butter melts. Pour over chicken pieces. Bake at 450 degrees 20 minutes, then reduce to 300 degrees; bake 2 hours, basting often.

## OPULENT CHICKEN CASSEROLE

4 whole chicken breasts
  (8 halves)
Salt
Pepper
Paprika
½ c. butter
2-8½ oz. cans artichoke
  hearts
½ lb. fresh mushrooms,
  sliced
Pinch tarragon
3 T. flour
⅓ c. Sherry
1½ c. chicken bouillon

**Serves 8**

Split chicken breasts and spread thickly with salt, pepper and paprika. Saute in 4 tablespoons butter until golden brown. Place breasts in 3 quart flat casserole; put artichokes among them. Saute mushrooms in remaining butter; season with tarragon and cook 5 minutes. Sprinkle flour in gently; add Sherry and bouillon. Simmer until thickened; pour over chicken and artichokes. Cover and bake at 375 degrees 45 minutes.

## ORIENTAL CHICKEN WITH VEGETABLES

3 lbs. chicken pieces
2 T. butter or margarine
1¼ t. salt
½ c. water
½ c. onion, sliced
1-12 oz. jar apricot,
  pineapple, peach
  preserves, or orange
  marmalade
¼ c. vinegar
1 T. cornstarch
1 T. soy sauce
½ t. ginger
1-5 oz. can water chestnuts,
  drained, thinly sliced
1 green pepper, coarsely
  chopped
1 tomato, cut in thin wedges

**Serves 6**

Melt butter in skillet; brown chicken. Sprinkle with 1 teaspoon salt; add water. Simmer, covered, 45 minutes or until tender. Remove chicken from pan; keep hot. Add onions to pan drippings, cook until limp. Combine preserves, vinegar, cornstarch, soy sauce, ginger and remaining salt; blend well. Add to skillet. Cook stirring constantly until thickened. Add water chestnuts, green pepper and tomato; heat. Serve chicken and sauce over rice.

*Served with wild rice and a mixed salad for a good party menu.*

# OVEN BARBECUE CHICKEN

1 2 to 3 lb. fryer, cut up
Juice of 1 lime
¼ c. butter or margarine
2 T. Worcestershire
2 T. vinegar
2 T. catsup
1 t. Tabasco
½ t. salt

Serves 4

Place cut up chicken in shallow baking dish. Combine rest of ingredients in saucepan; heat to boiling and pour over chicken. Bake in 350 degree oven 1½ hours. This is easy and delicious.

# POLLO DELICADO

4 chicken breast halves,
  boned
2 T. honey
4 T. Sherry
Juice of 2 lemons
2 eggs
2 T. cream
1 t. salt
½ t. pepper
1½ t. onion juice
Bread crumbs
Butter

Serves 4

Brush chicken breasts lightly with honey. Marinate 2 hours in Sherry and lemon juice. Wipe dry; flatten out to ½ inch thickness. Beat eggs; add cream, salt, pepper and onion juice. Dip chicken in mixture; roll in bread crumbs. Saute in butter until golden brown on both sides. Serve with slices of lemon and parsley.

# POLLY'S APRICOT GLAZED CHICKEN

3 lbs. chicken pieces or 8
  breast halves
1-10 oz. jar apricot preserves
1-8 oz. bottle red Russian
  dressing
1 envelope dry onion soup
  mix

Serves 6 to 8

Place chicken skin side up on pan lined with foil. Combine remaining ingredients and spread over chicken. Bake, uncovered, at 350 degrees 1 hour. Baste occasionally.

# POLYNESIAN CHICKEN

2 whole chicken breasts,
  (4 halves)
¼ c. soy sauce
⅓ c. vegetable oil
1 t. powdered ginger
½ t. onion salt
2 T. onion, minced
½ c. flour
½ c. orange juice
1 c. pineapple tidbits with
  juice
2 t. cornstarch
¼ c. cold water
½ c. Mandarin orange
  sections
¼ c. slivered almonds,
  toasted

Serves 4

Remove bones and skin from chicken. Arrange breasts in single layer in a shallow pan. Combine soy sauce, 3 tablespoons oil, ginger, onion salt, minced onion. Pour over chicken; let stand 1 hour; turn once. Drain; save marinade. Coat chicken with flour. Heat remaining oil; brown chicken. Add orange juice, and pineapple juice to soy sauce mixture; pour over chicken. Cover; simmer 30 minutes or until chicken is tender. Remove chicken. Mix cornstarch with water; pour into skillet; stir until thickened. Add pineapple, oranges and chicken. Heat. Sprinkle with almonds just before serving. Serve over rice.

# RITZY CHICKEN CASSEROLE

1-3½ lb. chicken
1 stack Ritz crackers,
  crushed
2 cans cream of chicken
  soup
1 c. sour cream
4 T. melted butter or
  margarine
1-6oz. can mushrooms

Serves 4

Simmer chicken until tender; remove meat from bones and dice. Combine all ingredients, blend well. Pour into greased 3 quart casserole dish. Bake at 300 degrees 45 minutes. (Canned peas may be added if desired).

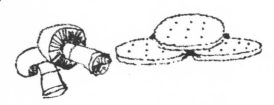

# SWEDISH CHICKEN BREASTS

8 chicken breast halves,
  boned
8 strips bacon
1 jar dried beef
1-8 oz. carton sour cream
1 can cream of mushroom
  soup
5 ozs. Sherry
3 oz. can sliced mushrooms
Lemon pepper
Dash Beau Monde
  seasoning
Parsley flakes

Serves 6 to 8

Wrap each breast in strip of bacon. Line shallow pan with dried beef. Place chicken breasts on top of beef. Combine sour cream, mushroom soup, Sherry and mushrooms. Sprinkle chicken with seasonings; cover with soup mixture. Bake covered with foil at 350 degrees 1 hour. Uncover; let brown slightly.

# BARBEQUED WILD DUCK

3 T. catsup
2 T. vinegar
1 T. Worcestershire
4 T. water
2 T. butter or margarine
3 T. sugar
1 t. salt
1 t. prepared mustard
1 t. chili powder
½ t. red pepper
½ t. black pepper
2 ducks
2 med. onions, quartered or
1 large onion and 1 apple,
  quartered
½ c. chopped celery

Serves 4

Blend together first eleven ingredients. Simmer together until butter melts. Set aside.

Cover ducks with water; add onions and celery. Parboil 10 minutes. Put ducks in roasting pan; salt and pepper; put onion in cavity. Pour sauce over ducks. Cover and roast at 350 degrees 2 hours. The last hour, skim top, add new potatoes (peel around middle). Remove cover to allow sauce to cook down.

# CHINESE DUCK

1 small onion, chopped
2 T. peanut oil
2 c. cooked rice
1 egg, beaten
2 T. soy sauce
½ c. slivered almonds
1 4-5 lb. duck
½ c. soy sauce
1 c. water
1 t. ground ginger

Serves 2

Brown onion in peanut oil; add rice. Cook a few minutes, separating grains by stirring. Add egg, 2 tablespoons soy sauce, add slivered almonds; fry until rice takes on a brown color. Stuff duck; place on trivet in roaster; pour soy sauce over it. Pour water in bottom of roaster; bake at 350 degrees 1 to 1½ hours (15 to 20 minutes per pound). Half way through roasting time, baste ducks with pan drippings; sprinkle with ginger and cook until tender.

# GLEN ACRES BRAISED DUCK

2 ducks, halved
2 T. vegetable oil
2 T. Sherry
2 T. tomato paste
3 T. flour
1½ c. strong bouillon
½ c. dry red wine
1 t. salt
¼ t. freshly ground pepper
½ lb. mushrooms, thinly
  sliced
1 bay leaf or ¼ t. marjoram

Serves 4

Remove and discard wings. Brown ducks in oil in a heavy Dutch oven until deep brown. Pour in Sherry turning ducks over a minute or two; remove from pan. Lower heat; stir in tomato paste. Sift in flour gradually, stirring until smooth. Gradually stir in heated bouillon. Add red wine. Bring mixture to boil; return duck halves to pan. Add salt, pepper, sliced mushrooms, bay leaf or marjoram. Cover and bake at 325 degrees two to three hours, or until ducks are tender. Remove to platter to keep warm. Strain sauce; degrease. Reheat and correct seasonings. Serve with wild rice garnished with crab apples.

# ROCK CORNISH HENS

2 Rock Cornish hens
½ c. butter
1 c. onion, minced
½ c. celery, chopped
½ c. shallots, chopped
½ c. ham, minced
1½ doz. oysters, drained,
 finely chopped; reserve
 liquid
2 eggs, lightly beaten
4 c. bread, cubed
2 T. fresh parsley, chopped
1 t. thyme
2 bay leaves, crushed
Salt and pepper
2 T. flour
1½ c. chicken stock
Sherry

Serves 2

Melt butter in skillet; saute chopped ingredients until transparent. Add drained oysters, heat through. Remove from heat; stir in eggs. Add bread which has been soaked in oyster liquid and squeezed dry. Return to heat, add parsley and seasoning. Stuff hens; brush with melted butter, sprinkle with salt and pepper. Bake in 350 degree oven 1 hour, or until done. Remove hens to platter; keep warm. Brown flour in pan drippings, stir in chicken stock; cook until thick and smooth. Strain. Add Sherry to taste. Serve over hens.

# TURKEY AND NOODLES ALFREDO

1 half turkey breast, cooked
1 egg yolk
2 T. milk
Flour
Olive oil
½ lb. butter
½ lb. cheddar cheese,
 grated
8 oz. pkg. noodles
½ c. thick cream
Salt and pepper to taste

Serves 4 to 6

Slice cooked turkey breast into ¼ inch slices. Beat egg yolk and milk together. Dip turkey slices in flour, then egg mixture, then flour. Fry in olive oil until golden brown. Boil noodles until just tender; drain well. Place in chafing dish. Add butter and cheese. Cook and stir with wooden spoon until well blended; add cream and seasoning. Pour over turkey slices.

*A very rich dish. One slice of turkey per person is sufficient.*

# TURKEY HAM CASSEROLE

½ c. chopped onion
2 T. butter
3 T. flour
½ t. salt
¼ t. pepper
1-3 oz. can broiled sliced
  mushrooms, undrained
1 c. light cream
2 T. dry Sherry
2 c. diced cooked turkey
1-5 oz. can water chestnuts,
  drained, sliced
1 c. diced cooked ham
½ c. grated Swiss cheese
1½ c. soft bread crumbs
3 T. butter, melted

**Serves 6**

Saute onion in butter until tender; blend in flour, salt and pepper. Add mushrooms, cream and Sherry; cook, stirring constantly until thickened. Add turkey, chestnuts and ham. Pour into 2 quart baking dish; sprinkle with cheese. Mix bread crumbs with 3 tablespoons butter; sprinkle with cheese. Bake at 400 degrees 35 minutes or until bubbly and browned.

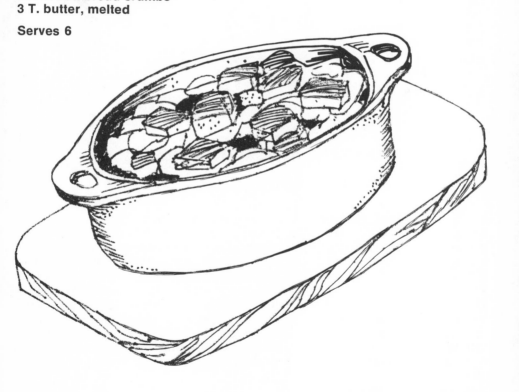

# SEAFOOD

## COURTBOUILLON

3 lb. red snapper or redfish
  filets
½ c. bacon drippings
½ c. flour
2 large onions, chopped
1 green pepper, chopped
1 c. celery, chopped
2 cloves garlic, minced
1-6 oz. can tomato paste
1 pt. water
1 c. red wine
Salt, pepper, cayenne, to
  taste
3 T. parsley, chopped
2 bay leaves
¼ t. sweet basil
¼ t. oregano

Serves 6 to 8

Saute onion, celery, garlic and pepper in bacon drippings until tender. Remove. Stir flour into drippings; brown. Add tomato paste; cook five minutes. Add vegetables, water, wine, seasonings. Simmer two hours. Put fish in 13x9 inch baking dish. Pour sauce over fish. Bake at 350 degrees one half hour or until fish is done. Serve sauce over fish.

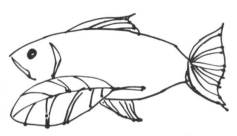

## CRAB AND AVOCADO CASSEROLE

1 c. green pepper, chopped
2 T. onion, minced
2 T. celery, minced
2 T. butter
2 T. flour
1 c. milk
½ c. sour cream
1 c. sharp cheese, grated
½ t. seasoned salt
½ t. Worcestershire
1-12 oz. pkg. frozen
  King crab
1 ripe avocado, sliced
1 T. lemon juice
½ c. bread crumbs
⅓ c. almonds, chopped

Serves 6

Saute green pepper, onion and celery in butter. Blend in flour; add milk then sour cream. Cook over low heat until thick. Add cheese, salt and Worcestershire. Stir until cheese melts. Fold in crab. Pour into one quart baking dish; sprinkle avocado slices with lemon juice; arrange over top. Sprinkle with bread crumbs and almonds. Bake at 350 degrees 20 minutes, or until lightly brown.

# CRABMEAT STUFFED AVOCADO

3 avocados
Lime juice
1 c. crabmeat, flaked
1 c. cream sauce
1 T. minced onion
1 c. sharp cheese, grated
Tabasco to taste

Serves 6

Cut avocados in half; remove seeds and sprinkle with lime juice. Mix crabmeat and cream sauce. Stir in seasonings. Fill halves with mixture; sprinkle each with cheese. Arrange in baking dish with ½ inch water in bottom. Bake at 350 degrees 20 minutes.

## CRAB CAKES

1 med. onion, chopped
1 med. green pepper, chopped
2 T. oil
2 med. potatoes
1 lb. white lump crabmeat
Salt and pepper to taste
1 egg, beaten
Corn flake crumbs

Serves 4

Saute onion and pepper in oil until tender. Boil potatoes with salt until done. Mash potatoes well. Combine onion and green pepper with crabmeat and potatoes. Season. Form into cakes about the size of hamburgers. Dip in beaten egg; roll in crumbs. Fry in oil until golden brown.

## CRAB RICE

1 c. onion, chopped
4 T. butter
1 clove garlic, chopped
1 3 oz. can mushrooms
Pinch basil, thyme, pepper
½ t. salt
½ bay leaf, crushed
1 (1 lb. 3 oz.) can tomatoes
½ lb. cheese, grated
1-6½ oz. can crab meat
1 t. Worcestershire sauce
4 c. cooked and salted rice

Serves 6

Saute onion in butter. Add all other ingredients, except rice; simmer until flavors have blended and cheese melted. Combine with cooked rice. Heat and serve.

# HEAVENLY CRABMEAT SOUFFLE

8 slices of bread
2-6 oz. cans good quality
  crabmeat
½ small onion, chopped fine
1 green pepper, chopped
  fine
1 c. celery, chopped fine
½ c. mayonnaise
4 eggs, well beaten
3 c. milk
1 can cream of mushroom
  soup
½ c. grated sharp cheddar
  cheese

Serves 8 to 10

Cube 4 slices of untrimmed bread; spread over buttered 13x9 inch pan. Mix vegetables, crabmeat and mayonnaise as for salad; spread on bread. Put remaining 4 slices of cubed bread on top. Combine eggs and milk and pour over all. Refrigerate overnight. Pour undiluted mushroom soup over all. Bake at 325 degrees 1 hour or until crusty. Fifteen minutes before serving, spread grated cheese on top and return to oven 10 minutes.

*This makes a nice meal served with slaw or tomato aspic. Vary it by using 2 pounds cooked shrimp instead of crabmeat.*

# CURRIED CRABMEAT CREPES

1 recipe crepes (see index)
Double recipe medium white
  sauce (see index)
7½ oz. can crabmeat
1 T. butter
1 t. shallot or green onion
½ c. dry white wine
1 t. curry powder
½ t. Worcestershire
⅛ t. pepper
Dash cayenne

Glaze:
1 egg yolk
4 T. butter, melted
¼ c. heavy cream, whipped
⅛ t. salt
2 t. lemon juice
Parmesan cheese

Serves 6

Separate crabmeat pieces. Saute onion in butter 1 minute; add crab, wine, curry powder, Worcestershire, pepper and cayenne. Simmer 3 minutes. Stir in 1 cup of white sauce; blend well. Fill crepes with crab mixture; arrange in shallow baking dish, seam side down. Cover with foil. Bake at 350 degrees 20-25 minutes, or until heated through. Uncover; spoon glaze over top. Sprinkle lightly with Parmesan cheese. Broil until browned.

Beat yolk and salt until foamy. Gradually beat in 2 T. melted butter. Mix remaining butter with lemon juice, and add to egg yolk mixture. Whisk in remaining white sauce. Fold in whipped cream.

# DEVILED CRAB

4 t. butter
3 t. flour
1 t. dry mustard
1 t. salt
2 eggs, hard-boiled,
  chopped
½ c. cracker crumbs
1 t. red pepper
1 c. milk
4 T. minced onion
¼ c. dry Sherry
2 c. cooked crabmeat
Lemon juice

Serves 4 to 6

Melt butter; stir in flour and add milk gradually; cook until thickened. Remove from heat; stir in crabmeat, seasonings and eggs. Add Sherry and lemon juice (to taste). Place in crab shells, sprinkle with cracker crumbs; dot with butter and bake at 400 degrees 15-20 minutes.

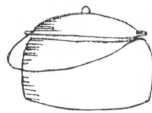

# FILETS EN PAPILLOTE D'ARGENT

8 small or 4 large fish filets
½ lb. mushrooms
½ lb. raw shrimp, cleaned
1 recipe medium white
  sauce (see index) seasoned
  with salt and lemon juice
1 t. salt
1 T. lemon juice
Dash paprika
Dash pepper
Chopped parsley

Serves 4

Prepare 4 pieces foil 14 inches long. Place 1 portion fish in center of each. Chop stems of mushrooms and lightly saute with caps in shortening. Arrange shrimp and mushrooms over filets equally. Season with salt, pepper and lemon juice. Spoon white sauce over each portion; sprinkle with parsley. Bring edges of foil together in double fold to make tight seal. Double fold ends to form tight square bag. Place on cookie sheet; bake at 425 degrees 40 minutes. Place on serving plates; snip through foil with scissors to form criss cross on top; fold back foil.

# AUSTRIAN STUFFED FLOUNDER

8 large flounder filets
Salt and lemon juice
10 slices toasted white
  bread, cubed
½ t. dried dill
6 ozs. Swiss cheese, diced
1 c. chicken broth
1 c. butter
1-6½ oz. can crabmeat
½ c. bread crumbs

Serves 8

Lay filets in greased baking dish; sprinkle with salt and lemon juice. In a large bowl, combine bread cubes, dill, Swiss cheese, chicken broth, crabmeat and ½ cup butter. Mix well. Place scoop of stuffing on one end of each flounder filet. Fold filets in half over stuffing. Melt remaining butter and spoon over filets. Sprinkle lightly with dill and crumbs. Bake at 350 degrees 30 minutes.

# BAKED STUFFED FLOUNDER

2 large flounder filets
Stuffing:
2 c. bread crumbs
½ c. clam juice
1 c. finely chopped clams
½ c. melted butter or
 margarine
¼ t. salt
1 t. seafood seasoning
1 T. finely chopped onion

Shrimp Sauce:
1 c. clam juice
4 T. butter or margarine
4 T. flour
½ c. water or Vermouth
½ c. cooked shrimp, split
Dash Accent

Serves 4

Combine all stuffing ingredients; mix well. Place one flounder filet in oiled baking dish; cover with layer of stuffing. Top with second flounder filet, pressing edges together, forming one fish. Salt lightly; brush with butter. Bake at 400 degrees 20 minutes (add small amount water to pan while baking). Place on serving dish; cover with shrimp sauce.

Heat clam juice and butter over low heat until butter melts. Dissolve flour in water or Vermouth; add to clam juice. Cook 10 minutes, or until thickened. Add shrimp and Accent; heat thoroughly.

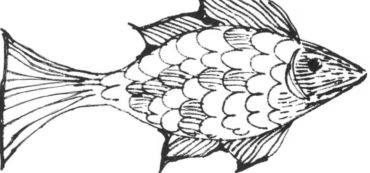

# BAKED HALIBUT STEAKS

2-1½ inch halibut steaks
1 can artichoke hearts
3 T. flour
3 T. butter or oleo
2 c. milk
1 T. fresh dill
Salt and pepper to taste
Pepperidge Farm stuffing

Serves 4

Cut steaks in bite-size pieces, removing skin and bone. Lay in four oven-proof dishes and divide artichokes among dishes. Make a roux of butter and flour; gradually add milk. Blend in chopped dill, salt and pepper. When thickened, pour over fish. Sprinkle Pepperidge Farm stuffing crumbs over dishes; dot with butter. Bake in 425 degree oven 30-40 minutes.

## DEVILED HALIBUT

1½ lbs. halibut steak (one
  piece)
¼ c. chopped green pepper
¼ c. minced onion
1 T. prepared mustard
1 t. Worcestershire
⅛ t. Tabasco
3½ T. lemon juice
½ c. butter, melted
2 c. bread or corn flake
  crumbs
Salt and pepper
2 T. Parmesan cheese

Serves 4

Combine green pepper, onion, mustard, Worcestershire, Tabasco and lemon juice. Mix butter and crumbs. Combine both mixtures, blending well. Spread half of mixture on top of steak, patting down well. Quickly turn crumb-side down on shallow greased casserole. Season top side; spread with remaining crumb mixture. Bake at 350 degrees 25-30 minutes, or until fish flakes easily. Spread cheese on top and brown under broiler, watching carefully.

## JAMBALAYA

1 large onion, chopped
1 bunch spring onions, 3
  inches of tops, chopped
1 green pepper, chopped
1 clove garlic, minced
1 stalk celery, chopped
½ lb. Italian or Spanish hot
  sausage, sliced
¾ c. cooked ham, diced
¾ lb. uncooked shrimp
5 fresh tomatoes, peeled,
  chopped
½ t. thyme
Salt, pepper, cayenne,
  to taste
1 bay leaf
5½ c. chicken stock
1¾ c. raw long grain rice

Serves 4 to 6

Saute onions, pepper, celery and garlic until tender. Remove. Brown sausage; remove. In sausage drippings, brown ham then shrimp. Combine onion mixture, ham, sausage, shrimp, tomatoes and seasonings. Add rice and chicken stock. Cover tightly and simmer one hour.

# FISH MOUSSE

2½ c. water
2 envelopes unflavored
  gelatin
1 small onion, sliced
2 t. salt
½ t. peppercorns
½ t. basil
1-16 oz. pkg. frozen flounder
  or sole filets
½ c. salad dressing or
  mayonnaise
1 T. lemon juice
½ t. hot pepper sauce
½ c. heavy cream, whipped

Serves 8

Sprinkle gelatin over water in saucepan. Cook over low heat, stirring constantly, until completely dissolved. Add onion, salt, peppercorns and basil. Heat to boiling. Reduce heat to low, cover and simmer five minutes. Add frozen filets; heat to boiling. Reduce heat to low; cover and simmer 15 more minutes, or until fish flakes easily. Remove fish; discard onion and peppercorns. Strain liquid; if necessary, add water to make 2¼ cups. Add fish, cover and refrigerate until mixture thickens. In blender, blend fish, liquid, salad dressing, lemon juice and hot pepper sauce until smooth. Put into large bowl; fold in whipped cream. Pour into 6 cup mold; chill until firm.

*This is a very versatile dish and can be served as an appetizer, first course, or luncheon dish.*

# DEVILED OYSTERS

½ pt. heavy cream
1 bay leaf
2 T. margarine
1 T. flour
2 egg yolks, beaten
Mace, salt, pepper
1 T. Worcestershire
3 T. catsup
1 T. parsley, finely chopped
3 doz. med. oysters,
  chopped
Toasted bread crumbs

Serves 4

Put cream and bay leaf in saucepan; bring to boiling point; remove bay leaf. Mix margarine and flour into smooth paste; add to milk; stir until well blended. Bring to boil; remove from heat. Add egg yolks, mace, salt, pepper, parsley, Worcestershire and catsup. Stir in oysters; mix well. Put in shells or baking dish with toasted crumbs on top. Bake at 400 degrees twenty minutes.
Variation: Omit catsup and mace; add 1½ teaspoon dry mustard and dash cayenne. May use scallops, crabmeat or lobster.

116

## OYSTERS JOHNNY REB

1 qt. oysters, drained
2 T. minced parsley
1 onion, minced
¼ t. salt
½ t. pepper
1 T. lemon juice
1¼ c. bread crumbs
½ c. butter
¾ c. milk
Red pepper to taste

Serves 8

Butter 1 quart shallow casserole and put in layer of oysters. Sprinkle with parsley, onions, salt, pepper, lemon juice and bread crumbs. Dot with butter. Make another layer of oysters and repeat. Cover with bread crumbs and dot with ample butter. Pour milk over all, making sure milk mixes well with oysters. Bake at 325 degrees 30 minutes or until bubbly and brown.

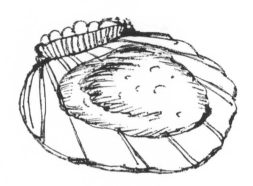

## OYSTERS ROCKEFELLER

8 oysters on half shell
1 c. minced onion
½ c. chopped parsley
1½ c. chopped spinach
½ c. flour
1 c. melted butter
1 c. water
2 cloves garlic, minced
½ t. salt
¼ t. cayenne pepper
1 T. anchovy paste
1 oz. Absinthe (optional)
½ c. bread crumbs
Rock salt

Serves 6 to 8

Fill pie pan with rock salt for each serving. Put into oven to heat. Grind onions, spinach, parsley together. Melt butter; stir in flour, cook but do not brown. Blend in water, garlic, salt and cayenne. Stir in chopped greens and anchovy paste. Simmer 20 minutes. Stir in Absinthe and cook until thick. Place half shell filled with oyster on rock salt. Put sauce on top of oyster and bread crumbs on top of sauce. Bake at 400 degrees 5-8 minutes or until edges of oyster curls.

## OYSTER ROCKEFELLER CASSEROLE

2 pkgs. frozen chopped
  spinach
2 pints oysters, drained
6 T. butter
1 c. crumbs
1 T. anisette (optional)
½ onion, grated
Tabasco, salt and pepper
½ tube anchovy paste
Parmesan cheese

Serves six as main dish
Serves eight as side dish

Slightly cook spinach; drain thoroughly. Add oysters mixed with all ingredients, except cheese. Top with Parmesan cheese. Bake covered 20 minutes at 350 degrees. Remove cover and bake 10 minutes more.

## SCALLOPED OYSTERS

1 pint oysters
1 pkg. Uneeda soda
  crackers (3½ oz.)
2 eggs
2 c. milk
½ c. melted butter
Salt and pepper

Serves 4

Cut oysters in half. Break crackers into coarse pieces. Beat eggs until very light. Mix all ingredients well, using half the melted butter. Put into a well buttered baking dish. Pour the rest of butter over the top. Bake at 375 degrees 45 minutes to 1 hour, until puffed and crusty on top.

## SALMON CROQUETTES

1–16 oz. can salmon, drained
2 eggs
¼ c. unsweetened
  cornbread mix

Serves 4

Remove all skin and bones from salmon. Combine all ingredients, mixing well. Shape into patties. Fry in hot fat until crusty on both sides.

*Here is an easy way to goodness. Try adding a small chopped onion or green pepper, or both!*

## SEAFOOD CASSEROLE

**Double recipe medium white
   sauce (see index)
Add: ¼ lb. Longhorn cheese
   or mild cheddar, grated
1 T. chopped canned
   pimientos
1 lb. cooked shrimp
1-7½ oz. can crabmeat
1-7½ oz. can lobster
1 small onion, diced
4 T. chopped green pepper
½ lb. mushrooms, chopped
   and sauteed in butter
1 c. very fine noodles,
   cooked barely done
3 hard-boiled eggs
Buttered bread crumbs**

**Serves 6**

Blend sauce with remaining ingredients, reserving eggs. Place in buttered 3 quart casserole. Slice eggs; place on top of mixture in casserole. Sprinkle top lightly with buttered crumbs; bake at 350 degrees 1¼ hours.

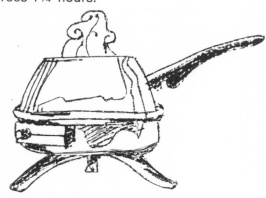

## QUICK SEAFOOD CASSEROLE

**1 pkg. Stouffer's macaroni
   and cheese
1 can cream of shrimp soup
1-4½ oz. can shrimp,
   drained
1-4½ oz. can crabmeat,
   drained
1 onion, chopped
3 T. dry Sherry
Toasted almonds**

**Serves 4**

Combine all ingredients. Pour into 1 quart casserole. Bake at 350 degrees 40 minutes. Sprinkle with toasted almonds and serve.

# SHRIMP AND ARTICHOKES

2 T. butter or margarine
2 T. flour
½ t. pepper
¼ t. cayenne
1 pt. half and half cream
1 T. catsup
1 T. Worcestershire
3 T. lemon juice
3 T. Sherry
1 8 oz. can artichokes, sliced
1 c. grated sharp cheese
2 lbs. shrimp, cleaned and
  deveined

**Serves 6**

Melt butter, add flour, pepper, cayenne. Mix well. Add cream; cook over low heat until thickened. Add catsup, Worcestershire, lemon juice and Sherry. Blend. Alternate layers of artichokes and shrimp in 2 quart baking dish. Pour in sauce and top with grated cheese. Bake at 400 degrees 30 minutes. Serve on patty shells or rice.

# BAKED SHRIMP IN SCALLOP SHELLS

¼ c. chopped green onion
1 clove garlic, crushed
2 T. butter or margarine
¼ c. flour
½ t. salt
2 T. cocktail sauce
1½ c. half and half cream
½ c. dry white wine
1 lb. boiled shrimp
1 small can water chestnuts,
  sliced
½ c. fresh bread crumbs
2 T. Parmesan cheese
2 t. chopped parsley
½ t. paprika
3 T. melted butter
Lime slices

**Serves 6**

Saute onion and garlic in butter until tender; blend in flour, salt and cocktail sauce. Remove from heat; stir in cream gradually. Heat to boiling, stirring constantly; boil 1 minute. Stir in wine, shrimp and water chestnuts, reserving a few shrimp for top. Spoon into 6 buttered scallop shells. Combine bread crumbs, cheese, parsley and paprika in small bowl; stir in melted butter. Sprinkle crumb mixture over shrimp filling. Bake at 350 degrees 15-20 minutes. Garnish with whole shrimp and lime slices on each.

## SHRIMP CHEF MONTEUR

24-30 raw jumbo shrimp,
  shelled and deveined
½ t. salt
½ c. olive oil
3 cloves garlic, crushed
½ c. brandy
1 c. heavy cream
¼ t. white pepper
½ t. oregano
1 small onion, minced,
  sauteed in
½ T. butter or margarine
½ c. dry white wine
2-16 oz. cans peeled
  tomatoes, drained and
  chopped

Serves 6

Split shrimp down the back and sprinkle with salt. Heat oil in a large skillet; cook garlic 2 to 3 minutes. Add shrimp; cook 5 minutes. Stir in brandy; continue cooking 3 to 4 minutes. Add cream; cook, stirring constantly, until brandy and cream are almost cooked down. Add pepper, oregano, sauteed onion, wine and tomatoes. Cook 10 minutes longer.

## SHRIMP-CRABMEAT BAKE

4 c. cooked shrimp
2 lbs. crabmeat
¾ c. minced onion
1½ c. thinly sliced celery
1 c. mayonnaise
2 T. Worcestershire sauce
1 t. salt
½ t. pepper
1 c. bread crumbs
4 T. butter
Lemon and parsley

Serves 6

Split shrimp in halves. Mix gently with crabmeat. Add all ingredients except bread crumbs and butter. Place in casserole. Melt butter, add to bread crumbs and spread over shrimp-crab mixture. Bake at 350 degrees 30 minutes. Garnish with sliced lemon and parsley.

# SHRIMP AND DEVILED EGGS

8 eggs, hard-boiled
⅓ c. mayonnaise
¼ t. dry mustard
½ t. salt
½ t. curry powder
½ t. paprika

Cut eggs lengthwise, remove yolks. Mash yolks with remaining ingredients and fill egg whites. Arrange in greased 13x9 inch baking dish. Cover with sauce.

Sauce:
1 can cream of shrimp soup
1 can cream of chicken soup
½ c. cheddar cheese, grated
1 c. soft bread crumbs,
  buttered
8 oz. pkg. frozen shrimp,
  thawed

Blend soups; add cheese and cook over low heat until cheese melts. Stir until smooth. Add shrimp and pour over eggs. Sprinkle with crumbs, dot with more butter and bake at 350 degrees 25-30 minutes.

Serves 6 to 8

## SHRIMP ETOUFFE

½ c. butter
1 med. onion, finely chopped
2 green onions, finely
  chopped
3 or 4 cloves garlic, minced
¼ c. celery, finely chopped
2 T. flour
2½ c. water
10½ oz. can tomato puree
2 bay leaves
1 T. Worcestershire sauce
4 drops Tabasco sauce
1 t. salt
½ t. sugar
½ t. whole thyme, crushed
⅛ t. pepper
1 lb. (3 c.) cleaned raw
  shrimp

Yield: 4 to 6 servings

In large skillet saute onion, green onions, garlic and celery in butter until tender. Add flour; cook and stir until lightly browned. Add water, tomato puree, bay leaves, Worcestershire, Tabasco and seasonings. Simmer uncovered, stirring occasionally, 40 minutes. Add shrimp; cook 15 minutes more. Serve over rice.

BAY LEAF

## GREEK SHRIMP

½ c. butter or margarine
½ c. olive oil
Juice of 1 lemon
¼ t. salt, pepper and
  garlic salt
½ t. paprika
2 lbs. shelled and deveined
  shrimp

Serves 4 to 6

Melt butter over high heat; add olive oil and lemon juice. Stir in all seasonings; bring to boil. Add shrimp; saute in sauce until pink and firm. Serve wtih sauce spooned over shrimp.

## SHRIMP AND GREEN NOODLE CASSEROLE

½ 8 oz. pkg. green spinach
  noodles
3 or 4 green onions, chopped
2 lbs. shrimp, cooked and
  deveined
1 can cream of mushroom
  soup
1 c. sour cream
1 c. mayonnaise
⅛ t. prepared mustard
½ c. sharp cheddar cheese,
  grated
3 or 4 T. dry Sherry

Serves 6

Cook green spinach noodles as directed on package. Toss chopped onions with noodles; place in bottom of 13x9 inch casserole. Cover noodles with shrimp. Combine cream of mushroom soup, sour cream and mayonnaise; add mustard and Sherry. Pour sauce over shrimp. Sprinkle cheese over top. Bake 30 minutes at 350 degrees.

## SHRIMP PASTE

1 lb. small cooked shrimp
½ lb. butter
Salt to taste

Serves 2

Grind shrimp using fine blade of food chopper. Cream butter and work thoroughly into the shrimp. Salt to taste. Pack into an oblong baking dish and bake at 375 degrees or until mixture leaves the sides of the dish and is a little brown on top. Cool. Place in refrigerator overnight, before slicing.

*This is very good sliced and served for lunch with hot grits and tossed salad.*

# SHRIMP PELLIEU

Cooked rice for 4
1 lb. raw shrimp, cleaned
2 T. butter
1 can cream of celery soup
¼ c. milk or cream
1 T. prepared horseradish
1 t. dry mustard
1 T. fresh lemon juice
Dash pepper
1 t. paprika

Serves 4

Place well drained shrimp in heavy fry pan; add butter. Saute, turning often until shrimp become pink. Do not overcook. Combine celery soup, milk, horseradish, dry mustard, lemon juice, pepper and paprika in a saucepan and heat; do not boil. Add shrimp; mix well. Serve at once over rice.

# SHRIMP VICTORIA

2 lbs. shrimp, shelled and
  deveined
1 lb. mushrooms, quartered
½ c. minced onion
½ c. butter or margarine
2 T. flour
1 t. salt
Dash freshly ground pepper
3 c. sour cream

Serves 6

Saute onion in butter until tender. Add mushrooms; cook 2 minutes; add shrimp. Cook 4 minutes, stirring constantly. Add flour, salt, pepper and sour cream. Simmer until heated and shrimp is done. Serve with rice.

Easy Gourmet

# BAKED TROUT

2 lbs. trout filets
½ c. Caesar salad dressing
1 c. potato chips, crushed
½ c. sharp cheddar cheese,
  grated

Serves 4

Dip filets in salad dressing; place in single layer, skin side down, in baking dish. Combine crushed chips and cheese; sprinkle over filets. Bake at 500 degrees 10-15 minutes.

## BAKED FLORIDA SPECKLED TROUT

8 filets sea trout, skin on
Corn oil
1 c. tomato juice
Salt and pepper
1 t. dried crushed basil
  leaves

Allow 1 to 2 filets per person
  depending on size

Place aluminum foil in flat open baking pan so that it comes up a little on all sides. Pour 2 or 3 tablespoons corn oil evenly on foil; dip upper side of each filet in oil and lay skin side down. Pour tomato juice evenly over filets covering edges. Season with salt and pepper; sprinkle each with basil. Bake at 400 degrees 10-20 minutes, until fish flakes easily with fork, but is not dry.

## TUNA HAWAIIAN

2 c. cooked rice
⅔ c. white sauce
1-6½ oz. can tuna
1 T. chopped parsley
1 t. salt
½ t. pepper
4 T. minced onion
1 c. grated cheddar cheese
10 slices pineapple
4 T. brown sugar, moistened
  with pineapple juice
½ c. crushed corn flakes

Serves 5 to 10

Combine white sauce with rice, tuna, parsley, salt, pepper, onions and ½ cup cheese. Place pineapple slices in a shallow baking pan and brush with brown sugar mixture. Spoon tuna-rice mix onto each slice, making mounds. Sprinkle with crushed corn flake crumbs; top with remaining cheese. Bake at 350 degrees 20 minutes.

SEAFOOD

# BAKED TUNA MOUSSE

3 6½ oz. cans tuna, drained
  and flaked
Dash pepper
¼ t. dry mustard
1½ c. sour cream
⅓ c. fresh chives
4 eggs, separated
Double recipe blender
  hollandaise (see index)
⅓ c. capers

Serves 6

Combine tuna with seasonings, sour cream and chives. Beat egg whites until stiff; fold in tuna mixture. Turn into greased 1 quart casserole or souffle dish. Bake at 350 degrees 50 minutes, or until browned. Using egg yolks, make double recipe blender hollandaise; stir in capers. Serve over mousse.

# BEER BATTER

¾ c. pancake flour
1 egg
Beer

Make a well in flour; drop in the egg. Mix well until egg is absorbed. Use enough beer to make thin batter. Dip fish into batter; coat evenly and fry in deep fat until lightly browned.

*Delicious, and no fish odor!*

# BUTTERMILK BATTER

Buttermilk
Buttermilk biscuit mix
Salt (dash)

Place pieces of fish in single layer in shallow dish. Pour buttermilk and salt over portions and let stand 30 minutes. Remove fish; roll in biscuit mix. Fry in hot oil until brown. Drain.

*Take the fish of your choice and fry it this way.*

# CHEESE, EGG, PASTA, RICE

## BRUNCH EGG CASSEROLE

**6 eggs, well beaten**
**4 c. milk**
**1 t. salt**
**¼ t. pepper**
**½ t. onion powder**
**½ t. dry mustard**
**2 c. croutons, flavored or**
**plain**
**½ c. sharp cheddar cheese,**
**grated**
**6 slices bacon, cooked dry**
**and crisp, then crumbled**

**Serves 6 to 8**

Spread croutons in bottom of a buttered 13 x 9 baking pan. Sprinkle with grated cheese. Combine eggs, milk, salt, pepper, onion powder and mustard; pour over croutons. (Croutons will rise to top). Sprinkle with bacon crumbs. Bake in 325 degree oven 1 hour or until firm. Test with silver knife.

## CHEESE BREAD SOUFFLE

**8 slices stale bread**
**1 onion, minced**
**2 lbs. sharp cheese, grated**
**6 eggs**
**2½ c. milk**
**Dash paprika**
**½ t. Worcestershire**
**¼ t. dry mustard**
**Salt and pepper**

**Serves 8**

Butter bread; spread layer in greased 13 x 9 baking dish. Combine onions and cheese; spread over bread. Repeat layers. Mix eggs, milk and seasonings; pour over all. Place in refrigerator overnight. Bake at 350 degrees 45 minutes or until set.

Variations: Fry 1 lb. bulk pork sausage and layer next to bread.
Fry ½ lb. bacon, crumble inside and on top.

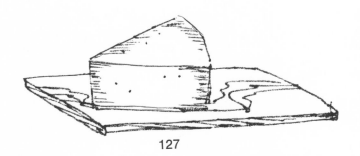

## CHEESE CROQUETTES

3 T. butter
½ c. flour
⅔ c. milk
½ t. Worcestershire
Salt and pepper
2 egg yolks
1½ c. sharp cheese, grated
Pinch dry mustard
1 egg, beaten
½ c. milk
Corn flake crumbs

Yields 1½ dozen small
  croquettes

Melt butter and add flour. Gradually add milk, blending well. Add egg yolks, cheese, Worcestershire sauce, salt, pepper and dry mustard. Cook over low heat until the cheese has melted. Pour into a pyrex dish and chill overnight. Shape into croquettes (or cut into squares). Beat egg and milk together; dip croquettes into egg-milk mixture, then into crumbs. Repeat. Fry in deep fat until nicely browned. Serve warm.

*Served hot topped with mustard sauce or wine sauce as a first course, or as a Sunday night supper.*

## TWO CHEESE PUDDING

4 eggs, beaten
¼ t. salt
½ t. paprika, cayenne
1 c. creamed cottage cheese
½ c. sharp cheddar cheese,
  grated

Serves 4

Combine all ingredients and mix well. Pour into buttered shallow 1 quart baking dish. Bake at 350 degrees 25 minutes or until set.

## UNBAKED CHEESE SOUFFLE

**1 pkg. unflavored gelatin**
**½ c. chicken broth**
**4 eggs, separated**
**1 c. milk**
**1 c. sharp cheese, grated**
**1 t. Worcestershire sauce**
**Dash salt, Tabasco**
**½ c. stuffed olives, chopped**
**1 onion, minced**
**1 c. heavy cream, whipped**
**8 soda crackers, crumbled**
**and buttered**
**Sliced pimiento**
**Olives**

**Serves 4 to 6**

Soften gelatin in broth 5 minutes; add egg yolks, milk, cheese, Worcestershire, salt and Tabasco. Stir over low heat until gelatin and cheese are melted (5-8 minutes). Chill, stirring occasionally until mixture thickens. Fold in olives, onion and whipped cream. Beat whites until stiff and fold in carefully. Turn into 1 quart dish, prepared with wax paper collar. Chill until firm. Remove collar and press the cracker crumbs around edge. Garnish with pimientos and olives.

*Delicious luncheon dish served with fruit salad.*

## CHEESE RICE SOUFFLE

**¼ c. rice**
**1 recipe cheese sauce (see index)**
**4 eggs, separated**
**½ t. salt**
**Cayenne pepper**

**Serves 6**

Cook rice; fold in cheese sauce, egg yolks and seasonings. Beat whites until stiff and fold in carefully. Turn into a greased 1½ quart casserole. Bake at 325 degrees 40 minutes. Serve immediately.

# SUNSHINE CHEESE SOUFFLE

1 can cream of mushroom
  soup
1 c. sharp cheese, grated
6 eggs, separated

Serves 4 to 6

Put 2½ quart casserole in shallow pan with boiling water up 1 inch. Put in 325 degree oven and let heat. Blend soup and cheese; heat until cheese melts. Add egg yolks. Beat whites until stiff; carefully fold into yolk mixture. Pour into hot casserole. Circle mixture with spoon one inch from side. Bake one hour, or until knife comes out clean.

# BAKED CHILI RELLENOS

1-4 oz. can green chili
  peppers
½ lb. sharp cheddar cheese
2 eggs
2 c. milk
½ c. flour
½ t. salt

Serves 5 to 6

In the bottom of an 8 inch square buttered pan arrange the peppers, seeded and cut into large squares. Cut the cheese and arrange in an even layer over the peppers. Beat eggs, milk, flour and salt and pour over cheese. Bake at 350 degrees 45-50 minutes. Cut and serve.

# MOTHER'S COLD EGGS

6 eggs, poached
6 slices toast
Anchovy paste
6 slices tomato
Mayonnaise
Cream
Parsley or paprika

Serves 6

Poach eggs about 5 minutes (yolks just sticky). Cut toast into rounds the size of eggs; spread each with anchovy paste. Place slice of tomato on toast, then egg. Refrigerate if making dish early. Before serving, thin mayonnaise to consistency of thick cream with milk or cream. Pour over the egg mounds. Garnish with chopped parsley or sprinkle paprika on top.

*These eggs were traditionally served with cold baked ham, a sauce made with red currant jelly mixed with mustard to accompany the ham, hashed brown potatoes, a tossed salad, and chocolate cake for dessert. It is a marvelous buffet for hungry people.*

## CREOLE EGGS

8 boiled eggs, sliced
1 onion, minced
1 green pepper, chopped
1 T. butter
1 t. salt
2 t. Worcestershire
2 t. chili powder
Dash pepper
1-16 oz. can tomatoes
1-17 oz. can young peas
2 c. medium white sauce
Bread crumbs (or cracker)
  mixed with butter
1 c. sharp cheese, grated

Serves 8

Saute onions and green pepper in butter; add seasonings, tomatoes and peas. Pour in white sauce; mix well. In buttered 2 quart casserole, place alternate layers of sauce and sliced eggs, ending with sauce. Top with crumbs and cheese. Bake at 350 degrees 15-20 minutes.

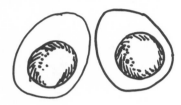

*This can be served over toast, rice or noodles.*

## EGGS HUSSARDE

4 slices Canadian bacon
1¾ c. Marchand de vin
  sauce (see index)
4 eggs, poached
¾ c. Hollandaise sauce
  (see index)
2 English muffins, split
Paprika

Serves 4

Saute bacon in butter until done. Toast and butter muffins. For each serving, place slice bacon on muffin and cover with Marchand de vin sauce. Put poached egg on top and cover with Hollandaise. Sprinkle with paprika.

## GARLIC GRITS

**1 c. grits**
**1 stick butter**
**1 roll garlic cheese**
**3 eggs, separated**
**⅔ c. milk**
**½ c. grated sharp cheese**

**Serves 6 to 8**

Cook grits according to package directions. While hot add butter and roll of cheese; stir until melted. Cool slightly. Beat egg yolks and add to milk; stir into grits. Beat egg whites until stiff; fold into grits. Pour into greased 1½ quart baking dish; sprinkle cheese on top and bake at 325 degrees 35-40 minutes, or until set.

*This is very good served with crushed fritos or bacon curls on top. To make it spicier, add 1 teaspoon cayenne pepper and 1 tablespoon Worcestershire.*

## GOLD RUSH BRUNCH

**1-5½ oz. box (dehydrated)**
**hash brown potatoes and**
**onion**
**4 T. butter or margarine**
**¼ c. flour**
**½ t. salt**
**½ t. pepper**
**2 c. milk**
**1 c. sour cream**
**2 T. chopped parsley**
**8 slices Canadian bacon,**
**¼ inch thick**
**8 eggs**

Prepare potatoes according to package. Melt butter over low heat; stir in flour, salt and pepper. Add milk and cook until thick. Stir in sour cream, parsley and potatoes. Pour into 13 x 9 inch baking dish; arrange Canadian bacon in a row down center, overlapping slightly. Bake at 350 degrees 20 minutes. Remove from oven and make 4 depressions on each side of bacon. Slip one egg into each depression. Sprinkle with salt and pepper; bake 10-12 minutes longer, or until eggs are set.

## GREEN CHILI PIE

½ onion, chopped
Oil
9 inch pie shell, partially
  baked
2 c. sharp cheddar cheese,
  shredded
1-4 oz. can green chiles
1 c. cream
3 eggs, barely beaten
¼ t. salt
¼ t. ground cumin
1 t. chili powder

Serves 6 to 8

Saute onion in oil until tender; remove from skillet. Sprinkle half the cheese over bottom of pie shell. Spread onions and chiles over cheese. Beat cream with eggs and add salt, cumin and chili powder. Pour into pie shell. Sprinkle remaining cheese over top and bake at 325 degrees 40 minutes or until middle of pie is set.

If you are daring and like hot sauce, then pour moderate amount over each slice.

## MEATLESS LASAGNE

½ lb. fresh mushrooms
4 T. butter
1½ lb. spinach lasagne
  noodles
½ c. cream
1 c. Ricotta or cottage
  cheese
2 pkgs. Mozzarella cheese
Parmesan cheese

Serves 6

Saute mushrooms in butter. Cook noodles, drain. In a 9 x 7 inch buttered baking dish, layer first one-half noodles; dot with butter. Spread half of cream, Ricotta and Mozzarella; sprinkle with Parmesan and mushrooms. Repeat, ending with mushrooms on top. Bake at 350 degrees 35 to 40 minutes.

## MACARONI AND CHEESE

**1 c. cooked macaroni**
**1 c. soft bread crumbs**
**1 t. onion, chopped**
**1 c. cheese, grated**
**1½ c. milk**
**2 eggs, beaten**
**1 t. green pepper, chopped**
**1 T. butter**
**Dash salt, pepper, paprika**

**Serves 4**

Combine all ingredients; place in greased 1½ quart casserole. Set in pan of warm water; bake at 350 degrees 45 minutes.

## MACARONI IN THE PINK

**2½ c. elbow macaroni**
**1 c. cream of tomato soup**
**1-8 oz. can tomato sauce**
**½ lb. cottage cheese**
**½ c. water**
**1½ t. salt**
**½ t. pepper**
**Dash garlic salt**
**1 onion, chopped**
**1 T. butter**
**½ bay leaf**
**Pinch thyme**

**Serves 6**

Cook macaroni according to package directions. Combine soup, tomato sauce, cottage cheese, water and seasonings. Saute onion in butter with bay leaf and thyme. Combine all this with the cooked macaroni. Turn in greased 1½ quart casserole and bake at 325 degrees ½ hour.

## MACARONI AND SAUSAGE

1 lb. bulk pork sausage
1 onion, chopped
1 c. elbow macaroni
1 can cream of celery soup
⅔ c. milk
3 eggs, beaten
1½ c. sharp cheese, grated
¾ c. corn flakes, crushed
2 T. butter, melted

**Serves 6**

Fry sausage and onion until done; drain off fat. Cook macaroni; drain. Combine sausage, macaroni, soup, milk, eggs and cheese. Pour into 8 x 8 baking dish. Mix corn flakes and butter; sprinkle over top. Bake at 350 degrees 40 minutes.

## NOODLE DOUGH

2 c. flour
½ t. salt
2 eggs, beaten
1 T. olive oil
1 T. warm water

**Yields about 1 pound**

Combine flour and salt; make a well in the center. Add eggs, olive oil and warm water. Mix well; add more warm water, drops at a time, to form firm ball. Knead on floured surface working in extra flour if dough seems sticky. Wrap in waxed paper and let rest 1 hour. Divide into 3 balls. Roll out each piece as thin as possible (paper thin) on lightly floured cloth-covered board. Place between 2 towels until dough is partially dry. Roll up dough as for jelly roll. With thin sharp knife cut into strips of desired width (⅛ inch for fine noodles, up to ½ inch for broad noodles). Shake out strips and allow to dry before using or storing. Cook in 6 to 8 quarts boiling salted water 5-10 minutes or until just tender.

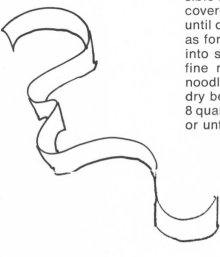

# DELICIOUS NOODLE PUDDING

½ lb. cooked wide noodles
⅓ c. sugar
3 eggs
1 c. milk
2 t. vanilla
½ c. butter, melted
1 t. salt
½ pt. sour cream
½ lb. cottage cheese
4 T. white raisins
6 oz. dried apricots
 (plumped in hot water)
8¾ oz. crushed pineapple,
 drained
8¾ oz. sliced peaches,
 drained

Topping:

1 c. corn flake crumbs
½ c. sugar
1 t. cinnamon

Serves 10 to 12

Beat eggs and sugar; add milk, vanilla, butter, salt, sour cream and cottage cheese. Mix well. Fold in noodles, raisins, apricots, pineapple and peaches. Pour into greased 13 x 9 inch pan. Sprinkle with topping, dot with butter and bake at 350 degrees ½ hour covered and ½ hour uncovered.

Mix cinnamon and sugar together and stir into corn flake crumbs.

# BAKED OMELET

2 dozen eggs
White Sauce:
1½ c. margarine
2 c. plus 1 T. flour
3 qts. milk
2 T. plus 1 t. salt
½ t. pepper

Serves 36 to 38

Beat eggs until well blended. Combine with white sauce.

Melt margarine in large sauce pan. Stir in flour; blend well. As mixture thickens, add milk gradually. Add salt and pepper. Cook until thickened; remove from heat. Mix eggs and white sauce; bake at 350 degrees 1 hour or until knife inserted comes out clean. One omelet will fit into a 21 x 13 inch pan. You may use two or three baking dishes. Serve with fresh fruit or jelly. Red pepper jelly is very good with it (see index).

*White sauce can be made a day ahead. Marvelous for a large brunch or Sunday night gathering.*

# OVERNIGHT LUNCHEON DISH

1 c. uncooked macaroni
1 c. cream of mushroom
  soup
1 c. milk
1-2½ oz. jar dried beef,
  washed and chopped
1 onion, chopped
¼ c. chopped green pepper
1 c. grated sharp cheese
Salt and pepper

**Serves 6 to 8**

Mix all ingredients. Pour into 1½ quart casserole; refrigerate overnite. Bake at 350 degrees 1 hour.

## PINEAPPLE STUFFING

½ c. butter
½ c. sugar
1 can (1 lb., 4 ozs.) crushed
  pineapple, well drained
5 slices white bread, cubed
4 eggs

**Serves 4**

Cream butter and sugar. Beat in eggs one at a time. Stir in pineapple; fold in bread cubes. Turn into greased 1½ quart casserole. Bake, uncovered, for 1 hour. Delicious with ham. Can be assembled the day before and refrigerated.

## SPAETZLES

2 c. flour, sifted
1 t. salt
2 eggs, slightly beaten
¾ c. milk
¼ c. dry bread crumbs
2 T. melted butter

**Serves 5 to 6**

Sift together flour and salt. Add eggs and milk; beat well. Place mixture in a coarse-sieved colander. Hold over large kettle of boiling salted water. Press batter through colander. Cook and stir 5 minutes; drain. Sprinkle with mixture of bread crumbs and butter.

## DELUXE CRAB QUICHE

**9 inch pie shell, partially baked**
**6 oz. pkg. frozen crabmeat**
**½ c. grated swiss cheese**
**⅓ c. minced onion**
**1 T. minced parsley**
**1 T. Sherry**
**⅛ t. leaf tarragon**
**3 eggs, slightly beaten**
**1 c. half and half cream**
**½ t. salt**

**Serves 6**

Bake pie shell at 425 degrees 10 minutes; do not brown. Sprinkle cheese over bottom. Thaw, drain and chop crab; toss lightly with onion, parsley, Sherry and tarragon. Arrange in layer over cheese. Beat eggs; blend with cream and salt, just to mix; pour gradually over the crab mixture. Bake at 325 degrees 45 to 50 minutes or until set. Let stand 10 minutes before cutting.

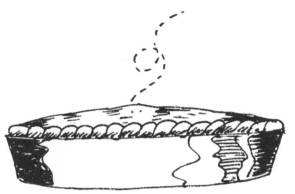

## QUICHE LORRAINE

**9 inch unbaked pie shell**
**6 slices bacon, fried crisp**
**6 thin slices Swiss cheese**
**4 eggs**
**2 c. light cream**
**1 T. flour**
**¼ t. nutmeg**
**½ t. salt**
**Dash pepper and cayenne pepper**

**Serves 6**

Crumble bacon into pie shell; arrange cheese over bacon. Combine eggs, cream, flour and seasonings; pour into shell. Bake at 400 degrees on lowest rack in oven 15 minutes. Reduce heat and bake at 325 degrees 30 minutes, or until set.

## QUICHE LORRAINE A LA RITZ

9 inch unbaked pie shell
1 onion, chopped
1 T. butter
½ lb. fresh mushrooms,
  sliced
½-1 c. ham, cooked and
  chopped
1½ c. Swiss cheese,
  chopped
4 eggs, beaten
1 c. cream
1 c. milk
Salt, pepper
Dash nutmeg
½ pkg. frozen spinach,
  thawed

Serves 4

Saute onion and mushrooms; line in bottom of uncooked pastry. Add chopped ham and cheese. Beat eggs; add milk, seasonings and pour over ham and cheese. Drain spinach; put in four corners of the pie. Bake at 350 degrees for 45 minutes or until set. Serve at once.

## RUSSIAN RAREBIT

2 T. chopped onion
2 T. chopped green pepper
1 T. butter, heaping
1 lb. longhorn cheese,
  grated
1 c. canned tomatoes
  (16 oz.)
1 t. salt
1 t. dry mustard
1 t. Worcestershire
Cayenne pepper and
  paprika to taste
1 c. cream
2 T. flour
1 egg, beaten

Serves 4 to 6

Saute onion and pepper in butter. In double boiler cook cheese, tomatoes, salt and mustard until cheese melts; add other seasonings. Stir until well blended. Just before serving mix cream, egg and flour and add to mixture. Serve over toast.

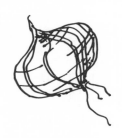

# CHARLESTON RICE

½ c. onions, chopped
½ c. celery, chopped
½ c. green pepper,
  chopped
2 T. butter
1-3 oz. can mushrooms,
  drained, chopped
3 c. long grain rice (cooked
  in chicken broth)
½ t. poultry seasoning
½ t. salt
¼ t. celery seed
¼ t. pepper
1 egg, beaten

**Serves 6 to 8**

Saute onions, celery and green pepper in butter until tender. Add mushrooms, rice and seasonings. Stir in egg. Turn into a greased 1½ quart shallow casserole. Cover and bake at 350 degrees 15 minutes.

# EASY RICE CASSEROLE

1 c. uncooked long grain
  rice
1 c. sharp cheese, cubed
1 small jar stuffed olives
1 c. tomatoes
1 onion, chopped
3 T. butter
1 c. water
Salt and pepper
3 T. Burgundy wine, optional

**Serves 6 to 8**

Mix all ingredients (it will be soupy) and pour into 1½ quart casserole. Cover and bake at 350 degrees 1 hour.

## GREEN BAKED RICE

2 c. cooked rice
Double recipe cheese sauce
  (see index)
3 med. onions
1 clove garlic
1 c. parsley
2 green peppers
1 T. salt

Serves 12

Finely chop vegetables in blender or food chopper. Mix rice, cheese sauce and vegetables; add salt. Pour into 2 quart baking dish. Bake at 350 degrees 1 hour. Can be prepared the day before.

## MEXICAN RICE

1 large onion, chopped
1 med. green pepper,
  chopped
2 T. butter
1 t. chili powder
1 can tomato soup
1 lb. can tomatoes
1 t. salt
½ t. pepper
4 c. cooked rice
¾ c. grated cheese

Serves 6 to 8

Saute onion and pepper in butter until tender. Blend in chili powder, soup, tomatoes, salt, pepper and rice. Pour into 2 quart casserole. Top with cheese. Bake at 375 degrees 30 minutes. If cheese is not brown, put under broiler flame.

## NASI GORING (INDONESIAN FRIED RICE)

1 c. rice, uncooked
⅓ c. cooking oil
1 large onion, chopped
½ c. green pepper, chopped
2-2½ c. water
1 T. soy sauce
1 t. salt
½ c. canned mushrooms,
 chopped
2 eggs, beaten

Serves 4

In a heavy skillet saute rice in oil until pale brown. Add onions, green pepper and ½ cup water, cooking and stirring until onions look transparent. Pour in additional water, about 1½ cups; add soy sauce and salt. Stir; cover pan. Reduce heat; cook about 20 minutes. If necessary add more water. Stir in mushrooms. Rice should be tender and will have absorbed all the liquid. Scramble eggs and serve over rice.

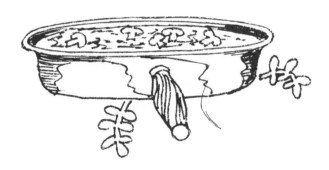

## PERSIAN RICE-PILAF

1 c. long grain rice
¼ c. onion, chopped
¼ c. plus 2 T. butter
¾ t. salt
2¼ c. boiling water
2 beef bouillon cubes
½ c. golden raisins
½ c. pecans, coarsely
 chopped

Serves 6

Saute rice and onion in ¼ cup butter until lightly browned, stirring frequently. Add salt, water, bouillon cubes and raisins. Cover; reduce heat and cook until rice is tender, 20 to 25 minutes. In a small pan melt 2 tablespoons butter; saute pecans 2 to 3 minutes. Sprinkle over rice just before serving.

# RANCH RICE CASSEROLE

*Easy Gourmet*

¼ c. butter or margarine
1 clove garlic, crushed
1 c. raw rice
1 can beef consomme
1 can onion soup
1-4 oz. can mushrooms with
   liquid

**Serves 6 to 8**

Melt butter in 1½ quart casserole; stir in crushed garlic. Add remaining ingredients. Stir gently. Bake, uncovered in 350 degree oven 1 hour.

## SHERRIED RICE CASSEROLE

2 c. heavy cheese sauce
   (see index)
1½ c. cooked rice
½ c. slivered almonds
½ c. flake coconut
1-6 oz. can or ½ lb. fresh
   mushrooms
1½ oz. Sherry
Curry powder

**Serves 4**

Add cheese sauce to cooked rice. Mix in almonds, coconut, mushrooms, Sherry; add curry powder to taste. Blend all together; place in greased casserole and bake at 350 degrees until bubbly. Especially good with chicken.

## WILD RICE AND OYSTERS

1 c. wild rice
¼ c. butter
2 c. fresh mushrooms, sliced
½ green pepper, chopped
½ c. sliced water chestnuts
1 c. dry white wine
2 c. fresh oysters
Salt and pepper

**Serves 6**

Cook rice. Melt butter; add mushrooms, green pepper and brown lightly; add salt and pepper to taste. Add 1 cup water and wine. Simmer 15 minutes; mix with rice. Add water chestnuts and mix well. Spread in casserole. Mix oysters with a little melted butter; arrange on top; bake at 350 degrees 30 minutes.

## WILD RICE A LA PUMP ROOM

2 c. cooked wild rice
¾ c. butter
6 green onions, with tops, chopped
½ c. chopped parsley
1 lb. mushrooms, sliced
2 large tomatoes, chopped
2 t. Worcestershire
Salt and pepper
2 T. heavy cream
3 T. Madeira wine
¼ c. brandy

Serves 6

Melt ½ cup butter in chafing dish; add onions, parsley and mushrooms. Cook and stir 3 minutes; add tomatoes and ¼ cup butter. Cook and stir 3 minutes. Add rice and heat. Blend in seasonings and cream; cook 1 minute. Add Madeira. Make well in center; add brandy and flame. Gently mix. Serve with baked Cornish hens.

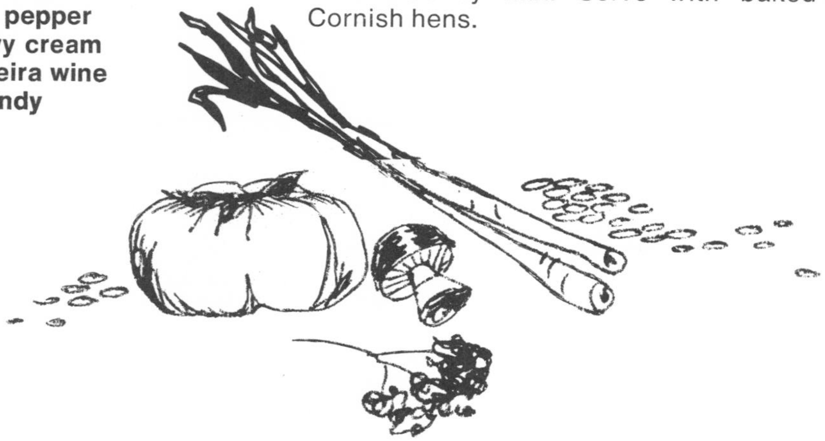

## WILD RICE CASSEROLE

1 c. wild rice
2½ c. tomatoes
1 c. cubed Velveeta cheese
½ c. chopped onion
½ c. chopped green pepper
½ lb. fresh mushrooms
⅓ c. butter
½ c. chopped ripe olives
1½ c. boiling water
1 t. salt
½ t. pepper
Dash sugar
½ t. oregano

Serves 12

Blend ingredients. Pour into 2 quart casserole; cover tightly. Bake at 325 degrees 2 hours. Stir after 1 hour.

SALADS
CHEESE
BEANS
VEGETABLES
ACCOMPANIMENTS
SAUCES AND RELISHES
BREADS

# VEGETABLES

## ARTICHOKES AU VIN BLANC

**4 artichokes**
**2 T. olive oil**
**1 clove garlic**
**1 small onion**
**Pinch of savory**
**2 t. salt**
**1 c. good white wine**

**Serves 4**

Trim tops and stems from artichokes. Put in pressure cooker. Sprinkle chopped onion, olive oil, garlic, savory, salt and white wine over artichokes. Cook in pressure cooker 10 minutes. Serve juices over artichokes.

## ASPARAGUS AS A VEGETABLE OR QUICHE

**2-10 oz. pkgs. frozen**
   **asparagus pieces**
**1 t. salt**
**12 slices of bacon**
**6 eggs**
**1½ c. light cream**
**⅛ t. nutmeg**
**⅛ t. salt**
**Dash pepper**
**¾ lb. Swiss cheese, grated**

**Serves 8 to 10**

Cook asparagus partially in salted water. Drain and put aside. Cook bacon until crisp; drain on paper towels. Mix eggs in bowl with rotary beater; add cream, nutmeg, salt and pepper. Mix until completely combined. Crumble bacon and sprinkle on bottom of 9 inch square pan. Add cheese and asparagus. Pour cream mixture on top. Bake at 375 degrees 40 minutes or until puffy and golden. For Asparagus Quiche, place above recipe in partially baked pie shell and bake at 350 degrees 45 minutes.

# ASPARAGUS SOUFFLE

1-15 oz. can asparagus,
save juice
4 T. butter or margarine
4 T. flour
1 c. milk
Dash salt
White pepper
3 eggs, separated

Serves 6

In top of double boiler, make thick cream sauce of butter, flour, milk and ½ cup of liquid from asparagus. Remove sauce from heat. Add salt and pepper. Blend in well beaten egg yolks. Cool. Add finely chopped asparagus. Beat egg whites until stiff. Fold into asparagus mixture. Pour into buttered 1½ quart souffle dish. Place in pan of water. Bake at 350 degrees 25 minutes. Sauce may be prepared ahead of time.

## BAKED ASPARAGUS

1-10 oz. pkg. frozen
asparagus
3-4 hard boiled eggs
2 level T. flour
Salt and pepper
4 T. butter, melted
1 c. half and half

Separate asparagus spears (leave frozen, do not pre-cook); lay on bottom of baking dish. Add eggs cut in pieces; sprinkle flour over eggs. Add salt, pepper and butter. Pour half and half over all. Bake at 350 degrees about 35 minutes.

## MARINATED ASPARAGUS

⅓ c. wine vinegar
¼ c. sugar
½ t. salt
3 whole cloves
1 stick cinnamon
¼ t. celery seed
2-15 oz. cans green
asparagus

Serves 4 to 6

Bring all ingredients, except asparagus, to boil. Pour mixture over drained asparagus while hot. Let stand a day or two in refrigerator before serving.

VEGETABLES

# BAKED BEANS

1 apple
¼ c. raisins
½ c. onion
Small piece ham
1 T. prepared mustard
¼ c. chili sauce
¾ c. brown sugar
½ c. bourbon
1 qt. baked beans

Serves 6 to 8

Grind or finely chop the apple, onion, raisins and ham together; mix with mustard, chili sauce, sugar and bourbon. Combine mixture with beans and bake at 375 degrees for 1 hour or until most of the liquid is absorbed.

# MRS. A'S GREEN BEANS

4 strips bacon
3 T. sugar
4 T. vinegar
2-16 oz. cans whole green
  beans, plus liquid
1 onion, chopped

Serves 6

Fry bacon; crumble. Set aside. Combine sugar, vinegar and beans in bacon drippings. Cook very low several hours. Serve topped with crumbled bacon and onion.

# BUTTER CRUNCH GREEN BEANS

1 lb. young green beans
3 T. butter
1 t. lemon juice
½ c. chopped cashew nuts
5 T. dry white wine
1 t. sugar
½ t. grated lemon peel

Serves 6 to 8

Cut beans in long thin slices on the diagonal. Place in cold water to cover; bring to boil over moderate heat. Cook 5 minutes. Drain. Melt butter in saucepan; add lemon juice, peel, wine and sugar. Add drained beans. Cover tightly and cook slowly, stirring occasionally, until crisply tender (about 15-20 minutes). Add cashews, and additional butter if desired.

# FAGIOLETTE AL OLIO E FUNGHI
## (GREEN BEANS IN OIL WITH MUSHROOMS)

2 can French style green
  beans
1 c. fresh sliced mushrooms
¼ c. olive oil
1 t. sugar
2 cloves garlic, minced
Salt and pepper to taste

Serves 4 to 6

Drain beans and saute them with remaining ingredients until mushrooms and garlic are cooked, about 15 minutes.

## GREEN BEANS SUPREME

½ c. onion, sliced
1 T. parsley, minced
2 T. butter
2 T. flour
1 t. salt
¼ t. pepper
½ t. grated lemon peel
1 c. sour cream
5 c. cooked green beans,
  drained
½ c. cheese, grated
2 T. butter, melted
½ c. bread crumbs

Serves 6

Saute onion and parsley in butter until tender, but not brown. Add flour, salt, pepper and lemon peel. Add sour cream and mix well. Stir in beans; heat well. Turn into 11 x 7 baking dish; top with cheese. Combine butter with crumbs and sprinkle over beans. Broil at low heat until cheese melts and crumbs brown. This may be prepared ahead, then heated in 350 degree oven 30-35 minutes. Broil to brown topping if needed.

## GREEN BEANS WITH BACON

1-16 oz. can whole green
  beans
3 strips bacon
French garlic dressing or
Italian dressing
Parmesan cheese

Serves 6

Drain beans; divide into 6 equal portions. Wrap each in ½ strip bacon; secure with toothpick. Pour dressing over beans; sprinkle with Parmesan cheese and marinate overnight. Put beans in pan; bake at 350 degrees 30 minutes or until bacon has cooked.

149

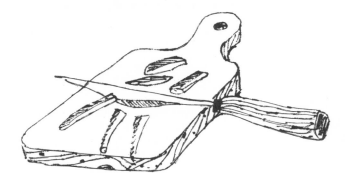

## SWEET-AND-SOUR GREEN BEANS

1 lb. fresh green beans, cut
   into 1-in. pieces
2 T. bacon drippings
1 c. boiling water
½ t. salt
1 T. cornstarch
3 T. vinegar
½ c. cold water
3 T. sugar
1 T. soy sauce
4 T. sweet pickle relish

**Serves 4 to 5**

Combine beans, bacon drippings, boiling water and salt in a saucepan; bring to a rapid boil. Cover and simmer 15-20 minutes or until beans are crisp-tender. Do not drain.

Combine cornstarch and vinegar; stir to blend. Add cold water, sugar, soy sauce, and pickle relish, stirring well. Pour over beans; cook over low heat, stirring constantly, until smooth and thickened.

## LIMA BEAN SURPRISE

1 c. onion, chopped
1 c. green pepper, chopped
1 clove garlic, minced
¼ c. vegetable oil
1 c. ripe olives
1 T. cornstarch
1 T. chili powder
1¼ c. bean liquid
4 c. cooked dried lima beans
1 c. grated cheese

**Serves 6**

Saute onions, green pepper and garlic in oil until tender. Blend in cornstarch, chili powder, olives, beans, liquid and half cup cheese. Mix well. Pour into 1½ quart casserole; top with remaining cheese. Bake at 350 degrees 30 minutes.

## CREOLE RED BEANS AND RICE

1 green pepper, chopped
1 T. oil
1 hambone
1 lb. red kidney beans, dried
3 med. onions, chopped
1 clove garlic, mashed
Salt and pepper
Dash cayenne or Tabasco

Serves 6 to 8

Saute pepper in oil until tender, not brown. Add hambone, washed beans, onions, garlic and pepper. Add water to top of beans. Simmer several hours—until "creamy" and thick. If beans appear watery, remove excess liquid before beans have completely cooked. Salt added early may toughen beans, therefore salt when beans are tender. (If ham is salty, salt may not be needed). At end of cooking time add pepper, cayenne or Tabasco to taste. Serve over rice.

## WILLIE'S PICKLED BEETS

1-16 oz. can sliced beets, drained
½ c. sugar (or to taste)
1 c. cider vinegar
½ c. water
1 T. whole cloves, tied in cloth bag

Serves 6

Bring sugar, vinegar, water and cloves to a boil. Pour over drained beets and let stand overnight.

## BROCCOLI AU GRATIN

2-10 oz. pkgs. frozen chopped broccoli
½ lb. Velveeta cheese
½ c. butter
1 stack Ritz crackers, crumbled

Serves 6 to 8

Cook broccoli according to package directions; drain. Blend in cheese and ¼ cup butter. Melt remaining butter and add to cracker crumbs. Pour broccoli mixture into 1½ quart casserole; top with crumbs. Bake at 350 degrees 25 minutes.

# EASY BROCCOLI CASSEROLE

2-10 oz. pkgs. frozen
  chopped broccoli, cooked
½ med. onion, chopped
½ c. slivered almonds
1 can cream of mushroom
  soup
1 roll garlic cheese
Bread crumbs

Serves 6

Cook broccoli according to package directions. Saute onion; add almonds and brown. Stir in soup and cheese and heat until cheese melts. Add broccoli to cheese mixture and pour into a greased 3 quart casserole. Cover with bread crumbs; dot with butter and bake at 350 degrees until brown, hot and bubbly.

# BROCCOLI SOUFFLE

2 c. cooked broccoli
3 eggs, beaten
1 c. mayonnaise
1 T. melted butter
1 T. flour
1 c. canned milk
½ t. salt

Serves 8

Drain and mash broccoli. Beat eggs and stir in Mayonnaise. Mix butter and flour and gradually stir in milk. Add to egg mixture along with salt. Blend all ingredients thoroughly with electric beaters or in blender until smooth. Pour into greased 2½ quart casserole; place in pan of water and bake at 350 degrees 30-40 minutes.

*Very easy to make and never fails.*

## BRAISED CABBAGE

5 strips bacon, minced
1 large onion, finely sliced
1 med. head cabbage,
  chopped
1 clove garlic, mashed
1 t. summer savory
3 T. butter
1 t. flour
1 c. beef or chicken stock
½ c. white wine
4 fresh tomatoes, quartered
1 t. tomato puree
1 T. parsley
Sour Cream
Parmesan Cheese

Serves 6 to 8

Saute bacon and onions until soft; add chopped cabbage, garlic, herbs, butter and flour. Stir lightly to blend; add stock and white wine. Cover and simmer until cabbage is almost tender. Add quartered tomatoes and the puree. Simmer until all is tender. Put into serving dish, garnish with a dollup of sour cream and sprinkle with parsley. Serve Parmesan cheese separately.

## GOURMET CABBAGE

½ head large cabbage,
  coarsely chopped
½ large onion, or 1 bunch
  scallions, chopped
3 T. butter
3 oz. pkg. cream cheese
Fresh or dried dill

Serves 6

Chop cabbage and put in salted, boiling water to cover. Cook about five minutes; drain in colander and set aside. Saute onion in butter until transparent; add drained cabbage and mix well. Break cream cheese into small pieces and stir into cabbage mixture; cover and cook slowly until cheese melts through the cabbage. When ready to serve, sprinkle dill lightly over top.

# WILTED CABBAGE

1 small head cabbage
¼ c. water
2 T. margarine or butter
¾ t. salt
¾ t. sugar
1 onion, thinly sliced
1 T. fresh lemon juice

Serves 4 to 6

Shred cabbage; add other ingredients and put into skillet with tight lid. Steam 3-4 minutes, no longer. Remove lid and brown mixture slightly. Do not overcook.

# CARROTS COINTREAU

2 lb. can small whole
    carrots
1 T. cornstarch
1½ t. frozen orange
    concentrate
1 t. grated orange rind
1 t. sugar
2 T. butter
¼ t. salt
Dash nutmeg, freshly grated
2 T. Cointreau
Chopped parsley

Serves 8 to 10

Drain carrots, reserving ¾ cup liquid. Blend orange concentrate, orange rind, sugar, salt, nutmeg and cornstarch with carrot liquid. Cook in double boiler until thickened; add carrots, butter and Cointreau. Sprinkle chopped parsley over carrots in serving dish.

# CARROT MOLD

3 c. pureed carrots
1 t. salt
1 t. pepper
2 T. onion
¼ c. butter
2 c. chopped celery, cooked
1½ c. cream
3 eggs, beaten
1½ c. bread crumbs

Put carrots, salt, pepper, onions, butter, celery and cream in blender. Blend until thoroughly mixed. Remove. Add eggs and bread crumbs. Pour into well greased 2 quart ring mold and place in a pan of hot water. Bake at 325 degrees 1½ hours or until set. Serve unmolded with green peas in center.

## COPPER PENNIES

2 lbs. carrots
1 small green pepper, sliced
  into rings
1 med. onion, thinly sliced
½ c. oil
1 c. sugar
¾ c. vinegar
1 t. prepared mustard
1 t. Worcestershire sauce
1 c. tomato soup, undiluted
Salt and pepper

Serves 10 to 12

Slice and boil carrots in salted water until fork tender. Cool. Alternate layers of carrots, pepper rings and onion slices in a bowl. Make a marinade of remaining ingredients, beating well until completely blended. Pour mixture over vegetables and refrigerate. Will keep several weeks. Can be used as a salad or relish.

## FAR EAST CELERY

4 c. celery
1-5 oz. can water chestnuts,
  sliced
1-2 oz. jar pimientos
½ c. slivered almonds,
  toasted
1 can cream of chicken soup

Topping:

½ c. crackers, crumbled or
  bread crumbs
¼ c. melted butter

Serves 6 to 8

Slice celery in 1 inch pieces; cook in small amount of water for 7 minutes (celery should be crisp). Mix celery, water chestnuts, almonds, pimientos and soup; place in buttered 1½ quart baking dish. Mix topping and spread on top. Bake at 350 degrees 30 minutes.

# CHINESE VEGETABLE CASSEROLE

1-16 oz. pkg. frozen green
  peas (or canned)
1 can bean sprouts
1 can water chestnuts, sliced
Soy sauce, pepper to taste
½ lb. sharp cheese, grated
1 can Chinese vegetables
1-6 oz. can mushrooms
¼ c. butter or margarine
1 can cream of mushroom
  soup
1 can French fried onions

**Serves 12 to 15**

Cook peas as directed on box; drain and place in bottom of well greased 2 quart casserole. Add bean sprouts, water chestnuts, pepper, soy sauce, ⅓ of cheese, ½ of Chinese vegetables, mushrooms, another ⅓ of cheese and remaining vegetables. Dot with butter; add mushroom soup, top with rest of cheese. Bake in 350 degree oven 30 minutes. Can be prepared in morning and refrigerated. To serve, reheat 10 minutes, put French fried onions on top, and bake an additional 5 minutes.

# CORN BAKE

3 c. cream style corn
1 green pepper, chopped
2 med. onions, chopped
1 c. herbed stuffing mix
Bread crumbs
Butter

**Serves 8**

Mix all together and put in well greased casserole. Sprinkle a few bread crumbs on top; dot with butter. Bake at 350 degrees 1 hour.

## CORN CASSEROLE

1 med. onion, chopped
½ green pepper, chopped
4 eggs
1 c. evaporated milk
2-16 oz. cans cream style
  corn
1 c. cracker crumbs
Salt and pepper to taste
3 T. butter

Serves 8 to 10

Saute onion and green pepper in a little butter. Beat eggs; add milk, corn, crumbs, salt, pepper, onions and green pepper. Mix well. Pour into 2 quart baking dish. If you desire a crunchy topping, add more crumbled crackers over top, then dot with butter. Place casserole in pan of water and bake in 350 degree oven 1 hour.

## MARGARET CHILE'S FRIED CORN

10 ears white corn
10 slices bacon
Salt and pepper
Milk

Serves 4 to 6

Ice down corn. Holding ears perpendicular to chopping board and using a very sharp knife, slice downward taking off just the tips of the kernels. With a kitchen knife, scrape the ears to remove remaining kernels. Fry bacon; remove. Put corn into bacon drippings and stir fry until corn is well coated and begins to turn clear; add milk to make it creamy. Do not boil. Simmer until corn is done. Adding a dash of sugar to mixture (optional).

*This recipe comes to us from our Senator's wife in Washington.*

## SCALLOPED CORN AND OYSTERS

2 eggs, slightly beaten
1-16 oz. can cream style
 corn
1 can (10 oz.) frozen oyster
 stew, thawed
½ c. milk
4 T. celery, minced
1 T. pimiento, chopped
¼ t. salt
Dash pepper
2 T. melted butter
1½ c. crushed saltines

Serves 6

Combine first eight ingredients. Stir in 1 cup of crackers. Cover and refrigerate until ready to bake. When ready to bake, sprinkle top of corn mix with the remaining ½ cup crackers that have been mixed with butter. Pour into 8 x 8 inch baking dish. Bake at 350 degrees 1 hour, or until knife comes out clean.

## EGGPLANT DELUXE CASSEROLE

2 large eggplants
3 or 4 strips of bacon, cut
 fine
1 large onion, chopped
3 stalks celery, chopped
2 t. Beau Monde seasoning
2 eggs, beaten
4 T. cracker crumbs
1 c. shredded cheddar
 cheese
Salt and pepper to taste

Serves 6 to 8

Peel eggplant; cut in 1 inch chunks. Cover with salt; let stand 20 minutes. Fry bacon slowly. When nearly done, push to edge of pan; add onion and celery. Continue to cook very slowly until vegetables are clear but not brown. Wash the salt off eggplant and boil until tender, about 15 minutes; remove from fire and drain. Chop or mash and drain again. Add 2 tablespoons cracker crumbs, and the bacon, celery and onion mixture; mix well. Add Beau Monde, salt and pepper. Stir in eggs and cheese. Pour into buttered 1½ to 2 quart casserole; sprinkle rest of cracker crumbs over top. Dot with butter. Bake at 325 degrees 1 hour. Delicious reheated.

## ROMAN EGGPLANT

1 med. eggplant, pared and
  cut into ½ inch slices
½ c. butter, melted
¾ c. fine dry bread crumbs
¼ t. salt
1-13½ oz. can spaghetti
  sauce with mushrooms
1 T. oregano
1 c. sharp cheese or
  Mozzarella cheese

Serves 4 to 5

Dip eggplant in butter, then in mixture of bread crumbs and salt. Place on greased cookie sheet; spoon sauce atop each slice. Sprinkle with oregano and cheese. Bake in 450 degree oven 10 to 12 minutes.

## STUFFED EGGPLANT

1 large eggplant
1 c. chopped onions
½ c. butter
2 large fresh tomatoes
½ c. pecans, broken
Cracker crumbs
Salt and pepper
Dash tabasco,
  Worcestershire
Bleu cheese

Serves 2 or 4

Slice eggplant in half; scoop out pulp, boil in salted water until tender. Drain. Saute onions in butter until tender; add tomatoes and pecans. Combine eggplant and onion tomato mixture. Add enough cracker crumbs to make firm consistency. Season highly. Put mixture into shells; sprinkle tops with cracker crumbs and bleu cheese. Place in shallow baking pan with 1 cup water in bottom. Bake at 350 degrees until bubbly and top browned.

## MUSHROOM, BEAN AND CARROT GLACE'

2 med. onions, sliced thin
  lengthwise
½ lb. fresh mushrooms
¼ c. butter or oleo
2 c. carrots cut lengthwise
  ½ x 3 in.
1-10 oz. pkg. frozen green
  beans, defrosted
1-10 oz. pkg. frozen wax
  beans, defrosted
2 t. salt
¼ t. pepper
1 t. Accent
½ t. garlic salt
1 t. rosemary
½ c. butter, melted
Glace' for vegetables,
  optional

Saute onions and mushrooms in ¼ cup butter until tender, not soft. Set aside. Combine carrot strips, defrosted green and wax beans. Steam in ½ inch of water, in a covered saucepan, until tender, but still colorful (about 7-8 minutes). In a large skillet combine onions, mushrooms, vegetables, all seasonings and ½ cup melted butter. Pour glace' over vegetables, blend gently and serve.

Glace' for vegetables:
1 T. cornstarch
2 T. water
1 c. clear chicken stock

Combine cornstarch with water. Add chicken stock. Cook, stirring constantly until thick.

**Serves 8**

## MUSHROOM CASSEROLE

½ c. onion, chopped
½ c. butter or margarine
1 c. beef bouillon
2 T. cornstarch
½ t. dried marjoram
1 lb. fresh mushrooms,
  chopped or 3-6 oz. cans,
  drained
2 T. dry Sherry
2 T. snipped parsley
½ c. coarsely crushed
  saltines
2 T. Parmesan cheese
1 T. butter or margarine

Cook onion in butter until tender. Blend beef bouillon with cornstarch and marjoram; stir into onion mixture. Add mushrooms; cook and stir until mixture thickens. Remove from heat. Stir in Sherry and parsley. Pour into 1 quart casserole. Combine crushed crackers, cheese and butter. Sprinkle over casserole; bake in 350 degree oven 20 minutes.

**Serves 6**

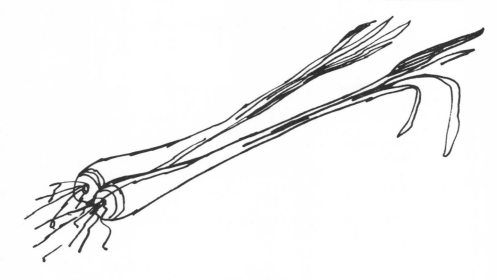

## OKRA AND TOMATOES

2½ c. okra, sliced
2 med. onions, chopped
Bacon fat
1½ c. cooked tomatoes
Salt and pepper to taste
2-4 slices fried bacon,
  crumbled

Saute okra and onions in bacon fat 5 minutes. Add tomatoes, salt and pepper; cook until done. Serve with crumbled bacon on top.

## BAKED ONIONS

4 large onions
½ c. butter
Salt and pepper to taste

Serves 6

*Wonderful accomaniment for steak.*

Cut onions in eighths. Place in 2 quart oblong baking dish. Dice butter; sprinkle over onions. Season. Cover tightly; bake at 400 degrees one hour. Stir frequently.

## ONION RINGS

3-4 large onions, thinly
  sliced
1 egg, beaten
1½ c. milk
2 c. buttermilk baking mix
Deep fat for frying

Serves 8 to 10

Separate onion into rings. Blend egg and milk; dip rings into mixture, a few at a time. Take out and drop into baking mix, being sure to coat well. Shake slightly and drop into hot fat, a few at a time; fry until lightly brown. Drain on paper towel. Keep hot until ready to serve.

*On a lazy day fry up several batches and freeze in plastic bags. Nice to have on hand for steak and seafood dinners.*

## SPINACH - STUFFED ONIONS

4 med. red onions
1 lb. fresh spinach, stems
  removed
2 T. melted butter
¼ c. half-and-half
Salt and white pepper to
  taste
Grated Parmesan or
  Gruyere cheese


Yield: 8 servings

Peel onions and cut in half horizontally; steam about 12 minutes or until tender but not soft and mushy. Cool; remove center of onions and dice. Leave shells intact. Wash spinach and cook 1 minute, using only water that clings to leaves; drain and chop. Saute spinach and diced onion in butter and half-and-half until fairly dry; season with salt and pepper. Fill onion shells with spinach mixture; sprinkle with cheese. Bake in a greased shallow pan at 350 degrees until onions are thoroughly heated.

## BAHAMIAN PEAS AND RICE

3 slices bacon
1 onion, chopped
3 slices ham, chopped
1 fresh tomato, chopped
2 T. tomato puree
1 can pidgeon peas
1 c. uncooked rice
1 c. water
Dash thyme
Salt and pepper
1 bay leaf

Serves 6 to 8

Cook bacon until done but not crisp. Add onion, ham, tomato and tomato puree. Cook 10 minutes. Add rice and peas; cover and cook 5 minutes. Add 1 cup water, seasonings and bay leaf. Cover; cook 20 minutes. Stir; cook 10 minutes more or until water is absorbed.

## PEAS IN CASSEROLE

1 c. mushrooms
1 small onion, grated
1 c. celery, diced
2 T. butter
2 c. cooked green peas
1 c. med. white sauce (see index)
4 eggs, hard cooked and sliced
1 can tomato soup
Bread crumbs

Serves 6

Saute mushrooms, onions and celery in butter. Layer peas, white sauce, mushroom mixture, eggs and tomato soup; repeat. Top with bread crumbs. Bake at 350 degrees 30 minutes.

Easy Gourmet

## BAKED POTATO ELEGANTE

1 baking potato
1 slice onion
1 strip uncooked bacon

Serves 1

Rub potato with bacon drippings; split lengthwise. Place onion slice between halves. Wrap bacon around potato, lapping on bottom. Wrap with foil; bake at 400 degrees one hour or until potato is done.

## BLENDER POTATO CASSEROLE

1 c. milk
3 eggs
1½ t. salt
¼ t. pepper
2 T. butter or margarine
1 c. cubed cheddar cheese
½ med. green pepper, diced
1 small onion, quartered
4 med. uncooked potatoes

Serves 8 to 10

Peel and cube potatoes. Combine all ingredients in blender in order listed. Cover and blend on high speed just until potatoes go through the blades. **Do not** over-blend. Pour mixture into greased 1½-2 quart casserole. Bake uncovered at 350 degrees 1 hour.

## FANNED POTATOES

6 med. potatoes
5 T. butter, melted
¼ c. dry bread crumbs
2 T. grated Parmesan
  cheese
1½ t. salt
Paprika

Serves 6

Wash and peel potatoes; place in bowl of cold water to prevent discoloration. Carefully cut each potato crosswise into ⅛ inch slices, cutting to within ½ inch of bottom (do not cut through completely). Return potatoes to cold water. Combine 2 tablespoons butter, bread crumbs and cheese; set aside. Drain potatoes and pat dry. Place in baking dish cut side up. Pour 3 tablespoons butter over potatoes; sprinkle with salt. Bake at 425 degrees 30 minutes or until tender. Sprinkle with crumb mixture. Bake 5-8 minutes until browned. Sprinkle with paprika.

# POTATOES A LA CAVE

Wash, scrub and peel as many medium-size potatoes as dinner guests. Slice potatoes VERY thin, almost like a potato chip. At La Cave they have a machine to do it.

Heat vegetable oil in a heavy skillet until VERY hot.

Fill skillet of hot oil about half full of potato slices. Amount of oil and number of slices will depend on skillet size. At La Cave they use an 8-inch skillet.

Fry slices on one side until golden brown. Slices will stick together. Turn carefully so pieces do not break off. Slices should be almost raw inside and crispy on outside. Cook second side until golden brown, too.

Use spatula to carefully remove pancake-like slices when done. Drain on paper towel. Let diners season as desired with salt and pepper.

Edmond Despointes

La Cave Restaurant

Indian Rocks Beach

# RATATOUILLE

1 large eggplant
2-3 zucchini
2 large onions, sliced
2 potatoes
1 med. green pepper, chopped
1-16 oz. can Italian plum tomatoes, undrained
2 cloves garlic, crushed
1 t. fresh basil
½ t. dried oregano
½ t. fennel seed
1 T. salt
¼ t. freshly ground black pepper
¾ c. olive oil

Serves 6 to 8

Dice unpeeled eggplant; slice unpeeled zucchini and dice potatoes. Combine with other ingredients in large heavy pot or Dutch oven. Mix thoroughly to coat vegetables with oil. Cook slowly, uncovered, 1½ hours, stirring occasionally. Allow to stand several hours. Can be served hot as a vegetable or cold as an appetizer. Freezes.

165

# "RED FOX INN" TOMATO PUDDING

**2-6 oz. cans tomato paste**
**1-46 oz. can tomato juice**
**1 t. salt**
**2 c. brown sugar**
**14 slices soft bread, cubed**
**1 c. butter, melted**

Boil tomato paste, juice and salt for 5 minutes; add sugar and stir until dissolved. Place cubed bread in 13 x 9 inch baking dish; pour melted butter over top. Add tomato mixture and bake uncovered 1 hour. May be frozen and reheated. Wonderful with meat.

## BAKED SAUERKRAUT

**10 slices bacon**
**2-4 oz. cans chopped**
**mushrooms**
**2 med. onions, diced**
**2 pts. sour cream**
**3 or 4-16 oz. cans sauerkraut**

**Serves 8**

Fry bacon; drain. Saute onions and drained mushrooms in bacon fat. Mix with sour cream; cook a few minutes. Pour over sauerkraut in 3-quart casserole. Bake at 350 degrees 1 hour.

## SAUERKRAUT MIT WEISWEIN

**2 lbs. sauerkraut**
**2 c. dry white wine**
**2 t. salt**
**1 T. caraway seed**
**1 t. allspice**
**½ c. butter**
**Sour cream**
**½ c. crisp cooked bacon,**
**crumbled**

**Serves 8**

Drain sauerkraut well; combine with wine, salt, caraway seed, allspice and butter. Cover and simmer 20 minutes. To serve, top with sour cream and bacon bits.

*Traditionally served with homemade bratwurst that has been boiled in beer and grilled over charcoal.*

## SPINACH AND ARTICHOKES

1-8½ oz. can artichokes
1 bottle garlic French
   dressing
Double recipe thick white
   sauce (see index)
8 oz. pkg. sharp cheese,
   grated
2 pkgs. frozen chopped
   spinach
Salt and pepper to taste
Dash Tabasco
Parmesan cheese

Serves 6

Cut artichokes in half and marinate in French dressing overnight. Make white sauce but do not let it get thick. Add cheese; cook until cheese melts and sauce thickens. Cook spinach according to package directions; drain well. Mix spinach with cheese sauce; blend thoroughly. Add salt, pepper and Tabasco to taste. Arrange artichokes on bottom of 2 quart casserole; pour spinach mixture over top. Put generous amount of Parmesan cheese over spinach. Bake in 350 degree oven until bubbly and cheese is slightly brown.

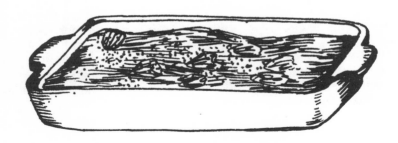

## SPINACH CHARLOTTE

1-10 oz. pkg. frozen chopped
   spinach
1 jar Old English cheese
8 ozs. cottage cheese
3 eggs
3 T. flour

Serves 6

Cook and drain spinach. Mix together softened Old English cheese, eggs and flour. Add well drained spinach and cottage cheese. Place in a buttered, standard-size quiche dish or pie plate. Bake at 350 degrees 30-45 minutes. Cut in wedges and serve.

# CREAMED SPINACH

2-10 oz. pkgs. frozen
  chopped spinach
3 T. butter
3 T. flour
1 med. onion, chopped
½ c. half and half
¾ c. chicken broth
Dash of nutmeg
Salt and pepper to taste

Serves 4 to 6

Cook spinach; drain well. Melt butter; stir in flour and chopped onion. Cook, stirring frequently until the onion and flour are slightly browned. Slowly add half and half and chicken broth while stirring mixture. Cook over low heat; continue stirring until sauce thickens. Add seasonings and spinach. Mix thoroughly.

# NEW ORLEANS SPINACH

2-10 oz. pkgs. chopped
  spinach
1-3 oz. pkg. cream cheese
½ c. butter
Salt and pepper to taste
Grated rind of one lemon
Pinch of mace (or nutmeg)
1 c. herb seasoned bread
  stuffing

Serves 6

Cook spinach; drain well. Add cream cheese and ¼ cup butter, and mix until blended. Add salt, pepper, lemon rind and mace. Put in 1½ quart greased casserole. Sprinkle dressing on top. Drizzle remaining ¼ cup melted butter over dressing. Bake at 375 degrees 25 minutes.

# STUFFED ACORN SQUASH

2 acorn squash, cut in half
1 c. unsweetened apple
  sauce
4 t. brown sugar
4 t. soft margarine
Cinnamon

Serves 4

Place squash halves cut side down in shallow baking pan. Cover bottom with water. Bake at 400 degrees 50-60 minutes, or until tender. Turn squash over. Fill each cavity with applesauce and brown sugar. Dot with margarine. Sprinkle with cinnamon. Continue baking until applesauce is bubbly, about 15-20 minutes.

## SQUASH-CARROT CASSEROLE

1½ lbs. summer squash
4 med. carrots
1-2 oz. jar pimientos,
  chopped
1 small onion, finely
  chopped
1 c. sour cream
1 can cream of chicken soup
1 pkg. seasoned stuffing
  mix
¾ c. butter, melted

Serves 4 to 6

Cook squash in salted water; drain and mash. Grate carrots; blend in. Add pimientos, onion, sour cream and chicken soup. Combine stuffing mix with butter; use one half of this mixture to line 1 quart casserole. Spread vegetable mixture on top; sprinkle with remaining dressing. Bake at 350 degrees 45 minutes.

## CREOLE SUMMER SQUASH

½ bell pepper, chopped
1 med. onion, chopped
2 T. butter
2 fresh tomatoes, peeled
  and chopped
5-6 squash, sliced
½ clove garlic, mashed
  (optional)

Serves 4

Saute pepper and onion in 2 tablespoons butter until tender;* add tomatoes and squash. DO NOT ADD WATER. Simmer on low fire until squash is tender, stirring occasionally to prevent sticking. Salt and pepper to taste.

* If garlic is used, add at this point.

## SQUASH PIE

8 med. yellow squash, sliced
1 med. onion, sliced
Salt and pepper to taste
1 can cream of mushroom
  soup
2 eggs
½ c. milk
¼ c. butter or margarine
1 lb. sharp cheddar cheese,
  grated

Serves 6

Cook squash and onion in water seasoned with salt and pepper until tender. Drain; add mushroom soup. Beat eggs in milk and add to soup mixture. Cut in butter and cheese. Pour into 2 quart casserole and bake at 375 degrees 25-30 minutes.

## SWEET POTATO PUDDING

3 c. diced raw sweet potato
¾ c. brown sugar
½ c. milk
2 eggs
½ t. ginger
¼ c. butter

Serves 6

Put all ingredients in blender; blend until completely mixed and potatoes are very smooth. Pour into buttered 1½ quart casserole. Cook at 325 degrees about 50 minutes or until knife inserted in center comes out clean.

## SWEET POTATO SOUFFLE

2 c. sweet potatoes, mashed
1 t. vanilla
½ c. raisins
¼ t. salt
1¼ c. sugar
½ c. butter
2 T. baking powder
3 eggs, beaten

Blend all ingredients thoroughly; put in shallow 1½ quart baking dish. Bake at 400 degrees 20 minutes. Remove from oven and cover with topping. Return to oven 10 minutes or until lightly browned.

Topping:

3 T. butter, softened
¼ c. brown sugar
1¼ c. corn flakes, crushed
¼ c. chopped nuts

Serves 8 to 10

## ZUCCHINI CASSEROLE

¼ c. butter or margarine
2 med. onions, chopped
4 med. zucchini squash
3 large fresh tomatoes
1 t. salt
Pepper to taste
1 c. diced Swiss cheese
½ c. fine bread or cracker
  crumbs
½ c. diced sharp cheddar
Butter

Saute onion in butter until onion is transparent, stirring frequently. Add sliced zucchini; steam 10 minutes. Combine mixture with diced tomatoes, salt, cheese and half of the bread crumbs. Mix thoroughly; pour into casserole. Add remaining crumbs and diced cheddar on top; dot with butter. Bake at 350 degrees 40 minutes, or until zucchini is done.

Serves 5 to 6

*Crabmeat may be added to this recipe to create a meal in one.*

## ZUCCHINI WITH WALNUTS

**4 c. sliced zucchini**
**⅓ c. sliced green onions,**
**with tops**
**2 T. butter or margarine**
**3 T. dry Sherry**
**½ t. salt**
**Sweet basil**
**¼ c. chopped toasted**
**walnuts**

**Serves 4 or 5**

Combine zucchini, onions and butter; cook uncovered over low heat 5 minutes. Add Sherry, salt and sweet basil. Cover; cook over low heat 3-5 minutes. Stir in walnuts; serve immediately.

## HOT CURRIED FRUIT

**1–1 lb. 4 oz. can pineapple**
**chunks**
**1–1 lb 4 oz. can sliced**
**peaches**
**1–1 lb. 4 oz. can apricot**
**halves, sliced**
**1–1 lb. 4 oz. can pear halves,**
**sliced**
**1 large jar maraschino**
**cherries**
**3-4 bananas**
**Curry powder**
**Light brown sugar**
**Butter**

**Serves 8 to 12**

Heavily grease 3 quart baking dish; sprinkle with brown sugar. Slice bananas lengthwise and place on bottom. Layer drained fruits over the bananas; sprinkle with curry powder and brown sugar. Repeat layers omitting bananas. Dot with butter; bake in 350 degree oven until casserole is bubbly and heated through.

*There are many versions of hot curried fruit, but this one is different and especially good.*

## FRUIT COMPOTE

**1 can (1 lb.) dark pitted
   sweet cherries
1 can (1 lb.) sliced peaches
   drained
1-12 oz. pkg. dried apricots
1 T. grated orange peel
1 T. grated lemon peel
½ c. orange juice
¼ c. lemon juice
¾ c. light brown sugar,
   packed**

**Serves 8 to 10**

Turn cherries and juice into 2 quart casserole. Add peaches, apricots, orange and lemon juices and peels. Sprinkle with brown sugar. Bake covered at 350 degrees for 1½ hours. Cool slightly. Cover and refrigerate overnight.

*This is also delicious served to accompany turkey or chicken.*

# SALADS

## MOLDED AMBROSIA

**1-3 oz. pkg. orange gelatin**
**1 c. hot water**
**1 c. crushed pineapple and juice**
**1 c. mandarin orange sections**
**½ c. grated coconut**
**1 c. sour cream**
**⅓ c. sugar**

**Serves 6**

Dissolve gelatin in water. Add pineapple juice. Blend in remaining ingredients. Pour into 5½ cup mold. Chill until firm.

## ANTIPASTO SALAD

**½ c. salad oil (may use**
  **¼ c. olive oil and**
  **¼ c. safflower oil)**
**¼ c. red wine vinegar**
**¼ t. salt**
**⅛ t. pepper**
**Garlic powder, to taste (optional)**
**¼ lb. sliced fresh mushrooms**
**½ c. pitted black olives**
**2 T. chopped pimientos**
**2 T. chopped fresh parsley**
**1 pkg. frozen artichoke hearts, cooked till tender, drained**

**Serves 4 to 6**

In glass jar pour oil, vinegar and seasonings; cover and shake well. Put in saucepan and heat. Shake again and pour over artichokes, mushrooms, olives, pimientos and parsley. Cover and chill for two hours. Serve on Romaine.

174

## CONGEALED ASPARAGUS SALAD

1 c. water
1 c. sugar
½ c. white vinegar
½ t. salt
2 pkgs. unflavored gelatin,
  dissolved in
½ c. cold water
1 c. chopped celery
½ c. pecans, cut small
1 small can pimiento
Juice of ½ lemon
1–16 oz. can asparagus, cut
  in small pieces
Grated onion, to taste
Mayonnaise

**Serves 8**

Bring first four ingredients to boil; add gelatin. When cold, add next six ingredients. Pour into pan and chill until firm. Cut into squares and arrange on lettuce leaves, with a dollop of mayonnaise on top.

*A decorative 6 cup mold may be used; chill until firm and unmold over a bed of lettuce.*

## ASPARAGUS VINAIGRETTE

24 fresh asparagus spears
½ c. salad oil
4 T. wine vinegar
½ t. salt
½ t. dry mustard
½ t. chopped onion
1 T. chopped pimiento
4 slices bacon, fried crisp,
  crumbled

**Serves 6**

Cook and drain asparagus; arrange in a dish. Combine oil, vinegar, salt, mustard, onion and pimiento; shake well and pour half over asparagus. Cover; refrigerate ½ hour. Arrange asparagus on lettuce leaves. Shake remaining dressing; pour over asparagus. Sprinkle with bacon.

# ARTICHOKE-TOMATO ASPIC

3 pkgs. lemon gelatin
6 c. tomato juice
3 t. onion juice
Juice of ½ lemon
2 t. Worcestershire sauce
Salt & pepper to taste
2 cans artichoke hearts,
   drained

Serves 18 to 20

Heat tomato juice to boiling; add lemon gelatin and stir until dissolved. Add the remainder of ingredients, except the artichokes. Oil a large ring mold (12 inches in diameter, or 2 smaller ones). Place artichokes in mold with a little of tomato juice mixture; refrigerate until congealed. Add rest of mixture; chill until firm. Unmold and decorate with salad greens or any other garnish.

# SPICY TOMATO ASPIC

1 pkg. lemon gelatin
1 c. boiling water
1-8 oz. can tomato sauce
1 t. grated onion
1½ T. vinegar
½ t. salt
¼ t. pepper

Serves 4 to 6

Dissolve gelatin in boiling water. Add remaining ingredients and mix well. Pour into mold and chill until firmly set. Unmold over lettuce leaves. Pour cucumber sauce over aspic (see index).

# TOMATO-CHEESE ASPIC

2 T. unflavored gelatin
½ c. cold water
1 can tomato soup
6 ozs. cream cheese
1 c. mayonnaise
1 c. finely chopped celery
¼ c. shredded onion
1 lb. cooked shrimp
   (optional)
Salt and pepper to taste

Serves 8

Soften gelatin in cold water; add tomato soup and bring to boil, stirring until gelatin dissolves. Add cheese and mayonnaise; stir until smooth. Blend in remaining ingredients; season to taste. Pour into greased 5½ cup ring mold; chill until firm.

176

# BEET SALAD MOLD

**1-3 oz. pkg. lemon gelatin**
**1 c. boiling water**
**¾ c. beet juice**
**1½ T. vinegar**
**½ t. salt**
**2 t. onion juice**
**1 T. horseradish, creamed**
**¾ c. celery, diced**
**1 c. canned beets, shredded**

**Serves 6 to 8**

Dissolve gelatin in boiling water. Add beet juice, vinegar, salt, onion juice and horseradish. Chill until thick. Fold in celery and beets. Pour into 6 individual molds or 1-quart ring mold; chill until firm. Unmold on lettuce and serve with mayonnaise.

# BROCCOLI MOLDED SALAD

**1-10 oz. pkg. frozen chopped broccoli**
**1 envelope unflavored gelatin**
**½ c. water**
**1 c. condensed chicken broth**
**⅔ c. mayonnaise**
**⅓ c. sour cream**
**1 T. lemon juice**
**1 T. onion, finely chopped**
**3 hard-cooked eggs, chopped**

**Serves 8**

Cook broccoli according to package directions; drain. Soften gelatin in water over low heat; add chicken broth and stir until well dissolved. Blend in mayonnaise, sour cream, lemon juice and onion; mix well. Refrigerate until slightly thick. Add broccoli and eggs; fold into gelatin mixture. Pour into 4 cup mold or individual molds; refrigerate until very firm. Unmold and serve on lettuce.

## CAESAR SALAD

2 cloves garlic, crushed
¾ c. olive oil
2 c. croutons
2 to 3 heads romaine lettuce
Freshly ground pepper
½ t. salt
2 eggs, boiled one minute
  (coddled)
3 T. lemon juice
6 to 8 anchovy fillets, cut up
½ c. grated Parmesan
  cheese

Serves 6 to 8

Combine garlic and olive oil; let stand overnight. Saute croutons in ½ cup garlic-oil mixture, stirring carefully, until golden brown. Drain on paper towels.

Break romaine into large pieces in large bowl; add pepper, salt and ¼ cup garlic-oil mixture. Toss to coat each leaf. Break eggs into middle of lettuce. Top eggs with lemon juice; toss until romaine has a thick, creamy look. Add anchovies. Add cheese and croutons; toss. Serve at once.

## CHEESE SALAD

1 c. grated cheese
1 c. mayonnaise
1 c. crushed pineapple,
  drained (reserve juice)
1 c. evaporated milk
1-3 oz. pkg. lemon gelatin
1 T. sugar

Serves 6 to 8

In large bowl mix cheese, mayonnaise, crushed pineapple and evaporated milk; set aside. Add water to pineapple juice to make 1 cup; bring to boil in saucepan. Add lemon gelatin and sugar; stir until dissolved. Blend gelatin mixture with ingredients in large bowl; pour into 6 cup mold. Refrigerate overnight.

## CHICKEN APPLE SALAD

5 c. cooked chicken, cut
  into chunks
2 c. unpared, cubed apples
Lemon juice
2 c. diced celery
⅔ c. sliced stuffed olives
½ c. slivered almonds
⅓ c. salad dressing
½ c. heavy cream, whipped
  or sour cream
2 t. salt
Bibb lettuce
Curly chicory
Unpared, cored apple rings

Serves 8 to 10

Dip apple chunks in ½ cup lemon juice; combine with chicken, celery, olives and almonds. Blend dressing, whipped cream, 2 tablespoons lemon juice and salt; toss well; refrigerate. At serving time, heap mixture on bed of lettuce and chicory. Dip apple rings in lemon juice and lay rings around salad; tuck chicory in each ring and on top of salad.

## CHICKEN SALAD - A LA TIZ

4 chicken breasts
Salted water
1 c. chopped celery
1 c. chopped green pepper
¼ c. chopped onion
6 thin slices cucumber
1-15½ oz. can drained
  pineapple chunks,
  reserving liquid
½ c. salad dressing
½ c. coleslaw dressing
1 t. lemon juice
¼ t. dill weed
¼ t. salt
¼ t. pepper
¼ t. curry
1 T. pineapple juice
1 small pkg. slivered
  almonds, toasted
1 small pkg. pecans, toasted

Serves 6

Cover chicken with salted water and cook until fork tender; cool in refrigerator 1 hour. Remove from water; skin, bone and cut into bite size pieces. In large bowl mix celery, green pepper, onion, cucumber, pineapple chunks and chicken. Combine salad dressing and coleslaw dressing; add lemon juice, dill weed, salt, pepper, curry and pineapple juice. Add dressing to chicken mixture and stir lightly. Chill. Serve on lettuce; top with toasted nuts.

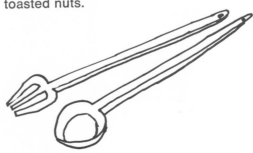

# ORIENTAL CHICKEN SALAD

3 c. cooked chicken
2 c. mayonnaise
2 T. lemon juice
2½ T. soy sauce
1 T. curry powder
1 T. onion juice, or finely
grated onion
1 T. chutney
1½ c. chopped celery
1 can pineapple chunks,
drained
2 c. grapes
¾ c. water chestnuts,
drained, sliced
¾ c. slivered almonds,
toasted, salted

**Serves 8**

Cut chicken into bite-sized pieces; set aside. Mix mayonnaise, lemon juice, soy sauce, curry powder, onion juice and chutney. Combine meat, celery, pineapple chunks, grapes and water chestnuts; add mayonnaise mixture and toss gently. Refrigerate several hours, preferably overnight. Just before serving, toss with almonds. Serve on lettuce.

*Turkey may be substituted for chicken; or you may use 1 1/2 cups each of crabmeat and shrimp.*

# FOUR HOUR COLESLAW

1 large head of cabbage,
shredded
1 large onion, cut in thin
slices
1 or 2 peeled carrots, grated
½ c. sugar
1 c. vinegar
¾ c. salad oil
1 t. dry mustard
1 t. celery seed
1 t. mixed salad herbs
Salt and pepper to taste

**Serves 8 to 10**

Combine last six ingredients in saucepan; bring to rolling boil. Remove from heat and let stand until cold. Place cabbage, onion and carrots in large bowl and sprinkle with sugar; pour dressing over the mixture. Do not stir. Cover tightly; refrigerate at least 4 hours. Stir and serve.

## LU'S FROZEN SLAW

2 large heads cabbage,
  shredded
2 large bell peppers, finely
  chopped
4 large onions, finely
  chopped
4 c. sugar
3 c. cider vinegar
¼ c. salt
4 carrots, grated

**Serves 16 to 20**

Mix all ingredients until well blended. Put into a 4-quart dish and refrigerate or freeze.

*You may want to reduce the sugar by half.*

## SOUTHERN COLESLAW

4 c. shredded cabbage
½ carrot, grated
3 T. chopped green pepper
3 T. chopped onion
½ c. mayonnaise
1½ T. sugar
1½ T. vinegar
¾ t. celery salt
Dash pepper
Dash Worcestershire sauce
2 T. cream plus milk to make
  ¼ c.

**Serves 6**

Mix cabbage, carrot, green pepper and onion in large bowl. In blender combine remaining ingredients; blend well. Pour over cabbage mixture; cover and chill. Stir occasionally.

## SUPER SLAW

1 med. head cabbage,
  shredded
2 c. seedless white grapes
1 c. cashew nuts, chopped
1 c. mayonnaise
1 T. onion juice
1 t. garlic powder
1 t. salt, sugar, dry mustard
2 T. vinegar

**Serves 8**

Shred cabbage; add grapes and nuts. Combine mayonnaise, onion juice and other ingredients; pour over cabbage slaw and chill.

## CORN SALAD WITH CURRY

1 chicken bouillon cube
1 c. water
1-10 oz. pkg. frozen corn
1 t. curry powder
2 T. lemon juice
1 envelope plus 1 t.
  unflavored gelatin
2 T. green onion, minced
  (use some of green top)
2 whole pimientos, drained,
  chopped
Mayonnaise
Chutney, to taste

**Serves 6**

Mix bouillon cube and ½ cup water in saucepan; bring to boil. Add corn and cook, covered, according to package directions; drain, reserving broth. Refrigerate corn. Add curry powder and 1 tablespoon lemon juice to broth. Dissolve gelatin in ½ cup water over low heat, stirring constantly. Add water to gelatin mixture to make 2 cups; stir into broth. Chill until slightly thickened. Mix in corn, onion and pimiento. Pour into 4-cup mold or individual molds and refrigerate until firm; unmold, serve over lettuce. Mix mayonnaise, chutney and 1 tablespoon lemon juice; pour over molded gelatin mixture.

## KING CRAB SALAD

1-7½ oz. can Alaska King
  crab or ½ lb. frozen Alaska
  King crab
1 c. pineapple chunks
2 T. pineapple liquid
¼ c. vinegar
¼ t. salt
¼ t. ginger
¼ t. monosodium glutamate
1 t. soy sauce
1 lb. can bean sprouts
½ c. green pepper, diced

**Serves 4**

Drain pineapple; reserve 2 tablespoons liquid. Mix vinegar, pineapple liquid, salt, ginger, monosodium glutamate and soy sauce. Drain crab; cut into bite size pieces. Pour vinegar mixture over crab and chill for one hour. Drain and rinse bean sprouts. Combine crab, pineapple, bean sprouts and green pepper; mix well. Serve over lettuce leaves.

## CUCUMBER WITH LABAN

2½ c. Laban (yogurt)
1 c. peeled chopped
  cucumbers
½ t. salt
3 cloves garlic
1 t. dried mint

Stir laban until smooth. Combine with cucumbers. Work garlic to paste with salt and mix it with a spoonful of laban before adding to cucumber mixture. Add mint. Finely shredded lettuce may be substituted for cucumber when out of season.

**Serves 6**

*Mint gives this summer salad a particularly refresing taste. Good with Kibbeh.*

# EGG SALAD MOLD

2 envelopes unflavored
  gelatin
¾ c. water
3 T. vinegar
1 t. Worcestershire sauce
1 t. salt
¼ t. dry mustard
1½ c. mayonnaise
¾ c. chopped celery
⅓ c. chopped green pepper
⅓ c. chopped pimiento
1 T. chopped scallions
8 hard boiled eggs, chopped
Pepper to taste
Chili Mayonnaise:
1 c. blender mayonnaise
1 T. chili powder
1 t. each green pepper and
  scallions (green tops only),
  minced fine

Dissolve gelatin in water in top of double boiler. Add vinegar, Worcestershire, salt and mustard. Cool 10 minutes. Stir in mayonnaise. Add celery, green pepper, pimiento, scallions and eggs. Blend lightly, but well. Adjust seasonings. Pour into 6-cup crown or ring mold. Refrigerate until set. Unmold and fill center with chili mayonnaise (best made a day or two ahead).

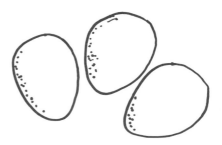

# SOUR CREAM FRUIT SALAD

1 #303 can pineapple
  chunks, drained
1 can Mandarin oranges,
  drained
1 can white, seedless
  grapes, drained
2 c. marshmallows, small
  size
4 medium bananas, sliced
Pecans or walnuts, chopped,
  if desired
Salt to taste
2 heaping T. sour cream

Serves 8

Combine first seven ingredients carefully. Chill in refrigerator. Mix in sour cream just before serving.

## SUNSHINE CITY SALAD

6 oranges
1 grapefruit
1 fresh pineapple, cut in
  bite-size cubes, or
  bite-size canned
12 fresh strawberries
12 pecan halves
Lettuce leaves

Serves 12

Cut down on each segment of peeled or-anges and grapefruit. Arrange sections and pineapple chunks in lettuce lined bowl. Garnish with strawberries and pecan halves. Serve with honey cream dressing (see index).

## MOLDED GAZPACHO SALAD

1 envelope unflavored
  gelatin
1-18 oz. can tomato juice
2 T. vinegar
2 T. salad oil
½ t. salt
Tabasco sauce, to taste
Freshly ground black
  pepper, to taste
1-16 oz. can cut green beans
1 large cucumber, peeled
  and diced
¼ c. green pepper, diced
¼ c. onion, finely chopped
1 small can mushrooms,
  drained, chopped

Serves 6

Place tomato juice and gelatin in sauce-pan; heat over low heat until gelatin is dissolved. Add vinegar, oil, salt, Tabasco and pepper. Combine beans, cucumber, green pepper, onion and mushrooms. Stir in tomato mixture and chill until firm. Serve over lettuce.

185

# LOUIS PAPPAS FAMOUS GREEK SALAD

**Potato salad:**
**6 boiling potatoes**
**2 med. onions or 4 green onions**
**¼ c. finely chopped parsley**
**½ c. thinly sliced green onions**
**½ c. salad dressing**
**Salt**
**Salad ingredients:**
**1 large head lettuce**
**3 c. potato salad**
**12 sprigs watercress (or roka)**
**2 tomatoes cut into 6 wedges each**
**1 cucumber, peeled and cut lengthwise into 8 fingers**
**1 avocado peeled and cut into wedges**
**4 portions Feta (Greek cheese)**
**1 green pepper, cut into 8 rings**
**4 slices canned cooked beets**
**4 peeled and cooked shrimp**
**4 anchovy filets**
**12 black olives (Greek style)**
**12 med. hot Salonika peppers**
**4 fancy cut radishes**
**4 whole green onions**
**½ c. distilled white vinegar**
**¼ c. each olive and salad oil, blended**
**Oregano**

Make potato salad. Line a large platter with outside lettuce leaves. Place 3 cups of the potato salad in a mound in the center of the platter. Cover with the remaining lettuce which has been shredded. Arrange the roka or watercress on top of this. Place the tomato wedges around the outer edge of salad with a few on the top, and place cucumber wedges in between the tomatoes, making a solid base of the salad. Place the avocado slices around the outside. Slices of Feta cheese should be arranged on the top of the salad, with the green pepper slices over all. On the very top, place the sliced beets with a shrimp on each beet slice and an anchovy filet on the shrimp. The olives, peppers and green onions can be arranged as desired. The entire salad is then sprinkled with the vinegar (more may be used) and then with the blended oil. Sprinkle the oregano over all and serve at once. Garlic toasted Greek bread is served with this salad.

*Louis Pappas called this a "Salad for 4 persons".*

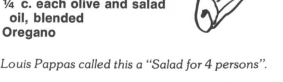

# GUACAMOLE I

4 c. thickly sliced avocado
1 c. fresh pineapple wedges,
  or canned pineapple
  chunks
⅓ c. salad oil
⅓ c. vinegar
1 clove garlic, crushed
Salt and pepper to taste

Serves 6

Combine avocado and pineapple. Blend oil, vinegar, garlic, salt and pepper. Pour over fruit and refrigerate, turning occasionally. Serve on lettuce.

# GUACAMOLE II

5 ripe avocados
3 small diced tomatoes
2 red onions, finely diced
½ t. chopped fresh
  coriander or coriander
  seed
Juice of 3 lemons
Salt to taste
½ hot pepper, minced

Serves 8 to 10

Peel avocados and chop fine; add tomatoes, onions and coriander. Mix; sprinkle with lemon juice. Add salt and hot pepper. Serve on lettuce.

# HEARTS OF PALM SALAD

1 head lettuce
4 c. hearts of palm, cut up in
  bite-size pieces
2 c. pineapple chunks
Tiny bits of crystallized
  ginger and dates, to taste
3 c. mayonnaise
1 c. vanilla ice cream
½ c. crunchy peanut butter
Green food coloring

Serves 10 to 12

Combine hearts of palm, pineapple chunks, ginger and dates. Arrange on a bed of lettuce. Blend last four ingredients; spoon over salad.

# KONA CANOE SALAD
## from The Garden Room at Robinson's

1 whole fresh pineapple
24 orange sections, fresh
12 strawberries, fresh
3 c. celery, ¼ inch dice
1 c. salad dressing or
  mayonnaise
½ t. seasoned salt
2 lbs. turkey breast or
  chicken (¾ inch dice)
1 t. ground ginger
¾ c. sliced almonds

Serves 4

Combine salad dressing, seasoned salt and ginger; toss with sliced almonds, turkey and diced celery.

Cut pineapple into quarters, leaving leaves attached to each quarter. Core and pare into 1 inch cubes. Place pineapple rind into bottom of oblong dish. Spoon ¼ of salad mixture into pineapple rind. Arrange pineapple cubes around outside top area. Cover top of salad with 6 orange slices and 3 strawberries.

Served with fresh flower garnish opposite pineapple leaves.

# KOREAN SALAD

1 bag fresh spinach
1 can bean sprouts, drained
2 hard boiled eggs
6 slices bacon, cooked and
  crumbled
1 can water chestnuts,
  sliced
Dressing:
1 c. salad oil
½ c. sugar
¼ c. vinegar
Small onion, grated
1 T. Worcestershire sauce
Salt and pepper

Serves 6 to 8

Combine salad ingredients.

Blend dressing ingredients well; add to salad ingredients and toss lightly.

## LOBSTER SALAD

10 c. cooked lobster meat
3 cloves garlic, crushed
6 t. salt
¾ t. pepper
¾ c. wine vinegar
3 c. olive oil
1½ c. chopped shallots
6 T. chopped parsley
2 c. minced celery
3 t. chopped onion
Juice of 1 lemon
1⅓ c. mayonnaise

Serves 10 to 12

Mix garlic, salt and pepper; add vinegar and mix well. Blend in oil, shallots and parsley. Pour over lobster meat which has been cut into bite sized pieces; toss lightly. Refrigerate several hours or overnight. Remove lobster from marinade; add celery, onion, lemon juice and mayonnaise. Chill well and serve on lettuce.

## MANGO SALAD

1 c. ripe mango, peeled
1 c. ripe tomatoes
8 strips bacon, fried crisp,
   crumbled
⅓ c. Roquefort cheese
4 to 6 t. mayonnaise

Serves 4 to 6 people

Cut mango and tomatoes into bite sized pieces; mix gently with bacon. Crumble cheese over all; serve on lettuce leaves. with dollop of mayonnaise.

# MARINATED MUSHROOMS AND ARTICHOKE HEARTS

**2 pkgs. frozen or canned
  artichoke hearts
2 lbs. small mushrooms,
  canned
1½ c. water
1 c. cider vinegar
½ c. oil
1 clove garlic, halved
1½ T. salt
½ t. peppercorns
½ t. dried thyme
½ t. oregano**

**Serves 16 to 20 people**

Cook artichoke hearts, if frozen, according to package directions; drain. Slice mushrooms in half through stem; combine with artichokes. Combine water, vinegar, oil, garlic, salt, peppercorns and herbs; mix well. Add vegetables and toss lightly. Refrigerate in covered bowl. Stir occasionally. Leave overnight. Drain before serving.

# SALADE NICOISE

**1 head Boston or Romaine
  lettuce
2 to 3 med. potatoes, cooked
Salt and freshly ground
  pepper to taste
1 c. string beans, cooked
1 large can tuna fish,
  drained, or any other fish
12 flat anchovies, drained
4 hard cooked eggs,
  quartered
2 large or 4 small ripe
  tomatoes, quartered
16 black olives, preferably
  Greek olives
¼ c. red wine vinegar
½ c. olive oil
Salt and pepper**

**Serves 4 for lunch
  or 6 for first course at
  dinner**

Wash lettuce leaves, pat dry; place in bowl. Cut potatoes into ¼ inch slices; spread over lettuce, sprinkle with salt and pepper. Spread string beans on top of potatoes. Make a mound of tuna fish in center and place anchovies around it. Surround anchovies with eggs, tomatoes and olives. Cover bowl; refrigerate. In small bowl mix vinegar, oil, salt and pepper. Pour over salad and serve.

## OLD KENTUCKY SALAD

1-3 oz. pkg. lime jello
1 c. finely cut marshmallows
¼ c. sugar
Dash salt
1 c. boiling water
Juice of ½ lemon
1-3 oz. pkg. cream cheese
1-15¼ oz. can pineapple
  chunks, drained
½ c. chopped pecans
½ pt. heavy cream, whipped

Serves 8

Combine jello, marshmallows, sugar, salt and water; heat until ingredients are dissolved. Add lemon juice; cool until slightly thickened. Add cream cheese (cut in small pieces), pineapple and pecans. Fold in whipped cream; pour into well oiled individual molds.

## OVERNIGHT SALAD

1 large head lettuce, torn
1 c. chopped celery
1 c. chopped bell pepper
1 c. chopped red onion
1 small can petite point
  peas, drained
Mayonnaise
1 T. sugar
½ c. Parmesan cheese

Serves 12

Place all vegetables in large bowl; completely cover top with layer of mayonnaise. Sprinkle sugar over top. Spread Parmesan cheese over all; seal and set in refrigerator overnight. Mix well before serving.

## PERFECTION SALAD

1½ c. hot water
1 pkg. lemon-flavored
  gelatin
3 T. lemon juice
1 T. sugar
½ t. salt
9 oz. can crushed pineapple
  and juice
1½ c. finely shredded red or
  green cabbage
1 head of lettuce or endive
Mayonnaise
Paprika

Serves 5 to 6

Add hot water to gelatin; stir until dissolved. Add lemon juice, sugar, salt and pineapple juice; chill until gelatin begins to set. Combine cabbage and pineapple and fold into mixture. Pour into 4-cup mold. Chill until firm. Unmold on lettuce bed, top with mayonnaise and a dash of paprika on top.

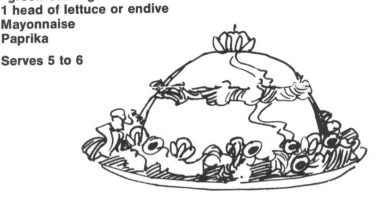

## PICNIC SALAD BOWL

2 very large Bermuda onions
3 oz. pkg. blue cheese,
  crumbled
½ c. salad oil
2 T. fresh lemon juice
1 t. salt
Pepper, to taste
Paprika, to taste
½ t. sugar
2 heads of lettuce

Serves 10 to 12

Cut onions into thin slices and separate into rings; put them in bowl. Combine all other ingredients except lettuce; pour over onion rings and chill for several hours. Just before serving break lettuce into bite size pieces and toss with onions and dressing.

## GERMAN POTATO SALAD

8-10 med. sized new
  potatoes
8 strips bacon, cooked
1 med. onion, finely chopped
Salt and pepper to taste
2 T. bacon drippings
2 T. flour
½ c. water
1 c. vinegar
½ c. sugar
Chopped parsley

Serves 8

Boil potatoes (unpeeled) in salt water; cook until just done. Cool, peel and thinly slice. In bowl layer potatoes, onions, bacon, salt and pepper; continue until all potatoes are used. Warm drippings; add flour and stir constantly. Mix water, sugar and vinegar; slowly add to drippings and flour mixture. Stir until thickened; pour over potatoes. Refrigerate 12 hours. Before serving, warm to room temperature and garnish with fresh chopped parsley.

## PRIZE WINNING POTATO SALAD

4 c. cubed cooked potatoes
¼ c. French dressing
3 hard cooked eggs, cut up
1 c. diced celery
3 T. chopped onion
3 T. chopped green pepper
¼ c. diced cucumber
¼ c. sweet pickle relish,
  well drained
1 T. celery seed
1 c. cooked ham (optional)
  diced
½ c. mayonnaise
Salt and freshly ground
  pepper to taste

Serves 6

Cook potatoes in skins; cool and remove skins. Marinate potatoes in French dressing 2 or 3 hours; add remaining ingredients. Serve in lettuce lined bowl; garnish with sliced hard cooked eggs, stuffed olives and parsley.

# RASPBERRY SALAD

**1-3 oz. box raspberry
gelatin
1 c. tomato juice
1 c. V-8 cocktail juice
1 t. fresh lemon juice
⅛ t. salt
Optional: ½ t. grated onion
½ c. chopped celery**

**Serves 4**

Heat tomato juice; dissolve gelatin. Add cocktail juice; stir in salt and lemon juice. If desired, add onion and celery. Pour into molds and refrigerate. When firm, unmold on shredded lettuce. Top with mayonnaise or favorite dressing.

# ROQUEFORT MOUSSE

**1 envelope unflavored
gelatin
¼ c. lemon juice
1 c. boiling hot water
¼ lb. Roquefort cheese
1 c. grated cucumber
4 T. parsley, chopped
2 T. pimiento, chopped
1 T. capers, chopped
1 t. grated onion or onion
juice
Salt and freshly ground
pepper
1 c. heavy cream, whipped**

**Serves 6**

Mix gelatin with lemon juice to soften; add to hot water. Mash cheese. Combine cucumber, parsley, pimiento, capers, onion, salt and pepper; add to mashed cheese. Stir in gelatin mixture. Chill until barely set; fold in whipped cream. Pour into 6 cup ring mold; chill until firm. Unmold on serving platter. You may fill center with seafood or chicken salad.

## SALMON CUCUMBER MOLD

2 envelopes unflavored
  gelatin
1 c. water
1 t. salt
3 T. lemon juice
1 c. salad dressing
1 lb. can red salmon, drained
  and flaked
2 c. finely chopped
  cucumber
1 c. finely chopped celery
2 T. dried dill weed
1 T. chopped chives, frozen
  or freeze dried

Serves 6 to 8

Sprinkle gelatin over cold water in medium saucepan. Place over low heat. Stir constantly until gelatin dissolves. Remove from heat; stir in salt and lemon juice. Gradually add to salad dressing; blend until smooth. Add salmon and remaining ingredients. Mix well. Turn into 6 cup mold. Chill until firm, several hours or overnight.

## SEAFOOD - AVOCADO SALAD

1 large avocado
¼ lb. cooked, cleaned and
  peeled shrimp, cut in half
¼ lb. cooked lobster meat,
  diced
¼ lb. fresh crabmeat
½ c. celery, diced
1 t. salt
¼ t. freshly ground pepper
Juice of 5 limes
1 t. prepared mustard
4 T. mayonnaise
1 head Boston lettuce
Yolks from 2 hard-cooked
  eggs
1 ripe tomato
1 bunch parsley
1 ripe olive

Serves 3

In a bowl combine seafood, celery, seasonings, juice of 2 limes, and mayonnaise; let stand. Peel avocado and cut into 3 equal slices. Remove pit and place slices in a bowl. Squeeze juice of 3 limes over avocado and let stand a few minutes. Place lettuce leaves on plates; arrange avocado slices on lettuce; arrange seafood over the avocado. Sprinkle sieved egg yolks over seafood. Place slices of ripe olive on top; garnish plates with quartered tomato and parsley. Serve cold.

# SEAFOOD - CUCUMBER SALAD

1-6 oz. pkg. frozen crabmeat
  or small frozen shrimp
2 large cucumbers
2 t. salt
¼ c. white vinegar
3 T. sugar
2 T. lemon juice
½ t. ground ginger
½ t. monosodium glutamate
1 t. toasted sesame seeds

Serves 4

Thaw crabmeat in refrigerator overnight; drain and set aside. Score cucumbers and cut in half lengthwise; remove seeds and pulp, cut in thin slices. Place in bowl and sprinkle with 1½ teaspoons salt; mix well and let stand 20 minutes, tossing occasionally. Combine vinegar, sugar, lemon juice, ½ teaspoon salt, ginger and monosodium glutamate; mix well. Drain, rinse cucumbers and pat dry; add seafood and toss. Arrange on bed of salad greens and pour dressing over it. Sprinkle with toasted sesame seeds.

# FROSTED SEVEN-UP SALAD

2-3 oz. pkgs. lemon gelatin
2 c. boiling water
2 c. Seven-Up
20 oz. can crushed
  pineapple, drained (reserve
  juice)
1 c. small marshmallows
2 bananas, sliced
½ c. sugar
2 T. flour
1 c. pineapple juice
1 egg, beaten
1 c. cream, whipped

Serves 15

Dissolve gelatin in boiling water; add Seven-Up and pour into 13 x 9 inch pan. Let partially set. Mix pineapple, marshmallows and bananas; add to gelatin mixture. Chill until set. Cook until thick sugar, flour, pineapple juice and egg; cool. Fold in whipped cream. Spread over set gelatin. Cut into squares and serve on lettuce.

*For a dinner salad, sprinkle with grated cheese and top with maraschino cherries. For a dessert salad, omit cheese.*

## CREOLE SHRIMP SALAD

2 lbs. large shrimp
⅔ c. finely chopped celery
¼ c. thinly sliced green
  onions
2 T. finely chopped chives
2 c. salad oil
½ c. chili sauce
3 T. lemon juice
2 T. horseradish
1 T. prepared mustard
½ t. paprika
½ t. salt
1 or 2 dashes hot sauce

Serves 8

Cook shrimp; peel, devein and chill in large bowl. Add celery, onion and chives. Combine remaining ingredients; pour over shrimp; mix gently. Cover; refrigerate 12 hours, stirring 2 or 3 times. Serve in lettuce cups.

## SHRIMP - CRAB - TUNA SALAD

2 c. seafood of your choice
1 cucumber, chopped fine
1 c. celery hearts, chopped
  fine
*4 sweet pickles, chopped
  or 4 T. pickle relish
4 hard-boiled eggs, grated
¼ t. salt
⅛ t. paprika
⅛ t. pepper
Mayonnaise, enough to
  moisten

Serves 6 to 8

Combine ingredients and chill. Add sufficient mayonnaise to moisten. Serve on crisp lettuce.

* Omit pickles with shrimp or crab.

## SHRIMP MACARONI SALAD

¾ lb. shrimp
2 c. cooked macaroni
1 c. cauliflower, chopped
1 c. celery, diced
¼ c. parsley, chopped
¼ c. sweet pickle, chopped
½ c. mayonnaise or salad
  dressing
3 T. garlic French dressing
1 T. lemon juice
1 t. grated onion, or onion
  juice
1 t. celery seed
1 t. salt
¼ t. pepper

**Serves 6**

Cook, peel and devein shrimp; combine with macaroni, cauliflower, celery, parsley and pickle. Mix mayonnaise, French dressing, lemon juice, onion, celery seed, salt and pepper. Add to macaroni mixture; toss and refrigerate. Serve on lettuce.

## SHRIMP - RICE MOLDED SALAD

¾ lb. shrimp
4 c. cold, cooked rice
½ c. chopped celery
½ c. peeled, chopped
  tomato
2 T. chopped green pepper
2 T. chopped pimiento
3 T. salad oil
2 T. tarragon vinegar
1¼ t. salt
½ t. dry mustard
¼ t. sugar

**Serves 6**

Cook, peel and devein shrimp; chill. Combine and toss rice, celery, tomato, green pepper and pimiento. Blend oil, vinegar, salt, mustard and sugar; add to rice mixture and mix well. Pack into 5 cup ring mold; chill. Unmold on lettuce. Fill center with shrimp and serve with Remoulade Sauce (see index).

## SPINACH SALAD

1-3 oz. pkg. lemon jello
1½ T. vinegar
½ c. mayonnaise
¼ t. salt
¼ c. chopped celery
1 T. onion, minced
1 c. frozen chopped spinach
¾ c. cottage cheese

Serves 6

Dissolve jello in ¾ cup boiling water; add one cup cold water. Stir in vinegar, mayonnaise and salt. Put in freezer tray and chill until firm one inch around sides of tray. Turn into bowl and beat until fluffy. Add celery, onion, spinach (thawed and drained), and cottage cheese. Place in 1 quart mold and chill in refrigerator until firm. Best done a day ahead.

## "WEEPING" SALAD

1 head lettuce
Mayonnaise
1 sweet Bermuda onion
Sugar
1 carton frozen peas,
  cooked
Swiss cheese
Crumbled bacon

Serves 6 to 8

In large salad bowl, place layer of lettuce broken into small chunks; spread several spoonsful of mayonnaise over it. Add layer of paper thin slices of onion; sprinkle lightly with sugar. Add layer of peas; then layer of Swiss cheese cut into strips. Repeat layers until bowl is full. Use no salt or pepper. Do not toss. Place in refrigerator two hours. Sugar causes onion to "weep" and this, with mayonnaise, makes the dressing. When ready to serve, cover salad with crumbled bacon.

# DRESSINGS

## AVOCADO DRESSING

1 medium avocado, peeled
  and mashed
¾ c. salad oil
½ c. sour cream
2 T. cider vinegar
1½ t. lemon juice
1 t. grated onion
¼ t. salt
⅛ t. pepper

**Yields 2 cups**

Place ingredients in a blender and puree 30 seconds. Stir before serving. Keep refrigerated.

## BLENDER BLUE CHEESE DRESSING

5 oz. jar blue cheese spread
1 clove garlic, crushed
½ pt. mayonnaise
½ pt. sour cream
1 T. lemon juice

**Yields 3 cups**

Put mayonnaise in the blender and add the lemon juice, sour cream, cheese and garlic (in this order) at low speed for about 2 minutes. Pour in a jar; cover and refrigerate until ready to use. May be used also as a dip.

## BLUE CHEESE - APPLE DRESSING

¼ c. wine vinegar
¼ t. salt
⅛ t. pepper
¾ c. plus 2 T. vegetable oil
½ c. sour cream
½ c. applesauce
¼ c. crumbled blue cheese

**Yields 2 cups**

Blend vinegar, salt and pepper; slowly add oil while blender runs at low speed. Add sour cream, applesauce and blue cheese; blend until smooth.

## CELERY SEED DRESSING

1 c. salad oil
½ c. sugar
1 t. dry mustard, salt,
  celery seed
1 T. onion juice (more if
  desired)
⅓ c. vinegar

**Yields 2 cups**

Mix sugar, dry mustard, salt and celery seed in mixer bowl or blender. Moisten the dry ingredients with a small amount of vinegar. Gradually add oil while beating, and then the onion juice and the rest of the vinegar. Continue beating until the sugar is dissolved and all ingredients well homogenized.

## CHAR-TETTE'S FRENCH DRESSING

½ bottle catsup
½ c. cider vinegar
Juice of 1 lemon
1 t. paprika
2 t. salt
¾ c. (scant) sugar
1 c. vegetable oil
Garlic salt or garlic
  (optional)

**Yields 2½ cups**

Combine catsup, vinegar, lemon juice, paprika, salt and sugar. Put in blender; mix until sugar dissolves. Gradually add oil; blend well. Refrigerate.

## FRENCH DRESSING

1 c. salad oil
¾ c. catsup
½ c. sugar
¼ c. vinegar
Juice of 1 lemon
1 t. salt
1 t. paprika
1 clove garlic

**Yields 2½ cups**

Shake well, or put in blender for 30 seconds. Keep in refrigerator in covered jar.

# FRENCH VINAIGRETTE

¾ c. plus 2 T. vegetable oil
¼ c. red wine vinegar
3 T. chopped hard-cooked
  eggs
3 T. chopped green olives
2½ t. chopped shallots
¼ t. garlic powder
¼ t. salt
⅛ t. pepper

**Yields 1½ cups**

Combine all ingredients. Shake well before serving. Keep refrigerated.

# GINGER FRUIT SALAD DRESSING

2 T. crystallized ginger,
  diced
1 T. sugar
½ t. salt
3 T. red wine vinegar
1 clove garlic, crushed
⅓ c. salad oil
¼ c. crushed pineapple,
  drained

**Yields ⅔ cup**

Pour ingredients in blender container; blend at high speed. Keep in refrigerator in covered jar. Good on fruit salads.

# GREEN GODDESS SALAD DRESSING

2 anchovies, minced
1 T. tarragon vinegar
1½ t. lemon juice
1 c. parsley, minced
2 T. chives, chopped
¾ c. mayonnaise
3 T. milk

**Yields 2 cups**

Combine all ingredients; pour into jar, cover. Refrigerate until ready to use. Good on salad greens.

## GREEN HERB DRESSING

¾ c. plus 2 T. vegetable oil
¼ c. red wine vinegar
3½ t. finely chopped chives
2 t. finely chopped parsley
2 t. dried thyme, crushed
¼ t. salt
⅛ t. pepper

Yields 1¼ cups

Combine all ingredients. Shake well before serving. Refrigerate.

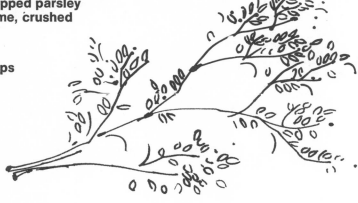

## HONEY CREAM DRESSING

2 T. honey
1 c. heavy cream, whipped
1 t. prepared mustard

Yields 2 cups

Mix mustard and honey together; stir in whipped cream.

## ITALIAN DRESSING

¾ c. plus 2 T. vegetable oil
¼ c. red wine vinegar
2 t. dried crushed oregano
1½ t. dried crushed basil
1½ t. grated onion
¼ t. garlic powder
¼ t. salt
⅛ t. pepper

Yields 1¼ cups

Combine all ingredients. Shake well before serving. Keep refrigerated.

# PRINCESS DRESSING

1 qt. mayonnaise
1 c. sugar
¾ c. Maraschino cherries,
  chopped
½ c. nuts, chopped
½ c. cherry juice
½ c. chopped pineapple
¾ c. pineapple juice
½ c. whipped cream

**Yields 2 quarts**

Mix all ingredients in blender at low speed. Makes a beautiful pink dressing, excellent on fruit salads. Keep in refrigerator in a covered jar.

# ROQUEFORT DRESSING

¼ c. Roquefort cheese,
  crumbled
¼ c. milk
¾ c. mayonnaise
1 t. Worcestershire sauce
⅛ t. salt
⅛ t. garlic powder
⅛ t. white pepper

**Yields 1¼ cups**

Combine all ingredients; pour into jar; cover; refrigerate. Good on salad greens.

# RUSSIAN DRESSING

1 c. mayonnaise
¼ c. chili sauce
2 T. sweet relish
2 T. chopped ripe olives
1 pimiento, minced
Juice of ½ lemon
Worcestershire sauce, to
  taste
Tabasco sauce, to taste

**Yields 2 cups**

Combine all ingredients in blender and blend for a few minutes. Keep in refrigerator in covered jar until ready to use.

## SOUR CREAM - HORSERADISH DRESSING

¾ c. sour cream
¾ c. vegetable oil
¼ c. crumbled crisp bacon
5 t. prepared horseradish
2 t. chopped dill
¼ t. salt
⅛ t. pepper

**Yields 1¾ cups**

Mix all ingredients. Put in blender for 30 seconds; stir before serving. If dressing becomes too thick, add a little more sour cream or milk.

## SWEET DRESSING

½ c. mayonnaise
1 T. honey
1 T. lemon juice
1 t. grated orange rind

**Yields ½ cup**

Mix all ingredients and serve over fruit salad.

## $1,000 DOLLAR DRESSING

1 c. vegetable oil
¼ c. vinegar
⅓ c. catsup
¼ c. sugar
½ lemon, juiced
1 T. grated onion
1 t. salt
1 t. pepper
1 t. celery seed
1 t. paprika
1 clove garlic, chopped

**Yields 2½ cups**

Combine ingredients. Put in glass jar and shake hard each time before serving.

# THOUSAND ISLAND DRESSING

1 T. chili sauce
1 T. sweet pickle relish
1 hard-cooked egg, chopped
3 T. milk
⅔ c. mayonnaise

Yields 1 cup

Mix all ingredients; pour into jar. Cover and refrigerate until ready to use. Good on salad greens or Chef's salad.

# TOP O' THE MOUNTAIN SALAD DRESSING

4 hard-boiled eggs
2 green peppers
½ bunch parsley
½ c. pimientos
1 small onion
1 pt. mayonnaise
1 bottle chili sauce

Yields 1 quart

Chop the first five ingredients. Blend mayonnaise with chili sauce; add egg mixture. Chill; stir again. Serve.

# WATERCRESS DRESSING

¼ c. water
1 T. lemon juice
¼ c. dry milk powder
¼ t. salt
¼ t. paprika
1 t. minced watercress
Dash Worcestershire sauce

Yields ½ cup

Mix water and lemon juice. Combine dry milk powder and salt. Sprinkle over surface of liquid. Beat with electric mixer until stiff enough to form soft peaks (about 8-10 minutes). Fold in seasonings. Chill before serving.

# BREADS

## BASIC STEPS TO BREAD MAKING

1.  Yeast — To soften yeast — Active dry yeast will soften in warm liquid of 105-115°F. Compressed yeast should be dissolved in liquid no warmer than 95°F.

2.  Flour — Add only enough flour to make a dough that can be handled. As dough is kneaded, a little more flour may be worked in.

3.  Kneading — Lightly flour work surface and your hands. Turn dough onto surface and shape into a ball. Press ball flat with the palms of your hands. Fold it over toward you, then with the heels of your hands, push down and away. Turn it one-quarter of the way around and repeat. Keep folding, pushing and turning until dough looks smooth and no longer feels sticky. This will take anywhere from 4 to 10 min. To test whether the dough has been kneaded enough, make an indentation in it with your fingers; it should spring back. Sometimes blisters will form on the surface of the dough and break, which is another sign that kneading is sufficient.

4.  Rising — Grease inside of bowl lightly. Press the top of dough in the bowl, then turn the dough over. Cover with a clean towel and set the bowl in a warm place (80-85°) free from draft, for the dough to rise until doubled in bulk.

5.  Test for doubled in bulk — Press dough with the tip of your fingers, making a dent about ½-in. deep. If dent disappears, let dough rise a little longer and test again. If the dent remains, the dough has risen enough and is ready to punch down.

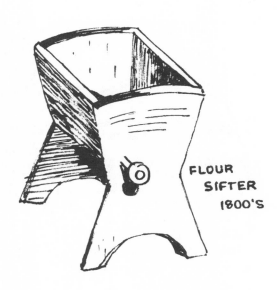

FLOUR
SIFTER
1800'S

6. Punching down — Punch dough down by pushing fist deep in the center. Fold the edges of the dough into the center and turn the ball of dough over completely.

7. Shaping — After punching down, divide dough into the required number of portions by cutting with a large knife. Cover, let dough "rest" for 10 min. An easy method for shaping is as follows: with lightly floured rolling pin or palms of your hands, form a rectangle about 12"x8". Starting with the 8" side, tightly roll dough jelly-roll fashion, pinch seam to seal. With sides of your hands press ends of roll to seal and tuck under; place seam-side down in greased loaf pan. To make round loaves or rolls — pull edges of dough under until ball is rounded and smooth, place on greased baking pan.

8. Testing for lightness — After shaping, allow breads to rise until doubled in bulk. To tell if they have risen enough, press the bread lightly near the bottom or edge with your finger. If the small dent remains, the dough has risen enough and is ready for baking.

9. Baking temperatures — Baking temperatures for yeast breads vary from 350°F. to 450°F. The lower temperatures are used for rich doughs. Rolls are usually baked at 400-425°F. while bread may be started at 425°F. then reduced after 15 min. to 350°F. If baked the entire time at the higher temperature, a browner crust results.

10. When bread has finished baking — To test, rap the top of the loaf with your knuckles. When done, it will sound hollow. There will also be a hollow sound when tapped on the bottom of the pan, and bread will have shrunk slightly from the sides.

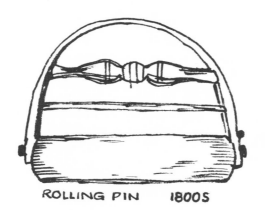

ROLLING PIN    1800S

# QUICK BREADS

## BANANA NUT LOAF

2 large or 3 small bananas
2 c. sifted flour
½ t. baking powder
¾ t. baking soda
½ t. salt
½ c. shortening
1½ c. sugar
2 eggs
1 t. vanilla
¼ c. buttermilk
1 c. finely chopped pecans

Break bananas into chunks; put into small bowl of electric mixer and beat on medium speed until mashed. Sift dry ingredients. Cream shortening, sugar and eggs; add vanilla. Beat on high speed 1½ minutes. Add dry ingredients alternately with bananas. Stir just enough to mix together. Add buttermilk and nuts. Pour into greased and waxed paper lined loaf pan. Bake at 350 degrees 1 hour or until just done.

## BEER BISCUITS

*Easy Gourmet*

2 c. biscuit mix
2 T. sugar
½ c. beer

Serves 12

Combine biscuit mix and sugar. Add beer and mix until just moist. Spoon into lightly greased muffin tins. Bake at 400 degrees for 10 minutes.

## CORN PONES

2 c. corn meal
½ t. salt
½ c. butter
Boiling water

Yields about 12

Put meal and salt into large bowl. Cut butter into small pieces and add to meal mixture. Pour enough boiling water over meal mixture, stirring constantly, to hold mixture together. Not too dry. Drop by large tablespoon onto a greased cookie sheet. Bake at 450 degrees until golden brown.

*These can also be dropped by teaspoon into a skillet and fried. They are very good with vegetable soup.*

# MATTIE'S CORN CAKES

**1 c. corn meal**
**1 T. flour**
**½ t. salt**
**½ t. sugar**
**1 egg**
**Buttermilk**
**Vegetable oil**

**Serves 2**

Mix corn meal, flour, salt, sugar; add egg and enough buttermilk to just hold batter together. Pour two tablespoons batter, one at a time, into hot fat. When bubbles form on top, turn over. Stack with butter between. Yields five.

# BASIC CREPES

**1 c. cold water**
**1 c. cold milk**
**4 large eggs**
**¼ t. salt**
**1½ c. instant-blending flour**
**2 T. butter, melted**

**Yields 24 (6 inch)**

**DESSERT CREPES**
**¾ c. cold milk**
**¾ c. cold water**
**3 egg yolks**
**1 T. sugar**
**3 T. Cointreau, rum or Cognac**
**1 c. plus 2 T. instant-blending flour**
**5 T. butter, melted**

Place liquids in blender, then eggs and salt. Blend 15 seconds. Add flour, then butter. Cover and blend at top speed 1 minute. Place small skillet, 6 inch, over medium heat; brush with oil. Heat oil. Remove from heat and spoon in 2 tablespoons batter, only enough to coat bottom of pan. Swirl pan quickly to cover bottom; pour off any excess batter. Cook until golden brown, lifting edge to be sure. Flip it over and cook reverse side about half a minute. Repeat process. Stack crepes between layers of foil if not using immediately.Refrigerate and warm when needed.

## CRANBERRY FRUIT NUT BREAD

2 c. flour
1 c. sugar
1½ t. baking powder
½ t. baking soda
1 t. salt
¼ c. shortening
¾ c. orange juice
1 T. grated orange rind
1 egg, well beaten
½ c. chopped nuts
1-2 c. fresh cranberries,
    coarsely chopped

Sift dry ingredients. Cut in shortening until mixture resembles cornmeal. Combine orange juice, rind and egg. Pour into dry ingredients, mixing just enough to moisten. Carefully fold in cranberries and nuts. Spoon into greased loaf pan. Spread corners and sides higher than center. Bake at 350 degrees 1 hour. Remove from pan. Cool. Store overnight for easy slicing.

## DATE-NUT BREAD

1 c. boiling water
1 t. baking soda
1 c. dates, chopped or
    1 c. raisins
1½ c. black walnuts,
    chopped
2 T. butter
2 eggs
1 t. vanilla
2 c. all-purpose flour
1 t. baking powder
1 c. sugar
½ t. salt

Serves 24 people

Pour boiling water over soda, dates and nuts. Add butter. Cool. Beat eggs; add vanilla and combine with dates and nuts. Sift flour and baking powder, add sugar and salt. Mix and blend well. Pour into greased and floured pyrex loaf pan. Bake at 350 degrees 45 minutes or until straw comes out clean. Cool on rack. Cut into thin slices to serve.

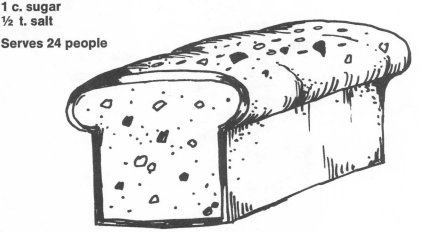

# DEEP FRIED PUFFS

**2 c. flour**
**¼ c. sugar**
**1 T. baking powder**
**1 t. salt**
**1 t. nutmeg**
**¼ c. melted shortening**
**¾ c. milk**
**1 egg**

Sift dry ingredients; add oil, milk and egg. Blend thoroughly. Drop by small teaspoonfuls into deep fat (375 degrees). Fry until golden brown. Drain on paper towel. Roll while warm in powdered sugar or a mixture of sugar and cinnamon. Batter may be kept in refrigerator several days.

*Wonderful for morning coffees. Children love them!*

# FRENCH BREAKFAST MUFFINS

**⅓ c. shortening, partly
  butter**
**½ c. sugar**
**1 egg**
**1½ c. sifted flour**
**1½ t. baking powder**
**½ t. salt**
**¼ t. nutmeg**
**½ c. milk**
**6 T. butter, melted**
**½ c. sugar, mixed with**
**1 t. cinnamon**

**Yields 8**

Cream shortening and sugar; add the egg. Sift together flour, baking powder, salt and nutmeg. Add to sugar egg mixture alternately with milk. Fill greased muffin cups ⅔ full. Bake at 350 degrees 20-25 minutes or until golden brown. Immediately roll in the melted butter, then in sugar cinnamon mixture. Serve hot.

## HUSH PUPPIES

1½ c. cornmeal
½ c. flour
1 onion, finely chopped
1 egg
Dash salt
2 T. baking powder
½ t. soda
1 c. buttermilk
4 T. melted shortening

Blend all ingredients well and drop by teaspoonfuls into hot fat (deep fat is better) and brown. They should be light and crunchy.

*Don't have a fish fry without these tender goodies.*

## IRISH SODA BREAD

2 c. flour
½ c. sugar
1 t. baking powder
½ t. baking soda
⅛ t. salt
1 egg
¼ c. vegetable oil
1 c. buttermilk or sour milk
½ c. raisins
1 t. caraway seeds (optional)

Serves 8 to 10

Combine dry ingredients in large bowl. Beat egg and oil together; add to buttermilk or sour milk. Mix liquids into dry ingredients. Stir in raisins and caraway seeds. Pour batter into greased and floured loaf pans (4 small or 2 medium). Bake in 350 degree oven 45-60 minutes.

# KRINGLE CHRISTIANIA

**Crust:**
**1 c. flour**
**½ c. butter**
**1 T. cold water**

Blend ingredients like pie crust. Divide in 2 equal parts; press in 3 inch wide strips on cookie sheet.

**1 c. water**
**½ c. butter**
**1 c. flour**
**3 eggs**
**½ t. almond extract**

Bring water to boil; add butter. Remove from heat and add flour. Stir until smooth. Add eggs one at a time, beating well after each. Add flavoring. Spread equal amount on each strip, mounding. Bake at 400 degrees 45-50 minutes. Cool slightly. Ice.

**Topping:**
**1 c. powdered sugar**
**1 t. butter**
**1 t. almond extract**
**Cream**

Combine powdered sugar, butter and flavoring. Add enough cream to make of spreading consistency. Drip over pastry.

*Wonderful for a morning coffee. They will think you have been working for hours.*

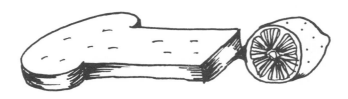

## LEMON BREAD

**½ c. butter**
**½ c. sugar**
**2 eggs**
**½ c. milk**
**1½ c. flour, sifted**
**1 t. baking powder**
**½ t. salt**
**Grated rind of 1 lemon**
**Juice of 1 lemon and**
**½ c. sugar mixed together**
**for topping.**

**Serves 12 to 16**

Cream butter and sugar. Add eggs, one at a time: Beating well after each addition. Add dry ingredients alternately with milk. Add lemon rind. Bake in greased loaf pan 45 minutes at 350 degrees. Cool a half hour. Pour combined lemon juice and sugar over bread. Freeze, if desired in moisture-vapor proof paper. Thaw in freezer wrapping. Serve cold or warmed.

Variation: ½ c. finely chopped nuts may be added to mixture.

# MAGIC MUFFINS

1 c. boiling water
1 c. 100% bran flakes
1½ c. sugar
1 c. margarine
2 eggs
2½ c. flour
2½ t. baking soda
1 t. salt
2 c. buttermilk
2 c. All-Bran or Bran Buds
  cereal

**Yields about 30 muffins**

Pour boiling water over bran; let cool. Cream together sugar, oleo and eggs. Mix together flour, soda and salt. Add alternately with buttermilk to creamed mixture. Stir in cooled bran mixture, then gently add All-Bran or Bran Buds cereal. Fill greased muffin tins or custard cups ½ full. Bake in 375 degree oven 20 minutes. If muffins remain in tins a few moments after leaving the oven, they will be easier to remove. To keep dough in the refrigerator and use as needed, fill wide-mouth glass jars with mixture, cover tightly. Will keep for 6 weeks.

# MEXICAN CORNBREAD

1½ c. cornmeal
3 t. baking powder
½ t. salt
2 eggs
½ c. shortening
1 med. onion, chopped
1 c. sour cream
1 small can cream-style corn
1 c. grated sharp cheese
½ c. chopped jalapeno
  peppers

**Yields 12 muffins**

Sift dry ingredients together. Add remaining ingredients. Mix well. Fill greased muffin pans ½ full and bake 15 minutes in 400 degree oven.

(You may bake in a well-greased 10 inch pan for 30-40 minutes. This will yield 8 servings)

# POPOVERS

3 eggs
1 c. milk
3 T. vegetable oil
1 c. flour, sifted
½ t. salt

**Yields 12**

Beat eggs, milk and oil together well. Mix flour and salt; sift over egg mixture and beat until smooth. Pour into lightly greased custard cups and bake at 400 degrees 50 minutes. If using popover pans, grease lightly get sizzling hot then pour in batter and bake 40 minutes.

# PUMPKIN BREAD

1 c. canned pumpkin
⅓ c. water
⅓ c. vegetable oil
2 eggs
1½ c. sugar
1⅔ c. flour
¼ t. baking powder
¾ t. salt
1 t. baking soda
½ t. cinnamon
¼ t. cloves
½ c. chopped nuts

Combine pumpkin, water and oil. Stir in eggs and sugar. Sift dry ingredients; add to pumpkin mixture. Fold in nuts. Pour into greased loaf pan (9x5). Bake at 350 degrees 70 minutes. Can be frozen.

Variation: Add 1 c. white raisins, pinch ginger, ½ t. nutmeg.

*The spicier the better!*

# SOUR CREAM COFFEE CAKE

½ c. butter
1 c. sugar
2 eggs
2 c. flour
1 t. baking powder
1 t. baking soda
¼ t. salt
1 c. sour cream
1 t. vanilla

**Topping:**
⅓ c. sugar
1 t. cinnamon
½ c. finely chopped nuts
⅓ c. raisins

Cream butter and sugar; add eggs one at a time. Sift dry ingredients. Add sour cream alternately with dry ingredients to sugar mixture. Stir in vanilla. Pour half of batter into a well greased and floured tube pan. Sprinkle in half of topping mixture. Pour in rest of batter then topping last. Bake at 350 degrees 45 minutes.

Mix sugar, cinnamon, nuts and raisins together thoroughly.

# SPOON BREAD

1½ c. water
1 t. salt
1 c. corn meal
3 T. butter
2 eggs, separated
1 c. milk

Serves 4

Boil water and salt; stir in cornmeal and butter. Cook until thickened. Add egg yolks. Stir in milk gradually. Beat whites until stiff. Fold into cornmeal mixture. Pour into greased 2 quart baking dish. Bake at 350 degrees 40-45 minutes. Serve at once with butter or gravy.

# SUWANNEE HOTEL SPOON BREAD

1 c. cornmeal
1 t. salt
1½ c. boiling water
2 T. butter or margarine
1½ c. milk
3 eggs
2 t. baking powder

Serves 4 to 6

Mix cornmeal and salt, stir in scalded water, giving a quick stir. Cover tightly. Melt butter in warmed milk (reserve ⅓ cup milk). Mix cornmeal, milk, butter and eggs. Mix baking powder in ⅓ cup milk and gently stir in mixture. Pour into a well greased 1½ quart baking pan. Bake at 350 degrees 40 minutes. Serve immediately. (Buttermilk may be used, if so substitute ¼ teaspoon soda for baking powder).

# TJOCK PAN CAKA

4 eggs
½ t. salt
1½ c. flour
1½ c. milk
½ c. butter

Serves 6

Beat eggs. Melt butter in 9 x 11 pan. Add salt, flour and milk. Mixture will be very thin. Bake 30 to 40 minutes in 400 degree oven.
Serve warm topped with lingonberries, cranberry sauce, applesauce, or maple syrup. Sausage or bacon will provide a brunch or light supper.

217

# ZUCCHINI BREAD

3 eggs
2 c. sugar (1 white, 1 brown)
1 c. vegetable oil
1 T. vanilla
2 c. zucchini, unpeeled,
  grated, drained
1½ c. flour
½ c. whole wheat flour
¼ t. baking powder
2 t. baking soda
1 t. salt
1 T. cinnamon
½ c. chopped nuts
½ c. chopped raisins
          or
Instead of nuts and raisins
¼ c. wheat germ
¾ c. raisins

Yields 2 loaves

Beat eggs until fluffy; add sugar, oil and vanilla. Blend well. Stir in zucchini. Sift dry ingredients; blend into cream mixture. Fold in nuts and raisins. Bake in 2 greased, floured loaf pans at 350 degrees 1-1½ hours or until done.

# YEAST BREADS

## BUTTERMILK BREAD

2 c. flour
3 T. sugar or honey
2 t. salt
⅓ t. baking soda
1 pkg. active dry yeast
1 c. buttermilk
1 c. water
⅓ c. margarine
1 egg, room temperature
3½ to 4½ cups flour

**Yields 2 loaves**

Mix first 5 ingredients in large bowl. Combine buttermilk, water and margarine; heat until warm. Add slowly to dry mixture. Beat 2 minutes; add egg and 1 more cup of flour. Beat well for 2 minutes more. Add enough flour to make a soft dough. Turn out on floured board and knead about 10 minutes, or until dough is smooth and satiny. Place dough in buttered bowl; turn to coat dough with butter. Cover and let rise in warm place until doubled in bulk, about 1 hour. Punch down dough; remove to floured board and shape into 2 loaves. Place in well greased loaf pans (8x4 or 9x5). Let rise again, covered, until almost doubled in bulk. Bake in 375 degree oven about 35 minutes, until golden brown and has hollow sound when tapped on crust. Cool on racks.

## "SNOW BISCUITS"

1 pkg. yeast
¾ c. lukewarm water
2 t. melted shortening
1½ t. sugar
1 t. salt
2 c. flour, sifted
Melted butter

Mix first 5 ingredients; add 2 cups sifted flour. Turn out onto floured board and cut into squares ¼ inch thick. Dip into melted butter; let rise 1 hour. Bake 425 degrees 12 minutes.

# BUTTERMILK YEAST BISCUITS

5 c. self-rising flour, unsifted
1 t. baking soda
¼ c. sugar
1 c. shortening
2 c. warm buttermilk
3 pkgs. active dry yeast,
dissolved in ½ c. warm
water

**Yields 2 to 3 dozen**

Mix flour, soda and sugar; cut in shortening. Add warm buttermilk and yeast; mix well. Turn out on lightly floured board the amount of dough you need and roll to ¼ inch thickness; cut with biscuit cutter and place on oiled baking sheet, flipping biscuit over so both sides will be coated with oil. Bake in 350 degree oven 12-15 minutes. Dough may be stored in refrigerator three to four weeks and used as needed. If dough has been stored, place biscuits on oiled baking sheet and allow to stand at room temperature for 10 minutes before baking.

# CINNAMON TWISTS
# (MAAS BROTHERS)

½ c. warm water
2 pkgs. yeast
2 eggs
½ c. warm milk
½ c. sugar
½ c. shortening
1 t. salt
1 t. vanilla
4½-5 c. flour
½ c. melted butter
1 c. sugar
2½ T. cinnamon

**Makes about 40 twists**

Dissolve yeast in water. Add eggs, milk, sugar, salt, shortening, vanilla and 2½ cups of the flour. Mix until creamed and smooth. Add enough flour to make dough easy to handle. Knead on floured board for 5 minutes. Put in greased bowl; cover. Let stand at room temperature 1½ hours. Punch down. Let rise 30 minutes. Cut dough into two pieces. Roll out each piece to approximately 8x16 inches. Brush one side with melted butter. Mix sugar and cinnamon together; sprinkle over rectangles. Fold outer edges of dough to center of strip. Repeat brushing with melted butter and sprinkle with cinnamon sugar mixture. Fold dough over, one edge to another. You will now have 4 layers of dough. Roll out strip to a width of 4 inches. Cut strip every ¾ inch. The piece of dough, now ¾x4 inches, is given one twist and placed in a shallow greased pan. Place each twist against each other. Brush tops of twists with melted butter and sprinkle with cinnamon sugar mixture. Bake at 375 degrees for 30 minutes or until done.

*This recipe comes from Maas Brothers and is one of their specialties.*

## COTTAGE CHEESE BREAD

1 pkg. active dry yeast
¼ c. warm water
1 c. creamed cottage
  cheese, heated to
  lukewarm
2 T. sugar
1 T. butter or margarine
1 t. salt
¼ t. baking soda
1 unbeaten egg
2¼ c. presifted flour

**Yields 1 loaf**

Soften yeast in warm water. Mix cottage cheese with yeast; add remaining ingredients, beating until smooth. Cover with cloth and let rise in warm place about one hour, or until double in bulk. Take from bowl; knead in enough flour to keep from sticking. Place in warm, greased medium-sized casserole or 9x5 inch loaf pan; cover with cloth. Place again in warm place until double in bulk. Bake at 350 degrees 40-45 minutes.

Variation:
One tablespoon minced onion and two teaspoons dill or caraway seed may be added with dry ingredients.

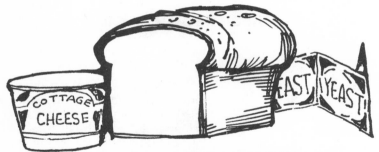

## HONEY WHOLE WHEAT BREAD

4 c. whole wheat flour
½ c. nonfat dry milk
1 T. salt
2 pkgs. dry yeast
3 c. water
½ c. honey
2 T. vegetable oil
4-4½ c. flour

**Yields 2 loaves**

Combine 3 cups whole wheat flour, dry milk, salt and yeast. Heat water, honey, oil until warm. Pour warm liquid over flour mixture. With mixer, blend at low speed 1 minute then medium speed 2 minutes. Stir in remaining whole wheat flour. Add regular flour. Turn out on floured surface and knead until smooth. Place in buttered bowl, turn to coat top. Cover; let rise in warm place until double in bulk (45-55 minutes). Punch down; divide in half. Place in two 9x5 inch loaf pans; let rise until almost double in bulk. Bake at 375 degrees 40-45 minutes.

# HOT CROSS BUNS

**1-13¾ oz. pkg. hot roll mix**
**¼ c. chopped glazed**
**pineapple**
**¼ c. chopped glace cherries**
**¼ c. chopped pecans**
**1¼ c. sifted powdered sugar**
**5 t. milk**
**1-8 oz. jar stemmed**
**Maraschino cherries**

**Yields 18 buns**

Prepare hot roll mix according to directions; add chopped pineapple, cherries and pecans. After rising, shape into 1½ inch balls and place on greased baking sheets. Let rise in a warm place until double in size. Cut deep cross on each with scissors. Bake at 400 degrees 10-15 minutes. Cool. Combine powdered sugar and milk until smooth, and pour over crosses. Top with stemmed cherries.

*This is an easy way to bake these traditional and good-tasting buns.*

# IRISH BROWN BREAD

**5 c. whole-wheat flour**
**2½ c. all-purpose flour**
**⅓ c. sugar**
**2 t. baking soda**
**1 t. salt**
**1 c. butter**
**2 eggs**
**2¼ c. buttermilk**

**2 round loaves**

In a large bowl combine the dry ingredients. By hand work in butter until the mixture resembles fine bread crumbs. In a separate bowl beat eggs until frothy, stir in buttermilk. Make a well in the center of dry ingredients and gradually add egg mixture, mixing by hand until stiff dough is formed. Turn out dough on floured board and knead thoroughly. Divide dough in half and shape into 2 round balls. Flatten tops slightly and with pointed knife cut an X about an inch deep. Put loaves on oiled baking sheet and bake in a 375 degree oven about 45 to 50 minutes or until brown and baked through. Cool before cutting into thin slices.

## ICE BOX ROLLS

**2 c. milk**
**½ c. sugar**
**½ c. vegetable shortening**
**1 pkg. active dry yeast**
**5 cups flour (approximately)**
**1 t. salt**
**1 heaping t. baking powder**
**½ t. soda**

**Yields 2 to 3 dozen rolls**

Scald milk; add sugar and shortening and let cool. Dissolve yeast in some of the warm milk, then add to cooled mixture. Add enough flour to make a thin cake batter. Let stand, covered, in a warm place for 2 hours. Add salt, baking powder and soda; make into dough, using enough flour to knead well. Put in large greased bowl, cover with damp towel, place in ice box; let stand 2 hours before baking. When ready to use, shape the rolls and put in greased pan. Let rise until double in bulk, about 1 to 1½ hours. Bake at 400 degrees 12-15 minutes. Can be kept in refrigerator several weeks.

## ITALIAN BREAD

**4-5½ c. unsifted flour**
**1 T. sugar**
**1 T. salt**
**2 pkgs. dry yeast**
**1 T. soft margarine**
**1¾ c. hot water**
**Cornmeal**
**Peanut oil or vegetable oil**
**1 egg white**
**1 T. cold water**

**Yields 2 loaves**

In mixing bowl combine 1½ cup flour, sugar, salt, yeast and margarine. Gradually add water to dry ingredients and beat 2 minutes medium speed, scraping bowl. Add ¾ c. flour. Beat at high speed 2 minutes. Stir in enough flour to make stiff dough. Turn out on floured surface; knead until smooth (8-10 minutes). Cover with plastic wrap, then towel. Let rise 20 minutes. Divide in half. Roll each half into oblong 15x10 inches. Beginning at wide side, roll up tightly, pinch seams to seal, taper ends. Cover greased baking sheets with cornmeal. Place loaves on sheets and brush with oil. Cover loosely with plastic wrap; refrigerate 2 to 24 hours. To bake, let stand at room temperature 10 minutes. Make 3 or 4 diagonal cuts on top of each loaf with razor blade or sharp knife. Bake at 425 degrees 20 minutes. Remove; brush with egg white and cold water. Return to oven. Bake 5-10 minutes longer or until golden brown.

# MANNA BREAD

2 pkgs. active dry yeast
3-4 c. sifted flour
¼ c. dry onion soup mix
8 slices bacon, fried crisp
12 oz. can beer
¼ c. milk
2 T. cornmeal

**Yields 16 rolls**

In mixing bowl combine yeast, 1¾ cup flour and onion soup mix. Heat together 2 tablespoons bacon drippings, beer, milk and sugar. Add to dry ingredients. Beat at low speed, then high, 3 minutes. Stir in crumbled bacon and enough flour to make stiff dough. Knead until smooth and elastic. Place in greased bowl; turn to grease top. Cover let rise until double. Punch down. Shape into 16 rolls. Place in two round 9 inch pans, brush with butter, sprinkle with cornmeal, cover and let rise 25 minutes. Bake at 375 degrees 20 minutes.

# MOLASSES BRAN YEAST ROLLS

2 pkg. dry yeast
1 c. warm water
¾ c. boiling water
1 c. shortening
⅔ c. molasses
3 c. whole bran cereal
1 t. salt
3 eggs
4½ c. flour, unsifted

**Yields about 3 dozen**

Dissolve yeast in warm water. Pour boiling water over shortening, molasses, bran and salt. Stir until shortening melts. Cool to lukewarm. Add yeast mixture and beat in eggs. Gradually add flour, mixing well until soft dough is formed. Cover. Let rise until double in bulk. Punch down and spoon into greased muffin tins, filling half full. Cover and let rise until almost double (30 minutes). Bake at 375 degrees 20-25 minutes.

# MYSTERY BREAD

2 c. boiling water
1 c. rolled oats (not quick)
½ c. molasses or honey
2½ t. salt
2 T. soft vegetable
  shortening
2 pkg. active dry yeast
⅓ c. lukewarm water
6 c. flour
1 c. dark raisins (optional)

Combine boiling water and oats; let stand ½ hour. Add salt, shortening, molasses and raisins. Dissolve yeast in lukewarm water; add to oat mixture. Stir in 2 cups flour. Beat until batter is smooth. Add 3 more cups flour, a little at a time, first by spoon and then by hand. Mix until dough leaves the sides of the bowl. Turn out onto lightly floured surface, knead in remaining 1 cup flour. Knead until dough is no longer sticky. Put in lightly greased bowl; turn dough to grease top. Cover with dry cloth and let rise in warm place until doubled in bulk (about 2½ hours). Divide into two parts. Roll into a rectangle 18x7. Roll up like a jelly roll, sealing with each turn. Fold ends under and place loaf in a greased loaf pan (9x5). Repeat with other piece. Cover loaves and let rise until double in bulk. Bake at 325 degrees 50 minutes. Cool away from drafts.

# NEW ORLEANS FRENCH DOUGHNUTS

1 c. boiling water
¼ c. shortening
½ c. sugar
1 t. salt
1 c. evaporated milk
1 pkg. active dry yeast
½ c. lukewarm water
2 eggs, beaten
7 c. flour (approximately)

**Coffee au Lait:**
**Very strong coffee with**
  **chicory, mixed with equal**
  **amounts of hot milk.**

**Yields 3 to 4 dozen**

Pour boiling water over shortening, sugar and salt. Add milk and cool to lukewarm. Dissolve yeast in lukewarm water and stir into cooled mix. Add beaten eggs; stir in 4 cups flour. Beat. Add enough flour to make soft dough. Place in greased bowl. Brush with melted butter and cover bowl with damp cloth. Chill until ready to use. Roll out dough ⅛ inch thick. Cut in squares about 2½ inches in diameter. Fry in hot fat (360 degrees) until brown. **Do not let dough rise before frying.** Drain on paper towels. Sprinkle with sifted powdered sugar. Serve hot with Coffee au Lait.

# SALLY LUNN

2 c. milk, scalded
1 yeast cake
½ c. butter
¼ c. sugar
3 eggs, beaten
1 t. salt
4 c. flour

Serves 10

Dissolve yeast in cooled milk. Cream butter and sugar; add eggs. Sift dry ingredients and add alternately with milk to sugar mixture. Beat until smooth. Cover and let rise until double in bulk. Punch down and pour into a well greased 9 inch tube pan. Let rise until double in bulk. Bake at 350 degrees 45 minutes.

# SYRIAN BREAD (PITA)

1 pkg. active dry yeast or
  1 cake
5 lb. flour (about 20 c.)
2 T. salt
1 T. oil
6 c. lukewarm water

Yields 36 (7 inch) rounds

Dissolve yeast in 1 cup warm water. Pour flour, salt and oil in large bowl; add dissolved yeast and rest of water. Mix well and knead until dough is smooth and no longer sticky. Put in greased bowl, turning over to coat top surface with grease. Cover with dry cloth; set in warm place to rise (about 1½-2 hours). To test make indentation in dough with two fingers. If dough Does Not spring back, it is ready. Make balls the size of oranges and roll between hands. Cover balls and allow to rise about 30 minutes. Flatten dough; spread with palm of hand to size of pancake. Set aside; keep covered with dry cloth. Take one at a time, spread each piece until you can flap it from one hand to another. It will become very thin. Place 3 to 4 pieces of dough on cookie sheet. Bake at 500 degrees, with oven rack one notch above center until dough rises with a balloon like appearance (about 5 minutes). Remove from oven. Can be frozen.

*This bread is so good for so many things. Try your hamburgers inside or split it, butter it, sprinkle with Parmesan cheese and toast it. You'll have to hide it or it will never make it to the freezer.*

# MISCELLANEOUS BREADS

## BAKED TOAST

1 loaf day old bread
¼ c. lemon juice
½ t. oregano, rosemary, thyme
1 lb. butter or margarine

Trim crusts from bread; slice in half diagonally. Combine lemon juice and spices. Let stand 15 minutes. Melt butter. Blend lemon mixture and butter. Spread both sides of each piece bread. Place on cookie sheet; bake at 325 degrees until golden brown. Not necessary to turn bread. Store tightly covered in refrigerator. Keeps one to two months. Can be reheated, or eaten cold.

## HERBED BREAD

1 large loaf French bread
1 c. butter or margarine, melted
2 T. chives
2 T. parsley flakes
1 t. sweet basil
1 t. marjoram
Lemon juice
        or
1 t. tarragon
1 t. thyme
1 t. sage or rosemary
1 t. dry mustard

Combine herbs of your choice. Add a little lemon juice; refrigerate a few minutes. Slice bread and spread with melted butter. Sprinkle each slice with herbs. Re-shape into a loaf; wrap in foil and heat at 350 degrees 10 to 12 minutes.

## ONION-SOUR CREAM BREAD

**1 loaf French or Vienna
  bread
1 can French fried onions
½ c. butter or margarine,
  melted
1 c. sour cream**

**Serves 6 to 8**

Slice bread 1½ to 2 inches thick. Place French fried onions in bowl; crush a little. Mix butter and sour cream. Dip slices into butter-sour cream then into the crushed onions. Place on shallow baking pan, single layer. Bake at 350 degrees 20-25 minutes or until crusty brown.

## PAIN PERDU (LOST BREAD)

**4 slices bread, sliced
  1 inch thick
3 eggs
¼ c. sugar
3-4 T. Curacao or other
  orange liqueur
¼ t. vanilla
2 T. butter
2 T. oil
Powdered sugar**

**Serves 4**

Beat eggs and sugar until well combined. Add Curacao and vanilla. Mix well. Add bread slices turning them in egg mixture to moisten both sides. Let bread soak for 30 minutes. In a heavy iron skillet, heat butter and oil until hot, but not smoking. Fry bread about 2 minutes on each side, or until golden brown. Drain on paper towels; sprinkle with powdered sugar. Serve immediately.

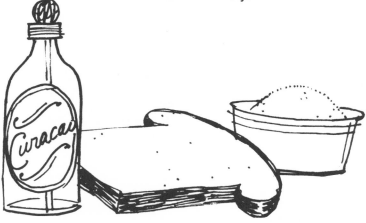

## SUPER CRUSTY FRENCH BREAD

1 loaf French Bread
1 c. butter, softened
1 pkg. onion flavored Four
  Seasons salad mix

Slice bread into rounds 1 inch thick. Combine softened butter with pkg. of salad mix. Arrange bread slices on cookie sheet and spread each slice GENEROUSLY with seasoned butter. Bake about 30 minutes in 200 degrees. Turn so unbuttered side is up and spread GENEROUSLY with remaining seasoned butter. Return to oven and bake for 30 minutes more. Use enough butter so entire slice is saturated. The slow baking makes it deliciously crisp all the way through.

## DILL BREAD

1 pkg. dry yeast
¼ c. warm water
1 c. creamed cottage
  cheese, heated to
  lukewarm
2 T. sugar
3 T. minced onion
1 T. butter
2 t. dill
1 t. salt
¼ t. baking soda
1 egg, beaten
2¼-2½ c. flour

Yields 1 loaf

Soften yeast in water; combine in mixing bowl with all other ingredients except flour. Add flour gradually, stirring after each addition, until the dough has a smooth elastic texture and can be handled without sticking. Knead well and let rise in covered bowl in a warm place until doubled in size. Punch down; remove from bowl and place in well-greased loaf pan. Let rise again until just above the edge of the pan. Bake at 350 degrees 35-45 minutes, or until brown. Remove from pan, place on rack and let cool.

# PRESERVES AND RELISHES

## CALAMONDIN MARMALADE

1 qt. calamondins
Water
Sugar
½ lemon, juiced

Yields 6 half pints

Cut calamondins in half; seed. Cover completely with water. Cook until fruit is soft. Cover and let stand overnight. For each cup of fruit mixture add corresponding cup of sugar. Mix. Add lemon juice and bring to boil. Boil 15 minutes, stirring constantly (no longer than 20 minutes). Remove from fire; pour into sterilized jars.

*Wonderful way to use this hardy and prolific fruit.*

## CANDIED DILLS

1 qt. dill pickles (not kosher)
2 T. mixed pickling spices
½ c. tarragon vinegar
  (optional)
2¾ c. sugar

Yields 1 quart

Drain pickles; cut lengthwise into ¼ inch strips or use a crinkle cutter and cut into ¼ inch rounds. Combine spices and sugar. Place layer of pickles in a jar, (or earthenware bowl) then a layer of spice-sugar mixture. Repeat layers. Cover or seal and let stand 5 days at room temperature. Turn jar upside down (or stir) twice a day.

*These pickles are very crisp, clear and spicy. After they are gone, use the juice in potato salad or deviled eggs or mix some with brown sugar for a good ham topping.*

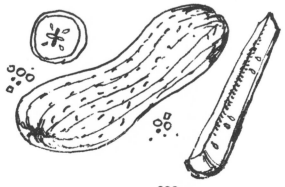

## HOT PEPPER JELLY

* 1½ c. bell pepper,
  chopped
¼ to ½ c. green hot
  peppers, chopped
1½ c. cider vinegar
1 bottle Certo
5½ c. sugar

**Yields 7 half pints**

Put peppers into blender with vinegar; blend thoroughly; combine with sugar in large sauce pan. Bring to boil; boil two minutes. Add Certo; skim. Pour into sterilized half pint jars.

* To make red hot pepper jelly use red bell peppers and red hot peppers.

*Excellent served with pork or lamb. Makes an unusual appetizer when served with cheese and crackers.*

## MANGO CHUTNEY

6 c. mangos
¾ c. vinegar
⅜ c. lemon juice
1½ c. raisins
1½ c. slivered crystalized
  ginger
⅔ c. chopped onions
1 t. allspice
½ t. cinnamon, cloves,
  nutmeg
1 T. salt
1½ c. firmly packed brown
  sugar
5¼ c. white sugar

**Yields 3 pints**

Peel and dice fruit; pour into large saucepan. Add all other ingredients; bring to full rolling boil, stirring constantly. Skim. Simmer until fruit is soft, not mushy. Pour into sterilized jars; cover with paraffin at once.

# ROSE PETAL JAM

8 c. rose petals
3 c. water
3 c. rose liquid
3 lbs. sugar
¼ c. lemon juice
1 bottle Certo

**Yields 6 cups**

Use unsprayed rose petals. Wash and measure. Add petals and water; bring to boil. Cook 10 minutes. Strain and reserve liquid and petals. Combine rose liquid, sugar, lemon juice and bring to full boil; add rose petals. Cook 10 minutes. Add Certo and bring to full boil. Remove from heat and skim. Pour into sterilized jars; top with melted paraffin immediately.

# STRAWBERRY FIG JAM

7 c. peeled figs
6 c. sugar
4-3 oz. pkgs. strawberry jello
½ c. water
Dash salt

Dissolve jello in water. Combine all ingredients. Cook over low heat 1 hour. Stir frequently. Put in jars.

# STRAWBERRY PORT JAM

1-20 oz. pkg. frozen,
  unsweetened strawberries
  (4½ cups)
1½ c. ruby port
1½ t. grated lemon peel
¼ t. ground nutmeg
1¾ ozs. powdered fruit
  pectin
4 c. sugar

**Yields 3 pints**

Chop berries; reserve juice. Add enough water to berries and juice to make 2½ cups. Combine berries with juice, port, lemon peel and nutmeg. Mix thoroughly. Add pectin; mix well. Cook over high heat, stirring constantly until mixture comes to hard boil. Stir in sugar; bring to full rolling boil. Boil hard 1 minute, stirring constantly. Remove from heat; skim off foam. Stir and skim for 10 minutes to cool slightly and prevent floating fruit. Ladle into hot clean jelly glasses. Cover with hot paraffin.

# GREAT GRANDMOTHER FAY'S CHILI SAUCE

25 large ripe tomatoes
8 large red bell peppers
5 large sweet onions
4 c. sugar
3 c. white vinegar

**Yields 6 pints**

Put first three ingredients through fine blade of food chopper; add the rest. Pour into large pot and cook slowly for four hours. Stir often as mixture tends to settle to the bottom and stick.

*The original recipe, which is well over one hundred years old, calls for five cups of sugar, which makes it a bit sweet. It also says to peel the tomatoes and peppers, which although unnecessary, does make for a finer sauce.*

# SPICED CRANBERRY APRICOT RELISH

1 lb. can whole cranberries
2 c. diced dried apricots
1 c. white raisins
1 T. grated orange rind
¼ t. ground ginger
2½ c. water
1 c. sugar

**Yields 1 quart**

Combine fruit, orange rind, ginger and water. Bring to boil; reduce heat and simmer 10 minutes, stirring constantly. Remove from heat; stir in sugar. Mix until sugar melts. Cool. Store in refrigerator. Will keep 6 weeks.

*This is a sweet tart relish. It is good served over pound cake or ice cream. Very versatile.*

# CRANBERRY CONSERVE

1 box cranberries
1 c. water
2⅔ c. sugar
1 orange, juiced
½ c. nuts, chopped

**Yields 2 pints**

Cook berries in water until skins burst. Add orange juice and sugar, blend well. Boil until mixture thickens, ten minutes or more. Remove from heat; add nuts. Pour into container. Keeps indefinitely in refrigerator.

## SPINACH RELISH

1 pkg. frozen chopped
  spinach
½ c. celery, diced
½ c. red or green bell
  peppers, chopped
2 T. onion, chopped
2½ T. horseradish
1 hard-boiled egg, diced
Salt and lemon to taste
Green Goddess salad
  dressing

Cook spinach according to package directions and drain well. Chop into fine pieces. Add spinach to other ingredients and moisten with salad dressing. Let season in refrigerator several hours.

## GREEN TOMATO RELISH
## (OR COLD MEAT SPREAD)

18 green tomatoes
6 bell peppers
6 red bell peppers, or 8 ozs.
  pimientos
6 large onions
2 T. salt
1 c. flour
4 c. sugar
1 t. tumeric
3 c. vinegar
1 pt. yellow mustard

**Yields 9 pints**

Grind together the tomatoes, peppers and onions. Add salt and let stand overnight. Drain well. Combine flour, sugar, tumeric, vinegar and mustard. Heat until boiling. Add vegetables. Simmer 1 hour or until transparent. Pour into hot sterilized jars. Seal at once.

# SAUCES

## HOT AVOCADO SAUCE

4 T. butter
2 T. boiling water
4 T. catsup
2 t. white vinegar
2 t. Worcestershire
½ t. salt
3-4 drops Tabasco

Combine all ingredients; bring to boil. Boil 5 minutes, stirring constantly. Serve warm over avocado halves.

## BEARNAISE SAUCE

4 egg yolks
1 lemon, juiced
2 c. butter, melted
Salt and pepper
2 T. capers
¼ c. chopped parsley
1 T. tarragon vinegar
2 t. minced onion
2 t. fresh tarragon flakes

Yields 2 cups

In top half of double boiler, beat egg yolks and lemon juice. Cook slowly over low heat, never letting water boil. Slowly add melted butter, stirring constantly with wooden spoon. Add salt, pepper, capers, parsley, vinegar, onion and tarragon flakes. Stir to blend.

## EASY BEARNAISE SAUCE

1 c. blender Hollandaise
  sauce (see index)
Salt and pepper
¼ c. chopped parsley
2 t. minced onion
2 t. tarragon flakes
1 T. tarragon vinegar
2 T. white wine

Yields 1½ cup

Stir to blend.

# BORDELAISE SAUCE

2 carrots, chopped
2 stalks celery, chopped
¼ c. chopped shallots
½ t. thyme
½ t. salt
¼ t. pepper
2 c. red wine
1 c. beef broth
2 T. butter, melted
1 T. flour

**Yields 3 cups**

Combine carrots, celery, shallots, thyme, salt, pepper and red wine in saucepan. Bring to boil. Cook, uncovered, over low heat 10 minutes. Add broth and cook 10 minutes. Strain sauce (optional). Blend butter and flour; add to a little of the sauce in a cup; mix until smooth and stir into sauce. Simmer until well blended and thickened.

*This is excellent served with beef tenderloin.*

# CHEESE SAUCE

1 lb. yellow cheese (rat cheese)
¾ c. milk
2 eggs
1 t. salt
Pepper

**Yield: 2 cups**

Melt cheese in double boiler; add other ingredients and cook until mixture thickens. Stir often. May be used as a sauce for vegetables or served on toast points. May be re-heated; will not separate.

Variation: Use 1 recipe thick white sauce (see index), ½ cup cheddar cheese. Yield: 1 cup

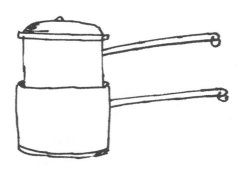

## COME BACK SAUCE

1 c. mayonnaise
¼ c. chili sauce
¼ c. catsup
1 t. mustard
½ c. vegetable oil
1 t. Worcestershire
1 t. pepper
1 T. minced onion
1 T. minced garlic
Juice of 1 lemon

Yields 1½ pints

Blend together well. Refrigerate overnight before using.

*This is very good served with vegetable salad or shrimp.*

## COCKTAIL BARBEQUE SAUCE

2 med. onions, finely
  chopped
2 cloves garlic
1-15 oz. can tomato sauce
1-6 oz. can tomato paste
3 T. Louisiana hot sauce
4 t. Worcestershire
1 t. prepared mustard
1 t. liquid smoke
Juice of 1 lemon
1 lemon quartered
Salt and pepper

Combine all ingredients; simmer 4 hours.
Remove garlic. Refrigerate until ready
to use.

*Wonderful to have handy for chicken or shrimp. Will cover up to 8 pounds of
cocktail weiners. Delicious.*

# CUCUMBER SAUCE

½ c. mayonnaise
½ c. sour cream
1½ t. lemon juice
½ t. dry mustard
1½ t. chopped chives
Dash dill weed
1 unpeeled cucumber,
  grated

Combine all ingredients; chill.

Yields 2 cups

*Serve over tomato aspic or as a dip for raw vegetables or as a regular salad dressing.*

# FISH BARBEQUE SAUCE

½ c. finely chopped onions
¼ c. olive oil
1 c. tomato paste
2 T. Worcestershire
½ c. honey
1 t. basil
1 t. salt
½ c. red wine

Saute onions in olive oil until tender. Add tomato paste, Worcestershire, honey and seasonings. Simmer 5 minutes, stirring constantly; add wine. Strain.

Yields about 2 cups

*The next time you broil or grill fish, try basting with this sauce. It is so different and so good.*

# GALLIANO BARBEQUE SAUCE

2 c. catsup
1 c. chili sauce
½ c. Galliano
2 T. Worcestershire
½ c. dark brown sugar
¼ c. lemon juice

Blend all ingredients and heat until sugar melts.

Yields 1 quart

*Can be used for hot dogs, hamburgers, spare ribs, seafood or chicken.*

## BLENDER HOLLANDAISE

**2 eggs**
**½ c. butter**
**3 T. fresh lemon juice**
**Dash Tabasco**
**1 t. salt**
**½ c. boiling water**

**Yields 2 cups**

Put eggs, butter, salt, Tabasco, lemon juice in blender. Mix well. Slowly add scant half cup boiling water; blend. Pour into top of double boiler. Cook over barely simmering water until just thick. Stir often. Do not let water boil. Can be stored in refrigerator, covered.

## MARCHAND DE VIN SAUCE

**¾ c. butter**
**⅓ c. finely chopped**
  **mushrooms**
**½ c. minced ham**
**⅓ c. finely chopped shallots**
**½ c. finely chopped onion**
**2 T. garlic, minced**
**2 T. flour**
**½ t. salt**
**⅛ t. pepper**
**Dash cayenne**
**¾ c. beef stock**
**½ c. red wine**

**Yields 2 cups**

In a skillet, melt butter; saute mushrooms, ham, shallots, onion and garlic until golden brown. Add flour, salt, pepper and cayenne. Brown well. Blend in stock and wine. Simmer over low heat 35 to 45 minutes.

## MUSHROOM SUPREME SAUCE

1½ lbs. fresh mushrooms
⅓ c. butter
1 t. salt
⅛ t. cayenne
⅛ t. nutmeg
1 T. parsley
1 T. grated onion
1 T. prepared mustard
1½ T. flour
1 c. heavy cream

Serves 8

Halve the mushrooms; place in buttered 1½ quart casserole. Combine softened butter with salt, cayenne, nutmeg, parsley, onion, mustard and flour. Dot butter mixture over mushrooms; pour heavy cream over all. Bake at 375 degrees 60 minutes.

## REMOULADE SAUCE

1 jar Mister Mustard
¼ c. vinegar
2 T. paprika
¼ c. horseradish
Salt and pepper to taste
½ c. olive oil
1 bunch green onions, minced
2 T. parsley

Yields 1 pint

Combine vinegar, mustard, paprika, salt, pepper and horseradish. Add olive oil and mix with rotary beater until well blended. Stir in the onions and parsley. Serve with boiled shrimp.

## SESAME OIL SAUCE

* Sesame seeds

Mix one cup taheeni* with several tablespoons lemon juice and enough water to make a sauce the consistency of mayonnaise. Crush a few cloves of garlic (quantity according to individual taste) with half teaspoon salt. Work the garlic salt thoroughly into the taheeni.

240

## STEAK OR BEEF SAUCE

1-14 oz. bottle catsup
1 bottle chili sauce
1-5 oz. bottle Worcestershire
1 bottle A-1 sauce
1 bottle chutney
⅓ bottle English pickled
   black walnuts
10 drops Tabasco

**Yields 2 quarts**

Chop the chutney and walnuts; combine with other ingredients. Store in refrigerator in two 1 quart bottles.

*This will keep a very long time and is great.*

## WHITE SAUCE

|  | Thin | Medium | Thick |
|---|---|---|---|
| Butter | 1 T. | 2 T. | 3 T. |
| Flour | 1 T. | 2 T. | 3 T. |
| Milk | 1 c. | 1 c. | 1 c. |

Melt butter or margarine on low heat. Stir in flour until smooth and bubbly. Slowly stir in milk. Cook until thick, stirring constantly. Season with salt and pepper to taste.

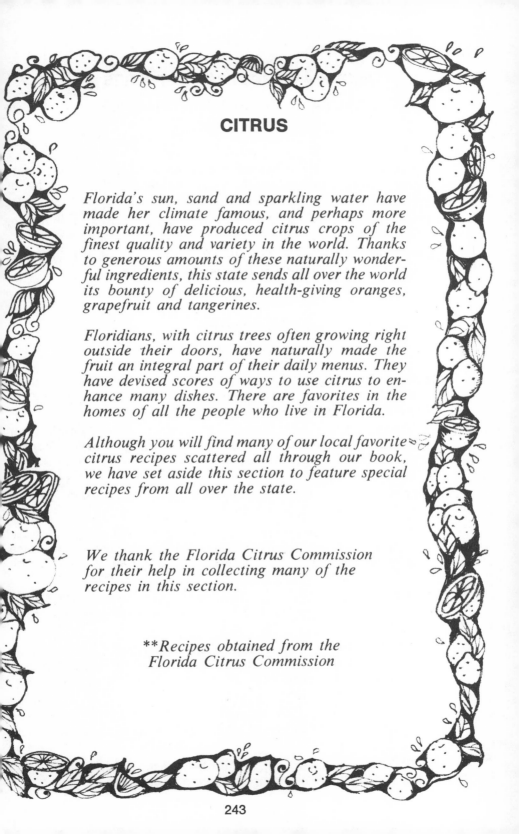

# CITRUS

*Florida's sun, sand and sparkling water have made her climate famous, and perhaps more important, have produced citrus crops of the finest quality and variety in the world. Thanks to generous amounts of these naturally wonderful ingredients, this state sends all over the world its bounty of delicious, health-giving oranges, grapefruit and tangerines.*

*Floridians, with citrus trees often growing right outside their doors, have naturally made the fruit an integral part of their daily menus. They have devised scores of ways to use citrus to enhance many dishes. There are favorites in the homes of all the people who live in Florida.*

*Although you will find many of our local favorite citrus recipes scattered all through our book, we have set aside this section to feature special recipes from all over the state.*

*We thank the Florida Citrus Commission for their help in collecting many of the recipes in this section.*

*\*\*Recipes obtained from the Florida Citrus Commission*

# FLORIDA CITRUS FRUIT VARIETIES
## EARLY AND MID-SEASON ORANGES

**NAVEL** (Nov. to Jan.) Extra large fruit, deep yellow color, usually seedless. May be peeled and sectioned easily. Of all the early varieties the Navel orange is best adapted to "hand eating."

**HAMLIN** (Oct. to Dec.) An excellent juice orange, medium size, thin skin, usually seedless.

**PINEAPPLE ORANGE** (Dec. to Feb.) Widely acclaimed for its juicy sweetness. Deep orange color, medium to large size, some seed.

## LATE ORANGES

**VALENCIA** (March to July) Orange colored flesh, abundant golden juice of fine flavor and aroma. Oval shape, deep orange color, large size, smooth thin skin, usually seedless or not more than 6 small seeds.

**TEMPLE ORANGES** (Jan. to March) Peels and sections easily, rich flavor all its own, generally regarded as the finest eating orange grown in Florida. Small size, oval shape, deep orange color. Sometimes pebbly skin. Few seeds.

**MURCOTT** (Feb. to April) Comparatively new variety. Sweet and juicy. Rich exterior and interior color, superior for hand eating.

**TANGELO** (Dec. to March) A cross or hybrid between the sweet tangerine and the tart grapefruit; it combines the rich golden sweetness and the ease of peeling of the tangerine with the luscious, invigorating flavor of the grapefruit. Easily separated into sections. Looks like high color orange.

**TANGERINE** (Dec. to Feb.) Rich, sweet flavor, spicy aroma. Called the "ZIPPER SKIN FRUIT". Small or medium size, flat ends, deep orange or red color, few seeds.

**DUNCAN GRAPEFRUIT** (Oct. to May) Usually thin skin, large size, pale yellow color, often tinged with green or russet. Cluster of seeds. Many say time required to remove seed is worthwhile for Duncan's superior flavor and greater juice yield.

**SEEDLESS GRAPEFRUIT** (Nov. to June) Easy to cut and serve, seldom more than 8 seeds. Smooth yellow skin, small medium size, usually flat at ends.

**PINK SEEDLESS** (Oct. to May) Many users believe the pink meat enhances its appearance; similar to the March seedless grapefruit.

## FLORIDA DERBY DAIQUIRI **

½ oz. fresh lime juice
1 oz. fresh orange juice
½ oz. simple syrup (or scant
   t. sugar)
1½ ozs. white rum
1 c. crushed ice

Serves 1

Pour into blender and blend 10 seconds.
Serve unstrained in chilled cocktail glass.

## FLORIDA GATORS **

1 jar (1 lb. processed)
   cheese spread
½ c. soft butter
3 T. orange juice
   concentrate, thawed,
   undiluted
1 T. grated orange rind
2 dashes Worcestershire
   sauce
Dash Tabasco
2 c. sifted all-purpose flour
½ t. cayenne
1 t. salt
¾ c. finely chopped pecans

Yields about 7 dozen

Cream together cheese and butter. Add
undiluted concentrate, rind, Worcestershire sauce and Tabasco. Sift together
flour, cayenne and salt; add to cheese
mixture. Mix well. Stir in pecans. Chill
until firm or freeze if desired. To bake,
drop by teaspoonfuls on baking sheet,
press flat with fingers or floured glass
bottom. Bake at 400 degrees 7 to 8
minutes.

*Bake these and take along to the next football game. The orange juice gives them a
zip other cheese snacks don't have.*

## ORANGE PECANS

1 c. sugar
Juice of 2 oranges
Grated rind of 1 orange
1 lb. shelled pecan halves

Mix sugar, juice and rind in saucepan;
bring to boil. Cook slowly 15 minutes. Remove from heat; stir in pecans. When well
coated, drop from tip of spoon onto
greased cookie sheet or waxed paper.

*EasyGourmet*

## ORANGE MELON BALLS **

¼ c. frozen orange juice concentrate, thawed, undiluted
¼ c. Kirsch
½ c. light corn syrup
4 c. honeydew melon balls
4 c. cantaloupe balls

**Serves 8**

Combine undiluted concentrate, Kirsch and corn syrup. Pour over melon balls. Chill several hours. If desire, garnish with sprigs of mint.

*Serve these at your next special brunch. Easy and good too.*

## SAUTEED CHICKEN LIVERS ON GRAPEFRUIT HALVES **

2 T. flour
¼ t. onion salt
¼ t. salt
⅛ t. pepper
8 large chicken livers
1 T. butter or margarine
4 grapefruit

**Yields 8 servings**

Mix flour, onion salt, salt and pepper; roll chicken livers in mixture. Heat butter; add livers and cook until tender, about 5 minutes, turning occasionally. To serve, place one chicken liver on each prepared grapefruit half.

## ENGLISH MUFFINS L'ORANGE**
## JOCKEY CLUB, MIAMI

6 English muffins, split
6 eggs
½ c. orange juice
½ c. light cream
2 T. butter

Beat eggs, orange juice and cream. Soak muffins. Fry in butter.

Sauce:
¼ c. Curacao
1 c. orange juice
¼ c. sugar
30 orange sections
2 t. cornstarch
Brown sugar
Coconut

Serves 6

Combine Curacao, orange juice and sugar; bring to boil. Pour over individual muffins. Garnish with orange sections; sprinkle with brown sugar. Top with coconut and brown under broiler.

## ASPIC SUZANNE **

3 rounded T. unflavored
   gelatin
⅓ c. lemon juice
2 c. orange juice
4 chicken bouillon cubes
¼ t. Lowry salt

Serves 2 to 4

Dissolve gelatin in lemon juice. Combine other ingredients in sauce pan and heat until bouillon cubes are dissolved. Add two mixtures together. Pour into 3 cup mold; chill. Remove from mold and decorate with dark cherries and slices of preserved kumquats.

## MEDITERRANEAN SALAD **

1 c. olive or salad oil, divided
2 cloves garlic, minced
¼ lb. mushrooms, sliced
1¾ c. Florida grapefruit
juice
½ c. catsup
1 t. sugar
2 t. salt
2 T. prepared mustard
¼ t. Tabasco pepper sauce
1 green pepper, cut in
squares
2 large carrots, pared and
cut in julienne strips
2 large ribs celery, cut in
diagonals
1 c. drained canned chick
peas
1 c. (15 ozs.) artichoke
hearts, drained
1 tomato, cut in 8 wedges
2 cups cauliflowerets
8 small scallions

Yields 6 servings

Heat 3 tablespoons oil in saucepan; add garlic and mushrooms and cook until tender. Add remaining oil, grapefruit juice, catsup, sugar, salt, mustard and Tabasco; heat to boiling. Place remaining ingredients in large bowl; pour grapefruit mixture over vegetables. Cover and marinate in refrigerator 12 hours or more, stirring occasionally. Drain well; arrange on large platter.

## SUNNY SKY SALAD **

½ c. diced chicken
¼ c. chopped pecans
1 c. diced celery
1 c. cut orange sections

Mix together well.

Dressing:
1 c. orange sherbert
½ c. sour cream
¼ c. mayonnaise

Serves 2

Beat until smooth and add to salad. Serve in a grapefruit basket.

## LOW-CALORIE DRESSING **

2 t. cornstarch
1 t. sugar
¾ t. salt
½ t. paprika
½ t. dry mustard
1 c. Florida orange juice
2 T. salad oil
¼ t. Tabasco
¼ c. catsup

Yields 1¼ cups, 25 calories
per tablespoon

Combine dry ingredients in saucepan; stir in orange juice. Place over medium heat and bring to a boil, stirring constantly. Boil 1 minute. Remove from heat; stir in remaining ingredients. Chill. Stir before serving.

*Who among us could not use this tasty salad dressing?*

## SWEET 'N PUNGENT FLORIDA SHRIMP **
## JOCKEY CLUB, MIAMI

2 lbs. Florida shrimp, fresh
   or frozen
6 Florida oranges, sectioned
1 c. vinegar
¼ c. soy sauce
2 c. Pina Colada (¾
   coconut, ¼ pineapple
   juice)
6 T. cornstarch
2 green peppers, cut in strips
2 tomatoes, cut in strips
8 black olives, cut in strips
3 c. cooked wild rice
   combined with
½ c. whole toasted almonds

Serves 8

Cook shrimp. Drain juice from orange into sauce pan. Add brown sugar, vinegar, soy sauce, orange juice and 2 cups Pina Colada. Add to sugar mixture. Cook, stirring constantly, until thickened. Add green peppers, orange sections and cut tomatoes. Cool five minutes. Add Florida shrimp and cook to heat shrimp through. Serve with wild rice almond mixture.

CITRUS

## CUTLETS OF SWEETBREADS "PRINCESS" **
## FROM WALT DISNEY WORLD

1½ lbs. calve's sweetbreads
1 small onion
¼ c. vinegar
1 t. salt
1 bay leaf
2 eggs, slightly beaten
½ c. flour
½ c. butter or margarine
2-10 ozs. pkgs. frozen
  asparagus spears, cooked

Grapefruit Hollandaise:
3 egg yolks
¼ c. Florida grapefruit juice
½ c. butter or margarine
Salt and pepper to taste

Yields 6 to 8 servings

Place sweetbreads in saucepan with enough water to cover. Add onion, vinegar, salt and bay leaf. Bring to a boil, reduce heat, cover and simmer 45 minutes or until tender. Drain sweetbreads; cool. Cut into ½ inch slices to make cutlets. Dust with flour and dip in beaten egg. Melt butter in large skillet; add cutlets and brown on both sides. Serve with asparagus and Grapefruit Hollandaise.

Beat egg yolks and grapefruit juice in top of a double boiler. Add butter cut into pieces, and place over hot water. Stir mixture constantly until butter melts and sauce thickens. Remove from heat.

## ORANGE BALLS

1 pkg. vanilla wafers,
  crushed
¾ c. coconut
¾ c. powdered sugar
½ c. orange juice

Mix crumbs, sugar and coconut. Add juice and mix well. Form into 1 inch balls. Roll in powdered sugar. Put in covered container. Better when a day old.

## BANANA-TANGERINE DESSERT

1 orange
1 lemon
½ c. butter
½ c. sugar
¼ c. tangerine juice
½ c. Curacao
8 firm ripe bananas
1 pt. vanilla ice cream

**Serves 8**

Grate orange and lemon rinds, lightly. Squeeze and strain juices. Melt butter and stir in sugar. Add juices, rind and Curacao. Bring to boil. Peel bananas and split lengthwise. Add to sauce and simmer until soft but NOT mushy. Baste often but do not turn. In individual serving dishes, place bananas, then scoop of ice cream, then warm sauce.

*Florida's answer to Bananas Foster.*

## GRAPEFRUIT ALASKA

*Easy Gourmet*

2 grapefruit
Brown sugar or Kirsch to
  taste
3 egg whites
9 T. sugar
½ t. vanilla
1 pt. orange sherbert
            or
1 pt. vanilla ice cream

**Serves 4**

Halve grapefruit. Remove sections. Cut away all membrane. Place fruit in bowl, sprinkle with brown sugar or Kirsch to taste. Chill rinds and fruit. Beat whites until frothy, add sugar gradually and beat until stiff. Drain grapefruit. Put ¼ cup sherbert in bottom of shell, top with ¼ of fruit sections and top with another ¼ cup sherbert. Spread meringue over top to seal. Place on cookie sheet and broil until meringue is lightly browned. Serve at once.

*What a wonderful way to end a dinner party. It is a beautiful dessert.*

## ORANGE ICE CREAM SAUCE FLAMBE

2 c. orange sections
2 T. butter
2 T. brown sugar
½ t. cinnamon
1½ bananas, peeled and
  sliced
⅓ c. rum
⅓ c. brandy
Vanilla ice cream

Serves 6

Melt butter in saucepan. Stir in brown sugar; add cinnamon, sliced bananas and drained orange sections. Stir in rum and heat thoroughly. Slowly pour brandy over sauce and light to flame. Spoon over ice cream.

## GLAZED ORANGES

8 navel oranges
4 c. water
¼ c. Grand Marnier
2 c. sugar
⅔ c. water

Serves 8

Remove orange part of skin with vegetable peeler. Cut removed skin into narrow 1½ inch strips. Place strips in saucepan; add 4 cups water. Simmer 20 minutes. Drain. Combine 2 cups sugar and ⅔ cups water. Stir until dissolved and bring to a boil. Add orange strips and simmer another 20 minutes. Remove from heat; add ¼ cup Grand Marnier. Cover and let stand 20 minutes.

With a sharp knife, peel off white membrane from oranges, section and place in a dish; pour syrup over orange sections. Refrigerate 6 to 8 hours. Baste occasionally. Serve with baked chicken or other meats.

## CHALET SUZANNE ORANGE SOUFFLE **

1 c. milk
¼ c. sugar
¼ c. cornstarch
2 T. butter
6 egg yolks
8 egg whites
1 c. orange sections which
  have been marinated in
Curacao or Kirsch Liquor
  Liquor
1 t. orange extract

**Serves 8**

Bring milk to a boil with sugar. Add corn-starch which has been mixed with a little water. Cook 2 minutes, remove from fire. Add butter, yolks and 1 teaspoon of orange extract. Add last, the stiffly beaten whites of 8 eggs.
As mixture is poured into mold, lay the well-drained orange sections in mold in an attractive pattern. Bake in 300 degree oven. When about done, sift confectioner's sugar over top and glaze quickly in oven.

Orange Sauce:
3 egg yolks
½ c. sugar
Dash salt
½ pt. heavy cream, whipped
½ t. orange extract

**Serves 8**

Blend together egg yolks, sugar and a pinch of salt; fold in whipped cream with orange extract. Serve over warm souffle.

*One of Florida's most famous restaurants. This dish is one of their specialties.*

## COLD TANGERINE SOUFFLE

2 envelopes unflavored
  gelatin
1⅓ c. sugar, divided
⅛ t. salt
8 eggs, separated
1⅓ c. fresh tangerine juice
1 T. fresh lemon juice
½ t. grated tangerine rind

Combine gelatin, ⅔ cup sugar and salt. Beat egg yolks and tangerine juice; stir into gelatin mixture. Place over low heat, stir until gelatin dissolves and mixture thickens. Remove from heat. Stir in lemon juice and rind. Chill until mixture mounds slightly when dropped from spoon. Prepare souffle dish by making a collar with foil that extends 2 inches above rim of dish. Fasten with tape. Beat whites until soft peaks form. Gradually beat in remaining ⅔ cup sugar; beat until stiff. Fold into tangerine mixture. Pour into prepared dish. Chill.

**Serves 8**

## ORANGE HERB SAUCE **

3 T. butter or margarine
3 green onions, minced
¾ t. dried tarragon
1¼ c. orange juice
3 T. slivered orange peel
⅓ c. currant jelly
¼ t. dry mustard
¼ t. salt
1½ c. orange sections

**Yields 1½ cups**

Saute onions and tarragon in butter until tender. Add orange juice, slivered peel, jelly, dry mustard and salt. Stir and bring to boil. Cover and simmer 15-20 minutes. Add orange sections; heat. Serve over meat.

*This sauce is especially good with ham, chicken or turkey.*

## FESTIVE GRAPEFRUIT HALVES

Drip 1 tablespoon honey over each half; refrigerate overnight. Add maraschino cherry, sprinkle with ginger or cinnamon and broil.

Decorate halves by placing a bacon curl in the center of each. Dip small bunches of grapes in egg white then sugar; chill. Place in the center of grapefruit halves. Place a scoop of lime sherbert in the center of each and garnish with mint.

## GRAPEFRUIT BASKETS

Cut grapefruit in half. Insert two toothpicks ½ inch apart on opposite sides of grapefruit. To make handle, cut through the peel ¼ inch below the top of the half; do not cut between the toothpicks. Cut around each section, loosening fruit from membrane. Cut around entire edge of grapefruit. Lift handles and tie together. Attach flower to handle; add place card if desired.

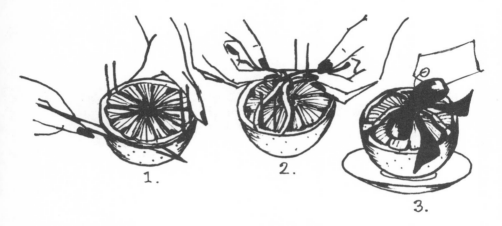

*Not too difficult to make and so pretty for serving fresh fruit, chicken or shrimp salads. Note the recipe for Sunny Sky Salad.*

## SLIVERED PEEL

Wash fruit; using vegetable peeler, remove very thin outer layer in strips. With scissors or knife, cut to desired size. Use to flavor biscuits, breads, puddings or as garnish for rice and other vegetables.

## GRATED RIND

Wash fruit; using medium grater, remove only the outer, orange-colored layer which contains the flavor-giving oils. (One medium orange makes about 2 tablespoons grated rind).

DESSERTS

# DESSERTS

## UPSIDEDOWN APPLES

5 small baking apples
2 T. sugar
¼ t. cinnamon

**Batter:**

1 egg, beaten
2 T. butter, melted
½ c. sugar
½ c. sifted flour
⅛ t. salt

Serves 10 to 12

Peel and core apples; cut into eighths and roll in mixture of sugar and cinnamon. Place apples in 10 to 12 greased custard cups. Spread batter over apples; bake at 375 degrees 45 minutes or until apples are tender.

To make batter: Cream egg, butter and sugar. Sift flour and salt. Combine lightly.

## GRANDMA MAMIE'S HEAVENLY BREAD PUDDING

2 c. bread or rolls, broken
1-13 oz. can evaporated milk
1 can water
4 eggs
½ c. sugar
1 T. vanilla
4 T. butter
Cinnamon

Combine milk, water and bread. Beat eggs; add to mixture with sugar and vanilla. Mix half of butter into pudding; mix well. Pour into 1½ quart casserole. Top with other half butter; sprinkle with cinnamon, generously. Place casserole in pan of boiling water half way up dish. Bake at 350 degrees 1 hour, or until set.

Serves 8

*This recipe is over a hundred years old! It would be a great addition to your Centennial celebration.*

CINNAMON STICKS

# PARTY BREAD PUDDING

3 eggs
1 c. sugar
2 c. milk
8 slices bread, crusts
removed
1 T. vanilla

Cream eggs and sugar. Combine bread and milk; stir in sugar mixture, blending well. Add vanilla. Pour into 1½ quart baking dish. Place dish in pan of water half way up dish. Bake at 350 degrees 45-50 minutes, or until set. Serve warm topped with hard sauce, then white sauce.

Hard Sauce:
1 c. sugar
4 T. butter
¼ c. sweet Sherry

Cream butter and sugar; add Sherry and cook over low heat until sugar melts. Pour over bread pudding while pudding is still hot.

White Sauce:
2 T. flour
Hot water
½ c. sugar

Add enough hot water to flour to make a thin paste. Stir in sugar and cook over low heat until thickened. Pour over hard sauce when serving pudding.

Serves 8

*If you don't think bread pudding is quite special enough for company dinner, try this. You'll receive many compliments for your efforts.*

# CHOCOLATE ANGEL WHIP

1-6 oz. pkg. chocolate bits
2½ T. water
2 eggs, separated
½ c. nuts, chopped
2 T. powdered sugar
½ pt. heavy cream, whipped
1 loaf angel food cake

Serves 10 to 12

Melt chocolate bits in water, add egg yolks, one at a time. Beat egg whites until stiff, add sugar then nuts. Fold egg whites and whipped cream into chocolate mixture. Tear cake into small pieces. Place layer of cake in 8 x 12 inch dish and cover with ½ of the chocolate mixture. Add another layer of cake and top with the remaining chocolate.
Refrigerate overnight. Serve with more whipped cream on top.

# CREAM PUFFS
# AND
# ECLAIRS

**Cream Puffs**

**1 c. water**
**½ c. butter**
**1 c. flour**
**½ t. salt**
**4 eggs**

**Yields 12**

Bring butter and water to boil. Add flour and salt all at once, stirring vigorously until mixture forms a smooth ball. Remove from heat; add eggs one at a time beating well after each addition. Drop by tablespoon 2 inches apart on ungreased cookie sheet. Bake at 400 degrees 35-40 minutes. Cool. Fill with vanilla pudding (see index).

**Yields 12 Eclairs**

Shape dough into fingers 4 x 1 inch using ¼ cup dough for each. Bake at 400 degrees 35-40 minutes. Cool. Fill with vanilla pudding (see index) and frost with chocolate frosting (see index, using half recipe).

**Yields 36 Tiny Puffs**

Drop from scant teaspoon on ungreased cookie sheet. Bake about 20 minutes. Fill with chicken salad, tuna salad, etc. These are always a hit at teas or cocktail parties.

# CREME BRULEE

**2 c. heavy cream**
**3 T. sugar**
**4 egg yolks**
**1 t. vanilla**
**1 t. brandy**
**½ c. sifted dark brown**
**  sugar for top**

**Serves 6**

Scald cream in heavy pan; add sugar and cook until sugar is dissolved; do not boil. Beat egg yolks; add milk mixture to eggs slowly, stirring constantly. Pour into 1½ quart baking dish; place in pan with two inches hot water. Bake at 300 degrees 45-50 minutes or until knife comes out clean. Cover and cool. To serve, sprinkle top with brown sugar; set dish in pan of ice cubes. Broil long enough for sugar to melt, do not burn! Chill and serve.

## GRANDMOTHER'S CUSTARD

**6 T. butter**
**1½ c. sugar**
**1 T. flour**
**4 eggs**
**2 t. vanilla**
**2 c. milk**

**Serves 6 to 8**

Cream butter and sugar; add flour. Stir in eggs one at a time, beating slightly. Gradually add milk then vanilla. Pour into ungreased 2 quart pyrex baking dish. Put in pan with water half way up bowl. Bake at 450 degrees 15 minutes then 300 degrees 40 minutes or until set. **Serve warm.**

*Old fashioned rich, smooth custard. Never fails to please.*

## FLAN

**⅔ c. sugar**
**1 T. water**
**4 eggs**
**1 c. sugar**
**1 t. vanilla**
**2-13 oz. cans evaporated milk**

**Serves 8**

Heat sugar and water in small heavy skillet over low heat, stirring constantly, until sugar melts and is golden brown. Divide syrup among custard cups; rotate cup to coat bottom. Allow syrup to harden in cup 10 minutes. Cream eggs and sugar; add vanilla and milk. Pour over caramel. Put cups in pan of water half way up cups. Bake at 350 degrees 45 minutes or until set.

## GREEN GRAPES AND BRANDY

*EasyGourmet*

1½ lbs. green seedless
  grapes
1 c. brandy
1 c. honey
1½ t. lemon juice
3 T. powdered sugar
1 c. sour cream

**Serves 8**

Wash, stem and dry grapes. Put into deep bowl. Mix brandy, honey, lemon juice and sugar; pour over grapes. Chill for at least 5 hours. Serve in small bowls (juice and all) with dollop of sour cream on top.

*This is very good served after a duck, wild game or very filling meal.*

## KUMQUATS GONE BANANAS

2 c. kumquats
2 med. bananas, peeled
1 c. flaked coconut
9 oz. non-dairy whipped
  topping
½ c. glazed cherries,
  chopped

**Serves 8**

Wash kumquats, cut in half, remove seeds and put fruit through food grinder, using medium blade. Slice bananas into ¼ inch rounds. Fold fruit and coconut into whipped topping. Chill. Serve in dessert dishes garnished with chopped cherries.

*Try using ice cream instead of the whipped topping. You'll go bananas too!*

## LEMON BUTTER CURD

6 tart shells
1½ c. sugar
3 eggs, beaten
2 T. butter
6 T. water
¼ c. lemon juice
¼ t. grated lemon rind

**Serves 6**

Cream sugar and eggs. Add remaining ingredients. Stir together over heat; let come to boiling point. Remove from heat; beat a moment; pour into a bowl and cool. Pour into tart shells.

*Delicious served on a salty cracker. Very different snack.*

## LEMON CUSTARD CUPS

2 T. butter
1 c. sugar
4 T. flour
⅛ t. salt
5 T. lemon juice
Grated rind of 1 lemon
3 eggs, separated
1½ c. milk

**Serves 6**

Cream butter, add sugar, flour, salt, lemon juice and rind. Add beaten egg yolks and milk. Beat egg whites until stiff. Gradually blend the two together. Pour into 6 buttered custard cups. Set cups in pan and fill pan with water halfway up the cups. Bake at 325 degrees 30-40 minutes or until set and lightly brown.

*This is another one of those great upside down desserts.*

## MELTING LEMON MOMENTS

4 c. heavy cream
1 c. fresh lemon juice
1 c. sweetened condensed
  milk
1 c. sugar
Few drops yellow food
  coloring

**Serves 8 to 10**

Combine cream, lemon juice and condensed milk in a large bowl. Chill several hours. Stir in sugar and whip until mixture is very thick and heavy. Pour into chilled crystal serving bowl or spoon into individual serving dishes. Refrigerate covered until firm (2 hours).

## DANISH RUM PUDDING

3 t. unflavored gelatin
¼ c. cold water
4 egg yolks
½ c. sugar
¼ t. salt
2 c. light cream
3 T. rum
½ pt. heavy cream, whipped

Serves 6

Soften gelatin in cold water; set aside. Beat egg yolks; add sugar, salt and cream; beat well. Cook in top of double boiler, stirring constantly, until mixture coats a spoon. Remove from heat; strain through fine strainer. Stir in gelatin, stirring until dissolved. Cool. Stir occasionally. Add rum; stir until blended. Pour into a 3 cup rounded mold and chill overnight. Unmold and serve with whipped cream.

*A toast to Denmark! Serve with crushed sweetened raspberries, strawberries, or sliced fresh peaches.*

## MACAROON PUDDING

1 doz. macaroons
1 envelope unflavored
  gelatin
2 c. milk
4 eggs, separated
1 c. sugar
4 T. powdered sugar
1 t. almond extract
½ pt. heavy cream, whipped
2 T. rum
Glazed cherries, cut in half
Fresh mint

Serves 8

Soak gelatin in half cup milk. Combine yolks, sugar and remaining milk. Cook in top of double boiler until thickened. Stir in gelatin until dissolved. Beat whites until stiff. Add two teaspoons powdered sugar and almond extract. Fold into custard. Crumble six macaroons and fold in. Pour into 1½ quart dish. Crumble remaining macaroons on top. Refrigerate. Whip cream. Add rum and remaining powdered sugar. Pour on top and garnish with cherries and fresh mint.

# BITTER CHOCOLATE MOUSSE

3 eggs, separated
¾ c. superfine sugar
3 T. brandy
1 t. vanilla
5 oz. unsweetened
  chocolate
4 T. soft butter
3 T. strong coffee
1 T. sugar
½ c. heavy cream, whipped

Serves 8

Beat egg yolks, brandy and vanilla. Cook in top of double boiler until thick and pale yellow. Beat with hand beater until slightly foamy, about 5 minutes. Cool. Melt chocolate and butter together. Slowly stir into egg yolks and mix until smooth. Add coffee. Beat egg whites until foamy, add 1 tablespoon sugar and continue to beat until stiff. Gradually fold into chocolate mixture until no streaks remain. Fold in whipped cream; pour into 8 individual serving dishes. Refrigerate.

*If you think you can stand any more calories, serve with brandy flavored whipped cream on top.*

# FRENCH CHOCOLATE MOUSSE

1-6 oz. pkg. chocolate bits
2 T. butter
2 T. sugar
4 eggs, separated
2 t. confectioners sugar
  (heaping)

Serves 8

Melt chocolate bits with butter in top of double boiler. Add sugar and beat until sugar is dissolved. Separate eggs. Beat yolks; add chocolate sugar mixture and beat, beat. Add vanilla. Beat whites; add sugar a little at a time. Fold in whites gently. Pour into small dishes and chill. Plan on 2 tablespoons per serving, it's quite rich.

# MINCEMEAT CREPES

1 recipe dessert crepes (see index)

**Mincemeat filling:**
Juice of 2 oranges
1 c. sugar
½ c. butter
Grated rind of 1 lemon
1 orange skin sliced long and thin
1 t. cornstarch
1 oz. Cointreau
2 oz. brandy
1-18 oz. jar mincemeat

Serves 8

Prepare crepes and keep warm.

Heat orange juice, sugar, butter, lemon rind and orange peel. Moisten cornstarch in water and stir in. Cook until thickened and clear. Add Cointreau and half of brandy. Cook until orange peel is transparent. Spoon mincemeat along diameter of each crepe and roll up. Place side by side in a 13 x 9 inch oven dish. Pour sauce over casserole and re-heat in oven. To serve, pour remaining brandy over crepes and ignite.

# PEANUT BRITTLE PYRAMID

½ c. butter
4 egg yolks, beaten
2 c. powdered sugar
1 pt. heavy cream, whipped
1 t. vanilla
3 T. very strong coffee
1 pound cake, loaf size (cut into 10 slices)
1 c. crushed peanut brittle

Serves 6 to 8

Cream butter and egg yolks. Slowly blend in powdered sugar and then whipped cream. Add vanilla and coffee. On a large serving platter, place 4 slices pound cake; cover with creamed mixture. Add 3 slices pound cake and cover with creamed mixture; add 2 slices and cover, then 1 slice. Cover entire pyramid completely with cream mixture. Sprinkle evenly with crushed peanut brittle. Refrigerate one hour or more before serving. To simplify recipe, layer cake and cream mixture in 8 x 8 inch pan and cut into squares.

## PEACH CUSTARD DESSERT

½ c. butter
1½ c. sifted flour
½ t. salt
1-16 oz. can sliced peaches
½ c. sugar
½ t. cinnamon
1 egg, slightly beaten
1 c. evaporated milk

Serves 8

Mix flour and salt. Cut in butter until mixture resembles coarse meal. Press into bottom of 8 x 8 inch pan. Drain peaches, reserving half cup juice. Arrange peaches on crust. Sprinkle with sugar and cinnamon. Bake at 375 degrees 20 minutes. Mix half cup juice, egg and milk. Pour over peaches and bake 30 minutes longer.

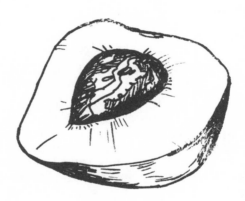

## GOLDEN PEACHES

1 c. dark brown sugar
1 c. Sherry
1-16 oz. can peach halves
2 T. cornstarch
4 oz. sour cream
Dash dehydrated orange
 rind

Serves 6

Drain juice from peaches and slice in rather thick pieces. Mix cornstarch with sugar. Add Sherry and cook mixture until slightly thickened, stirring frequently. Add peaches and serve warm in individual dishes with tablespoon sour cream on top of each serving. Sprinkle with orange rind.

# PEACH MELBA

1 or 2 peach halves per
  person
1 scoop ice cream per
  person

Sauce:
2½ c. canned raspberries
4 t. cornstarch
¼ c. sugar
Dash salt
1 T. butter
2 T. lemon juice
¼ c. Port wine

Yields 2 cups sauce

Force raspberries and juice through fine sieve; removing all seeds. Mix cornstarch, sugar and salt; stir in raspberry puree. Cook, stirring constantly, until mixture boils. Remove; add butter and stir. Add lemon juice and wine. Chill. Serve over peaches and ice cream.

# SOUFFLE FROID AU CHOCOLAT

2 squares (1 oz. each)
  unsweetened chocolate,
  melted
½ c. confectioner's sugar
1 c. milk, heated
1 envelope unflavored
  gelatin, softened in 3 T.
  cold water
¼ t. salt
¾ c. granulated sugar
1 t. vanilla
2 c. heavy cream, whipped

Serves 6 to 8

Combine chocolate and confectioner's sugar; gradually add hot milk, stirring constantly. Put over low heat and stir until mixture reaches boiling point, but do not boil. Remove from heat, stir in softened gelatin, sugar, vanilla and salt. Chill until slightly thickened. Beat with rotary beater until light and fluffy. Fold in whipped cream and pour into 2 quart serving dish. Chill 2-3 hours.

# TRIFLE

**Custard:**
**½ c. sugar**
**3 eggs**
**1 t. cornstarch**
**2 c. milk**
**½ t. almond extract**

**½ pound cake (11 inch)**
**½ c. raspberry or strawberry**
  **jam**
**¼ c. sweet Sherry**
**¼ c. Cognac**
**2 c. custard**
**1 c. heavy cream, whipped**
**¼ c. slivered toasted**
  **almonds**

**Serves 8 to 10**

Cream eggs and sugar, beating well. Add cornstarch and milk. Cook slowly until mixture coats spoon. Take off heat; add almond extract. Cool.

Break pound cake into inch thick slices and coat with jam. Place slices, jam side up, in bottom of large bowl. Combine Sherry and Cognac; pour over cake. Let stand 30 minutes or more. Layer soaked cake and custard in individual serving dishes or a 1½ quart casserole. Chill. Serve topped with whipped cream and toasted almonds.

# BING CHERRY ICE CREAM DESSERT

**1-16 oz. can pitted Bing**
  **cherries**
**½ c. bourbon or brandy**
**1 c. pecans, chopped**
**3 doz. small macaroons,**
  **crumbled**
**½ gal. vanilla ice cream**

**Serves 8 to 12**

Halve cherries; combine with juice and bourbon. Let stand overnight. Soften ice cream; add nuts, macaroons and cherry mixture. Freeze in 13 x 9 inch pyrex container and cut into squares or freeze in parfaits and top with whipped cream and a cherry.

*A very good frozen Cherries Jubilee.*

# HEAVENLY DESSERT

**1 doz. large almond
  macaroons
4 T. rum
1 qt. coffee ice cream
Chocolate syrup
½ pt. heavy cream, whipped**

**Serves 4 to 6**

Place macaroons in flat bowl; pour rum over. Spread slightly softened ice cream over next. Top with chocolate syrup and freeze. Serve topped with whipped cream.

# PARRISH PEARS

**1 c. Ruby Port
3 T. brown sugar
1-16 oz. can pears, drained
Sour cream**

**Serves 3 to 4**

Combine port and sugar; bring to boil. Add pears and simmer 10 minutes. Chill. Serve topped with dollop of sour cream.

# SHERRY BAKED PEARS

**½ c. Sherry
½ c. water
½ c. brown sugar
2 T. fresh lemon juice
3 T. butter
4 fresh pears**

**Serves 4**

Simmer Sherry, water, sugar, lemon juice and butter for 5 minutes. Halve pears, pare and core. Arrange in 13 x 9 inch baking dish. Pour syrup over pears and cover. Bake at 350 degrees for 35-40 minutes, or until pears are just tender. Serve warm, plain or with whipped cream.

## PINEAPPLE ICE BOX DESSERT

1 lb. vanilla wafers, crushed
1 box powdered sugar
1 c. butter
4 eggs
1-16 oz. can crushed
  pineapple, drained
1 c. pecans
1 pt. heavy cream, whipped

Serves 16

Spread thin layer wafer crumbs over bottom of 13 x 9 inch pan. Cream butter and sugar. Add eggs one at a time; beat until creamy. Spread over crumbs. Blend pineapple, pecans and whipped cream; spread over egg butter mixture. Sprinkle remaining crumbs over top. Refrigerate 24 hours before serving. Freezes well.

## RAISIN-WALNUT TORTE

3 eggs, separated
1 c. sugar
1 c. grapenut cereal
1 c. chopped walnuts
¼ t. salt
1 t. vanilla
1 t. baking powder
½ c. raisins

Serves 4 to 6

Add sugar to egg yolks; beat until well blended. Add cereal, nuts, salt, vanilla and baking powder. Beat egg whites until stiff peaks form; fold cereal mixture carefully into egg whites. Pour into 8 x 8 inch pan; bake at 350 degrees 25 minutes.
May be served as is, or any additional topping such as ice cream or whipped cream may be used.

# RAVANI

1 c. butter
1½ c. sugar
6 eggs, separated
2 c. milk
2 c. farina (baby)
2 c. flour
4 t. baking powder
1 c. pecans, chopped
½ t. cinnamon
1/8 t. salt

Syrup:
3 c. water
6 c. sugar
½ lemon, juiced

Yields approximately 60
  small squares

Cream butter and sugar, add egg yolks mixing until smooth. Add milk, farina, flour, baking powder, pecans and cinnamon; mix well. Beat egg whites with salt until stiff. Fold into mixture and turn into well buttered 12 x 18 inch pan. Bake at 350 degrees 45 minutes to 1 hour. While still hot pour on syrup topping. When syrup is absorbed and pastry is cooled, cut into squares.

Syrup: Bring to high boil then lower to soft boil until syrup is slightly thickened. Pour over pastry as described above.

# SNOWBALL CAKE

1 Angel Food cake
1-3 oz. pkg. lemon jello
1 c. boiling water
½ c. undiluted orange juice
  concentrate
1 fresh lemon, juiced
Dash salt
2 pts. heavy cream, whipped
  and sweetened
Coconut

Serves 8 to 10

Prepare the night before. Mix jello and water until jello melts. Add orange juice, lemon juice and salt. Refrigerate until set. Fold half of whipped cream into jello mixture. Line a large rounded mixing bowl with waxed paper, allowing paper to lap over bowl's edge. Put layer of jello mixture on bottom. Pull off hunks of cake (egg size) and add a layer. Alternate layers of cake and jello mixture, ending with jello. Refrigerate overnight. Turn mold upside down on serving dish and peel off waxed paper. Cover with other half whipped cream. Sprinkle all over with coconut and serve.

## GRAPE JUICE SHERBERT

2 c. boiling water
3 c. sugar
3 large lemons, juiced
1½ pts. grape juice
1 qt. milk
1 qt. cream

**Yields 1 gallon**

Dissolve sugar in water. Add juices and pour into gallon freezer. Freeze until mushy. Add milk and cream and continue freezing.

## TOFFEE ICE CREAM DESSERT

1 recipe meringue shell
 (see index)
½ pt. heavy cream,
 whipped
Brandy
8 Heath bars, crushed
Coffee ice cream (little over
 a quart)

**Serves 8**

Use basic meringue shell recipe; make 8 individual meringue shells. Mix whipped cream, brandy to taste and crushed Heath bars. Ice meringues with this mixture; top with scoop of ice cream. Put remaining whipped cream mixture over ice cream and serve.

*Drizzle hot fudge sauce over each serving! Unbelievably good!*

## KIDDIE DELIGHT

Bananas, peeled
Canned chocolate fudge
 sauce
Nuts, finely chopped
Popsickle sticks

Insert popsickle stick in one end of banana. Dip in fudge sauce, then in nuts. Wrap in waxed paper and freeze.

# CAKES

## APPLE CAKE

1 c. sugar
¼ c. melted butter or
  margarine
1 egg
1 c. flour
1 t. baking soda
½ t. cinnamon
¼ t. salt
2 c. tart apples, peeled and
  thinly sliced

Cream sugar and shortening; add eggs, blending well. Sift dry ingredients and blend in egg mixture. Stir in apples. Batter should be very thick. Bake in ungreased 8 x 8 inch pan at 350 degrees 40 minutes. Serve warm, topped with vanilla ice cream or whipped cream.

## THELMA'S APPLE CAKE

3 eggs
1 c. oil
1 c. brown sugar
¾ c. sugar
2 c. flour
1 t. each salt, baking soda,
  cinnamon
4 c. diced apples
½ c. chopped walnuts or
  pecans

Beat eggs; add sugar gradually, mixing well. Add oil and flour alternately. Add sifted dry ingredients. Stir in apples and nuts. Pour into 13 x 9 inch greased pan, bake at 350 degrees 45-50 minutes. Serve topped with ice cream or cool whip.

## APRICOT BRANDY CAKE

3 c. sugar
1 c. butter or margarine
6 eggs
3 c. flour
¼ t. baking soda
½ t. salt
1 c. sour cream
½ t. rum extract
½ t. lemon extract
¼ t. almond extract
1 t. orange extract
1 t. vanilla
½ c. apricot brandy

Cream butter and sugar; add eggs one at a time, beating well after each addition. Sift dry ingredients. Combine sour cream, flavorings and brandy; add to sugar mixture alternately with flour. Mix until just blended. Pour into a greased and floured tube pan. Bake 1 hour 15 minutes or until done.

## APRICOT NECTAR CAKE

1 pkg. yellow cake mix
5 eggs, separated
¾ c. vegetable oil
¾ c. apricot nectar
3 t. lemon extract

Beat egg yolks; add oil, apricot nectar and cake mix. Mix thoroughly. Add lemon extract. Beat egg whites until stiff; fold into cake mix. Pour into greased and floured 10 inch tube pan. Bake at 325 degrees 45-50 minutes, or until done. Cool slightly. While still warm, pierce with holes and ice.

Icing:
2 c. powdered sugar
2 lemons, juiced or apricot
   nectar

Combine sugar and lemon juice, or enough of the apricot nectar to make icing (about ½ cup).

275

# BANANA NUT CAKE

2 c. flour
½ c. butter
3 ripe bananas
1½ c. sugar
2 eggs
1 t. soda
1 t. baking powder
4 T. buttermilk
1 c. chopped nuts
1 t. vanilla

**Icing:**
½ c. butter
2 bananas
1 box powdered sugar,
  sifted
½ c. chopped nuts
Vanilla

Cream butter and sugar; add bananas and eggs, one at a time. Sift dry ingredients; add alternately with buttermilk. Add nuts and vanilla. Pour into two greased and floured 9 inch baking pans. Bake at 350 degrees 30 minutes.

Cream butter; add bananas, sugar, nuts and vanilla. Ice between layers, top and sides of cake.

# BLACK FOREST CAKE

1 c. butter
2 c. sugar
3 ozs. unsweetened
  chocolate, melted
4 eggs
2 c. sifted flour
¼ t. salt
1½ t. baking soda
⅔ c. buttermilk
1 t. vanilla

Cream butter and sugar; add melted chocolate. Beat in eggs one at a time until mixture is light and fluffy. Sift flour and salt. Mix baking soda with buttermilk; add alternately with flour to creamed mixture. Add vanilla. Pour into 3 greased and floured 9 inch cake pans. Bake at 325 degrees 30-35 minutes. Cool 10 minutes; turn out.

Cherry Filling:
1-17 oz. can pitted dark
  sweet cherries
Liquid from canned cherries
2 T. cornstarch
¼ c. water

Bring cherry juice to boil. Mix cornstarch with water; stir into juice. Cook until clear. Add cherries. Cool.

Chocolate Butter Cream
  Filling:
4 T. butter
2 c. sifted powdered sugar
1 egg white, unbeaten
1 t. vanilla
1½ ozs. semi-sweet
  chocolate, melted

Cream butter; add sugar, egg white and vanilla. Add chocolate; beat well until smooth.

Whipped Cream:
2 c. heavy cream, whipped
½ c. sugar
¼ c. Kirsch

Sprinkle sugar into whipped cream; mix well. Fold in Kirsch.

To assemble: Place one layer of cake on large cake plate. Spread cherry filling over first layer; put on second layer and spread with chocolate butter cream filling. Prick top of third layer with fork; sprinkle with 2 tablespoons Kirsch. Cover top and sides of cake with whipped cream. Decorate top of cake with stemmed maraschino cherries and the sides with semi-sweet chocolate curls or shavings. Refrigerate.

## BOURBON CAKE

½ lb. butter
2 c. sugar
5 eggs
¼ t. salt
1 t. vanilla
2 c. sifted flour

Cream butter and sugar; add eggs one at a time, beating well. Add salt and vanilla. Mix in sifted flour. Pour in greased, floured tube pan. Bake at 325 degrees 1 hour 10 minutes. Remove from oven. Pierce top of cake thoroughly. Glaze with topping while still hot.

Topping:
1 c. sugar
½ c. water
½ c. butter
½ c. bourbon

Mix sugar, water and butter. Heat until sugar dissolves. Add bourbon and pour over hot cake. Cool cake completely before removing from pan.

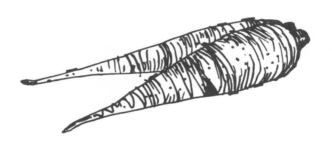

## CARROT CAKE

2 c. self-rising flour
2 c. sugar
1 t. baking soda
1 t. cinnamon
1 t. salt
4 eggs
1½ c. Wesson Oil
3 c. finely shredded carrots

Sift dry ingredients; add oil, eggs and carrots. Mix well. Pour into 3 greased, waxed-paper lined 9 inch cake pans; bake at 350 degrees about 40 minutes or until done. Ice.

Icing:
1-8 oz. pkg. cream cheese
½ c. butter
2 t. vanilla
1 box powdered sugar
1½ c. chopped walnuts

Cream the cheese and butter. Add sugar, beating well. Stir in nuts and vanilla.

## CHOCOLATE FRUIT CAKE

½ c. butter
1 c. sugar
3 eggs
3 squares unsweetened
  chocolate
2 c. flour
2 t. baking powder
1 t. salt
1 t. cinnamon
⅓ c. milk
3 c. mixed chopped
  candied fruits
1 c. raisins
1 c. broken pecans

Cream butter and sugar; add eggs one at a time, beating well. Stir in melted chocolate. Sift dry ingredients; add to cream mixture alternately with milk. Stir in fruits and nuts. Pour into greased, paper lined 10 inch tube pan. Bake at 275 degrees 1 hour 45 minutes or until done. Cool. Remove from pan and wrap in bourbon-soaked cloth for several weeks.

## CHOCOLATE MOCHA POUND CAKE

2 c. cake flour, sifted
⅔ c. shortening, softened
1¼ c. sugar
1 T. instant coffee
1 t. salt
½ t. cream of tartar
¼ t. soda
½ c. water
1 t. vanilla
3 eggs
2 1-oz. squares unsweetened
  chocolate

Sift cake flour into soft shortening; add sugar, instant coffee, salt, cream of tartar and soda. Add water and vanilla; mix until flour is dampened. Beat vigorously for 2 minutes. Add eggs and chocolate; beat 1 minute longer. Pour into 9 x 5 x 3 loaf pan which has been lined with paper. Bake in 325 degree oven 70 minutes. Cool in pan 10 minutes; remove. When thoroughly cool, sift confectioners sugar over top.

## CHOCOLATE POUND CAKE

1 c. butter
½ c. shortening
3 c. sugar
5 eggs
3 c. flour
½ t. baking powder
5 T. cocoa
½ t. salt
1 c. milk
3 t. vanilla

Cream butter and shortening; add sugar; mix well. Add eggs one at a time, beating well. Sift dry ingredients with cocoa three times; add alternately with milk. Add vanilla. Pour into greased, floured tube pan and bake 1 hour (or until just done, not dry) at 325 degrees. Let cool in pan.

## SCOTCH CHOCOLATE CAKE

2 c. sugar
2 c. flour
½ c. butter
½ c. shortening
4 T. cocoa
1 c. water
2 eggs
½ c. buttermilk
1 t. baking soda
1 t. vanilla

Blend sugar and flour. In sauce pan bring to boil the butter, shortening, cocoa and water; add to flour-sugar mixture. Stir in eggs, buttermilk (with soda dissolved in it) and vanilla. Pour into greased 13 x 9 inch pyrex baking dish; bake at 350 degrees 50 minutes. Ice while hot.

Icing:
½ c. butter
4 T. cocoa
6 T. milk
1 t. vanilla
1 box powdered sugar
1 c. chopped pecans

Heat together butter, cocoa, milk and vanilla; pour over powdered sugar; mix well. Stir in chopped nuts. Ice cake right from oven.

## COCONUT CAKE

1 c. butter
2 c. sugar
5 eggs
1 t. baking soda
Dash salt
2¾ c. cake flour
1 t. baking powder
1 c. buttermilk
1 t. vanilla
½ t. coconut extract
3 c. fresh grated coconut

Cream butter and sugar; add eggs, beating after each addition. Sift dry ingredients and add alternately with buttermilk. Stir in vanilla and coconut extract. Pour into 3 greased and floured 9 inch layer pans. Bake at 350 degrees 25-30 minutes. Cool. Make double recipe Seven Minute Frosting (see index). Sprinkle coconut between layers and on top.

*Old South cake that is especially good at Christmas time.*

## COCONUT POUND CAKE

1½ c. butter or margarine
3 c. sugar
6 eggs
½ t. coconut extract
½ t. vanilla extract
3 c. flour
½ t. baking soda
¼ t. salt
8 oz. sour cream (or 1 c. milk)
1 pkg. coconut, thawed

Cream butter and sugar; add eggs one at a time, beating well, after each addition. Add flavorings. Sift dry ingredients and add alternately with milk or sour cream. Fold in coconut. Pour into greased and floured tube pan. Bake at 325 degrees until done. This will take about 1 hour or until pick inserted in middle comes out clean.

# COLA CAKE

2 c. flour
2 c. sugar
1½ c. chopped
  marshmallows
½ c. shortening
½ c. butter
3 T. cocoa
1 c. cola drink
½ c. buttermilk
1 t. baking soda
2 eggs, beaten

Sift dry ingredients; stir in marshmallows. Put aside. In a sauce pan put shortening, butter, cocoa and cola. Boil until shortening and butter melt. Remove from heat and stir into flour mix. Stir in buttermilk (with soda dissolved in it) and eggs. Pour into tube pan and bake at 350 degrees 45 minutes. Cool in pan. Be sure you **do not beat** the cake. Frost when cold.

Frosting:
½ c. butter
3 T. cocoa
6 T. cola drink
1 box powdered sugar, sifted
1 c. chopped pecans

Bring to boil butter, cocoa, and cola. Remove from heat and stir in sugar and pecans.

# DATE AND LEMON CAKE

¾ c. butter
1 c. sugar
2 eggs
1 c. chopped nuts
1 lb. pkg. dates, chopped
1 c. buttermilk
1 t. soda
2½ c. flour
1 t. baking powder

Cream butter and sugar; add eggs. Sift dry ingredients; add to butter mixture alternately with buttermilk. Fold in dates and nuts. Pour into a tube pan. Bake at 350 degrees 1 hour. Ice while cake is still hot.

Icing:
1 c. powdered sugar
Juice of 2 lemons

Sift sugar; add juice and mix well.

282

## HARVEY WALLBANGER CAKE

1 pkg. orange cake mix
1 pkg. instant vanilla
  pudding mix
½ c. vegetable oil
4 eggs
¾ c. orange juice
2 oz. Vodka
2 oz. Galliano

Mix together thoroughly cake mix and pudding mix. Blend in vegetable oil. Add eggs one at a time, beaitng well. Stir in the orange juice, Vodka and Galliano. Mix well and pour into tube pan that has been greased and floured. Bake at 350 degrees 45-50 minutes.

Frosting:
1 c. powdered sugar, sifted
1 T. orange juice
1 T. Vodka
1 T. Galliano

Sift the sugar and add the other ingredients. Beat well and spread over top of cake while the cake is still warm.

## HAWAIIAN FRUIT CAKE

1 c. butter
2 c. brown sugar
4 eggs
3 c. flour
½ t. salt
1 t. each: cinnamon,
  allspice, cloves, nutmeg,
  soda
1½ c. buttermilk
1 c. chopped raisins
1 c. pitted dates
1 c. chopped nuts

Cream butter and sugar. Add eggs, one at a time, beating well. Sift dry ingredients; add alternately with buttermilk. Dust raisins, dates and nuts with flour and fold in. Pour into three greased and floured 9 inch layer pans. Bake at 325 degrees 1 hour or until cake leaves sides of pan. Let cool.

Filling:
2 c. coconut
2½ c. sugar
2 T. flour
Grated rind and juice of
  two lemons
1½ c. hot water

Mix coconut and sugar in saucepan. Add flour, grated lemon rind, juice and hot water. Cook over medium heat until thickened. Cool slightly and put between layers.

# HERSHEY SYRUP CAKE

4 eggs
½ c. butter
1 c. flour
1 c. sugar
1 t. baking powder
1 t. vanilla
1-16 oz. can Hershey
  chocolate syrup

Cream butter and sugar; add eggs one a
a time. Sift dry ingredients and add. Sti
in vanilla and chocolate syrup. Pour batter into two 9 inch well-greased round o
square pans. Bake at 350 degrees 35
minutes. Cool. Frost with your favorite
chocolate frosting.

(This cake does not rise very much.)

# ITALIAN CREAM CAKE

½ c. margarine
½ c. shortening
2 c. sugar
5 eggs, separated
2 c. flour
1 t. baking soda
1 c. buttermilk
1 t. vanilla
1-7 oz. can flaked coconut
¼ c. chopped pecans

Frosting:
8 oz. cream cheese, softened
½ c. margarine
1 box powdered sugar,
  sifted
1 t. vanilla
¼ c. chopped pecans
¼ c. coconut

Cream margarine and shortening; add
sugar; beat until smooth. Add egg yolks;
beat well. Combine flour and soda; add
alternately with buttermilk. Stir in vanilla,
coconut and pecans. Beat egg whites
until stiff; fold in. Pour into three 9 inch
greased and floured pans. Bake at 350
degrees 24 minutes, or until cake tests
done. Frost.

Beat softened cream cheese and margarine until smooth. Add sugar and vanilla; beat until smooth. Sprinkle top with
pecans and coconut.

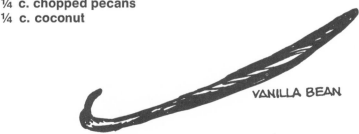
VANILLA BEAN

# LANE CAKE

1 c. butter
2 c. sugar
1 t. vanilla
3¼ c. sifted flour
3½ t. baking powder
¾ t. salt
1 c. milk
8 egg whites

Cream butter and sugar; add vanilla. Sift dry ingredients; add to butter mixture alternately with milk. Beat egg whites until stiff but not dry. Fold whites into batter. Divide batter equally between four greased and floured 9 inch pans. Bake at 375 degrees 15 minutes or until done. Cool.

**Frosting:**
8 egg yolks
1¾ c. sugar
½ t. salt
¾ c. butter
½ c. bourbon
1½ c. each chopped
  pecans, raisins, glazed
  cherries
1½ c. frozen coconut

Put egg yolks in top of double boiler; beat slightly. Add sugar, salt and butter. Cook until sugar is dissolved and mix has thickened. Remove and add the bourbon. Beat 1 minute. Stir in nuts, raisins, coconut and cherries. Spread frosting between and on top and sides. Cover closely and store for several days to ripen. Can be frozen.

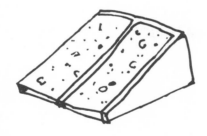

# LEMON CRUNCH CAKE

1 pkg. yellow cake mix
1 pkg. lemon instant pudding
½ c. oil
1 c. water
1 T. grated lemon rind
4 eggs, beaten
½ c. ground coconut
½ c. ground nuts

Put cake mix and pudding mix into a bowl; add oil, water and lemon rind. Mix well. Stir in beaten eggs; blend well. Grease tube pan and sprinkle bottom and sides with the ground coconut and nuts (most will settle to the bottom). Pour batter into pan. Bake at 350 degrees 55-60 minutes. Cool completely. Ice with glaze.

**Glaze:**
⅓ c. lemon juice
2½ c. sifted powdered sugar

Mix together well.

285

## MILKY WAY CAKE

8 Milky Way bars
1 c. butter (2 sticks)
2 c. sugar
4 eggs, separated
2½ c. flour
½ t. baking soda
1¼ c. buttermilk
1 c. chopped pecans

Frosting:
2½ c. sugar
1 c. evaporated milk
6 oz. pkg. chocolate chips
1 c. marshmallow creme
½ c. butter or margarine

Melt candy bars with 1 stick butter over boiling water. Cream sugar and remaining butter. Add candy mixture to this and stir. Add egg yolks one at a time, beating well after each. Dissolve soda in buttermilk, then add flour and buttermilk alternately, ending with flour. Add nuts. Fold in stiffly beaten egg whites. Bake in greased, floured tube pan at 325 degrees 1 hour and 10 minutes. Cool. Frost.

Cook milk, margarine and sugar until soft ball forms in cold water. Add the chocolate bits and marshmallow creme. Stir until smooth and frost cake.

## MISSISSIPPI MUD CAKE

2 c. sugar
½ c. butter
½ c. shortening
4 eggs
1½ c. flour
¼ t. salt
⅓ c. cocoa
2 t. vanilla
1 c. chopped pecans
1–10 oz. bag miniature
  marshmallows

Frosting:
½ c. butter
⅓ c. cocoa
1 box powdered sugar
½ c. evaporated milk
1 c. pecans, chopped
1 t. vanilla

Cream sugar and shortenings; add eggs one at a time, beating well. Sift flour, cocoa and salt. Add to creamed mixture. Stir in vanilla and nuts. Pour into greased, floured 13 x 9 inch baking dish. Bake at 300 degrees 30-40 minutes. Spread marshmallows over top. Set back in oven for 3-4 minutes, or until marshmallows have melted enough to spread. (Spread with greased spatula). Pour frosting over hot cake.

Bring butter to boil; add cocoa and milk. Pour over sifted powdered sugar. Add vanilla and nuts.

## ORANGE CAKE

⅔ c. butter
1½ c. sugar
2 t. grated orange peel
3 eggs
2½ c. sifted cake flour
2½ t. baking powder
1 t. salt
1 c. orange juice

Cream the butter and sugar; add peel. Beat in eggs one at a time, mixing well. Sift dry ingredients and add alternately with orange juice to creamed mixture, beating well. Bake in two 9 inch greased, floured cake pans at 350 degrees 25-30 minutes. Cool and remove from pans. Fill layers with orange filling; frost with seven minute icing. (see index)

**Filling:**
⅔ c. sugar
3 T. flour
1 c. orange juice
2 T. butter
2 egg yolks

To make the filling: Combine the sugar and flour in a sauce pan; add the orange juice and egg yolks. Cook and stir until mixture boils; cook one minute more. Stir in the butter; cool. Spread between the layers.

*This cake is shown on the cover.*

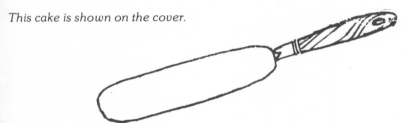

## ORANGE CHIFFON CAKE

1¾ c. cake flour
3 t. baking powder
1 t. salt
1½ c. sugar
½ c. safflower oil
5 egg yolks, unbeaten
¾ c. orange juice
2 t. orange rind
1 c. (7 or 8) egg whites
1 t. cream of tartar

Sift dry ingredients and put into large bowl; add sugar and blend. Make a well in the center, pour in oil, egg yolks, orange juice and rind. Blend well; beat 2 minutes on medium speed. Beat egg whites in large bowl until foamy; add cream of tartar and beat until stiff. Fold in egg yolk mixture gently. Pour into a 10 inch tube pan (ungreased). Bake on lower rack at 325 degrees 55 minutes to 1 hour, then 10 to 15 minutes more at 350 degrees. Invert pan and let cool. Sprinkle with powdered sugar or orange flavored frosting.

287

# ORANGE-CRANBERRY CAKE

2¼ c. flour, sifted
1 c. sugar
¼ t. salt
1 t. baking powder
1 t. soda
1 c. chopped walnuts
1 c. chopped dates
1 c. whole cranberries
2 eggs, beaten
¾ c. vegetable oil
1 c. buttermilk
Grated rind of 2 oranges
1 c. orange juice
1 c. sugar, scant

Sift dry ingredients together. Stir in nuts, dates, cranberries and orange rind. Combine eggs, milk and salad oil. Add fruit mixture to flour; stir until blended. Pour into greased 10 inch tube pan. Bake at 350 degrees 1 hour. Let stand in pan until lukewarm. Place on rack and set over wide dish. Combine orange juice and remaining cup of sugar; pour over cake; repeat several times. Wrap in heavy foil and refrigerate 24 hours before serving. Serve plain or with whipped cream. Keeps well in refrigerator for about 2 weeks, also freezes well.

# ORANGE DATE NUT CAKE

1 c. butter
2 c. sugar
4 eggs
4 c. flour
1 t. baking soda
1⅓ c. buttermilk
1 pkg. dates, chopped
1 c. chopped nuts

Cream butter and sugar well. Add eggs one at a time, beating well. Mix ¼ cup of flour with the chopped dates and nuts. Sift remaining flour with soda. Add milk and flour alternately to butter mixture. Add floured dates and nuts. Put waxed paper in bottom of a large tube pan; grease the sides. Pour in the batter. Bake at 350 degrees one hour. While cake is still hot, pour on the sauce.

Sauce:
1⅓ c. fresh orange juice
2 c. sugar
1 T. grated orange rind

Put all ingredients together in a sauce pan; heat until the sugar dissolves. Pour over hot cake. Let cool in pan.

*To make the cake a Christmas Cake, use one cup orange wine or brandy and orange juice.*

## PINEAPPLE CAKE

1 can (1 lb. 4 oz.) crushed
  pineapple
2 c. buttermilk baking mix
1 c. flour, sifted
1 t. baking soda
1 c. sugar
¾ c. sour cream
½ c. butter
2 t. vanilla
2 eggs
2 T. rum

Glaze:
¾ c. sugar
¼ c. butter
¼ c. pineapple juice
2 T. rum

Drain pineapple, saving syrup. Mix baking mix, flour and soda. Cream sugar, sour cream, butter and vanilla, beating well. Add eggs and blend. Stir in flour mixture; beat well. Mix in pineapple and rum. Pour into 9 inch tube pan. Bake at 350 degrees 45 minutes, or until cake tests done. Pour half of glaze over hot cake; let stand 15 minutes. Turn out onto plate. Spoon over remaining glaze. Cool.

Mix together all ingredients and cook over low heat until sugar dissolves and butter melts. Stir in rum.

## PINEAPPLE POUND CAKE

½ c. shortening
1 c. butter
2¾ c. sugar
6 eggs
3 c. flour
1 t. baking powder
½ t. salt
¼ c. milk
1 t. vanilla
¾ c. undrained crushed
  pineapple

Topping:
1½ c. powdered sugar
1 c. drained crushed
  pineapple
¼ c. butter

Cream shortening, butter and sugar. Add eggs one at a time, beating well. Add sifted dry ingredients alternately with milk. Add vanilla and stir in crushed pineapple; mix well. Pour into well greased and floured 10 inch tube pan. Place in cold oven. Turn oven to 325 degrees; bake 1½ hours or until just done. Let stand. Carefully remove; make holes with toothpick. Pour icing over while still hot.

Cream butter and sugar; stir in drained pineapple.

## POPPY SEED CAKE

1 pkg. yellow cake mix
1-3 oz. pkg. instant lemon
  pudding
4 eggs
1 c. water
½ c. oil
½ c. poppy seeds

**Glaze:**
2 lemons, juiced
2 T. butter
1½ c. powdered sugar

Using an electric mixer, beat all ingredients 2 minutes. Pour into well greased spring form or tube pan. Bake at 350 degrees 50-60 minutes. Cool 7 minutes. Prick cake with fork and pour glaze over cake while still warm.

Heat juice, butter and sugar until sugar melts. Pour over cake.

## PRUNE CAKE

1 c. vegetable oil
1½ c. sugar
1 c. buttermilk
1 c. cooked prunes
3 eggs
2 c. flour
1 c. chopped pecans
1 t. baking soda
1 t. salt
1 t. cinnamon, nutmeg,
  allspice
1 t. vanilla

**Frosting:**
1 c. sugar
½ c. buttermilk
1 T. white corn syrup
½ c. butter
½ t. vanilla
½ t. baking soda

Cream oil and sugar; add eggs and mix well. Sift dry ingredients; add alternately with buttermilk. Add vanilla, chopped prunes and nuts. Pour into greased, floured 13 x 9 inch pan. Bake at 300 degrees 1 hour. Cool.

Blend ingredients. Cook until soft ball stage. Remove from heat and beat 2 minutes. Pour over cake in the pan.

## PUMPKIN CAKE

2 c. sugar
1½ c. vegetable oil
2 c. canned pumpkin
4 eggs
2 c. flour
2 t. baking soda
2 t. cinnamon
1 t. salt
1 c. chopped nuts
½ c. coconut

Blend sugar, oil and pumpkin; stir in eggs, one at a time. Sift dry ingredients; add to creamed mixture. Blend in nuts and coconut. Pour into 3 greased 9 inch cake pans. Bake at 350 degrees 35 minutes. Cool. Frost with Butter Frosting (see index). Sprinkle top of cake with more chopped pecans and coconut if desired.

## EASY PUMPKIN CAKE

1 box (2 layer) spice cake
  mix
½ t. baking soda
1 c. milk
1 c. canned pumpkin
½ c. chopped pecans
½ c. finely chopped dates
1 c. heavy cream, whipped
2 T. honey
1½ t. cinnamon

Blend cake mix and soda. Follow package directions, using milk in the place of water in the first addition, and pumpkin for the second addition of liquid. Fold in the nuts and dates. Pour into two greased and floured 9 inch pans. Bake at 350 degrees 25-30 minutes. Whip cream with honey and cinnamon. Spread between layers and on top of cake.

# RICOTTA CHEESE CAKE

**1-3 lb. can ricotta cheese**
**2¼ c. sugar**
**½ c. flour (potato)**
**8 egg yolks**
**Grated rind of 1 lemon**
**1 t. vanilla**
**½ c. heavy cream, whipped**
**8 egg whites**
**Graham crackers**

Beat ricotta until smooth; gradually add 2 cups sugar and egg yolks, beating well after each addition. Beat in flour, lemon rind and vanilla. Beat whites with ¼ cup sugar until stiff. Fold whipped cream and whites into ricotta mixture. Turn into a 12 inch spring form pan which has been well buttered and sprinkled with graham cracker crumbs. Bake at 425 degrees 10 minutes then at 350 degrees 1 hour. Turn off heat and allow to remain in oven for 1 hour or longer.

*Variations:*

*1. Add raisins, chopped citron or chopped Maraschino Cherries to filling.*

*2. Before pouring in filling, cover bottom of pan with crushed pineapple, apple sauce or sliced apples.*

# RUM NUT CAKE

**½ c. chopped pecans**
**1 pkg. golden cake mix**
**1-3¾ oz. pkg. vanilla instant pudding**
**½ c. light rum**
**½ c. water**
**½ c. oil**
**4 eggs**

**Hot Rum Glaze:**
**1 c. sugar**
**½ c. margarine**
**¼ c. rum**
**¼ c. water**

Mix together cake and pudding mix. Add rum, water, oil and eggs. Mix 2 minutes. Pour batter into greased and floured tube pan with pecans sprinkled on bottom. Bake at 325 degrees 45 minutes. Pour hot rum glaze over cake while hot (will cause cake to settle). Cool.

Put all ingredients in sauce pan and bring to boil. Boil for 2-3 minutes. Pour over hot cake.

*This cake is especially good using bourbon or bandy instead of the rum, either way it is a great cake to have on special occasions.*

## SAUSAGE CAKE

½ lb. mild bulk sausage
1¼ c. sugar
2 eggs
2½ c. flour
¼ t. baking soda
½ t. salt
2 t. baking powder
½ t. nutmeg, allspice
¼ t. cloves
1 c. milk
1 c. shredded apples
½ c. chopped pecans
1 t. cinnamon

Cream sausage and sugar; add eggs and beat five minutes. Sift dry ingredients and add alternately with milk. Fold in apples and pecans. Pour into 10 inch tube pan and bake at 350 degrees 50-55 minutes. Cool. Serve with whipped cream.

## SOUR CREAM POUND CAKE

3 c. sugar
1 c. butter
6 eggs, separated
¼ t. baking soda
1 c. sour cream
3 c. flour
1 t. vanilla

Cream butter and sugar; add egg yolks one at a time, mixing well. Dissolve soda in sour cream. Add flour and sour cream alternately to sugar mixture. Beat whites and fold in. Add vanilla. Pour into greased and floured 10 inch tube pan. Bake at 350 degrees 1 hour and 15 minutes.

## TRUE SPONGE CAKE

1 c. sifted flour
¼ t. salt
Grated rind of ½ lemon
1½ T. lemon juice
5 eggs, separated
1 c. sugar

Sift flour and salt together 4 times. Combine lemon rind and juice with beaten egg yolks and mix until thick. Beat egg whites until stiff but not dry. Fold in sugar in small amounts. Add yolks to whites carefully. Sift about one fourth of flour at time over the surface of the mixture and fold in. Do this until flour has been used up. Bake in greased tube pan at 350 degrees 1 hour. Invert pan and let stand until cool.

293

## GATEAU DES FRAISES AU DOUBLE CREAM
## (STRAWBERRY CREAM CHEESE CAKE)

11 ozs. cream cheese
2 eggs
½ c. sugar
½ t. vanilla
2 c. sour cream
¼ c. sugar
¼ c. toasted whole almonds
6-8 whole strawberries
4 T. currant jelly
2 T. water
1 T. crystallized ginger
(optional)

Blend cream cheese until smooth; add eggs one at a time, beating well. Add ½ cup sugar gradually; blend in vanilla. Pour into a 9 inch spring form pan that has been buttered and lined with graham cracker crumbs. Bake at 350 degrees 25 minutes. Blend the sour cream and ¼ cup sugar; add almonds. Spread over cake and return to oven 10 minutes. Cool, then chill until set. Place strawberries on top of cake. Mix currant jelly, ginger and water. Pour over strawberries to glaze. If ginger is not used, reduce water to one tablespoon.

## STRAWBERRY PECAN CAKE

1 pkg. white cake mix
1-3 oz. pkg. strawberry
 gelatin
1 c. vegetable oil
½ c. milk
4 eggs
1 pkg. (10 oz.) frozen
 strawberries with juice
1 c. coconut
1 c. chopped pecans

Frosting:
½ c. butter
1 box powdered sugar, sifted
1 pkg. (10 oz.) frozen
 strawberries, drained
½ c. coconut
½ c. chopped pecans

Sift together cake mix and gelatin. Add oil and milk. Add eggs, one at a time, beating well. Stir in strawberries, coconut and pecans. Pour mixture into 13 x 9 inch pyrex baking dish. Bake at 350 degrees 40-50 minutes. Pour frosting over cake **while still hot.** Cool. Cut into squares.

Melt butter and mix with sugar. Stir in drained strawberries, coconut and nuts.

# TENNESSEE POTATO CARAMEL CAKE

⅔ c. butter
2 c. sugar
4 eggs, separated
½ c. milk
4 sq. unsweetened
 chocolate
1 c. hot mashed potatoes
2 c. flour
1 t. baking powder
1 t. each cinnamon, cloves
 nutmeg
1 c. chopped pecans

Frosting:
2 c. brown sugar
1 c. cream
½ c. butter
½ t. vanilla

Cream butter and sugar; add beaten egg yolks and milk. Melt chocolate in mashed potatoes. Sift dry ingredients; add to sugar mixture. Add mashed potatoes. Beat egg whites and fold in. Add nuts. Bake in two greased, floured 9 inch layer pans at 350 degrees 25 to 30 minutes. Cool and frost.

Mix sugar and cream. Add butter and cook to soft ball stage. Add vanilla and beat until of spreading consistency.

# TEXAS PECAN CAKE

½ lb. butter
4 c. flour
2 c. sugar
1 t. salt
2 t. baking powder
6 eggs
4 c. pecan halves
1½ lbs. raisins
1 t. nutmeg
½ c. brandy or bourbon

Cream butter and sugar. Add eggs one at a time. Sift dry ingredients. Add bourbon, raisins and nuts to creamed mixture, blending well. Add dry ingredients, one cup at a time, mixing well after each addition. Put mixture in a greased and floured 10 inch tube pan. Bake at 300 degrees 1½ hours or until cake tests done.

# WELSH CHEDDAR CHEESECAKE

Crust:
1-6 oz. box Zwieback
 crackers
3 T. sugar
6 T. butter

Crush the crackers; add to melted butter and sugar. Press into a 9 inch lightly buttered spring form pan. Chill.

Filling:
4-8 oz. pkgs. cream cheese
8 ozs. cheddar cheese,
 shredded
1¾ c. sugar
3 T. flour
5 eggs
3 egg yolks
¼ c. beer

Soften cream cheese; beat together with cheddar cheese until smooth. Add sugar and flour. Add eggs and yolks, one at a time, beating well after each addition. Stir in beer. Pour into pan; bake at 475 degrees 12 minutes, then at 250 degrees 1½ hours. Turn off oven and let cake remain 1 hour.

295

# FROSTINGS

## FROSTINGS FOR ANGEL FOOD CAKES

**Creamy Chocolate:**
1 pt. heavy cream, whipped
3 T. cocoa
3 T. sugar
Dash salt
1 t. vanilla
Toasted almonds

Combine all ingredients (except almonds) and let stand in refrigerator several hours, or overnight. The next day, beat at high speed until thick. Spread between layers, on top and sides. Sprinkle with almonds.

**Creamy Coffee:**
½ pt. heavy cream, whipped
2 T. powdered sugar
1 t. instant coffee
1 t. vanilla

Combine all ingredients; refrigerate.

**Between layers:**
2½ c. powdered sugar
2 T. soft butter
1 t. instant coffee
1 t. vanilla

Cream sugar and butter. Add coffee and vanilla. Stir in just enough cream to spread. Spread between layers. Spread whipped cream topping over sides and top.

**Creamy Orange:**
1 egg, beaten
¾ c. sugar
3 T. flour
Juice of 1 orange
Grated rind of 1 orange
1 T. lemon juice
½ pt. heavy cream, whipped

Combine all ingredients except cream in top of double boiler; cook until thick. Chill. Fold in whipped cream and ice top and sides of Angel food cake. For special occasions, cut cake in half and put lemon icing between layers before frosting.

**Lemon Icing:**
2½ c. powdered sugar
2 T. soft butter
Lemon juice

Cream sugar and butter; add just enough fresh lemon juice to spread.

## BUTTER FROSTING

⅓ c. soft butter
3 c. powdered sugar
1½ t. vanilla
2 T. milk (or more)

Blend butter with sugar. Stir in vanilla and milk; beat until of spreading consistency. Will frost two 9 inch layers or 13 x 9 inch cake.

*For Orange Butter Frosting, leave out vanilla and use orange or lemon juice instead of milk; add 2 teaspoons grated orange or lemon peel.*

## CHOCOLATE FROSTING

3 T. butter
3 ozs. unsweetened
  chocolate
2 c. powdered sugar
¼ t. salt
⅓ c. milk
1 t. vanilla
¼ c. chopped nuts
  (optional)

Melt butter and chocolate. Stir in the other ingredients and beat until smooth. Will frost two 9 inch layers or a 13 x 9 inch cake.

*For Mocha Butter Frosting, add 1 1/2 teaspoons powdered instant coffee with sugar.*

## PINEAPPLE FROSTING

¼ c. butter
¼ c. pineapple juice
2 egg whites, beaten
1 lb. powdered sugar, sifted
1 t. almond extract

Cream butter; blend in juice. Add beaten egg whites alternately with sifted sugar. Blend in almond extract. Spread lightly on cake. Allow to dry well before serving.

# SEVEN MINUTE FROSTING

1 c. sugar
⅓ c. water
¼ t. cream of tartar
⅛ t. salt
2 unbeaten egg whites
1 t. vanilla

Combine sugar, water, cream of tartar, and salt in saucepan. Bring to boil, stirring until sugar dissolves. Very slowly add to **unbeaten** egg whites in mixing bowl, beating constantly with electric mixer until stiff peaks form. Beat in vanilla. Will frost 2 9-inch layers or a 10-inch tube cake.

*This frosting is excellent for fresh coconut cake; just add coconut to the icing.*

# PIES

## MOM'S APPLE PIE

Pastry for 2 crust pie
½ c. seedless raisins,
  plumped*
12 pitted dates, cut in
  quarters
16 dried apricots, cut in
  quarters
1-16 oz. can apple pie filling
¼ c. brandy
¼ t. cinnamon
¼ t. nutmeg

*to plump raisins, place
  them in a small bowl; cover
  with hot water until puffed
  and no longer wrinkled.

Combine raisins, dates, apricots, apple pie filling, brandy and spices; set aside. Roll out half of pastry and fit into 9 inch pie pan. Spoon filling mix into shell. Roll out remaining pastry; cut a 5 inch circle on top for steam vent. Place on top of fruit filling and seal edges; crimp decoratively. Bake at 400 degrees 45 minutes, or until crust is golden. Cool on wire rack. Serve slightly warm.

*Guild the lily by adding a scoop of vanilla ice cream on top.*

## BLACK BOTTOM PIE

16 gingersnaps, crushed
½ c. butter, melted

2 c. scalded milk
4 egg yolks
½ c. sugar
1½ T. cornstarch
1½ squares unsweetened
  chocolate
1 t. vanilla

1 T. unflavored gelatin
2 T. cold water
2 T. brandy
4 egg whites, beaten
½ c. sugar
¼ t. cream of tartar

Serves 8

Crush gingersnaps; add melted butter. Press into 9 inch pie pan. Bake at 400 degrees 10 minutes. Cool.

Combine sugar, cornstarch and eggs; beat well. Add milk. Cook in top of double boiler 20 minutes, stirring constantly until thickened. Remove from heat; reserve 1 cup. To this cup of custard add melted chocolate and vanilla. Pour into crust.

Dissolve gelatin in cold water. Add remaining custard. Beat egg whites until stiff; add sugar and cream of tartar, beating well. Add brandy. Fold custard mixture into whites. Pour over chocolate layer. Cool. Cover with whipped cream and chocolate curls.

# BROWNIE PIE

3 egg whites
⅛ t. salt
1 c. sugar
¾ c. chocolate wafer
crumbs
½ c. chopped walnuts
½ t. vanilla
2 c. heavy cream, whipped

Serves 6

Beat egg whites and salt until peaks form. Gradually add sugar, beating until stiff. Fold in crumbs, nuts and vanilla. Spread evenly in lightly buttered 9 inch pie plate. Bake at 350 degrees 35 minutes. Cool. Spread top with the whipped cream. Chill for 3-4 hours. Garnish with shaved chocolate curls.

# BUTTERMILK PIE

9 inch pie shell, unbaked
3 eggs
1½ c. white sugar
½ c. butter
⅓ c. buttermilk
1 T. flour
1 t. vanilla
1 small can Angel Flake
Coconut (optional)

Serves 6 to 8

Beat eggs slightly. Melt butter. Combine butter, sugar, eggs, milk, flour, vanilla and coconut. Pour into pie shell. Bake at 350 degrees 45 minutes.

# CALAMONDIN CREAM PIE

9 inch pie shell, baked
3 T. cornstarch
1¼ c. sugar
¼ c. calamondin juice
3 egg yolks
1½ c. boiling water
1 T. butter or margarine
3 egg whites
6 T. sugar

Combine cornstarch, sugar and fruit juice. Add beaten egg yolks; stir until smooth. Gradually add boiling water. Heat over boiling water until thickened, stirring constantly. Add butter; remove from heat. Cool. Pour into pie shell.

Beat egg whites until stiff; beat in sugar. Spread over top of pie sealing in filling. Bake at 400 degrees 5 minutes. Chill.

## SPEEDY CHEESECAKE PIE

**9 inch graham cracker crust**
**1  8 oz. pkg. cream cheese**
**½ c. sugar**
**1 T. lemon juice**
**½ t. vanilla**
**⅛ t. salt**
**2 eggs**
**1 c. sour cream**
**2 T. sugar**
**½ t. vanilla**

**Serves 8**

Blend cream cheese until fluffy; add next four ingredients. Add eggs one at a time, beating well after each. Pour into crust. Bake at 325 degrees 30 minutes or until set. Combine sour cream, sugar and vanilla; spoon over top. Bake 10 minutes longer. Chill. Serve with fresh or frozen strawberries over top.

## RICOTTA CHEESE APPLE PIE

**9 inch pie shell**
**3 c. thinly sliced apples**
**¼ c. sugar**
**½ t. nutmeg**
**2 eggs, beaten**
**1 c. ricotta cheese**
**½ c. sugar**
**½ c. heavy cream**
**⅛ t. salt**
**1½ t. grated lemon rind**

**Serves 6 to 8**

Place apples in pie shell; mix ¼ cup sugar with cinnamon and nutmeg. Combine eggs, ricotta, ½ cup sugar, cream, salt and lemon rind. Mix; pour over apples, covering evenly. Bake at 425 degrees 10 minutes, then at 350 degrees 30 minutes.

## CHESS PIE

**9 inch pie shell, unbaked**
**1 c. sugar**
**2 eggs**
**⅓ c. melted butter**
**1 T. cornmeal**
**1 t. vinegar**

**Serves 6 to 8**

Combine all ingredients and blend together well. Pour into pie shell and bake at 450 degrees 6-8 minutes, then at 300 degrees 20 minutes or until knife comes out clean.

## CHESS PIE

½ c. butter
1½ c. sugar
1 T. vinegar
1 t. vanilla
3 eggs
Dash salt

**Serves 6-8**

Cook the first three ingredients over low heat until sugar is dissolved. Pour this over slightly beaten eggs. Add vanilla and salt. Beat, beat, beat. Pour into pie shell and bake at 350 degrees 30 minutes or until pie is set.

## CHESS TARTS (ENGLAND)

1 recipe pie crust (2 crust)

½ c. butter, softened
1 c. brown sugar, firmly
  packed
2 eggs
1 t. grated lemon rind
½ c. dairy sour cream
¾ c. chopped walnuts
¾ c. cut-up dates
½ c. raisins
Sour cream
Walnut halves

Roll out pastry, cut into 5 inch rounds; fit into foil tart pans (3 inch in diameter, ⅓ cup capacity).

Cream butter and brown sugar; beat in eggs, one at a time. Stir in lemon rind, sour cream, walnuts, dates and raisins.

Place tart shells on jelly-roll pan; spoon in filling. Bake at 450 degrees 10 minutes; lower heat to 350 degrees for 25 minutes or until filling is firm. Remove tarts from oven; cool on wire rack.

Carefully remove tarts from pans. Serve topped with cream and walnut halves, if desired.

**Serves 10**

302

## CHOCOLATE CHESS PIE

**10 inch pie shell, unbaked**
**3 squares unsweetened**
**chocolate**
**½ c. butter**
**1½ c. sugar**
**3 T. white corn syrup**
**⅛ t. salt**
**4 eggs**
**1 t. vanilla**
**1½ oz. bourbon**
**½ c. chopped pecans**

**Serves 6 to 8**

Melt butter and chocolate together. Cool. Mix in sugar, corn syrup and salt. Add eggs one at a time, beating well. Stir in vanilla, bourbon and nuts. Pour into pie shell. Bake at 350 degrees 25-30 minutes.

*Very good served with bourbon flavored whipped cream on top.*

## FRENCH SILK CHOCOLATE PIE

**9 inch pie shell, baked**
**½ c. butter**
**¾ c. sugar**
**2 oz. unsweetened**
**chocolate, melted**
**1 t. vanilla**
**2 eggs**

Cream butter and sugar; stir in melted chocolate. Add eggs one at a time, beating 5 minutes after each addition. (With electric mixer use medium speed.) Turn into cooled pie shell. Chill 1 to 2 hours. May garnish with whipped-cream and nuts.

Variation: Fold in 2 cups Cool Whip and chill or freeze.

303

## CHOCOLATE MARVEL PIE

9 inch pie shell, baked
1-6 oz. pkg. chocolate chips
3 T. milk
2 T. sugar
4 eggs, separated
1 t. vanilla
½ pt. heavy cream, whipped

**Serves 6 to 8**

Combine chocolate chips, milk and sugar in top of double boiler. Heat until chocolate melts. Add egg yolks one at a time, beating well. Cook until thickened. Remove from heat; add vanilla. Beat egg whites until stiff; fold into chocolate mixture. Pour into pie shell; chill several hours before serving.
Add whipped cream and serve.

## VIRGINIA'S SATIN PIE

2 c. Club Cracker crumbs
1 c. finely chopped pecans
½ c. melted butter
¾ c. butter
1 c. powdered sugar
¾ c. cocoa
4 eggs
1 t. vanilla
½ t. almond extract
1 c. heavy cream, whipped
¼ c. Maraschino cherries, chopped

**Serves 10**

Combine crackers, pecans and butter; press into 9 inch pie plate. Bake at 375 degrees 10 minutes.
Cream butter, sugar and cocoa, if mixture is stiff add one of the eggs. Beat well. Add eggs and whip on high speed in electric mixer until consistency of whipped cream. Add flavorings; beat well. Pour into pie shell. Chill until set (about 2 hours). Add cherries to whipped cream and spread over pie.

# COCONUT CHERRY PIE DELIGHT

½ c. butter
7 oz. coconut
2  1 lb. cans dark, sweet
  cherries
1½ pts. vanilla ice cream,
  softened
2 t. cornstarch

Serves 6

Melt butter; add coconut. Mix together well; press into 9 inch pie pan. Bake 10 minutes; cool. Drain cherries, reserving liquid. Fold cherries into ice cream quickly, then pour into pie shell. Cover with foil and freeze. Add cornstarch to reserved juice; cook until slightly thickened and pour over pie.

## DAIQUIRI PIE

1 pkg. unflavored gelatin
1 c. sugar
¼ t. salt
⅓ c. lime juice
⅓ c. water
3 eggs, separated
½ t. grated lime rind
2 drops green food coloring
¼ c. light rum
⅓ c. sugar

Mix together gelatin, sugar and salt in a saucepan. Add lime juice, egg yolks and water. Cook until mixture boils and gelatin dissolves. Remove from heat; add lime rind and food coloring. Cool. Stir in rum. Chill until partially set. Beat egg whites to soft peaks; stir in sugar and beat until stiff. Fold in gelatin mixture. Chill until filling mounds. Pour into pie shell. Chill until firm. Top with whipped cream.

## GRASSHOPPER PIE

16 crushed Oreo cookies
½ c. melted butter
½ c. milk
24 large marshmallows
½ pt. heavy cream, whipped
3 T. Creme de Menthe
3 T. White Creme de Cocoa

Add melted butter to crushed cookies. Press into 9 inch pie pan.

Melt marshmallows in milk over low heat, stirring constantly. Cool to room temperature. Add Creme de Menthe and Creme de Cocoa to whipped cream. Fold cream mixture into marshmallow mixture. Pour into pie shell. Chill or freeze.

Serves 6 to 8

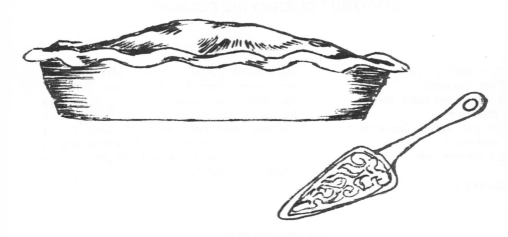

## HONEY SHERRIED CRUNCH PIE

9 inch pie shell, baked
1 T. unflavored gelatin
½ c. medium dry Sherry
1 pkg. (3½ oz.) vanilla
  pudding mix (not instant)
1½ c. milk
¼ c. honey
1 c. heavy cream, whipped
1 c. coarsely crushed peanut
  brittle

Serves 8

Soften gelatin in Sherry. Prepare pudding mix according to package directions using 1½ cups milk as liquid. Remove from heat; add softened gelatin and Sherry; stir until dissolved. Stir in honey. Cool filling 1 hour until partially thickened. Fold in whipped cream. Spoon in pie shell. Cover top with crushed peanut brittle, patting down with hand. Chill.

*This pie cuts to perfection after it has been chilled several hours or overnight.*

## JAPANESE FRUIT PIE

1 c. sugar
2 eggs, beaten
½ c. butter
1 T. white vinegar
½ c. raisins
½ c. chopped nuts
½ c. coconut

Combine first 4 ingredients. Add raisins, nuts and coconut. Pour into 9 inch unbaked pie shell; bake at 325 degrees 40 minutes.

## KAHLUA PIE

16 chocolate cookies, crushed
¼ c. melted butter
1 c. coconut
1 pkg. unflavored gelatin
½ c. sugar
½ t. salt
1⅓ c. milk
2 t. instant coffee
2 oz. unsweetened chocolate
3 eggs, separated
¼ c. Kahlua
¼ t. cream of tartar
½ c. sugar
½ pt. heavy cream, whipped

Mix crushed cookies, butter and coconut. Press into 9 inch pie pan.

Combine first 6 ingredients; cook in top of double broiler until well blended and gelatin is dissolved. Cool. Add beaten egg yolks to chocolate mixture. Return to heat; cook until thickened, about 5 minutes. Add Kahlua; chill until slightly thick. Beat egg whites until frothy, stir in cream of tartar and beat until stiff, adding sugar gradually. Fold into chocolate mixture. Chill. Whip cream; fold in. Spoon into pie shell. Chill.

## LEMON CHIFFON PIE

9 inch pie shell, baked
1 c. sugar
Juice of three lemons
½ t. grated lemon rind
1 envelope unflavored gelatin
¼ c. lukewarm water
4 eggs, separated

**Serves 6 to 8**

Mix yolks and half cup sugar. Add lemon juice and rind. Cook in top of double boiler. Stir until thickened. Dissolve gelatin in lukewarm water; add to mixture. Beat egg whites until frothy, add remaining sugar; beat until stiff. Fold egg whites in carefully. Pour into pie shell; chill 4 hours. Serve with whipped cream.

## LEMON MERINGUE PIE

9 inch pie shell, baked
1 c. sugar
5 T. flour
1 large lemon, juiced
4 eggs, separated
1 c. milk
1 T. butter
3 T. sugar

Serves 6 to 8

Mix flour and sugar; add lemon juice and grated rind. Beat yolks and milk together; stir in flour-sugar mixture. Cook in top of double boiler until thick. Add butter; cool. Pour into pie shell. Beat egg whites until stiff; add the 3 tablespoons sugar gradually, beating well. Put meringue on pie sealing well. Bake at 400 degrees 15 minutes or until brown.

## SLICED LEMON PIE

1 recipe 2 crust pie shell
4 eggs, beaten
2½ c. sugar
¼ c. water
2 T. butter, melted
Dash salt and nutmeg
Rind of 2 lemons
3 lemons, sliced

Serves 6 to 8

Combine eggs and sugar; add butter, water, salt and nutmeg. Grate rind from two lemons and remove all white membrane. Slice very thin. Thinly slice the other lemon, skin intact. Add lemon rind and slices to egg mixture. Pour into pastry shell. Cover with pastry and crimp edges well. Bake at 400 degrees 10 minutes; at 350 degrees 30 minutes more. Cool and serve.

## KEY LIME CHIFFON PIE
## SEA GRAPE LODGE

9 inch pie shell, baked
2 egg yolks, slightly beaten
1¼ c. sugar
¼ t. salt
½ c. fresh key lime juice
1 t. grated lime rind
1 T. unflavored gelatin
½ c. cold water
4 drops green food coloring
2 egg whites, beaten stiff
1 c. heavy cream, whipped

Serves 6

Combine 1 cup sugar, egg yolks, salt and ¼ cup lime juice; cook over boiling water until thick, stirring constantly. Soften gelatin in cold water; add to hot mixture. Stir until dissolved. Set pan aside to cool. Add remaining ¼ cup lime juice, green coloring and rind. Cool until mixture begins to jell. Add remaining sugar to egg whites slowly, beating well. Fold this into the cooled mixture carefully. Fold in whipped cream; pour into baked shell. Chill 3-6 hours. Serve topped with whipped cream.

## OATMEAL PIE

**9 inch pie shell, unbaked**
**¾ c. sugar**
**½ c. butter**
**2 eggs**
**⅛ t. salt**
**¾ c. dark corn syrup**
**¾ c. uncooked oatmeal**
**1 t. vanilla**

Cream butter and sugar; add eggs, one at a time, slightly beating. Fold in salt, corn syrup, oatmeal and vanilla. Pour into pie shell; bake at 325 degrees 40 minutes or until set.

*No pecans? Try this pie and you will never worry about running out of pecans again. It's sooo good.*

## PEANUT BUTTER CHIFFON PIE

**9 inch graham cracker crust**
**1 envelope unflavored gelatin**
**¼ c. sugar**
**¼ t. salt**
**1 c. milk**
**2 egg yolks, beaten**
**½ c. crunchy peanut butter**
**2 egg whites, beaten**
**¼ c. sugar**
**2 c. Cool Whip, thawed**

Mix gelatin, sugar and salt in top of double boiler. Add yolks. Scald milk; add to egg mixture, stirring constantly until thickened. Remove from heat and add peanut butter. Blend. Chill. Beat egg whites until foamy. Add sugar gradually, beat until stiff. Fold into peanut butter mixture. Fold in Cool Whip and spoon into crust. Chill until firm. Garnish with whipped cream and grated chocolate.

**Serves 6 to 8**

*So wonderfully light and yummy*

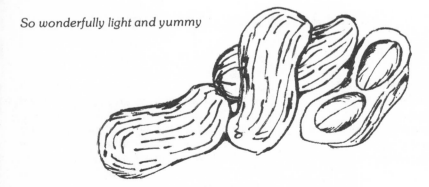

309

# PECAN PIE

9 inch pie shell, unbaked
2 eggs, beaten
1 c. light corn syrup
⅛ t. salt
1 t. vanilla extract
1 c. light brown sugar
2 T. melted margarine
1 c. pecans, coarsely broken

Mix eggs, syrup, salt, vanilla, sugar, margarine together. Stir in pecans. Pour into unbaked pie shell. Bake at 400 degrees 15 minutes. Reduce heat to 350 degrees; continue baking 30 minutes.

Serves 6

*This pie can be frozen unbaked, but defrost before baking.*

# SOUTHERN PECAN PIE

9 inch pie shell, unbaked
1 c. dark corn syrup or
  molasses
¾ c. sugar
3 eggs
1 t. vanilla
1 c. pecans, chopped
3 T. butter

Mix syrup and sugar; bring to boil and cook 3 minutes. Remove from heat. Beat in eggs one at a time. Add butter, vanilla and pecans. Pour into pie shell. Bake at 375 degrees 45-50 minutes.

Serves 6 to 8

# PONCHATRAIN ICE CREAM PIE

10 inch pie shell, baked
2 c. egg whites
1½ c. sugar
2 pts. ice cream (2 different
  flavors)
Chocolate sauce

Spoon softened ice cream into pie shell that has been baked and cooled. Beat egg whites until stiff; add sugar gradually, beating all the while. Spread whites over ice cream and broil about 1 minute or until brown. Freeze. To serve, cut into pieces and pour warm chocolate sauce over top.

## UNCOOKED PUMPKIN PIE

**9 inch pie shell, baked
2 pkg. instant vanilla pudding mix
1-16 oz. can pumpkin pie
  mix
1-9 oz. carton Cool Whip
1½ c. milk
Pecan halves**

**Serves 8**

Blend pudding mix, pie mix and milk. Pour into pie shell. Chill until set. Decorate with Cool Whip and pecans.

## RASPBERRY MOUSSE PIE

**9 inch graham cracker crust
1 pkg. frozen raspberries,
  thawed
1-3 oz. pkg. raspberry
  gelatin
1 c. hot water
16 marshmallows
1 c. heavy cream, whipped**

**Serves 6 to 8**

Drain raspberries; reserve juice. Mix juice, gelatin, and hot water; cook over low heat until gelatin dissloves. Add marshmallows. Simmer, stirring often until marshmallows melt. Chill until thickened. Beat thickened gelatin in electric mixer until it doubles in size. It should be light pink and mound slightly. Fold in raspberries gently. Fold whipped cream into raspberry mixture. Spoon into pie shell and chill until set. Sprinkle top with almonds.

# RHUBARB CREAM PIE

1 recipe 2 crust pie shell
1½ c. sugar
3 T. flour
½ t. nutmeg
1 T. butter
2 beaten eggs
3 c. cut rhubarb

Serves 6 to 8

Blend sugar, flour, nutmeg and butter. Add beaten eggs; beat until smooth. Pour over rhubarb in pastry lined pan; top with pastry cut in fancy shapes. Bake at 450 degrees 10 minutes, then at 350 degrees about 30 minutes.

# SOUR CREAM PIE

9 inch pie shell, unbaked
1 c. sour cream
½ c. raisins, finely chopped
½ t. cinnamon
⅛ t. cloves
1 c. sugar
3 eggs, separated
1 t. salt

Combine egg yolks and one egg white. Beat well; stir in all other ingredients except egg whites. Bake at 350 degrees 40 minutes. Beat remaining whites with salt until stiff. Pour on pie and return to oven and brown.

# STRAWBERRY PIE

9 inch pie shell, baked
1 qt. strawberries
1 c. sugar
3 T. cornstarch
Whipped cream

Serves 6 to 8

Clean berries, drain well. Mash half of the berries and mix with one cup of sugar and cornstarch. Cook this until thick and transparent. Cool. Put the other half of the berries in pie shell and pour cooked mixture over them. Top with sweetened whipped cream and a few pretty berries. Chill.

## STRAWBERRY MERINGUE PIE

3 egg whites
½ t. baking powder
1 c. sugar
10-2 inch soda crackers,
  rolled fine
½ c. coarsley chopped
  pecans
1 qt. unsweetened fresh
  strawberries
½ c. heavy cream, whipped

Serves 8

Beat egg whites and baking powder until stiff. Add sugar gradually; beat well. Fold in nuts and crackers. Spread in well greased 9 inch pie pan. Bake at 300 degrees 30 minutes. Cool. Fill with strawberries; top with whipped cream. Chill several hours.

## FRESH STRAWBERRY TART

½ c. soft butter
3 T. sugar
1¼ c. flour
¼ c. chopped nuts

1 pt. fresh strawberries
½ pt. heavy cream, whipped

¾ c. red currant jelly
2 T. hot water
Slivered almonds
Green food coloring

Serves 6 to 8

Combine butter, sugar, flour, nuts; mix with pastry blender. Form into a ball, roll out and fit into a 9 inch pie pan. Score bottom; bake at 400 degrees 15 minutes or until brown. Cool.
Wash and prepare strawberries. Spread whipped cream on bottom of cooled shell. Arrange berries over cream in a pattern. Heat jelly and water over low heat until jelly melts. Cool. Pour over berries. Decorate with almonds that have been colored green to resemble leaves. DO NOT fill shell sooner than 6 hours before serving, or later than 2 hours.

# VANILLA PUDDING OR PIE FILLING

¾ c. sugar
⅓ c. flour
2 eggs, beaten
2 c. milk
1 t. vanilla
2 T. butter
Dash salt

**Yields filling for a 9 inch
pie shell**

Mix flour and sugar; add eggs (if recipe calls for meringue, add only yolks here), blending well. Stir in milk; cook over low heat until thick. Add butter and vanilla and mix well. Cool. Pour into baked pie shell or use as pudding. If pudding gets lumpy while cooking, just beat with hand mixer until smooth.

**Basic Recipe can be
used for:**

## CHOCOLATE PIE

Increase sugar to 1 cup
2 oz. melted unsweetened
  chocolate
Whipped cream topping

## COCONUT CREAM PIE

¾ c. fresh coconut
Whipped topping

Add coconut with the butter and vanilla. You may wish to add toasted coconut on the top.

## DESSERT ANGEL FOOD CAKE

1 small Angel Food Cake
4 T. brandy

Slice cake into servings. Stir brandy into warm pudding. Pour over cake. Serve immediately.

*The above are just a few suggestions for this versitile recipe. It can also be used as a filling for cream puffs and eclairs or banana pudding.*

## MERINGUE SHELL

3 egg whites
¼ t. cream of tartar
6 T. sugar
½ t. vanilla

**Yields 9 inch pie shell**

Let egg whites stand at room temperature until tepid. Beat with cream of tartar until frothy; add sugar a little at a time beating all the while. Continue beating until very stiff. Add vanilla. Pile into a 9 inch pie plate, high on the sides and evenly on bottom, making a shell. Bake at 250 degrees 1¼ hours. Turn off heat; leave in oven half hour longer.

*There are many pies that require a meringue shell; here are a few:*

## ANGEL PIE

4 egg yolks
½ c. sugar
Grated rind of 1 lemon
3 T. lemon juice
2 T. water
½ pt. heavy cream, whipped

Mix first five ingredients; cook in top of double boiler until thick. Cool. Whip cream. Spread thin layer of whipped cream in meringue shell. Put cooked filling over cream; top with remaining whipped cream. Chill several hours.

## CHOCOLATE ANGEL

**1 bar German chocolate**
**(4 oz.)**
**3 T. Water**
**1 t. vanilla**
**1 c. heavy cream, whipped**

Melt chocolate and water over low heat, stirring constantly. Cool. Add vanilla. Fold in whipped cream. Pile into meringue shell; top with more whipped cream if desired.

## PEACH MERINGUE GLACE

**1½ c. milk**
**2 T. flour**
**⅓ c. sugar**
**⅛ t. salt**
**3 egg yolks**
**½ t. vanilla**
**½ t. almond extract**
**1 c. heavy cream, whipped**
**1 qt. sliced fresh peaches**
**½ c. fresh blueberries**

**Serves 8**

Scald milk in top of double boiler. Mix flour, sugar and salt; stir into milk. Cool until smooth and thickened. Pour over slightly beaten egg yolks; cook 10 minutes longer. Cool. Add flavorings then fold in whipped cream. Pour into meringue shell. Chill. Before serving, top with sliced peaches and sprinkle with fresh blueberries.

## PIE CRUST (TWO CRUST PIE)

**¾ c. vegetable shortening**
**¼ c. boiling water**
**1 T. milk**
**2 c. flour**
**1 t. salt**

Put shortening into bowl; stir in hot water. Add milk and break up shortening with fork. Tilt bowl and whip with fork until mixture is smooth and thick like whipped cream. Sift flour and salt together and add to shortening. Stir quickly round the bowl until mix clings together. Roll out between two sheets of waxed paper.

## PIE CRUST (ONE CRUST)

**½ c. vegetable shortening**
**3 T. boiling water**
**1 t. milk**
**1¼ c. flour**
**½ t. salt**

Follow the above directions.

## PIE CRUST

**⅓ c. margarine**
**⅓ c. shortening**
**2 c. sifted flour**
**⅓ c. ice water**

Blend with pastry blender until mix holds together. Add ice water, enough to form a ball. Roll out. Enough for 2 small pies or a deep dish pie.

# PIE CRUST

3 oz. pkg. cream cheese
½ c. butter
1 c. flour

Mix all together and work until smooth. Chill about an hour. Makes 1 pie shell.

## PIE CRUST (ONE CRUST)

1 c. flour
½ c. butter
1½ T. sugar

Mix well with your hands and press into a 9 inch pie pan. Prick the bottom and bake at 350 degrees for 8 to 10 minutes. Very good for any fruit torte or cream pie using instant pie fillings that do not require baking.

## PIE CRUST (ONE CRUST)

1½ c. flour
6 T. shortening
½ t. salt
Ice water

Blend well together and add enough ice water to hold together. Roll out.

## GRAHAM CRACKER CRUST

20 Graham crackers
¼ c. soft butter or margarine
¼ c. sugar

Roll crackers to fine crumbs. Pour crumbs into a bowl and add the butter and sugar. Blend these well. Pour into a 9 inch pie pan and press firmly to make even layer on sides and bottom.

## BROWN SUGAR PASTRY

½ c. butter or margarine
1 c. flour
¼ c. brown sugar, packed
½ c. chopped pecans

Place all ingredients in pie pan, do not mix. Bake at 400 degrees for 15 minutes. Remove from oven and stir well with fork at once! Pat out into 9 inch pie pan.

*This is an especially good crust for any cream pie or chiffon pie.*

## SANDBAKKELS

1 c. shortening
1 c. white sugar
1 egg, beaten
Dash salt
1 t. almond extract (or ½ t. each vanilla & almond)
2¾ c. flour

Cream shortening and sugar; add egg and cream well. Add salt, flavoring and flour (fairly stiff). Press small ball of dough into Sandbakkel tin, trimming off excess. Place tins on ungreased cookie sheet; bake at 375 degrees 12-15 minutes. When cool, turn out of tins. Store in cool place; when ready to serve, fill with pie filling and top with whipped cream.

## $3,000.00 PIE CRUST (CHARLOTTE HUGHES HERBERT)

3 c. plus 6 T. flour
½ c. water
1½ t. salt
1 c. plus 2 T. shortening

Makes 2 or more pie crusts according to size of pan.

Measure and sift flour; measure again and reserve ½ cup. Dissolve salt in water; add ½ cup flour and make a paste. Set aside. To rest of flour add shortening; mix until it looks like cornmeal. Now add salt, flour and water paste; mix until it forms a firm ball. Place in refrigerator until ready to use. This dough can be reworked, frozen and handled quite a bit. There is no waste. Roll it out like any other pie crust on a floured board. Be sure it is thin.

*To prevent a soggy crust, just brush melted butter on the inside of unbaked crust and refrigerate a few hours.*
*Leftover bits of pie crust? Use around olives, stuffed dates, sausages, franks and bake. Freeze for later use.*

# COOKIES

## BON BON COOKIES

½ c. butter
¾ c. sifted powdered sugar
1 T. vanilla
1½ c. sifted flour
Salt

Icing:
1 c. powdered sugar
2 T. cream
1 t. vanilla
  (for chocolate, add 1
  square)

For Top:
Coconut
Nuts
Colored sugar

Yields 2 dozen

Mix butter, sugar and vanilla. Blend in flour and salt thoroughly by hand. Wrap dough around cherries, nuts, dates or chocolate. Bake at 350 degrees 12-15 minutes, or until set. Dip in icing and top each with any of topping ideas.

## BRANDY WAFERS

½ c. molasses
½ c. butter
1¼ c. sifted flour
¼ t. salt
⅔ c. sugar
1 T. ginger
3 T. Brandy

Yields 5 dozen

Heat molasses to boiling; add butter. Add sifted dry ingredients gradually, stirring constantly. Stir in brandy. Drop by half teaspoon 3 inches apart on greased cookie sheet. Bake a few at a time. Bake at 300 degrees 8-10 minutes. Cool one minute. Remove with spatula and roll at once around handle of wooden spoon. If removed too soon wafers will break, if not soon enough they will not roll. If they will not roll, reheat slightly.

# BROWNIES SUPREME

4 eggs
1 c. butter
⅓ c. cocoa
1½ c. flour
2 c. sugar
1 t. vanilla
Dash salt
1½ c. pecans, chopped
1 jar marshmallow creme

Combine eggs, sugar, salt, flour and vanilla. Melt butter; blend in cocoa and add to mixture. Beat well. Fold in nuts. Place in 13 x 9 baking dish and bake at 350 degrees 20-25 minutes or until just done. While still hot spread with marshmallow creme. Let cool.

Icing:
½ c. butter
⅓ c. cocoa
1 box powdered sugar
Dash salt
1 t. vanilla
Milk

Melt butter; stir in cocoa. Pour mixture in bowl that has the box of sifted powdered sugar in it; add salt and vanilla. Gradually blend in enough milk to make it spreadable; beat well. Put this icing over the marshmallow topping. Do not take out of pan until they have been cut and are cool.

Yields 2 dozen

# BUNEULOS
## (Fried Sweet Puffs)

3⅓ c. sifted flour
1 t. salt
1 t. baking powder
1½ T. sugar
¼ c. butter or margarine
2 eggs
½ c. milk
Vegetable oil for frying
Sugar or glazed coating

Sift dry ingredients. Add butter; work into flour until mixture is like coarse meal. Beat eggs with milk; pour into flour mixture and stir until dough forms solid mass. Turn dough out onto board, knead 2 minutes or until smooth. Cut into balls the size of marbles; let stand 15 minutes. Roll each ball on a lightly floured board into thin pancake 4 inches in diameter; cut hole in center with thimble. Place circles in single layer on waxed paper until you are ready to cook. Fry in hot deep fat (375 degrees) until puffed and golden brown; drain. Use one or both of following:

Sugar coating:
1 c. sugar
1 t. cinnamon

Mix sugar and cinnamon in paper bag. Reheat buneulos in 250 degree oven 5 minutes; shake gently, one at a time, in bag to coat.

Glazed coating:
½ c. each granulated sugar
 and light brown (firmly
 packed)
½ c. water
1 T. butter or margarine
1 t. cinnamon
1 T. dark corn syrup

Yields about 6 dozen

Place sugars and water in frying pan; add butter, cinnamon and corn syrup. Heat and stir until sugar melts; boil rapidly 1 to 2 minutes, until two drops of syrup run together off spoon. Remove from heat and cool 1 minute; spoon syrup over buneulos one at a time until well coated. Drain on wire rack 30 minutes. Coating will be slightly sticky but not drippy. Will glaze 20 buneulos.

# BUTTERSCOTCH BROWNIES

½ c. butter or margarine
2 c. light brown sugar
2 eggs
2 c. sifted flour
½ t. salt
2 t. baking powder
1½ c. pecans, chopped
2 t. vanilla

Yields 5½ dozen

Combine butter and sugar in sauce pan; stir until butter melts and sugar dissolves. Cool; add unbeaten eggs to mixture and beat well. Sift dry ingredients; add to sugar mixture. Stir in nuts and vanilla. Spread in greased and floured 13 x 9 inch shallow pan; bake at 350 degrees 30 to 35 minutes. While hot mark into squares; cool slightly. While still warm cut and remove from pan.

*The secret is not to let them overcook so that they will be chewy. The flavor is better too.*

## CHOCOLATE CHIP MERINGUE COOKIES

2 egg whites
¾ c. sugar
1 c. chocolate chips
½ t. vanilla

Yields 3 dozen

Beat egg whites until stiff; add sugar gradually, beating constantly. Stir in vanilla and chocolate chips. Drop by small spoon on cookie sheet. Preheat oven to 375 degrees; when heated turn off oven. Put cookies in oven and leave several hours or overnight.

## CHOCOLATE NUGGETS

½ c. butter
2 c. sugar
1 c. evaporated milk
1 c. chocolate chips
¾ c. flour
1 c. graham cracker crumbs
1 c. pecans, chopped
1 t. vanilla

Yields 2 dozen

In saucepan combine butter, sugar and milk; bring to boil, stirring constantly for 10 minutes. Add chocolate chips, flour, graham cracker crumbs, pecans and vanilla; beat mixture by hand. Remove from heat; pour into buttered 13 x 9 inch pan and cut into squares while warm.

## CHOCOLATE NUT SQUARES

½ c. white sugar
½ c. brown sugar
1 c. shortening
3 eggs, separated
1 T. cold water
1 t. vanilla
2 c. flour
¼ t. salt
1 t. baking soda
1 12 oz. pkg. chocolate bits
1 c. chopped walnuts

Topping:
Egg whites
1 c. brown sugar

Yields 2 dozen

Cream sugars, shortening, egg yolks, water and vanilla. Sift dry ingredients; add to creamed mixture (will be stiff). Put into greased 13 x 9 inch pan; spread evenly over bottom. Sprinkle chocolate bits and nuts over this. Beat egg whites until stiff; gradually add brown sugar (will be stiff). Carefully spread meringue over chocolate bits and nuts. Bake at 350 degrees 25 minutes. Rich and delicious.

# CHRISTMAS COOKIES

1 lb. butter or margarine
1 c. white sugar
1 c. brown sugar
3 beaten eggs
5 c. flour
1 T. cinnamon
1 t. cloves
Salt
2 t. baking soda
3 c. oatmeal
½ lb. candied fruit mix chopped
½ lb. dates, chopped
½ c. currants
½ c. raisins
1 c. walnuts or pecans,
  chopped
1 ring of candied pineapple,
  chopped
½ c. candied cherries, chopped

Cream butter and sugars; add eggs, half the flour and half the oatmeal. Sift other dry ingredients with remaining flour. Warm raisins and currants in top of double boiler over boiling water. Dust fruits and nuts with part of flour mix; stir them into mix. Blend in remaining flour and oatmeal. Shape into rolls and chill. Slice thin for crisp cookies, thick for soft. Bake at 325 degrees 20 to 30 minutes. (Can be kept soft in tightly sealed container with half apple or orange).

*Dough can be stored in quart milk cartons; when ready to bake, just cut in half lengthwise and tear carton away.*

# COCONUT COOKIES

½ lb. margarine
1½ c. brown sugar (pack
  down)
1 egg
1¾ c. flour
1 t. baking powder
½ t. baking soda
1 t. salt
2 c. corn flakes
1 c. coconut

**Yields about 5 dozen**

Cream margarine and sugar together in electric mixer. Add other ingredients in order. Drop from spoon on cookie sheet. Bake 350 degrees 10 minutes.

## COCONUT CROWNS

1 lb. moist coconut
1 c. granulated sugar
3 eggs, unbeaten
½ c. butter
½ c. flour

**Yields 5 dozen**

Combine all ingredients; chill for several hours, or overnight. Shape into small balls; pull into a peak. Place on greased cookie sheet and bake at 350 degrees 12-15 minutes, or until peaks are touched with brown. Remove from sheet; cool and store in air tight container.

## COOKIE JAR COOKIES

1 c. sugar
1 c. brown sugar
1 c. less 2 T. shortening
1 t. vanilla
2 eggs, beaten
2 c. flour
½ t. salt
2 t. baking powder
½ c. nuts
1 c. raisins, seedless
1 c. coconut
2 c. cornflakes

**Yields 6 dozen**

Cream together sugars and shortening; add vanilla and eggs. Sift dry ingredients and add to mixture. Stir in nuts, raisins, coconut and cornflakes. Drop by teaspoons on ungreased cookie sheet; bake at 375 degrees 10 minutes.

## DATE CREAM CHEESE ROLL-UPS

1 c. butter
½ lb. cream cheese
2 c. sifted flour
¼ t. salt
Powdered sugar
Pitted dates

**Yields 8 dozen**

Cream butter and cheese together. Blend in flour and salt. Chill for several hours, or until firm enough to roll. Roll to ⅛ inch thickness on board sprinkled with powdered sugar. Cut into 1 x 3 inch strips with pastry wheel. Put a date in center of each strip and roll up; place folded side down on cookie sheet. Bake at 375 degrees 15 minutes. If desired, sprinkle with powdered sugar.

*For variety, substitute nuts or candied cherries for the dates.*

# DATE NUGGETS

**1 egg**
**¼ c. sugar**
**½ t. vanilla**
**1 pkg. pitted dates, chopped**
**1 c. chopped nuts**
**1 c. natural cereal with fruits**
**and nuts**
**Sugar to roll**

**Yields 5½ dozen**

Beat egg and sugar together and add vanilla. Add dates, nuts and cereal. Mix well. Press into buttered 8 inch square baking pan. Bake at 350 degrees 10 minutes. While warm cut into cubes and roll these into balls. Roll in sugar.

# DIAMOND COOKIES

**1 c. sugar**
**1 c. shortening**
**2 eggs**
**½ c. molasses**
**1 t. soda**
**Dash salt**
**½ t. cinnamon**
**½ t. cloves**
**½ t. ginger**
**3 c. flour**
**Sugar**

**Yields 5 dozen**

Cream sugar and shortening; add eggs and molasses. Blend in sifted dry ingredients. Spread on greased cookie sheet; sprinkle with sugar and bake at 350 degrees until light brown. Cut while warm and return to oven; turn oven off, leave door slightly open until cool. This will assure crisp cookies. They can be cut in squares but the Swedish way is always a diamond shape.

## DREAM BARS

¼ c. butter
¼ c. vegetable shortening
½ c. brown sugar, packed
1 c. flour

**Topping:**
2 eggs beaten
1 c. brown sugar
1 t. vanilla
2 T. flour
1 t. baking powder
½ t. salt
1 c. moist coconut
1 c. slivered almonds

**Yields 2½ dozen**

Cream shortening and sugar; stir in flour. Pat into bottom of ungreased 13 x 9 inch baking dish. Bake at 350 degrees 10 minutes. Spread with topping.

Mix eggs, sugar and vanilla. Combine wtih flour, baking powder and salt; stir in coconut and almonds. Return to oven and bake 25 minutes more. Cool and cut into bars.

## GINGERSNAPS

¾ c. shortening
1 c. sugar
4 T. molasses
1 egg
2 c. flour
2 t. baking soda
1 t. each cinnamon, cloves, ginger

Cream shortening and sugar; add molasses and egg, beat well. Sift dry ingredients; blend into sugar mixture, beating until smooth. Roll into small balls and sprinkle with sugar. Place 2 inches apart on greased cookie sheet. Bake at 375 degrees about 10 minutes.

327

# GLAZED GRAPE BROWNIES

**1-6 oz. pkg. butterscotch
  bits**
**¼ c. butter**
**½ c. grape jam**
**½ c. light brown sugar,
  firmly packed**
**2 eggs**
**½ t. vanilla**
**1 c. flour**
**1 t. baking powder**
**¾ t. salt**
**½ c. pecans, chopped**

**Frosting:**
**Powdered sugar**
**Grape juice**

**Yields 2 dozen**

Melt butterscotch bits and butter; stir in grape jam and brown sugar. Cool 5 minutes. Blend in eggs and vanilla. Stir sifted dry ingredients into butterscotch mixture; add nuts. Spread into greased and floured 13 x 9 inch pan. Bake at 350 degrees 25 minutes. Frost with powdered sugar and grape juice icing; cut into 2 inch squares.

# KISSES

**½ t. salt**
**4 egg whites**
**1¼ c. extra fine sugar**
**1 t. vanilla**
**2 c. shredded coconut**
**24 candied cherries**

**Yields 4 dozen**

Add salt to egg whites and beat until stiff but not dry. Sprinkle sugar over whites, one tablespoon at a time, beating just until granules are dissolved. Stir in vanilla and coconut, mixing lightly. Drop by teaspoonsful onto ungreased cookie sheet; bake at 350 degrees 20-25 minutes. Let stand 1 minute. Top with cherry half.

## LEMON BARS

½ c. butter
1 c. flour
⅓ c. powdered sugar
2 T. lemon juice
Grated rind of one lemon
2 eggs, beaten
1 c. sugar
2 T. flour
½ t. baking powder

Yields 16 squares

Combine butter, flour and powdered sugar; press into bottom of 8 inch square pan. Bake at 350 degrees 15 minutes or until light brown. Sift together sugar, flour and baking powder; stir in lemon juice, rind and eggs. Spread on baked crust and return to oven; bake about 25 minutes. Frost with powdered sugar mixed with lemon juice.

## SMOG BARS

Part I:
½ c. butter or margarine
¼ c. sugar
1 egg
4 T. cocoa
2 c. graham cracker crumbs
1 c. coconut
¼ c. walnuts

Mix butter, sugar, egg and cocoa; put in double boiler and stir until mix resembles custard. Combine crumbs, coconut and nuts and add to mixture. Press tightly into buttered 9 x 9 baking dish.

Part II:
¼ c. butter or margarine
3 T. milk
2 T. vanilla custard powder
2 c. sifted powdered sugar

Cream all ingredients together. Do not cook. Spread over Part I.

Part III:
4 squares semi-sweet
  chocolate
1 T. butter

Yields 2 dozen

Melt chocolate in top of double boiler; add butter and spread over Part II. Put into refrigerator and chill until set. Cut into small squares — very rich and delicious.

# MAGIC COCONUT BARS

½ c. butter or margarine
1½ c. graham cracker
  crumbs
1 c. nuts, chopped
1-6 oz. chocolate chips
1⅓ c. flaked coconut
1 can condensed milk

**Yields 4 dozen**

Melt butter in 13 x 9 baking dish; sprinkle evenly with graham crumbs. Over this in layer-fashion place chopped nuts, then chocolate chips and flaked coconut. Pour milk over all. Bake at 350 degrees 25 minutes or until light brown. Allow to cool 15 minutes before cutting into small squares.

# MAHMOOL

1 lb. butter
1 c. sugar
2 eggs
1 jigger whiskey
5½-6 c. flour
2 lbs. pitted dates, ground
Powdered sugar

**Yields about 90 pieces**

Cream butter and sugar; add eggs, mix well. Stir in whiskey and flour, cup by cup. Dough will get thick; if too thick for mixer, mix by hand. Make small ball (size of ping pong ball) and press thumb in center; place about ½ teaspoon ground dates in center. Work dough around to cover dates. Form oblong shape and pinch design with tweezers or fork. Put on ungreased cookie sheet and bake at 325 degrees 20 minutes or until lightly brown. Sprinkle with powdered sugar before serving.

# MELT IN THE MOUTH COOKIES

½ c. butter
1 c. light brown sugar,
  packed
1 t. vanilla
1 egg
¾ c. sifted flour
1 t. baking powder
½ t. salt
½ c. finely chopped nuts

**Yields 8 dozen**

Cream butter; add sugar, vanilla and egg and beat until light. Add sifted dry ingredients and nuts. Drop by scant teaspoon on cookie sheet; bake at 400 degrees 5 minutes. Cool ½ minute and remove.

## NANA'S CHOCOLATE DROP COOKIES

½ c. butter or margarine
1 c. brown sugar
2 eggs, separated
2 c. flour
½ t. soda
¼ t. salt
½ c. milk
2 squares chocolate
1 c. nuts (walnuts or pecans)

Frosting:
2 squares chocolate, melted
2 c. sugar
½ c. light cream
1 T. light corn syrup
½ t. salt
1 T. butter
1 t. vanilla
¼ c. chopped nuts

Yields 5½ dozen

Cream butter and sugar; add beaten egg yolks. Sift dry ingredients; add alternately with milk. Stir in melted chocolate. Fold in stiffly beaten egg whites and nuts. Drop from teaspoon onto ungreased cookie sheet. Bake at 350 degrees 12-15 minutes, or until firm to touch.

Butter sides of heavy 2 quart sauce pan. Combine melted chocolate, sugar ,cream, light corn syrup and salt; cook over medium heat, stirring constantly until sugar melts and mixture comes to boil. Cook to softball stage (238 degrees). Remove from heat; cool to lukewarm (110 degrees) **without stirring.** Add butter and vanilla; beat vigorously until fudge begins to lose its gloss. Add nuts. Frost cooled cookies at once.

## LUSCIOUS ORANGE SQUARES

Crust:
1 c. flour
¼ c. orange-flavored drink
  mix powder
½ c. butter, softened

Filling:
2 eggs
1 c. sugar
2½ T. fresh orange juice
Dash salt
Orange-flavored drink mix
  powder

Yields 1½ dozen

Sift flour and drink mix powder into bowl; blend in butter until well mixed. Pat evenly into bottom of 8 x 8 x 2 baking pan. Bake 20 minutes at 350 degrees.

Combine all ingredients; pour over baked crust and return to oven for 20 to 25 minutes at same temperature. Cool on rack. Cut in 2 inch squares; sprinkle with orange-flavored drink mix powder.

# OATMEAL COOKIES
## (AUNT HATTIE'S ORIGINAL RESTAURANT)

1½ c. firmly packed brown
  sugar
1½ c. butter or margarine
3 c. uncooked oatmeal
½ T. baking soda
3 c. sifted flour

**Yields 7 dozen**

Place ingredients in large bowl in order given and knead thoroughly. Form dough into small balls. Butter bottom of small glass. Dip into sugar and mash balls flat. Bake at 350 degrees 10-12 minutes. Allow cookies to cool slightly before transferring to paper towel.

# OATMEAL CRISPS

½ c. margarine, softened
½ c. brown sugar
½ c. white sugar
1 egg
½ t. vanilla
1½ T. molasses
¾ c. plus 2 T. flour
½ t. salt
½ t. soda
1½ c. quick oatmeal,
  uncooked
¼ c. nuts, chopped

**Yields 3½ dozen**

Cream margarine and sugars; add egg, vanilla and molasses. Blend in sifted dry ingredients; beat until smooth. Fold in oatmeal and nuts. Shape into rolls 2 inches in diameter; wrap in waxed paper. Chill several hours. Slice rolls into ¼ inch pieces; place on ungreased cookie sheet and bake in 350 degree oven 10-12 minutes. Remove immediately.

## ORANGE BLONDE BROWNIES

½ c. butter, melted
2¼ c. light brown sugar,
  firmly packed
¼ c. frozen orange juice,
  undiluted
4 eggs
2 c. flour
2 t. baking powder
1 t. salt

**Yields 24 squares**

Combine melted butter and sugar; stir in orange juice. Beat in eggs one at a time. Sift dry ingredients, blend in. Pour into well greased 13 x 9 inch baking pan. Bake at 350 degrees for 40 to 45 minutes. Cool. Cut into 2 inch squares.

## CRACKLED TOP PEANUT BUTTER COOKIES
## (AUNT HATTIE'S ORIGINAL RESTAURANT)

¾ c. margarine
¾ c. sugar
¾ c. brown sugar, packed
1 egg, slightly beaten
¾ c. peanut butter
1 t. vanilla
1¾ c. all-purpose flour
½ t. baking soda
½ t. salt

**Yields 5 dozen**

Cream margarine and sugars; blend in egg, peanut butter and vanilla. Add flour sifted with soda and salt; mix well. Chill 20-30 minutes. Form rounded teaspoon of dough into balls; roll in sugar and place on ungreased baking sheets. Bake at 375 degrees 10-12 minutes.

# PEANUTTY CHEWS

¼ c. firmly packed brown
   sugar
¼ c. corn syrup
1 T. butter or margarine
2 c. sugar coated corn flakes
½ c. salted cocktail peanuts

Yields 4 dozen

Measure sugar, corn syrup and butter into large saucepan. Cook over medium heat, stirring constantly, until mixture begins to bubble. Cook 2 minutes longer; remove from heat. Add sugar coated corn flakes and peanuts; stir until well coated with syrup. Drop by rounded measuring teaspoon onto waxed paper or buttered baking sheets. With buttered fingers, shape portions into balls.

# PECAN BARS

2 T. margarine
1 c. brown sugar
1 egg
1 c. flour
1 t. baking powder
¼ t. salt
½ c. chopped pecans

Yields 5 dozen

Melt margarine and add brown sugar; cool. Beat egg into mixture. Sift dry ingredients and blend into sugar-egg mixture; add nuts. Pour into 8 inch square pan and bake at 300 degrees 40 minutes. Cut into squares while hot.

# PINEAPPLE BARS

Part I:
2 c. crushed pineapple
1½ c. sugar
6 T. cornstarch
Dash salt

Partially drain pineapple. Blend all ingredients together; cook until clear and thick, stirring constantly.

Part II:
2 c. Quaker oats
2 c. light brown sugar
2 c. flour
½ t. salt
2 t. baking powder
1 c. margarine

Yields 4½ dozen

Combine all ingredients in large bowl; put half of mix in bottom of 13 x 9 inch baking dish. Spread pineapple mixture over top; cover with other half of mix.

Bake at 350 degrees 30 minutes.

# SKILLET COOKIES

½ c. butter
2 egg yolks
1 pkg. dates, diced
1 c. pecans, chopped
2 c. rice crispies
1 t. vanilla
Coconut

**Yields 4 dozen**

Melt butter in large skillet. Combine egg yolks, dates and pecans and add to skillet. Cook over low heat 2 minutes, stirring constantly; remove from heat. Stir in rice crispies and vanilla; mix well. While warm shape into small balls; roll in coconut.

# SNAPPY SNACK COOKIES

½ c. butter or margarine
1 c. brown sugar
2 c. quick-cooking oats
¼ t. salt
1 t. baking powder
½ c. chopped dried figs

**Yields 24**

Combine butter and sugar in saucepan; cook until butter melts. Stir in remaining ingredients. Spoon into greased 8 inch square pan; press down lightly with back of spoon. Bake at 350 degrees 20-25 minutes. Cool; cut into squares or bars.

# SNOW BALL MELTS

1 c. soft butter
½ c. sifted powdered sugar
1 t. vanilla
2¼ c. sifted flour
¼ t. salt
¾ c. finely chopped pecans

**Yields 4 dozen**

Mix together butter and powdered sugar; add vanilla. Sift flour and salt; stir into butter mixture. Add finely chopped nuts. Chill dough; roll into 1 inch balls. Place on ungreased cookie sheet; bake at 400 degrees 10-12 minutes. Do not brown. While still hot roll in sifted powdered sugar. Cool; roll in sugar again.

## SPIRITED RAISIN COOKIES

1 c. raisins
½ c. warm rum, or 3 T. rum
  extract in ½ c. water
1 c. butter, softened
½ c. powdered sugar, sifted
2 c. flour
¼ t. salt
¼ t. baking powder

**Yields 12-2 inch cookies**

Bring raisins to boil in rum; remove from heat. Cover, let stand 30 minutes; drain. Cream butter and sugar. Sift dry ingredients and add to butter mixture. Stir in raisins. Roll out to ½ inch thick; cut in desired shapes. Bake at 375 degrees 20 minutes.

## WORLD'S BEST SUGAR COOKIES

1 c. butter
1 c. vegetable oil
1 c. granulated sugar
1 c. powdered sugar
1 t. vanilla
1 t. almond extract
2 eggs, beaten
5 c. flour
½ t. salt
1 t. baking soda
1 t. cream of tartar

**Yields 12 dozen**

Cream butter, oil and sugars; add extracts. Stir in eggs one at a time, beating well. Sift dry ingredients and add to creamed mixture. Chill and roll into balls the size of walnuts; flatten with glass dipped in sugar. Bake at 350 degrees 10-12 minutes. Very crisp. Recipe may be halved.

# YUM YUMS

**Crust:**
**1 c. brown sugar, firmly packed**
**½ c. butter**
**2 egg yolks, slightly beaten**
**Dash salt**
**1½ c. flour**
**2 t. baking powder**
**½ t. vanilla**

Cream sugar and butter; add egg yolks, salt and sifted dry ingredients. Blend in vanilla. Pat into 9 x 9 inch pan.

**Topping:**
**2 egg whites**
**1 c. brown sugar**
**½ t. vanilla**
**Dash salt**
**1 c. nuts**

**Yields 1 dozen 2 x 2 inch squares**

Beat egg whites until stiff; add brown sugar gradually. Stir in vanilla, salt and nuts. Spread over first mixture in pan and bake at 350 degrees about 28 minutes. Cool and cut into squares. Serve plain or with ice cream.

# GOOD FOR YOU FOODS

## HOMEMADE GRANOLA

2½ c. old fashioned rolled
  oats
1 c. shredded coconut
½ c. coarsely chopped
  almonds
½ c. sesame seeds
½ c. shelled sunflower
  seeds
½ c. unsweetened wheat
  germ
½ c. honey
¼ c. vegetable oil
½ c. chopped dried apricots
½ c. raisins

Yields 6½ cups

Combine oats, coconut, almonds, sesame seeds, sunflower seeds and wheat germ. Mix honey and oil together; stir into oat mixture. Spread out in 13 x 9 inch pan and bake at 300 degrees 45-50 minutes or until golden brown. Remove from oven; stir in apricots and raisins. Remove to another pan to cool. Stir occasionally to prevent lumping. Store in tightly covered jars or plastic bags. To store more than two weeks, seal in plastic bags and freeze.

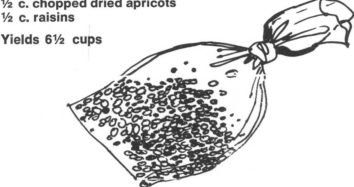

## APRICOT RAISIN GRANOLA

5 c. quick or old fashioned
  oats, uncooked
⅓ c. firmly packed brown
  sugar
½ c. wheat germ
⅓ c. vegetable oil
¼ c. honey
¼ t. almond extract
1 c. raisins
1 c. chopped dried apricots

Yields 8½ cups

Heat oats in ungreased 13 x 9 inch baking pan at 350 degrees 10 minutes. Combine oats, brown sugar and wheat germ. Add oil, honey, almond extract and fruit, mix until ingredients are well coated. Bake in ungreased 13 x 9 inch baking pan at 350 degrees 20-25 minutes, stirring frequently until brown. Cool. Stir until crumbly. Store in tightly covered container in refrigerator.

## PEANUTTY MOLASSES GRANOLA

**4 c. quick or old fashioned
oats**
**⅓ c. firmly packed brown
sugar**
**⅓ c. wheat germ**
**⅓ c. flaked or shredded
coconut**
**1 c. chopped peanuts**
**⅓ c. vegetable oil**
**¼ c. molasses**
**1 t. vanilla**

**Yields 6½ cups**

Heat oats in an ungreased baking pan at 350 degrees 10 minutes. Combine oats, brown sugar, wheat germ, coconut and peanuts. Add oil, molasses and vanilla; mix until dry ingredients are well coated. Bake in ungreased 13 x 9 inch baking pan at 350 degrees 20-25 minutes, stirring until brown. Cool. Store in tightly covered container in refrigerator.

YOGURT MAKER

## HOMEMADE YOGURT

**1 qt. milk, whole or skim**
**½ c. non-fat dry milk powder**
**¼ c. yogurt**

Combine milk and dry milk powder in small saucepan; bring to boil. Immediately remove from heat, and cool for about 15 minutes. Add a little lukewarm milk to plain yogurt starter and beat lightly with wire whisk. Add to remaining cool milk and beat briefly. Pour mixture into a deep casserole, cover with clean cloth and secure with a rubber band. Place in unlit oven for about 4½ hours, for a mild yogurt, longer for a tangier curd. After yogurt has fermented, chill before using. Save a small amount for use as a starter.

341

## BANANA ORANGE MUFFINS

1½ c. flour
½ c. sugar
3 t. baking powder
¼ t. salt
1 c. wheat germ (regular)
1 c. mashed bananas
  (2 small)
½ c. orange juice
¼ c. vegetable oil
2 eggs

**Yields about 18**

Sift together flour, sugar, baking powder and salt. Stir in wheat germ. Make a well in the center. In another bowl, combine banana, orange juice, oil and eggs. Add to flour mixture all at once. Stir enough to blend. Fill well greased muffin tins ¾ full. Bake at 400 degrees 20-25 minutes.

## BULGHUR PILAF

½ c. bulghur (cracked
  wheat)
2 c. water
3 T. butter or margarine
1 onion, finely chopped
1 c. chicken broth
¼ t. sage
Salt
⅛ t. summer savory
1 T. chopped parsley
1 c. fresh mushrooms

**Serves 4**

Rinse bulghur in cool water; drain. Place bulghur and water in saucepan. Bring to boil; simmer covered 40 minutes or until tender, adding more water if necessary. Spread out on baking sheet; dry in 200 degree oven, stirring as needed to dry evenly. Saute dried bulghur and onion in butter 5 minutes. Add broth, salt, savory sage and parsley. Cover tightly; simmer until water is absorbed, about 25 minutes. Saute mushrooms and add before serving.

## SESAME CHEESE BALLS

**1-3 oz. pkg. cream cheese**
**¼ c. crumbled blue cheese**
**¼ c. finely minced dried**
**beef**
**Dash cayenne pepper**
**¼ c. toasted sesame seeds**

**Yields about 10 to 12**

Blend cheese with dried beef and seasonings. Shape into small balls. Chill. Roll in toasted sesame seeds.

Toast in dry skillet until golden.

## CRANBERRY WHEAT GERM BREAD

**2 c. flour, sifted**
**1 c. sugar**
**2 t. baking powder**
**½ t. baking soda**
**1½ t. salt**
**1 c. raw cranberries, halved**
**½ c. chopped pecans**
**½ c. wheat germ**
**3 T. grated orange peel**
**1 egg, slightly beaten**
**½ c. orange juice**
**¼ c. warm water**
**2 T. vegetable oil**

Sift together flour, sugar, baking powder, baking soda and salt. Stir in cranberry halves, pecans, wheat germ and orange peel. Combine egg, orange juice, water and oil. Add to flour mixture; stir just enough to moisten ingredients. Spoon into greased loaf pan 9 x 5 x 3 inches. Bake at 350 degrees 50 to 60 minutes or until done. Cool in pan 5 minutes before removing; finish cooling on rack.

*Good served at a "coffee" or at breakfast.*

## CRUNCHY FRUIT NUGGETS

**1-6 oz. pkg. semi-sweet**
**chocolate bits**
**1-6 oz. pkg. butterscotch bits**
**2 c. Apricot Raisin Granola**
**(see index)**

Melt chocolate and butterscotch bits in top of double boiler until well blended. Stir in granola. Drop by teaspoon onto waxed paper. Chill until firm. Store in refrigerator.

## GRANOLA RICE STUFFING

1 small orange
1½ c. cooked rice
1 c. Homemade Granola
 (see index)
1 small apple
½ t. salt
¼ t. ground cinnamon
⅓ c. chopped celery
¼ c. chopped onion
2 T. butter or margarine
Orange juice

Peel and section orange over bowl, to catch juice; set juice aside. Chop orange sections (⅓ cup). Combine rice, Homemade Granola, apple (pared, chopped), orange, salt and cinnamon. Saute celery and onion in butter until tender; add to rice mixture; blend well (add orange juice if desired to moisten). Stuff lightly into Cornish hens or chicken.

## GRANOLA RIPPLE CAKE

1 pkg. white cake mix,
 2 layer
1-3¾ oz. pkg. instant
 butterscotch pudding mix
1 c. water
½ c. vegetable oil
4 eggs
2 c. Homemade Granola
 (see index)
Powdered sugar

Combine cake mix, pudding mix, water and oil. Beat on medium speed in electric mixer 2 minutes or until smooth. Add eggs one at a time, beating well after each addition. Pour ¾ batter into well greased 10 inch tube pan. Sprinkle granola onto batter; carefully add remaining batter on top. Bake at 350 degrees 50-55 minutes or until done. Cool 15 minutes in pan; remove. Cool. Sprinkle with powdered sugar.

## HIGH PROTEIN NECTAR

3 c. milk
2 T. honey
32 unbleached almonds

Serves 4

Blend until smooth. Pour into glasses and chill.

## MANGO BREAD

1¾ c. sugar
3 eggs
1 c. vegetable oil
2 c. flour
2 t. baking soda
2 t. cinnamon
½ t. salt
2 c. mango puree
1 t. vanilla
¼ c. walnuts
½ c. raisins
½ c. coconut

Cream sugar, eggs and oil. Sift dry ingredients; add to creamed mixture. Stir in mango puree, vanilla, nuts, raisins and coconut; blend well. Pour into two greased and floured loaf pans. Bake at 350 degrees 1 hour. Let stand 20 minutes before removing.

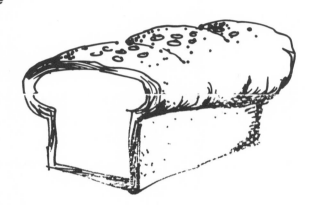

## NUT LOAF

3 T. butter
1½ c. chopped celery
1½ c. chopped onions
½ c. ground almonds
1 c. chopped walnuts
1 c. toasted cashews
2 T. rolled oats
¼ c. sesame seeds
2 T. sunflower seeds
1 lb. cottage cheese
½ c. cooked rice
2 t. salt, pepper
¼ t. herb blend for
  vegetables
3 eggs

Saute celery and onions in butter until tender. Combine remaining ingredients in a large bowl; add celery and onions. Blend together well. Pour into buttered loaf pan and bake at 400 degrees 1 hour.

*This is a wonderful substitute for meat.*

## OATMEAL DROP BISCUITS

1 c. flour
3 t. baking powder
½ t. salt
3 T. shortening
1 c. quick cooking rolled
 oats
1 egg, beaten
⅓ c. milk
2 T. honey

**Yields 10**

Blend flour, baking powder and salt. Cut in shortening until mixture resembles coarse meal. Stir in oats. Combine eggs, milk and honey; add all at once. Stir until blended. Drop by spoonfuls on greased baking sheet. Bake at 425 degrees 8-10 minutes.

## PEANUT BUTTER CAKE

2¼ c. sifted cake flour
3 t. baking powder
1 t. salt
1 t. ground ginger
½ t. ground cinnamon
¼ t. nutmeg
⅓ c. butter or margarine
½ c. creamy peanut butter
1½ c. sugar
2 eggs
1 c. mlik
1 t. grated orange rind
⅓ c. raisins, finely chopped
⅓ c. finely chopped prunes
⅓ c. chopped peanuts
1 recipe Seven Minute Icing,
 (see index)

Cream butter, peanut butter, sugar and eggs until fluffy. Sift dry ingredients. Add dry ingredients and milk alternately to creamed mixture. Stir in orange rind. Pour into two greased and floured 9 inch cake pans. Bake at 350 degrees 35-40 minutes. Remove and cool. Combine prunes, raisins and nuts. Mix 1 cup icing with prune mixture; spread between layers. Frost sides and top with remaining icing.

## PEANUT ICE CREAM PIE

1 t. butter or margarine
1½ c. Homemade Granola
 (see index)
1 qt. vanilla ice cream
½ c. crunchy peanut butter
1 c. whipped dessert topping
2 T. fudge sauce
Chopped peanuts

Serves 6 to 8

Using butter, generously grease bottom and sides of 9 inch pie pan. Sprinkle granola in bottom; bake at 375 degrees 5-6 minutes. While warm, press some granola up along sides of pie pan. Cool. Fold peanut butter into softened ice cream; fold in whipped topping. Spoon into crust. Freeze. Thin the fudge sauce and drizzle over top of pie. Freeze 5 hours. Remove 10 minutes before serving. Sprinkle top with chopped peanuts.

## PEANUTTY PEACH CRISP

4 c. canned peach slices,
 drained
⅓ c. sifted flour
½ c. firmly packed brown
 sugar
1½ c. Peanutty Molasses
 Granola (see index)
⅓ c. butter or margarine

Serves 6

Place peaches in greased 9 inch square baking pan. Combine flour, sugar and granola. Melt butter and add to flour mixture; mix until crumbly. Sprinkle over peaches. Bake at 350 degrees about 25 minutes. Serve warm with cream.

# BAKED SOY BEANS

1½ c. dried soy beans
4 c. water
¼ lb. salt pork, diced
¾ c. diced onion
2 T. dark molasses
1 T. dry mustard
1 T. prepared mustard
1 T. Worcestershire
½ c. beer
2 t. salt
2 T. brown sugar
3 drops Tabasco
1-8 oz. can tomato sauce

**Serves 6 to 8**

Bring beans in water to boil. Remove from heat; cover and let stand 1 hour. Place beans and liquid in 2 quart casserole dish. Add all ingredients (except tomato sauce). Bake covered at 300 degrees 3-4 hours or until beans are almost tender. Stir in tomato sauce and bake uncovered 2 hours or until tender. Add additional water if necessary. Best made the day before serving.

# SOYBEAN DIP

1 c. cooked cold soybeans
1½ T. chopped onion
2 T. tomato paste
2 T. chopped Greek olives
¼ c. toasted sesame seeds
2 T. chopped parsley

Mash beans. Stir in remaining ingredients. Mix and chill. Serve on oven toasted squares of whole wheat bread which have been spread with butter while hot.

# WHEAT GERM CORN BREAD

2 c. yellow cornmeal
1¾ c. flour
1¼ c. toasted wheat germ
½ c. sugar
1¾ t. salt
1 t. baking soda
2 c. buttermilk
½ c. oil
2 eggs, slightly beaten

**Yields 1 loaf**

In large bowl combine first 6 ingredients, blending well. In small bowl, beat buttermilk, oil and eggs. Stir egg mixture into flour mixture just until flour is moistened (batter will be lumpy). Quickly pour into a loaf pan, spreading evenly. Bake at 375 degrees 1 hour 10 minutes, or until toothpick comes out clean. Cool in pan 10 minutes; remove.

## WHEAT GERM MOLASSES SQUARES

**3 c. unsifted flour**
**½ c. sugared Honey Wheat Germ**
**1 t. baking powder**
**½ t. baking soda**
**2 t. cinnamon**
**¼ t. cloves**
**1 c. light molasses**
**½ c. sugar**
**4 T. butter or margarine**
**1 c. canned applesauce**
**1 egg, slightly beaten**
**1 c. raisins**
**½ c. chopped walnuts**

**Yields about 20**

Combine flour, wheat germ, baking powder, soda and spices; blend. Put molasses, sugar and butter in saucepan; cook until butter melts. Remove; stir in applesauce and egg. Add blended dry ingredients. Mix well. Stir in raisins and nuts. Spread in greased 13 x 9 inch pan. Bake at 350 degrees 35-40 minutes or until toothpick comes out clean. Serve warm with butter.

## YOGURT DIP

**1 c. yogurt (see index)**
**1 clove garlic, crushed**
**4 walnuts, crushed**
**1½ t. olive oil**
**1 t. lemon juice**
**1 cucumber, peeled, seeded, chopped**
**Salt and pepper**

Mix all ingredients together, chill and serve with assortment of raw vegetables (carrots, cauliflower, scallions, celery).

# YOGURT FRUIT DIP

**1-8 inch pie shell**
**1 c. yogurt (see index)**
**½ lb. small curd cottage**
  **cheese**
**1 t. vanilla**
**1 t. honey**
**1-10 oz. pkg. frozen**
  **blueberries or raspberries**
**2 t. brown sugar**

Whip together yogurt, cottage cheese, vanilla, honey. Line bottom of pie shell with fruit; top with yogurt mixture. Chill several hours. Sprinkle with brown sugar and serve with whipped cream on top.

# TURKISH YOGURT SOUP

**¼ c. pearl barley**
**4 c. chicken broth**
**2 T. butter**
**2 onions, finely chopped**
**2 t. chopped fresh coriander,**
  **or parsley**
**2 t. finely cut fresh mint**
**Salt and pepper to taste**
**2 c. yogurt (see index)**

Combine barley and broth in saucepan. Simmer until barley is done. Saute onion in butter until tender; add to broth. Stir in coriander, mint, seasonings and yogurt. Serve hot or cold.

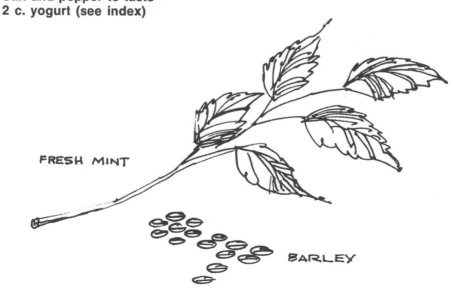

FRESH MINT

BARLEY

350

MEN'S COOKING

## MEN'S COOKING

There are many good cooks on the Suncoast and not all of them are women. Many a man here can turn out a delicious meal with just as much flourish as the women.

Our Suncoast men cooks come from all walks of life. They may be business men, members of the food service industry or professional men and they represent just about any part of the community.

In this part of Gourmet Gallery are some of the favorite recipes from some of the excellent men cooks in our area.

Mr. Frank Allen
Mr. Wilmot C. Arey
Dr. Russell C. Bane
Dr. Vance D. Bishop
Mr. John David Cowan
Mr. Robert Crisp
Mr. Raymond N. Fairfax
Mr. A. B. Fogarty
Dr. F. P. Fudge
Mr. Richard Hilburn
Mr. George R. Hoover, Jr.
Mr. Marvin A. Jackson
Mr. Rob Johnson
Mr. Thomas P. Johnson

Mr. Peter Kersker
Mr. William W.W. Knight
Mr. Leroy Lawson
Mr. George P. MacGregor
Mr. Morton D. May
Mr. John A. McNulty
Mr. Thomas S. Miller
Mr. Robert Montgomery, Jr.
Mr. Maurice Nichols
Mr. Angel P. Perez
Mr. Luther C. Pressley
Mr. Raymond W. Schuster
Mr. Herbert Smith
Mr. Edwin Lee White

# MEN'S COOKING

## CLAM DIP

1 clove garlic
8 oz. pkg. cream cheese
2 t. lemon juice
1½ t. Worcestershire sauce
½ t. salt
Dash of freshly ground
  pepper
7½ or 8 oz. minced clams,
  drained
¼ c. clam broth

Yield 1 pint

Peel and halve garlic clove; rub on interior of bowl. Leave cream cheese in bowl until it has reached room temperature. Cream with fork until smooth. Gradually add remaining ingredients, blending well.

If a thinner dip is desired, add additional clam broth. May be used with crackers or fresh vegetables.

## BAKED SOUP

1 can green pea soup
1 can turtle soup
Salt and pepper to taste
2 T. Sherry
2 T. sharp cheese to each
  cup
1 T. whipped cream to
  each cup

Serves 4

Mix soups with salt and pepper to taste; heat until very hot. Add Sherry and pour soup into ovenproof soup cups. Sprinkle grated cheese on top of each cup; top with whipped cream. Place under broiler until cheese melts a little.

## OLD FASHIONED BEAN SOUP

1 lb. navy beans
2 t. baking soda
Small piece of ham plus
  2 ham hocks
1 large onion, chopped
3 or 4 stalks celery, chopped
Salt and pepper

Soak beans overnight in water with 2 teaspoons baking soda added. Cut ham in 1 inch cubes; put in large kettle. Cover with water. Add hocks, chopped onions and celery; cook slowly 2 to 3 hours. Remove outer skin and bone from hocks. Drain beans and rinse in colander. Add beans to kettle; continue slow cooking until beans are tender, 2 hours or more. Add water as needed for soup consistency. Season to taste with salt and pepper. Leftovers may be frozen in plastic containers.

# RED SNAPPER SOUP

2 pts. fish stock*
¼ c. diced onions
½ c. diced celery
1 green pepper, diced
2 T. butter
1 pt. tomato and brown
  sauce**
1 c. diced red snapper
1 c. Sherry

Saute onions, celery and green pepper in butter; add fish stock and bring to boil. Add the tomato and brown sauce and bring to boil again. Stir in red snapper; cook until fish is tender (about 12 minutes). Just before serving, add Sherry.

*Fish stock
3 pts. water
1 c. dry white wine
1 med. onion stuck with
  cloves
6 peppercorns
½ bay leaf
1½ t. salt
2 sprigs parsley
1 carrot, cut in thin strips
Dash thyme

Put trimmings of the fish, bones, head and fins in large kettle; cover with water (3 pints). Add other ingredients; simmer 30 minutes. Strain.

**Tomato and brown sauce
3 T. flour
¼ lb. shortening
3 pts. beef stock
1 #2 can tomato puree

Yields 2 quarts

Brown flour in shortening. When light brown add beef stock and puree; cook 2½ hours. Can be stored in refrigerator in covered jar up to 1 week.

# SPINACH SALAD

1 large or 2 small bunches
  of fresh spinach
8 slices of bacon, diced
1 t. minced onions
2 t. red wine vinegar
2 T. dark brown sugar
2 dashes Worcestershire
1 T. Dijon mustard

Serves 4 to 6

Wash spinach and pat dry. At time of serving, have spinach at room temperature. Pan fry bacon; pour off grease and reserve. Put bacon chips aside. Return reserved grease to fry pan; when hot, add minced onions and bacon chips, stirring constantly. Allow onions to soften, but not brown. Add red wine vinegar, dark brown sugar, Worcestershire and Dijon mustard. Continue stirring until all ingredients are well combined and sugar has melted. Pour immediately over spinach in a very large bowl; toss and serve at once.

# SPANISH POTATO OMELET

3 med. potatoes, pared and
  sliced
1 c. olive oil
2 t. salt
1 small onion, finely
  chopped
3 eggs

Serves 2

Heat olive oil in heavy skillet until hot. Season potatoes with 1 teaspoon salt and put in pan. Stir until well covered with oil. Cook 8 minutes, turning occasionally; add onions. Cook until potatoes are brown; remove and drain. Take all but three tablespoons oil from skillet. Beat eggs with 1 teaspoon salt until frothy; add potatoes and onions. Pour all into hot skillet. Tilt skillet to distribute eggs. Cook until lightly brown on bottom. Hold dinner plate over skillet. Grasp skillet firmly and turn both over quickly to invert omelet and let it slide back into skillet to cook other side (3 minutes). Turn onto warm plate, fold over and tuck sides.

*This is a true Spanish omelet. Muy bueno!*

# BAKED STUFFED ONIONS

8 fairly large onions
4 T. butter
½ lb. sausage meat,
 crumbled
1¼ c. soft bread crumbs
⅓ c. milk
¼ c. chopped parsley
¼ t. thyme
Salt and pepper to taste
1 can beef bouillon
½ c. dry white wine

**Serves 8**

Scoop out the centers of onions, leaving a shell ⅛ to ¼ inches. Chop enough of centers to make 1½ cups. Blanch onion cases in boiling water 5 minutes; drain. In a skillet saute chopped onion in butter until it is tender. Add sausage meat and saute until it is no longer pink. Soak bread crumbs in milk and add; simmer 5 minutes, stirring constantly. Season with parsley, thyme, salt and pepper. Fill onion shells with stuffing. Arrange in buttered shallow pyrex dish just large enough to hold them. Pour in bouillon and wine. Bake at 350 degrees about 45 minutes, basting several times. Transfer onions to warm serving dish. Pour liquid into saucepan; reduce. Pour over onions and sprinkle with chopped parsley.

*You may wish to parboil the onions before scooping out centers; this makes it an easier task.*

# BURMESE RICE

3 c. cooked white rice
1 c. flaked coconut
1-6 oz. can sliced
 mushrooms
¼ c. butter
1 c. raisins
1 med. onion, thinly sliced
1-6 oz. pkg. blanched
 almonds
2 egg yolks, hard cooked

**Serves 8**

Combine coconut and rice. Saute mushrooms in butter; add raisins. When the raisins puff, add sliced onions and cook until tender. Push to one side; add almonds and brown. Blend with rice mixture; sprinkle chopped egg yolks over each serving.

*This may also be used as an entree by adding 2 cups of sliced cooked chicken.*

# BEEF BRACCIOLE

2½ lbs. bottom round
½ c. parsley, chopped
¾ lb. raisins
6 cloves garlic, chopped
2 T. olive oil
1 onion, chopped
1 lb. can whole tomatoes
Dash oregano
1 bay leaf
1 lb. green noodles, cooked
2 oz. Parmesan cheese,
  grated

**Serves 4 to 6**

Cut meat into 4 oz. steaks and pound between waxed paper until thin. Mix parsley, raisins and garlic; use as stuffing on each beef slice. Roll up each slice and tie with string. Brown rolls on all sides in olive oil. Place rolls in casserole. Saute onions; add tomatoes, oregano and bay leaf. Cook until tender; pour over beef rolls. Cover casserole and bake at 350 degrees 1 hour. Serve with green noodles and Parmesan cheese on top.

*This recipe comes from the New York Athletic Club.*

# LOT JU KAIN NGOW
# (SHANGHAI BEEF)

3 lbs. steak sliced very thin
4 green peppers sliced into
  rings
1⅓ c. oil
⅔ c. vinegar
1 c. Chinese soy sauce
1 T. oil
1 t. garlic powder
1 t. salt
2 t. sugar
2 t. onion powder
1 t. black pepper
2 T. soy sauce
3 t. cornstarch
1 T. cooking sherry
4 tomatoes, diced

**Serves 8**

In a large bowl, combine oil, vinegar and soy sauce. Mix well and marinate beef and peppers in this mixture an hour. Just before guests are due, heat up the tablespoon of oil in a heavy skillet.

Combine garlic powder, salt, sugar, onion powder, pepper and two tablespoons soy sauce. Mix in cornstarch and stir for two minutes. Add meat and green peppers.

Cook five minutes, stirring constantly; add sherry and tomatoes and cook three minutes. If the sauce seems to be disappearing, add some of the marinade.

# AREY'S ROLLED MEAT LOAF

**Group one:**
3 slices white bread minus
  crusts
½ c. water
1½ lbs. twice ground lean
  chuck
2 T. chopped parsley
  (or 1 T. dried)
1 clove garlic, minced
1 large egg, beaten
Salt and pepper to taste

**Group two:**
3 T. raisins
3 T. onion, chopped
1 T. juniper berries, chopped
2 T. pine nuts
2 T. grated Romano cheese
¼ lb. prosciutto, thinly
  sliced
Wax paper a little over a foot
  long
3 T. Spanish olive oil

**Group three:**
2 c. water
2 c. red wine
2-6 oz. cans tomato paste
½ t. basil
½ t. salt
Pepper to taste

Serves 4 to 6

Moisten bread in water; crumble. Add remaining ingredients in group one and mix well. Pat mixture onto wax paper in form of rectangle ½ inch thick (width of rectangle to fit dutch oven). Place ingredients in group two in layers on meat mixture. Starting at narrow end roll rectangle compactly, with aid of wax paper. Seal ends and seam with wet fingers. Wrap tightly in wax paper and place in refrigerator for at least 3 hours. Brown loaf in frying pan in olive oil and place in dutch oven. Add ingredients in group three to meat drippings. Mix well; simmer 15 minutes. Pour over meat roll; cover and simmer 1 hour. Remove meat to warm platter. Serve with noodles and the gravy.

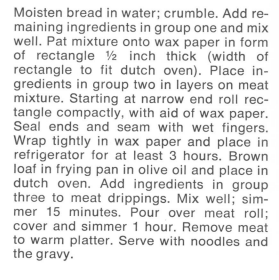

# SAUERBRATEN

4 lb. beef roast (rump is
  best)
2 c. vinegar
1 med. onion, thinly sliced
1 t. salt
½ t. pepper
3 bay leaves
4 whole cloves
½ c. water
2 T. honey
2 T. flour
4 T. small curd cottage
  cheese

Serves 6 to 8

Let roast soak 4 days in pickling solution of vinegar, onion, salt, pepper, bay leaves and cloves, turning once. Place roast in frying pan and brown lightly on all sides; transfer to roasting pan. Mix together one half of the pickling liquid, water and honey; pour into roasting pan. Roast, covered, 2½ to 3 hours at 350 degrees. Add water as necessary. Slice and place on serving platter. Make a gravy to go over meat as follows: Add flour to liquid in bottom of roasting pan; heat, stirring rapidly, until thickened. Add cottage cheese and stir until just dissolved. Pour over meat and serve immediately.

*Serve with parsley boiled potatoes and sauerkraut.*

# CHARCOAL BROILED STEAK

Estimate one pound per
  person; market weight
  Sirloin or Porterhouse cuts
  1½ to 2 inches thick
  preferred.

Steak: Buttered, broiled and
  then seasoned with butter,
  salt and pepper (optional).

One layer of red hot coals, with grill set approximately 5 inches above. Trim all fat from steak. Marinate in your favorite sauce (optional). Place in separate pieces of two to four pounds each on a grill approximately 5 inches from a full single tier of red hot briquets. Turn every three minutes until doneness desired, generally from 15 to 30 minutes, depending on the thickness and meat temperature at start. Test when you think ready by cutting and sampling. When about ready, butter and broil each side for a few seconds. Cut in quarter inch slices vertically or at an angle.

# CROCK POT BEEF STEW

2 lbs. stew beef
6 whole medium potatoes
6 carrots (or as many as
  you need)
1 c. chopped celery
6 whole small onions
1 can tomato soup
Salt and pepper

**Serves 6**

Put all ingredients in Crock pot. Cook at low temperature about 8 or 9 hours. Do not add water. This is good to put on before a day of shopping or when you will be away for a time. Can be served over rice or noodles.

# CALIFORNIA PORK CHOPS

6 loin or rib pork chops
  1 inch thick
Salt and pepper
¼ c. flour
Vegetable oil
2 oranges, peeled and sliced
5 T. brown sugar
2 t. cornstarch
½ c. chicken stock
1 c. orange juice
½ t. dried marjoram or ½ t.
  fresh, chopped
2 med. onions, sliced
2 T. chopped parsley

**Serves 6**

Season chops to taste; roll lightly in flour and brown well in hot oil. Arrange browned chops in large shallow casserole, preferably one that will enable you to crowd them in one layer. Sprinkle orange slices with 3 tablespoons brown sugar and let stand. Blend cornstarch with chicken stock, orange juice, marjoram, and rest of brown sugar; pour mixture over chops in casserole and arrange onions on top. Sprinkle onions with parsley; cover and bake at 350 degrees 1 hour. Arrange orange slices on top and bake 15 minutes more uncovered.

# COMPLETE MEAL

1 c. raw noodles
1 c. cooked pork, chopped
2 c. onions, chopped
2 c. celery, chopped
1 can tomato soup
⅓ c. water
¾ c. sharp cheese, grated
1 t. salt
1 t. pepper

**Serves 6**

Cook noodles until tender; drain. Brown meat in pan; add onions and celery. Cook 10 minutes. Add to drained noodles and other ingredients; mix well. Pour into 2 quart buttered casserole. Bake 45 minutes at 375 degrees. Leftovers remain tasty when re-heated.

# POULET A LA CREME
# (CHICKEN IN CREAM)

8 pieces chicken (broiler-
fryer)
3 T. butter (not margarine)
2 c. thinly sliced yellow
onions
½ t. salt
⅛ t. white pepper
¼ t. curry powder
½ c. dry white wine
3 c. whipping cream
Salt and pepper to taste
1 t. lemon juice
Fresh parsley

Serves 4 to 6

In a heavy skillet saute chicken in butter over medium heat 4 to 5 minutes. DO NOT BROWN. Remove chicken. Stir onions into skillet; cover and cook slowly 5 minutes. DO NOT BROWN. Return chicken to skillet; cook slowly 8 to 10 minutes. DO NOT BROWN. Turn once only. Add salt, pepper, curry powder and wine. Turn up heat and boil until most of liquid evaporates. Place 2½ cups whipping cream in small saucepan; bring to slow boil. Pour hot cream into skillet and simmer gently 25 to 30 minutes. Remove chicken to platter; keep warm. Ten minutes before serving, skim fat off sauce in skillet. Boil rapidly, stirring until sauce reduces, thickens, and will coat spoon. Add few drops lemon juice to taste and more salt and pepper, if needed. Smooth out sauce with rest of whipping cream. Place chicken in serving dish; pour sauce over, and garnish with parsley.

# CONNIE'S CASSEROLE

2 c. diced chicken (or
turkey)
1 c. cooked rice
1 c. diced celery
2 T. chopped onion
1 can water chestnuts,
thinly sliced
½ c. slivered almonds
1 c. sour cream
1 c. cream of chicken soup
undiluted
1 can chopped pimiento
Salt and pepper to taste
1 c. coarsely ground corn
flakes
¼ lb. melted butter or
margarine

Serves 4

Saute celery and onion in half of the melted butter. Combine and mix other ingredients except corn flakes, and turn into a casserole. Mix corn flakes with remaining butter and sprinkle on top. Bake 40 to 50 minutes in a 350 degree oven.

## FRUITED CHICKEN

2½ to 3 lbs. chicken pieces
¼ c. butter or margarine
1 T. cornstarch
1 t. dry mustard
⅛ t. ground ginger
⅛ t. cinnamon
½ t. salt
1 6 oz. can frozen orange
  juice
1 c. red currant jelly
Dash of Tabasco
1–1 lb. 3 oz. can sliced
  peaches
1–8¾ oz. can mandarin
  oranges
1–8¼ oz. can pineapple
  tidbits
1–16 oz. can dark cherries
Slivered almonds

Place chicken in greased baking dish. Melt butter and brush on chicken; bake at 350 degrees one hour, basting every 10 to 15 minutes. Drain peaches; save one cup of syrup. If more juice is needed add syrup from pineapple. Combine cornstarch, mustard, ginger, cinnamon and salt in a saucepan. Add syrup, a little at a time; heat over low heat. Blend in orange juice, jelly and Tabasco; cook, stirring constantly, until thickened. Spoon off all but about 2 tablespoons of chicken drippings. Pour ½ above mixture over chicken; bake at 375 degrees 15 minutes. Remove from oven; top with peaches, oranges, pineapple and cherries. Add remaining syrup mixture; bake 15 minutes at 375 degrees. Before serving, sprinkle slivered almonds (plain or toasted) over top.

# OLD TIME WILD DUCK RECIPE
## (ABOUT 1671)

With a few modern day seasonings added by the author.

Defrost ducks minimum 6 hours.

Use roasting pan with cover. Close steam vent. Pre-heat oven to 425 degrees. Wash ducks outside and cavity thoroughly with plain water.

Fill cavity with small chunks of whole orange, apple (including peel), onion, and celery. Cut chunks small enough to fill cavity with equal parts of orange, apple and onion. Sew cavity closed and tie legs together. Duck wings are unimportant and should be removed at the first joint before cooking.

Place ducks breast down in roasting pan. Fill roasting pan with mixture of ¾ parts water, ¼ part red cooking wine, touch of salt and ¾ level teaspoon of Accent per duck, plus left-over chopped chunks of orange, apple, onion and celery, should there be any.

Water level in pan should be brought almost to top of duck's back. Do not cover back. Have it barely out of water.

Cover with lid and place in oven one hour. Test with fork. Fork should enter breast easily. If not, replace in oven for additional 20 minutes. Re-test. If not ready, re-test at the end of an additional 20 minutes.

Remove from oven, turn oven to 325 degrees. Pour off all liquid except for about one inch in bottom of pan. Turn breasts up, sprinkle liberally with ground pepper and accent. Replace lid. Return ducks to oven 45 minutes. Remove lid and turn oven up to 400 degrees 15 to 20 minutes; baste liberally with remaining liquid. Remove.

Serve with wild rice and grape preserves. Red wine should be served to your taste — the drier, the better. Add whatever green vegetable or salad of your choice. A salad with Roquefort cheese dressing goes very well.

*Eat hearty!*

363

# SMOKED TURKEY

¾ c. butter, melted
8 oz. olive oil
4 garlic cloves, crushed
1 oz. liquid smoke
Salt and pepper
Hickory chips or shavings

**Temperatures per pound**

| | |
|---|---|
| 10 lbs. | 16-18 min. |
| 10-18 lbs. | 13-15 min. |
| Over 18 lbs. | 10-12 min. |

Select a turkey allowing approximately 1 pound per person. A self-basting butterball is preferred.

To prepare grill: Line coals along both sides of grill on the bottom, leaving center open. Start coals and let burn until white. Place hickory chips or shavings in container of water to soak. Once the smoke from starting the coals has cleared, place top on grill and let heat 10-15 minutes.

Take completely thawed turkey and wash thoroughly. Lock wings behind the back and tie legs and tail together securely. Combine melted butter with liquid smoke, olive oil and garlic. Rub turkey inside and out with this mixture; reserve remaining for basting. Salt and pepper turkey inside and out; place in aluminum baking pan. Place pan on grill over the open area; grill should be normal distance above the coals. Adjust vents to ¼-½ open. Once in the pan the turkey will not need turning. Replace lid on grill and begin timer. After ½ hour, use oil mixture to baste the bird. Also add a few hickory chips to coals. After this set the timer for every 20 minutes; baste with juices in the pan, and add a few hickory chips. About halfway through, you may need to add more coals, depending on the size of the bird. Allow turkey to cool 45 minutes before slicing.

*The smoke from the hickory chips tend to make the bird look browner on the outside than it is done on the inside. Cook well!!*

## CONNIE'S SEAFOOD CASSEROLE

½ c. butter
¼ c. flour
1 t. salt
¼ t. pepper
2 c. light cream
1 T. Worcestershire
⅓ c. catsup
3 T. lemon juice
3 T. dry white wine
1 pkg. frozen artichoke
  hearts, cooked
2 lbs. fresh shrimp, cooked
2-6 oz. cans crab meat,
  flaked
2 c. grated sharp cheese

**Serves 8**

Make sauce of first five ingredients over low heat. When desired consistency is reached, stir in Worcestershire, catsup, lemon juice and wine. Remove from heat and pour into baking dish. Stir in cooked and drained artichokes, peeled and deveined shrimp, crab meat and 1 cup cheese. Sprinkle remaining cheese on top; bake at 350 degrees 20 minutes.

## BOB'S SPECIAL SHRIMP

2½ lb. shrimp, raw,
  deveined
1 c. flour, seasoned with salt
  and pepper
½ lb. butter or margarine
3 cloves garlic, chopped
¼ c. chopped parsley
¼ c. chopped spring onions

**Sauce:**
Half bottle of catsup
Dash Tabasco (or more to
  taste)
2 T. Worcestershire
½ c. Sherry

**Serves 4 to 6**

Shake shrimp in paper bag with flour, salt and pepper until coated. Melt butter slowly in large shallow pan with garlic. Add shrimp in one layer on bottom of pan and cook slowly until lightly browned; turn shrimp over and cook until other side is browned. Sprinkle with onion and parsley and cook slowly 5 to 10 minutes. Add sauce.

Combine all ingredients; ladle sauce over shrimp in pan. Cook 15 minutes; stir well and serve.

## SHRIMP de JONGHE

3 lbs. fresh shrimp, cooked, peeled and deveined
1½ c. butter
6 cloves garlic, crushed
1½ c. dry breadcrumbs
¾ t. salt
¾ t. pepper
3 T. parsley, finely chopped or parsley flakes
4½ t. chives or onion leeks, finely chopped, including green
¾ t. Worcestershire
3 T. butter
Paprika to taste
½ c. Sherry

Serves 5 generously

Cream butter and crushed garlic. Mix 1 cup breadcrumbs, salt and pepper; blend with garlic butter. Add parsley, chives and Worcestershire sauce. Pat prepared butter into a long, narrow shape; wrap in waxed paper and refrigerate for one or two days. In skillet, over low heat, melt 3 tablespoons butter. Add shrimp; stir until well coated. Remove from skillet; place in casserole dish. Pour drippings from skillet over shrimp. Remove prepared butter from refrigerator and cut in ¼ inch slices. Place evenly over shrimp, sprinkle lightly with remaining bread crumbs and paprika; add Sherry. Bake at 400 degrees 20 to 25 minutes, or until crumbs are lightly browned.

## SHRIMP REMOULADE

½ c. olive or salad oil
1 t. salt
2½ T. paprika
¼ to ¾ t. cayenne
2 cloves garlic, minced
⅓ c. tarragon vinegar
⅓ c. horseradish mustard
2 T. catsup
½ c. chopped green onions and tops
3½ c. cooked, cleaned shrimp
Shredded lettuce

4 to 6 servings

Combine all ingredients except shrimp and lettuce. Cover and store in refrigerator several hours or overnight. Several hours before serving, add shrimp to sauce and chill thoroughly. Serve on bed of shredded lettuce.

# SOLE PAPRIKA

1½ lbs. filets of sole
Onion slices, paper thin
1 c. sour cream
1 T. flour
⅓ c. Sauterne, or other
  white wine
½ t. paprika
Salt and pepper to taste

Serves 4

Arrange filets in greased shallow baking dish; cover with onion slices. Pour mixture of sour cream, wine, flour and seasonings over filets. Bake in moderately hot oven, 375 degrees, about 25 minutes or until fish is tender.

# BAKED ALASKA (individuals)

6 ¾ inch thick slices pound
  cake
1 qt. vanilla ice cream
  (brick if possible)
3 egg whites
2 T. sugar
6-6-inch diameter aluminum
  foil discs

Serves 6

Place slices of pound cake on aluminum discs on cookie sheet. Place slices of ice cream on top of cake; put all into freezer until ready to serve. Beat egg whites and sugar until stiff. Pile on ice cream and cake, sealing well. Put into 500 degree oven long enough for meringue to brown (about 2 minutes).

# MACE CAKE

1 c. butter
3 c. sugar
5 eggs
3 c. flour
½ t. salt
1 c. buttermilk
1 t. vanilla
1 t. mace
⅓ t. soda in 1 T. hot water

16 servings

Have all ingredients at room temperature. Cream sugar and butter; add eggs, one at a time at medium speed, then slow speed. Sift flour and salt; add alternately with buttermilk, scraping sides often. Mix in seasonings, soda and water. Grease and flour tube pan; pour in batter and bake at 350 degrees 45-50 minutes. Rest upright until cake is cooled, then store.

*The flavor may be varied with almond flavoring.*

# BLACK WALNUT PIE

9 inch pie shell, unbaked
3 eggs
½ c. sugar
1 c. dark corn syrup
⅛ t. salt
1 t. vanilla
¼ c. melted butter
1 c. black walnut meats,
  broken

Serves 6 to 8

Beat eggs; add sugar, syrup, salt, vanilla and butter. Mix well. Spread nuts over bottom of raw pie shell and cover with mixture. Bake at 350 degrees 50 minutes.

# FRIED ICE CREAM SANDWICH

1 loaf-size pound cake
1 qt. brick chocolate ice
  cream
½ c. butter, melted

Serves 6

Cut pound cake in slices approximately ½ inch thick; brush melted butter on one side of cake. Place butter side down in hot frying pan, using two pieces of cake for each sandwich; brown. Slice brick chocolate ice cream into slices approximately ½ inch thick. When cake is browned, remove from pan; put slice of ice cream on one piece of cake. Top with second piece of cake to form sandwich — with browned sides on the outside. Serve immediately while outside is still hot and inside is cold and not melted. Pound cake that is not too porous is recommended.

It is suggested that brick ice cream be sliced in advance, separated with wax paper and returned to freezer until ready for use.

# IRISH COFFEE

1 c. hot and very strong
  coffee, depending on taste
¾ oz. Irish whiskey
½ oz. Kahlua
Whipped cream

Serves 1

Warm Irish coffee mugs; pour coffee up to ⅔ of the mug. Add whiskey and Kahlua. Top with whipped cream.

# BISHOP'S BARBEQUE SAUCE

½ c. onion, finely chopped
¼ c. salad oil
3 cloves garlic, crushed
1 c. catsup
2 T. Worcestershire sauce
¼ c. dry red wine
1 t. prepared mustard
¼ c. lemon juice
Few drops Tabasco sauce

Makes about 2¼ cups

In saucepan, simmer onion and garlic in oil 5-10 minutes. Add remaining ingredients and cook 10 minutes over low heat. Pour in a glass jar, cover and keep in refrigerator until ready to use.

# OCALA FOREST BARBECUE SAUCE

2 c. vegetable oil
1-28 oz. bottle catsup
6-8 oz. jar mustard
2 T. salt
1½ t. black pepper
1 c. vinegar
2 lbs. sugar

Makes 3 quarts

Blend all ingredients except sugar. Heat in pan; stir in sugar. Cook until sugar melts and does not feel gritty. **Do not boil.**

# BISHOP'S STEAK MARINADE

1 c. salad oil
½ c. dry red wine or Sherry
6 cloves garlic, crushed
2 t. salt
2 t. peppercorns, crushed
2 t. dry mustard
2 t. Worcestershire sauce
2 t. hickory smoke salt
½ t. Accent
4 T. Kitchen Bouquet
½ t. Season-all
¼ c. green onions, cut up
   fine

**Makes about 2 cups**

Combine all ingredients in a covered glass jar and keep in the refrigerator. Have steak at room temperature; pour marinade over it and let it stand about two hours before broiling.

## SESAME SEED DRESSING
## FOR FRESH SPINACH SALAD

1 T. peanut oil
4 T. sesame seeds
4 T. sugar
4 T. vinegar
1 T. soy sauce
3 slices bacon, crumbled

Heat oil in skillet; add sesame seeds and brown evenly. Use low heat as seeds can burn quickly. Remove from heat and add sugar, vinegar, soy sauce and stir.

Wash spinach. Wrap in toweling and place in refrigerator to crisp. To serve, heat sauce quickly and toss with cold spinach then sprinkle with bacon.

**Serves 4**

This is enough dressing for about 1 pound spinach.

## ALL CHILDREN'S HOSPITAL CHARITY BALL

*Ah, the cocktail party! St. Petersburg hostesses really outdo themselves each year for the pre-Charity Ball parties, most of which take place right on the dance scene at the city's Coliseum.*

*The following menu and recipes were submitted by these participating hosts and hostesses:*

> Mr. and Mrs. Robert A. Buenzli
> Mrs. Lowell Barnes
> Mr. and Mrs. Thomas M. Harris
> Mr. and Mrs. Richard Hilburn
> Mr. and Mrs. Thomas P. Johnson

Smoked Turkey
7-Up Glazed Ham and Pork Roast served with Barbecue Sauce
Swedish Meat Balls    Curry Dip    Cucumber Sandwiches    Crab Salad
Chicken Livers in Chafing Dish  Cheese Balls, Salmon Balls, Sausage Balls
Onion Dip    Alaskan King Crab    Cream Cheese and Chutney
Guacamole Dip    Benedictine Sandwiches    Cherry Tomato Delights

## CHARITY BALL CRAB DIP

1 lb. King crabmeat,
  shredded
1 c. celery hearts, finely
  chopped
6 eggs, hard boiled and
  grated
1 c. stuffed olives, sliced
Salt to taste
Lemon juice to taste
Tabasco to taste
½ c. mayonnaise

**Serves 25**

Combine ingredients; add seasonings. Stir in mayonnaise. Chill. Serve with crackers.

*When using fresh crabs (you may just catch them right off the dock in the back yard), measure mayonnaise carefully. Use only enough to moisten.*

## CHARITY BALL CURRY DIP

1 c. mayonnaise
1 T. curry powder
1 T. Worcestershire
1 T. prepared horseradish
1 lemon, juiced
Raw vegetables:
  radish roses, carrot curls,
  cauliflower, squash, celery

Serves 25

Blend together and serve as dip for raw vegetables.

## PARTY CHICKEN LIVERS

4 lbs. chicken livers (if large, split)
Salt
Pepper
Flour
1 c. butter or margarine
4 T. grated onion
3 T. parsley, finely cut
  fresh or dehydrated
½ c. dry Sherry

Salt and pepper each liver; dust with flour. Place in single layer in broiler pan. In skillet saute onions in butter or margarine. Pour over livers. Place in 375 degree oven; bake 10 minutes. Mix Sherry with parsley; drizzle over livers. Bake until almost dry. Serve on tooth picks. These are best when kept warm in chafing dish.

## CHERRY TOMATOES DELIGHT

3 boxes cherry tomatoes
2 cans crabmeat
Mayonnaise
Salt
Parsley

Cut stem end off tomatoes; scoop out seeds. Mix crabmeat, mayonnaise and salt together; fill tomatoes. Serve on a platter with parsley sprigs.

## CHARITY BALL FROSTY YULE LOG

**8 ozs. cream cheese**
**Milk**
**1 pkg. onion or garlic olive**
**dip mix**
**2-4¼ oz. cans deviled ham**
**Chopped nuts**
**Pimiento**

Soften cream cheese with milk. Spread enough of cream cheese mixture to form a strip 3 x 6 inches on serving plate. Reserve remaining cream cheese. Combine dip mix and deviled ham. Form into a 6 inch long roll. Place on cheese strip. Frost with remaining cream cheese. Cover with chopped nuts and garnish with pimiento.

# SPANISH DINNER
## Dr. and Mrs. Vance D. Bishop

*Although the Vance Bishop home is typically Southern Colonial, they entertain in a true Spanish manner. Isabel has a Spanish background and Vance a Southern one, and they prove that Southern and Spanish hospitality do blend beautifully. Dinner parties begin in the family room, progress to the dining room and end in the formal living room.*

Served in Family Room:   Choice of:   Daiquiri, Rum Manhattan
Margarita, Pina Colada (see index)
Mixed Drinks

                            Appetizer:   Fritas de Bacalao

                            Choice of:   Cucumber Soup (served cold) or
Peanut Soup (served hot)
Served in small mugs before sitting
down to dinner.

Served in Dining Room:   Carne Mechada or Pollo a la Andaluza
Tossed Green Salad
Arroz con Gandules
Herb Bread
Bienmesabe

Choice of Wines:   Marques de Riscal           Mateus
Bodegas Bilbainas

Served in Living Room:   Coffee or Demitasse
Felipe II Brandy

Harvey's Bristol Cream Sherry, Liqueurs

# DAIQUIRI

½ lime or lemon, juiced
1 t. sugar
1½ ozs. light rum

Serves 1

Blend ingredients. Put in shaker with cracked ice and shake until shaker frosts. Strain into cocktail glass.

# RUM MANHATTAN

1½ ozs. rum
1 T. Sweet Vermouth
Cherry
Lemon or orange twist

Serves 1

Blend well; pour over cracked ice. Stir and strain into cocktail glass or over ice. Add cherry. Garnish with lemon or orange twist.

# FRITAS DE BACALAO

½ lb. dried salted filet of
  codfish
1½ c. sifted flour
¾ t. salt
1 t. baking powder
1½ c. water
1 large clove garlic, crushed
4 peppercorns
Vegetable oil

Wash codfish; bring to boil in enough water to cover. Drain. Wash in cool water 2-3 times. Remove skin and bones. Shred. Soak in water 1 hour to remove excess salt. In saucepan, combine flour, salt and baking powder; stir in water. Pound garlic and peppercorns in a mortar; add flour mixture. Drain codfish well; add, blending well. Drop batter by teaspoonfuls into hot oil and fry until golden brown. Remove and drain on absorbent paper. Serve hot.

# PEANUT SOUP
## Hotel Rorarica, Surinam, South America

4 c. water
1 small fryer, cut up
2 ozs. cured ham
1 large onion, chopped
1 stalk celery, chopped
1 clove garlic, mashed in
  mortar
Salt and pepper to taste
¾ c. creamy peanut butter
Tabasco

Serves 6

Put first seven ingredients in saucepan; bring to boil. Cook until meat is tender. Pour broth into heavy pan. Cool. Skim off fat. Blend peanut butter in slowly, stirring constantly until mixture is smooth. Bring to boil. Season with Tabasco. Serve hot.

# CARNE MECHADA
## (Stuffed Eye-Round Roast)

1 med. onion
1 green pepper, seeded
1 T. capers
6 green olives, pitted
2 ozs. salt pork
2 ozs. cured ham
½ Chorizo (Spanish
  sausage)
1 T. oregano
1 T. Spanish olive oil
1 T. red wine vinegar
4 lb. eye of round roast
4 T. Spanish olive oil
6 c. water
1 T. salt
1 large tomato, peeled,
  seeded, chopped
1 large onion, chopped
½ green pepper, chopped
3 leaves fresh coriander or
  parsley (1 T.)
1 large clove garlic, mashed
½ c. red cooking wine
12 small new potatoes,
  peeled
½ c. tomato sauce
Parsley to garnish

Serves about 6

Put first 7 ingredients through food chopper. Mix well with next three ingredients. Remove skin and fat from beef; wipe with damp cloth. With sharp, slender knife, make several deep cuts almost through meat. Stuff with ham mixture, forcing filling in with fingers. Heat 4 tablespoons Spanish olive oil in heavy pan; sear meat on all sides. Brown slowly for about 10 minutes. Add next 8 ingredients. Cover; cook over medium heat 1½ hours, basting and turning occasionally. Skim excess fat from top of sauce. Add last ingredients. Cook uncovered over high heat until sauce thickens and potatoes are done. Remove roast. Cool. Slice into thick slices. Place in serving platter in form of whole roast. Surround with potatoes; garnish with parsley. Strain hot sauce into gravy boat and serve with meat.

# POLLO A LA ANDALUZA
## La Zaragozana Restaurant, San Juan, P. R.

3 large cloves garlic
½ c. chopped parsley
Salt
3 ozs. orange jucie
6 chicken breasts, boned
1 c. flour
1 c. Spanish olive oil
¾ lb. butter or margarine
6 oz. Spanish Manzanilla
  wine (dry Sherry)
6 T. raisins
6 T. slivered almonds
1 c. small Spanish olives,
  pitted

Serves 6

Soak raisins in Spanish Manzanilla two hours; remove and set aside, reserving wine. In mortar, crush garlic and parsley. Add salt and orange juice; mix well. Spread mixture over chicken; pound in with edge of saucer. Coat chicken with flour. Fry in hot olive oil until brown; remove. Pour oil from pan; add butter and Spanish Manzanilla; heat. Add raisins, almonds, olives and chicken. Cook over low heat 15 minutes.

# ARROZ CON GANDULES (PIGEON PEAS)

1 lb. lean pork
3 T. pork fat
2 ozs. cured ham
2 ozs. salt pork
1 large onion, chopped
½ t. capers
2 bay leaves
6 green olives, pitted,
  chopped
1 green pepper, seeded,
  chopped
1 leaf fresh coriander (may
  substitute 1 T. chopped
  parsley)
½ t. oregano
2 large cloves garlic,
  mashed
½ c. tomato sauce
¼ c. dry white wine
1 lb. gandules (pigeon peas)
1½ c. rice, washed
3 c. water
Salt to taste

Serves about 6

In heavy pan, fry pork over medium heat until well done; cut into ¾ inch cubes. Remove from pan; set aside. Pour pork fat into bowl; measure 3 tablespoons and return this to pan. Add ham, salt pork, onion, capers, bay leaves, olives, green peppers, coriander, oregano and garlic. Saute a few minutes. Add pigeon peas and their water; bring to boil. Cook for a few minutes. Add rice; mix well. Add water, salt and pork cubes. Bring to boil. Cook uncovered 20 minutes over moderate heat. Lower heat; cover and cook until dry. Turn and lift mixture with a large spoon (do not stir). Cover again and continue cooking until rice is tender.

## HERB BREAD

1 large loaf French, Cuban
  or Italian bread
¼ lb. butter or margarine
3 large cloves garlic
¼ t. each: dill weed,
  rosemary leaves,
  seasoned-salt,
  oregano
  Parsley flakes

Serves about 6

Crush garlic in mortar; add to butter; blend well. Cut bread into ¾ inch slices on a slant. Coat both sides with butter mixture. Place in center of large piece of aluminum foil and reshape slices into loaf shape. Cover top of crust with remaining butter. Sprinkle remaining ingredients over top. Wrap in foil. Warm in 350 degree oven 15-20 minutes. Serve hot.

## BIENMESABE

1 c. coconut milk
1½ c. sugar
3 egg yolks, beaten
6 T. grated coconut
3 inch stick cinnamon
1 8-inch sponge cake
2 egg whites
2 T. sugar

Serves 6

Combine coconut milk and sugar; heat to boiling without stirring; reduce heat. Cook 8-10 minutes or until thin syrup forms. Cool. Mix in egg yolks gradually; add cinnamon stick. Cook in top of double boiler over rapidly boiling water until custard is slightly thickened (don't over cook). Cool. Remove cinnamon stick. Cut cake into 6 squares; arrange in serving plates. Pour custard over cake. Beat egg whites until stiff; add sugar, beating well. Spoon meringue over each serving.

*You may want to brown the meringues before serving.*

379

# CHRISTMAS BELLES COFFEE

*One of the most anticipated events of a party-filled Christmas calendar in St. Petersburg is this coffee, given at a home of one of the members of the Christmas Belles, to benefit the Christmas Toy Shop. The annual membership gives an enriched Christmas to over 5,000 children in South Pinellas County. Current Hostess Belles are:*

| | | |
|---|---|---|
| *Mrs. Uphom Allen* | *Mrs. William Futch* | *Mrs. Ben Reed* |
| *Mrs. George Brussel* | *Mrs. Francis H. Langley* | *Mrs. Hubert Rutland, Jr.* |
| *Mrs. F. Joseph Burns* | *Mrs. E. H. McIntyre* | *Mrs. Robert Speakman* |
| *Mrs. Henry Douglas* | *Mrs. J. Curtis Merkel* | *Mrs. Rodney Waterman* |
| *Mrs. Joseph W. Fleece* | *Mrs. Steven Puffer* | *Mrs. J. Dean White* |

| | | |
|---|---|---|
| Tuna Quiche | | Shrimp Aux Belles |
| | Hot Sour Cream Deviled Eggs in Cheddar | |
| | Cheese Sauce | |
| Cheese Straws | Anise Wafers | Vanilla Horns |
| Meringues | Candied Strawberries | Date Tarts |
| Apricot Balls | Christmas Cookies | Brandy Balls |
| | Assorted Finger Sandwiches | |
| Buttermints | Marsipan Fruit | Fudge |
| Champagne Punch | | Coffee |

## BELLES DEVILED EGG CASSEROLE

**12 large eggs, hard boiled**
**4 t. prepared mustard**
**6 T. sour cream**
**½ t. salt**
**½ t. white pepper**
**4 T. margarine**
**1 c. chopped green pepper**
**⅔ c. chopped onion**
**½ c. chopped pimiento**
**1½ c. sour cream**
**2-10½ oz. cans mushroom**
**soup**
**1 c. shredded cheddar**
**cheese**

**Serves 6 to 8 for luncheon**
**24 for buffet**

Halve eggs lengthwise; remove yolks. Blend yolks, mustard, sour cream, salt and pepper. Fill whites.

In large skillet melt margarine. Saute onions and green pepper until tender. Remove from heat; stir in pimiento, soup and sour cream. Pour half of mixture in flat 3 quart baking dish. Arrange eggs, stuffed side up, in single layer lengthwise. Spoon remaining sauce over top. (This may seem thick and scant but sauce will thin out when heated). Sprinkle cheese over top. Bake at 350 degrees 20 minutes or until heated through.

*Casserole may be assembled in advance and refrigerated. Do not over heat or keep warm too long as whites will become tough and rubbery.*

# BELLES TUNA QUICHE

9 inch partially baked pie
  shell *
2 eggs, beaten
1 c. half and half cream
1 T. minced onion
1 t. Dijon mustard
¾ t. salt
Dash cayenne
1-7 oz. can white tuna, flaked
1½ c. shredded Swiss
  cheese
1 T. flour
Nutmeg

Beat together eggs, cream, mustard, salt and cayenne. In separate bowl, combine tuna, cheese and flour. Sprinkle this evenly in pie shell. Pour cream mixture over tuna cheese mixture. Sprinkle lightly with nutmeg. Bake at 325 degrees 50 minutes or until set. Cool 10 minutes before cutting.

* Prick sides and bottom of shell and bake at 450 degrees for 8 to 10 minutes.

# SHRIMP AUX BELLES

3 lbs. frozen shrimp
4 qts. water
1 clove garlic
1 t. cayenne
½ c. celery tops
½ c. chopped celery
6 peppercorns
3 eggs, hard boiled, diced
½ c. butter
½ c. flour
1½ t. salt
1 t. white pepper
1-5½ oz. can evaporated
  milk
1¾ c. milk
⅔ c. finely minced apple
6 t. lemon juice
1 T. curry powder
1 can pitted black olives,
  thinly sliced lengthwise
6 T. dry Sherry

Drop thawed shrimp in boiling water; add next 6 ingredients. Simmer 10 minutes. Cool in broth. Peel and devein. Cut into pieces. In top of double boiler, melt butter, blend in flour, salt, pepper, curry powder and both milks. When mixture thickens add apple, shrimp, eggs, lemon juice and olives. Warm thoroughly, add Sherry.

# STONE CRAB DINNER
## Dr. and Mrs. Charles Donegan

*Most of us consider ourselves very lucky to be living in Florida and never more so than during the stone crab season. A stone crab dinner is a very special occasion. The crab claws can be bought already cooked at local stores (fishermen only remove one claw from the crab before returning it to the water to grow another). Many Suncoast hostesses serve typical stone crab claw dinners and invite their fortunate friends to share this wonderful delicacy.*

**DINNER FOR SIX**

Stone Crab Claws
Tossed Salad
with
Italian Dressing
Fresh Fruit

*Dry White Wine      Pouilly Fuisse      Samillon or French Colombard*

*Cover table with newspapers. Make a centerpiece using stones, shells, small plants in individual pots and driftwood. Pass large lemon scented napkins before dessert.*

**10 lbs. cooked crab claws**
**1 lb. melted butter**
**6 lemons, juiced**

Break claws with hammer. Pile high on serving platter. Blend butter and lemon juice and pour into individual pots. Put pots on each plate. Serve each person claw crackers and picks.

# FOGARTY STONE CRAB DINNER
## Mr. and Mrs. A.B. Fogarty

Stone Crabs
Lemon Butter Cups
Pappas Famous Greek Salad (see index)
Buttered Cuban or French Bread
Key Lime Pie (see index)

Wine                    Beer                    Coffee

Tables are set around the pool with mats and napkins featuring a crab motif. Each guest is given a long apron to wear so they can relax and dig in.

# MUSEUM GARDEN PARTY

ιe curved Palladian facade of the Museum of Fine Arts has been compared to ιrms extending a gracious welcome."

s one enters the Great Hall, this impression increases. Volunteers in the Museum ιhop smile as they greet members. They tell of the current exhibition, the scheduled ιcture, film and musical presentations, and at which hour the Docents conduct ιurs through the flower bedecked galleries.

ιe membership garden pictured on the cover is the setting for special parties and r afternoon tea, served to members and their guests by volunteers who have ιund the following menu to be ever welcome:

Champagne      Iced Fruit Punch

Assorted Sandwiches

Coconut-Apricot Balls

Mints      Salted Nuts

## COCONUT-APRICOT BALLS

1 ½ c. dried apricots, ground
2 c. coconut flakes
⅔ c. sweetened condensed milk
Powdered sugar

Yields about 32

Combine apricots and coconut; add condensed milk. Blend well. Shape into small balls. Roll in powdered sugar. Let stand until firm.

Receptions for members are held in the beautiful courtyard garden or in the spacious Marly Room. Undoubtedly, the climax of the welcome spirit comes at Christmas time when Museum members greet every person in the community who wishes to come. A majestic green wreath hangs above the portico. A tremendous tree dominates the Great Hall, and the crystal chandeliers of the Marly Room shed their sparkling light on the lace and linen banquet cloths, the silver epergnes filled with fruit or flowers, the silver punch bowls and salvers that hold the array of delectible gourmet specialties.

Instant Spiced Tea (see index)      Iced Fruit Punch

Cheese Log with Assorted Crackers

Stuffed Dates      Fruit Cake

Cucumber Sandwiches      Cream Cheese and Strawberry Sandwiches

Brownies (see index)

# CHEESE LOG

5 lbs. sharp cheddar cheese
3 large jars pimientos
1 c. mayonnaise
Dash salt, Mexi-pepper or
  Tabasco
Chopped pecans

Grate cheese. In blender, chop pimient
and their juice and seasonings. A
cheese; blend well. Shape into a roll; r
in chopped pecans. Chill. Serve wi
crackers.

# CUCUMBER SANDWICHES

Cucumber
Melba thin bread, crusts
  removed
Mayonnaise
Salt and pepper

Slice cucumber into thin slices; soak i
salted ice water (with ice cubes) 30 mir
utes. Drain and dry. Spread bread wit
mayonnaise. Add cucumbers; season
Top with bread slice. Cut in triangles o
finger sandwiches.

# CREAM CHEESE AND STRAWBERRY SANDWICHES

Bread
Mayonnaise
Cream cheese
Milk
Strawberries, halved

Cut bread slices into rounds with biscuit
cutter. Mix cheese with enough milk to
make of spreading consistency. Spread
bread with mayonnaise then cream
cheese. Top with strawberry halves.

# PRESTON'S FORMAL CHINESE BANQUET

*A formal Chinese meal usually consists of from eight to twelve courses. It is customary to offer dishes differing from one another. For example, if the beef dish is stir-fried, the egg rolls are deep fried, the pork is braised and the other dishes steamed or served with cornstarch-thickened sauce. An informal Chinese meal may be served using only four of the dishes offered here: appetizer, cold dish, sauteed or fried dish, steamed or braised dish. Rice is always served. For frequent entertaining, Judy and Evan Preston find that their all-time favorite, and biggest hit with their guests, is this beautiful selection of Chinese food.*

Soy-colored eggs
Sweet corn and chicken soup
Spring roll-egg roll
Szechwan peppercorn chicken
Stir-fried shrimp with pea pods and water chestnuts
Beef with black bean sauce, tomatoes and onions
Red-cooked pork with braised bamboo shoots
Orange-spiced duck
Broccoli with water chestnuts

## SPRING ROLL - EGG ROLL

½ lb. egg roll wrapper, about 8 sheets
½ lb. ground fresh pork
½ c. bamboo shoots, shredded
¼ c. Chinese mushrooms, shredded
2 T. dry tree-ears, shredded
4 oz. bean sprouts
1 scallion, shredded
2 T. dry Sherry
2 T. soy sauce
1 t. sugar
½ t. salt
Oil for deep frying

Filling: Stir-fry pork in oil 2 minutes. Add mushrooms, scallion, bamboo shoots and tree-ears. Mix and cook for a minute. Add Sherry, soy sauce, salt and sugar. Mix well. Cook three minutes over medium flame. Add bean sprouts. Mix well and place in bowl. Cool thoroughly before using.

Assembly: Place about 3 tablespoons of filling mixture on center of wrapper, holding the ingredients together. Take piece of wrapper nearest you and fold over filling. Brush edges of skin with beaten egg. Fold both sides toward center, then roll close and tight. The size should be about 1½ inches in diameter — 4 inches long. Deep fry in oil at 375 degrees until golden brown.

385

# PLUM SAUCE DIP

½ c. Chinese plum sauce
½ c. peach preserve
½ c. apricot preserve
½ c. apple sauce
2 T. chili sauce
1 t. dry mustard
¼ t. garlic powder

Mix all ingredients and use as dip for egg rolls.

# SZECHWAN PEPPERCORN CHICKEN

2 whole chicken breasts
2 slices fresh ginger root
1 stalk scallion
4 c. lettuce shreds

Wash and clean chicken breasts. Boil 2 quarts water in sauce pan with ginger and scallion. Add chicken breasts and bring to boil. Cover, boil 15 minutes. Turn flame off and cool chicken in same water. Skin and bone chicken. Pull meat apart into coarse shreds.

## SAUCE "A"

3 T. peanut oil
3 T. chopped scallion
½ t. minced ginger
1 t. Szechwan peppercorn, crushed
¼ t. crushed chili pepper (or fresh hot pepper)

Mix sauce "B". Heat sauce "A" to boiling. Add "B" to "A". Mix lettuce with chicken and then pour sauce over chicken just before serving. Mix well and serve.

## SAUCE "B"

2 T. soy sauce
1 t. Hoisin sauce
1 T. Karo
2 cloves garlic, minced

# STIR-FRIED SHRIMP WITH PEA PODS
# AND WATER CHESTNUTS

1 lb. shrimp
1 T. cornstarch
2 T. Sherry
1 t. salt
½ lb. water chestnuts
½ lb. pea pods
1 clove garlic
2 slices fresh ginger root
1 T. cornstarch
2 T. water
3½ T. oil
¾ c. stock
1 scallion

Shell and devein shrimp. Split each shrimp and flatten. Combine 1 tablespoon cornstarch, Sherry and salt with ½ egg white; add to shrimp and toss to coat. Peel and slice water chestnuts. Remove strings from pea pods. Crush garlic. Mince ginger root and chop scallion. Blend remaining 1 tablespoon cornstarch and cold water to paste.

Heat oil (2 tablespoons). Add garlic, ginger and scallion. Stir-fry ½ minute. Add shrimp and stir-fry until pink (2-3 minutes). Remove from pan and place in serving dish. Heat 1½ tablespoon oil. Add water chestnuts and pea pods and stir-fry briefly to coat with oil. Pour in stock and heat quickly. Then cook covered over medium heat until nearly done (2 minutes). Return shrimp, stir-fry to reheat then stir in cornstarch paste to thicken. Serve at once.

## BEEF WITH BLACK BEAN SAUCE,
## TOMATOES AND ONIONS

1 lb. beef (sirloin or flank)
¾ c. yellow onions, sliced
  thin
¼ c. scallions, shredded
1 c. very ripe, fresh
  tomatoes, diced
2 T. black beans, minced
2 slices fresh ginger root
2 cloves garlic, minced
½ egg white
2 t. cornstarch
4 T. Sherry
2 t. light soy sauce
1 T. dark soy sauce
3 T. oil
1 t. sugar

FRESH
GINGER ROOT

Slice beef against the grain about ⅜ inch thick. Mix 1 tablespoon Sherry, 2 teaspoons light soy sauce, 1 teaspoon sugar, 1 teaspoon cornstarch and egg white with beef and refrigerate at least ½ hour.

Mince together black beans, garlic and ginger root.
Slice onions, shred scallions, dice tomatoes.
Mix 1 tablespoon dark soy sauce with 3 tablespoons Sherry and 1 teaspoon cornstarch. Place wok over high heat and add 2 tablespoons oil. When oil is hot, add black beans, ginger and garlic. Stir-fry a few seconds. Add beef mixture and stir-fry over high heat until beef has browned well (about 2-3 minutes). Set beef aside. Wash wok and return to high heat. Stir-fry onions and scallions in 1 tablespoon oil one or two minutes. Add tomatoes and stir-fry another minute.
Add cornstarch-soy sauce mixture and stir-fry over high heat until mixture thickens slightly. Add beef mixture and stir to blend flavors. Dish and serve immediately.

# RUTLAND RANCH WILD GAME DINNER

*The Rutland Dove Shoot is the St. Petersburg hunter's idea of truly good hunting; and the dinner served following it when wives join the hunters at the big Manatee County Ranch has to be the gourmet's idea of truly good eating. While the game is brought up from the fields and the hunters clean up, guests arrive and socialize over cocktails on the green lawn, contemplating the feast. It is a variety of game and Florida-keyed dishes that Ruth Rutland has collected and embellished over the years, adding a new dish or two each year.*

| | | | |
|---|---|---|---|
| Smoked Oyster Dip | Bolo Crabmeat | Chutney Dip | Chicken Wings |
| | Swamp Cabbage Slaw | | |
| Dove and Quail | Wild Turkey | Wild Boar | Manatee Duck |
| Turnip Greens | Hubert's Grits | Pea Pods and Pearl Onions | |
| Cornbread | | | Biscuits |
| Wine | Fruit | | Brandy |

## BOLO CRABMEAT

1 lb. crabmeat
1 cucumber, seeded and
  shredded
¼ c. chopped parsley
¼ c. chopped green onion
½ c. mayonnaise
¼ c. grapefruit juice
Juice of 1 lemon
Chopped parsley

Combine all ingredients except parsley. Let stand in refrigerator 2 hours; drain. Arrange in bowl, garnish with chopped parsley. Surround with crackers or Melba toast rounds.

## CHUTNEY DIP

4 eggs, hard-boiled
1-3 oz. pkg. cream cheese
1 T. Worcestershire
1 T. curry powder
Dash cayenne
2-3 dashes Tabasco
¼ t. celery seeds
2 T. mayonnaise
Salt and pepper to taste
3-4 T. chutney, chopped fine

Mash eggs with cheese. Add other ingredients, blending well. Add chutney. Chill. Serve as a dip. Will keep well in refrigerator several weeks.

## CHICKEN WINGS WITH ZIPPY DIP

Chicken wings
Garlic salt
Flour
Cornflake crumbs
Nutmeg
Red pepper
Egg batter

Unjoin wings. Cut off tips or have butcher do it. Wash and pat dry with paper towels. Sprinkle with garlic salt. In a bag, mix flour, cornflake crumbs or bread crumbs, nutmeg, red pepper. Shake wings in mixture until coated. Dip chicken in egg batter and then in mixture. Fry in deep fryer.

## ZIPPY DIP

1 pt. sour cream
⅓ c. pickle relish
1-3 oz. pkg. Roquefort
  cheese
2 t. mustard
Dash Tabasco sauce
Dash Worcestershire sauce
Dash curry powder

Blend all ingredients together. Serve in a bowl. Dip chicken wings into sauce.

# SWAMP CABBAGE SLAW

## (Hearts of Palm)

Shred hearts of palm, add finely cut celery and chopped pimiento and onion. Mix with sour cream dressing or onion dressing. Sprinkle with lemon juice and serve over crunchy green lettuce leaves.

## WILD BOAR

Cut meat in small thin chunks (3 inches long) and season well with cracked pepper. Dip chunks in Sweet Sour Sauce and barbeque over hot coals, basting frequently. Cook for 2-3 hours. The meat will be tender and sweet!

## SWEET SOUR SAUCE

1 T. dry mustard
3 T. garlic flavored red wine vinegar
½ c. catsup
1 t. horseradish
1 T. cornstarch
¼ t. curry powder
2-3 T. brown sugar
Salt and pepper to taste
¾ c. pineapple juice
2 T. soy sauce

Yields 1½ cups

Mix all ingredients together thoroughly. Cook until slightly thickened and clear. If too thick, add more pineapple juice. Serve hot or chilled.

## WILD TURKEY

Wash and dry bird. Grease inside and out with butter or margarine, pepper and salt. Rub dry onion soup mix all over, inside and out. Place in roasting pan. Baste all over with Sherry and add a little to water in bottom of pan. Cover well with foil and cook well done, according to weight.

## MANATEE DUCK

Wash and dry duck; rub with butter. Season with salt and pepper and sage. Grill over charcoal. Baste alternately with Sweet Sour Sauce and Sherry. Continue until done. An hour before serving put duck into foil. Pour more Sherry over duck; seal foil. Bake in moderate oven.

## TURNIP GREENS ALABAM

Wash and cut greens. Set aside roots. Boil and simmer greens in a pot with ham hocks, pepper and salt. When greens are almost done add pared and sliced turnips (or roots) and continue to cook until they are tender.

## HUBERT'S GRITS

Cook grits a bit stiffer than usual. Add plenty of garlic salt and black pepper for seasoning. Stir in large dollops of Cheese Whiz to taste. Add cream and butter, enough to make good consistency. Hubert's secret is the bold use of garlic and pepper!

## PEA PODS AND PEARL ONIONS
## ALA BERNICE

Prepare frozen pea pods as directed. Saute tiny pearl onions and few pimientos for color. Stir in sliced water chestnuts, butter, salt and pepper to taste. Serve warm.

*The Rutlands top this delicious meal off with a simple dessert of fruit and brandy . . . the perfect ending.*

# ORANGE SQUEEZE PARTY
# MR. AND MRS. GEORGE L. VAN SCIVER

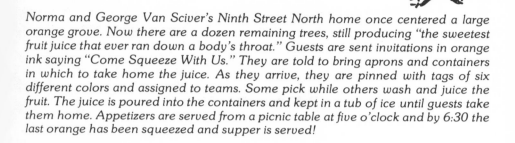

## "COME SQUEEZE WITH US"

*Norma and George Van Sciver's Ninth Street North home once centered a large orange grove. Now there are a dozen remaining trees, still producing "the sweetest fruit juice that ever ran down a body's throat." Guests are sent invitations in orange ink saying "Come Squeeze With Us." They are told to bring aprons and containers in which to take home the juice. As they arrive, they are pinned with tags of six different colors and assigned to teams. Some pick while others wash and juice the fruit. The juice is poured into the containers and kept in a tub of ice until guests take them home. Appetizers are served from a picnic table at five o'clock and by 6:30 the last orange has been squeezed and supper is served!*

PICKLED MUSHROOMS     SARDINE DIP
COLD HAM AND TURKEY
POTATO SALAD     MARINATED BEAN SALAD
BAKED EGGPLANT     DEVILED EGGS
BLENDER ORANGE AND CRANBERRY MOLD
ASSORTED BREADS     ORANGE BLOSSOM CUP CAKES
COFFEE     ICED TEA     ORANGE JUICE

\*    \*    \*    \*    \*

## PICKLED MUSHROOMS

2 c. white wine or cider
  vinegar
2 T. sugar
2 t. salt
2 shredded bay leaves
6 cloves
6 peppercorns
2 cloves garlic, sliced
2 slices lemon
1-16 oz. can large
  mushrooms

Combine vinegar, seasonings and mushroom liquor. Boil 3 to 4 minutes. Add mushrooms. Turn into a jar and let stand 1 to 3 weeks.

## SARDINE DIP

8 oz. pkg. cream cheese
2 cans sardine filets
3 T. minced chives
½ c. minced parsley
Salt to taste
Sweet cream

Soften cream cheese to room temperature. Mash sardines with oil. Blend cheese, sardines, chives and parsley. Add salt to taste and enough cream to thin mixture to dunking consistency.

## POTATO SALAD

10 large white potatoes
2 c. finely diced celery
½ c. finely diced onion
½ c. finely diced green
  pepper
½ c. finely diced sweet
  pickle
3 c. homemade mayonnaise
2 hard cooked eggs,
  chopped
2 T. vinegar
Salt, pepper, Tabasco to
  taste
Dash of mustard

Boil potatoes in jackets. Cool and peel; cut in small bite-sized pieces. Mix all other ingredients together; add potatoes. Correct seasonings. (Adding a little pickle juice helps the flavor).

## MARINATED BEAN SALAD

½ c. vinegar
¼ c. (or less) sugar
1 t. garlic vinegar
¼ c. oil (olive oil is good)
2 t. soy sauce
Celery salt to taste
1 c. (1 lb.) Blue Lake cut
  green beans
1 c. (1 lb.) kidney beans,
  drained
1 med. onion, sliced in thin
  slices
  (purple onion is best)
1 c. (5 oz.) water chestnuts,
  drained
1 small can tiny lima beans,
  drained
1 carrot, cut up
2 ribs celery, cut up
Dash Tabasco
Lemon pepper
Dry mustard

Blend all ingredients together and marinate several hours or overnight. Stir from time to time so marinade can get through all the beans. Other vegetables such as wax beans, raw cauliflower, green pepper, corn, olives and fresh mushrooms marinated in French dressing may be added if you like.

## BAKED EGGPLANT

1 eggplant
1 large Spanish onion, diced
1 large can mushrooms,
  drained
1–5½ oz. can water
  chestnuts, drained
½ t. thyme
½ c. sour cream
1 T. soy sauce
½ c. skim milk
Salt and pepper
Buttered cracker crumbs

Peel and cut eggplant into 1 inch squares. Cook in boiling, salted water until soft. Saute onion; mix all ingredients together except cracker crumbs. Pour into casserole and top with buttered crumbs. Bake in 375 degree oven 20 minutes, or until heated through.

## BLENDER ORANGE AND CRANBERRY MOLD

**2 envelopes unflavored gelatin**
**½ c. cold water**
**½ c. boiling water**
**½ orange, cut in pieces and seeded**
**1¼ c. sugar**
**3 c. fresh cranberries**

Sprinkle gelatin over cold water in blender container; allow to stand while assembling other ingredients. Add boiling water; cover and blend at high speed until orange is finely chopped. Stop blender and add cranberries. Cover and blend until cranberries are finely chopped. Turn into 4 cup mold or individual molds. Chill until firm.

## ORANGE BLOSSOM CAKE

**Use any prepared cake mix and frost with the following while cake is hot:**
**Grated rind and juice of 2 lemons**
**Grated rind and juice of 2 oranges**
**1¼ lbs. powdered sugar**

Sift sugar; add juices and rinds. Cream together until very smooth. It is **very** important that the sugar be sifted.

# MR. AND MRS. CHARLES WEDDING'S
# FISH FRY

*No Gulf Coast cookbook is complete without the classic fish and hushpuppy dinner. And for St. Petersburg, the fish must be mullet, and the mullet must be fresh. For the hushpuppies, the cornmeal must be water-ground. Toots Wedding's 24-hour slaw is splendid, and Charles himself is in charge of the mullet, frying it while guests are enjoying drinks poolside.*

DEEP-FRIED FRESH MULLET
RELISH TRAY          24-HOUR SLAW
BAKED GARLIC GRITS
MINCEMEAT TARTS WITH APRICOT BRANDY SAUCE

## FRIED MULLET

**Fresh Mullet**
**Salt and pepper**
**Cornmeal**
**Vegetable oil**

Mullet must be fresh. Season with salt and pepper. Roll in corn meal and deep fry until golden crispy.

## HUSH PUPPIES

**2 c. white water ground cornmeal**
**1 T. flour**
**1 t. baking powder**
**½ t. soda**
**1 t. salt**
**1 egg**
**6 T. chopped onion**
**1 c. buttermilk**

**Serves 10**

Mix all dry ingredients; add chopped onion, then milk and egg. Drop by spoonful into deep hot oil where fish are cooking. Turn over and allow to cook until lightly browned; place on paper to drain.

## 24 HOUR SLAW

¾ c. sugar
¼ c. vegetable oil
¼ c. vinegar
1 T. salt
1 T. dry mustard
½ t. celery seed
1 green pepper, sliced
3 lb. head cabbage,
  shredded
2 medium onions, sliced

**Serves 6**

Boil sugar, oil, vinegar, salt, mustard and celery seed together. Pour over green pepper, onions and cabbage. Put in covered dish and refrigerate for 24 hours before serving.

## MINCEMEAT TARTS WITH APRICOT BRANDY SAUCE

1 recipe 2 crust pie
1-18 oz. jar prepared
  mincemeat

**Yields 10**

Roll out pastry and cut in 3 inch circles. Put one spoonful of mincemeat on each circle and fold over. Press the edge with a fork. Bake at 350 degrees until lightly browned.

## APRICOT BRANDY SAUCE

2 cans apricots, drained
1 T. flour
¼ c. sugar
½ c. brandy

Seed apricots and put through sieve. Add rest of ingredients and cook slowly until slightly thickened.

# FAMILY CAMPING
## Mr. and Mrs. Richard Buckingham

*With year-round outdoor weather, camping out is a popular activity for the whole family in Florida. And to make the vacation a real one, here are some helpful ways to minimize cooking time and effort while serving tasty meals:*

ONE - POT TACOS
CAMPFIRE SALAD
FRUIT DESSERT

## ONE POT TACOS

**3 lbs. hamburger**
**1 large onion, chopped**
**2 pkgs. Taco mix**
**1-30 oz. can Ranch style or**
  **Kidney beans**
**1 head lettuce, shredded**
**4 tomatoes, chopped**
**2 lbs. sharp cheddar cheese,**
  **grated or sliced thin**
**2 large bags Fritos or**
  **Doritos**

**Serves up to 12**

Brown hamburger in large pan over grill or open fire; add onion. Sprinkle Taco mix in and add water; simmer. Add beans. Serve over Fritos, and let each person add their own tomatoes, lettuce and cheese.

## CAMPFIRE SALAD

Select one of these:

      Celery cut in sections
      Peanut butter spread in groove
      Add raisins

              or

      Cabbage leaves, washed and separated
      Spread lightly with peanut butter, then roll up and eat

Nutritious, delicious and SO EASY . . .

# FRUIT DESSERT

Wash, core and halve an apple. Spread with mixture of cream cheese, raisins and nuts . . . or one or the other. Great tasting!

## ANOTHER ONE-POT CAMPING SUPPER

**2 lbs. hamburger**
**2 pkgs. onion soup mix**
**2 cans whole kernel corn, drained**
**4 c. water**
**2 cans boiled potatoes**
**2 cans kidney beans**
**1 t. chili powder, optional**
**Pepper flakes (equivalent to one bell pepper)**

**Serves up to 12**

**A real filler!**

Brown hamburger. Add water, soup mix, pepper flakes, and chili powder. Simmer. Add corn, potatoes and kidney beans.

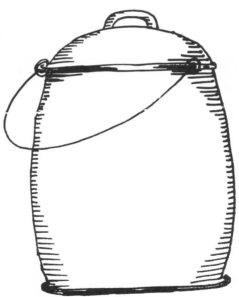

# HINTS AND MENUS FOR CAMPING AND BEACH PARTIES
## Mr. and Mrs. Richard Buckingham

### BEACH PARTY MENU

To Plan:

Bring blankets or plastic sit-upons, two card tables for serving, one large barbecue grill, charcoal and lighter fluid, heavy paper plates, roll paper towels, large plastic trash bag and plastic knives and forks. Everything served are "finger foods" and mostly "do-it-yourself".

MENU:       Tender ears of corn (In Husks) Plan 2 per person
Large Shrimp (unpeeled — 1 lb. per person)
Hot Dogs & Buns
Vegetable Salad
Iced Canned Beverages of your choice

CORN . . . . Soak corn on cob in husks overnight in large container of water. Grill in husks over charcoal, turning frequently. When outside is dry, even lightly charred, it's done. Melt stick of butter in pie pan on grill. Each person peels their own corn, rolls in butter, salts . . . hmn delicious! It's sure to be the hit of your party.

SHRIMP . . . Plan 1 lb. per person — use the large size because they are easier to peel and eat under casual circumstances. As soon as charcoal is burning well, place a large container of water on to boil. When boiling well, add 1 can of beer (or your favorite Seafood Boil), then add the Shrimp. Cook 3 minutes. Serve with melted butter, sprinkled with garlic salt (in pie pan) or bring along your favorite cold seafood sauce. Actually, the shrimp are great right out of the pot. And . . . everyone peels their own!

HOT DOGS AND BUNS . . . What's a picnic without them? Simply let each person broil their own over the dying coal as they're ready to eat them. These should be served after the corn and shrimp are done. You'll need several long handled barbecue forks, Catsup, Mustard, Relish, and cut-up sweet onions.

401

VEGETABLE PLATTER . . . Wash and cut-up vegetables and store in baggies (some with ice water to maintain freshness and flavor.

Peel carrots, cut in sticks
Cut celery in 4-inch sticks
Place these in double baggies with ice in cooler
Slice Cucumbers (do not peel)
Cauliflower . . . Sectioned into bite-size pieces
Zucchini & Yellow Squash . . . ¼-inch slices

Serve chilled on paper platters with bottled Catalina or French Dressing.

# HOW TO MAKE - SCOTCH BOX OVEN

Take dividers out of heavy Scotch whiskey box and line insides (including flaps) with heavy duty aluminum foil. Start your charcoal in metal pie pan. Plan one charcoal piece for each 50 degrees of heat, plus one for the box. Example: 350 degrees = 8 pieces charcoal.

Place charcoal in center (arranging box so flap is like an oven door you can open). Place 3 empty soft drink cans in triangle around charcoal as "burner". Cooks amazingly like your own oven for short term recipes. Add charcoal as necessary.

# MENU

Excellent for campfire breakfasts
Canned Cinnamon Rolls done in Scotch oven
Bacon and Eggs        "        "        "        "

You will need muffin tin (use teflon or spray well with Pam). Place one strip of bacon in each cup. Cook until half done; break an egg in center of each cup. Cook until all is done.

OTHER SCOTCH BOX OVEN USES . . .

Cup Cakes in Muffin Tins
Canned Biscuits or Cinnamon Rolls
Cake mixes, Gingerbread, One-Dish Casseroles

## MENU FOR BOATING

### Mr. and Mrs. Richard Misener

*Boating plays such a big part in the life of this waterfront town that boating hosts are continually planning parties afloat. With careful thought given to use of canned foods that can be stored aboard, the Richard Miseners have come up with an enticing shipboard menu.*

Chilled Gazpacho Soup (see index)
Chicken a la Can Can
Canned Asparagus with Pimiento Strips
Buttered French Bread
Canned Fruit and Cookies
Coffee, Tea or Milk

## CHICKEN A LA CAN CAN

**1 can cream of chicken soup**
**1 can cream of celery soup**
**1 soup can of water**
**1–12 oz. can boned chicken**
  **or 1½ cups boned, cooked**
  **chicken pieces**
**1 soup can minute rice**
**1 can French fried onions**

**Serves 4 to 6**

Combine soups, water and chicken; add minute rice, right from box. Stir to mix; bring quickly to boil. Cover, reduce heat; simmer 7 minutes. Top with onions heated according to directions on can.

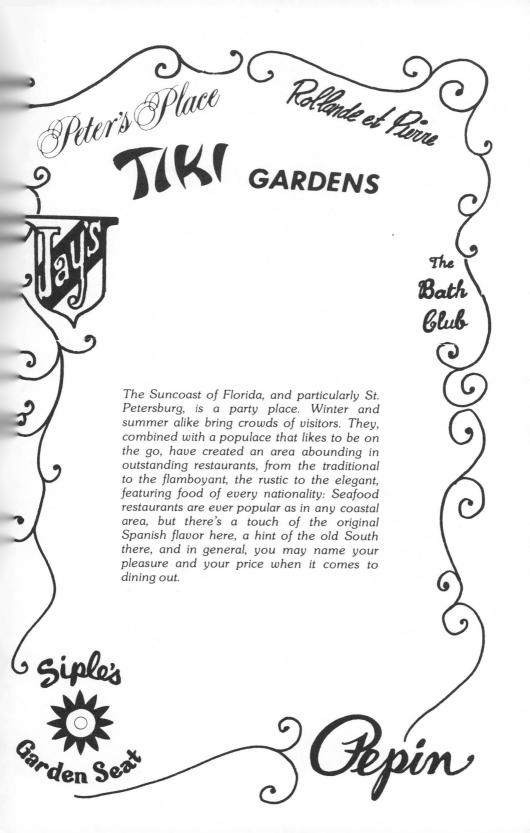

Peter's Place

Rollande et Pierre

# TIKI GARDENS

Jay's

The Bath Club

The Suncoast of Florida, and particularly St. Petersburg, is a party place. Winter and summer alike bring crowds of visitors. They, combined with a populace that likes to be on the go, have created an area abounding in outstanding restaurants, from the traditional to the flamboyant, the rustic to the elegant, featuring food of every nationality: Seafood restaurants are ever popular as in any coastal area, but there's a touch of the original Spanish flavor here, a hint of the old South there, and in general, you may name your pleasure and your price when it comes to dining out.

Siple's
Garden Seat

Pepin

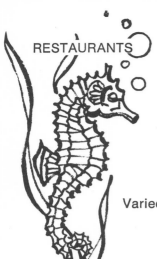

# The Bath Club

Escargots
Black Olive Soup With Melba Toast
Braised Celery Vinegarette
Filet of Beef Wellington
Frozen Pink Squirrel

Varied Cheeses                    Fresh Fruit

Coffee

*Since its opening in 1936, the Bath Club has been a social center and meeting place for St. Petersburg, Tampa and Gulf Beach residents. Famous for beach cookouts, patio parties and formal dining as well, the club, with Chef Josef Schoen, who's been in residence 20 years, has never waned in popularity and boasts a varied menu.*

## ESCARGOTS BOURGUIGNINNE

**48 snail shells**
**48 snails**
**1 c. chopped shallots**
**1 lb. butter**
**1 c. Burgundy wine**
**1 clove garlic, minced**
**Salt and pepper**
**1 t. rubbed tarragon**
**1 T. chopped parsley**
**1 T. Cognac**

**Serves 8**
 **(6 per serving)**

Drain escargots and wash with cold water. Saute shallots in butter until tender. Add escargots and simmer while adding the other ingredients. Simmer 15 minutes. Drain butter from mixture and reserve. Stuff shells with escargot mixture, one escargot per shell. When butter cools, whip to smooth consistency and top each individual escargot. Refrigerate. Bake a few minutes when ready to serve.

# OLIVE SOUP

**4 oz. ripe olives, minced**
**1 clove garlic**
**1½ c. chicken broth**
**1 egg, beaten**
**4 oz. cream**
**Salt and pepper**

**Serves 3 to 4**

Simmer olives with garlic in broth. Cook 15 minutes; remove garlic. Combine egg and cream; add to broth stirring constantly. Season to taste. Serve hot or chilled.

# BRAISED CELERY VINEGARETTE

Take ¼ heart of celery about 6 inches long and blanch. First scraping the celery thoroughly so there are no strings. After blanching and the celery is tender and cool, put it in a good vinegarette dressing. Let stand in the refrigerator overnight. Serve two per person with a strip of pimiento on top.

# BEEF WELLINGTON

**8 oz. pork**
**8 oz. beef**
**8 oz. veal**
**Handful bread crumbs**
**4 eggs**
**Chopped parsley**
**Salt, pepper, garlic,**
**  marjoram and nutmeg**
**1 whole beef tenderloin**
**Puff pastry**

Grind pork, beef and veal; mix with bread crumbs, eggs and seasonings. Mix to a smooth consistency. Season tenderloin and sear in pre-heated pan on all sides. Cool. Roll out puff pastry (buy it at a specialty store) to ⅛ inch thick, long and wide enough for meat to fit on it and sides pull over. Spread pork, beef, veal mixture on pastry. Lay filet in the center and roll pastry around meat. Close ends by overlapping tightly. Lay on baking pan, brush with water and bake at 400 degrees half an hour.

*We suggest you bake the tenderloin to almost the doneness desired the day before (or the day you prepare it) then wrap it in the pastry and bake until the pastry is golden brown.*

# PINK SQUIRREL

**1½ oz. Cream de Noya liquer (almond liquer)**
**1½ oz. Cream de Menthe**
**1 scoop vanilla ice cream**

Put all three ingredients in a blender for a few seconds or until well blended. The mixture should be nice and thick. Serve in medium sized brandy snifter or wine glass.

*This will serve as a dessert as well as an after dinner drink.*

Toasted Mushrooms a la Jay's
Minestrone Soup
Veal Ham Rolls
with
Spaghetti
Dessert

White Wine                    Trecciarossa Bianco

*Every area has its Italian restaurant, but few can excel "Jay's Ristorante Italiano." A family owned venture, it's doors opened in 1951 when Jay Basso put her cooking skills into practice using old world recipes. These same recipes are being used today and daughter and son-in-law, Jim and Ann Milano plus their son and daughter-in-law, Rich and Pam Milano have joined the business. Success is evidenced in the crowd of customers and continued expansion, for which more plans are being made. Veal dishes are a specialty, and a variety of local and imported wines are available.*

## TOASTED MUSHROOMS A LA JAY'S

**1 lb. medium size whole
  fresh mushrooms
2 c. sifted flour
3 eggs, beaten
½ c. milk
2½ c. breadcrumbs
Peanut oil for deep fryer**

Preheat oil in deep fryer to 350 degrees. Clean and drain mushrooms. Mix egg and milk together. In order, dust the mushrooms in sifted flour, coat in egg-milk mixture and roll in bread crumbs. When oil is hot, place mushrooms in deep fryer for approximately 3-4 minutes or until golden brown. Remove from fryer and drain excess oil.

**Cheese Sauce:
½ lb. cheddar cheese
2 ozs. dry Marsala wine
Chopped fresh parsley
Pepper**

Melt cheese until soft. Add wine, parsley and salt and pepper to taste. Keep warm over low heat stirring occasionally. Ladle the warm melted cheese sauce over mushrooms. Garnish platter with fresh sprigs of parsley.

# MINESTRONE SOUP

2 lbs. garbanzo beans (chick peas)
1 lb. great northern beans
2 lbs. beef, cut up
1 c. celery, diced
1 large Spanish onion
2 medium sized carrots, diced
½ head cabbage, shredded
2 T. salt
1 t. pepper
1 c. elbow macaroni
1 clove garlic, chopped
1 t. Beau Monde
2 T. butter

Serves 10 to 12

Boil garbanzo and great northern beans in 8 quarts water over low flame for 1 hour. Add beef and cook for 45 minutes more. Add vegetables and spices and cook until vegetables are tender. Saute onion and garlic in butter and add with elbow macaroni to soup about 20 minutes before serving.

# SALTIMBOCCO A LA JAY'S (VEAL-HAM ROLLS)

18 veal scallops
18 thin slices Proscuitto ham
18 thin slices Mozzarella cheese
18 pieces fresh pimiento
1 t. salt
¼ t. freshly ground black pepper
4 fresh sage leaves crumbled
4 T. butter
½ c. Marsala wine
1 t. Beau Monde seasoning

Serves 6

Pound veal slices as thin as possible. Season with salt and pepper. Cover each slice with proscuitto, cheese and pimiento. Roll tightly and fasten with a toothpick. Melt butter in skillet, add spices, brown scallops in it over high heat on all sides. Add Marsala and cook over low heat for 5 minutes or until veal roll is tender. Place on serving dish. Pour gravy mixture over rolls. Serve hot.

# SPAGHETTI

Spaghetti with sauce of ham strips, garlic butter and parmesan cheese.

# DESSERT

Chilled green seedless grapes with Grand Marnier or any assortment of fresh fruits and cheeses.

# Pepin

## AUTHENTIC SPANISH FLAVOR

Spanish Bean Soup
Salad
Filet Salteado
Rice
Flan
Sangria

*Spanish food is a great favorite in the St. Petersburg area, and a great favorite among Spanish restaurants is "Pepin's." Although the location is new, on Fourth Street North, Pepin's is actually a descendant of "Pepe's" in Tampa and Indian Rocks, opened in 1974 by Delia and Jose Cortez, Pepe's sister and brother-in-law. Spanish decor, white-washed walls, posters, candlelight, and the best in Spanish foods from the traditional black beans, rice and Sangria to the more elegant stuffed shrimp and the best in steaks and wines bring a steady stream of customers.*

## SPANISH BEAN SOUP

**1 lb. dried garbanzos
(chick peas)
½ lb. smoked bacon
1 ham bone
½ lb. flank steak
2 Chorizos (Spanish
sausage)
1 small whole onion
1 whole ripe tomato
Pinch saffron
3 medium potatoes (peeled
and cubed)
Salt**

**Serves 6**

Wash garbanzos, cover with cold water and soak overnight. Next morning, drain and rinse. Set aside. In a 4 quart soup kettle place bacon, ham bone, chorizos, flank steak, onion and tomato. Cover with water and bring to a rapid boil and skim several times. Lower heat to medium, cover pot and cook about 30 minutes. Add saffron, stir. Cover and cook until beans are tender (approximately another 30 minutes). Remove meat to platter and reserve for later use. Discard ham bone, onion and tomato. Add potatoes to beans. Correct salt to taste. Cover and cook until potatoes are done (30 minutes). Cut meat into small portions, slice chorizos. Return all to soup. Serve hot.

# FILETE SALTEADO

2 medium potatoes
½ c. olive oil
1 clove garlic
1 small onion, chopped
1 small green pepper,
  chopped
1 medium ripe tomato
¼ lb. cooked ham, diced
3 Chorizos, sliced (Spanish
  sausage)
4 filets of prime beef, cubed
  in large pieces
1 c. sliced mushrooms
  (cooked)
3 T. tomato sauce
¼ c. cooking Sherry
¼ c. cooked small peas
1 pimiento, cut in thin strips

Peel potatoes and cut in small cubes. Fry and set aside. Saute onion and green pepper until transparent. Add tomato and saute until vegetables are soft and mushy. Set aside. Saute ham and chorizos for about 5 minutes. Add cubed filet and sear quickly. Add potatoes, vegetables, salt. Stir and toss all ingredients well. Cook according to taste (medium, medium rare, etc.). When done scatter peas and pimiento on top and pour in wine. Serve with yellow rice.

## FLAN

6 c. milk
4 eggs
2 egg yolks
1½ c. sugar
1 t. vanilla
6 T. sugar

Scald 6 cups milk, add 1½ cups sugar. Set aside and let it cool. Beat 4 eggs, 2 yolks and add 1 teaspoon vanilla. Add egg mixture to milk, stirring constantly. Set aside. In a small iron skillet place 6 tablespoons sugar. Place skillet over low heat and cook unitl a foamy golden caramel is obtained. Immediately pour into 1½ quart casserole and quickly coat the bottom evenly. Let it set for a few seconds.

Strain egg mixture into casserole. Place in shallow pan with hot water. Set oven at 275 degrees. Cook for approximately 45 minutes or unitl done. Do not allow water to boil. Do not overcook. Cool and serve.

## SANGRIA

1 pt. imported Spanish Red
  Wine
2 T. sugar
½ jigger brandy
3 slices orange
3 slices lemon
Cinnamon
Ice

In a pitcher place oranges, lemons, 2 tablespoons sugar. Add wine, sprinkle dash of cinnamon on top. Stir well and serve, straining ice.

*a touch of elegance...*

## Peter's Place
### CAFE INTERNATIONAL

*menu*

### Dinner for eight

Crepe King Crab au Sherry
Mixed Green Salad
Dressing a la Peter's Place

Ash Spumante

Onion Soup Parisienne
Prime Filet Cordon Bleu

Beaujolais

Sauce Bernaise         Rice

Peanut Butter Pie
"Chantilly"
Peter's Coffee

*Practicing attorney Peter Kersker wondered if his dream would materialize. The dream was of a superbly elegant French restaurant featuring the kind of dining done only in a leisurely manner, each course a cherished specialty. For decor he would have the finest in crystal chandeliers, Oriental rugs, linen, silver bud vases and the best in china and flatware.*

*The dream has come true in the form of "Peter's Place," a tiny French restaurant opened next to his law office on Beach Drive in 1973. Tiny, it has a surprisingly big and delightfully elegant selection of appetizers, soups, entrees, and desserts. Such a selection, in fact, that one is sorely tempted to come frequently and try them all in varying combinations.*

# CREPE KING CRAB AU SHERRY

1 recipe crepes (see index)
2 c. medium white sauce
1-12 oz. pkg. Alaskan King
  Crab, thawed and drained
1 T. (scant) freeze dried
  onions
⅛ t. nutmeg
1 T. chives, freeze dried
2 T. Sherry
Dash salt and ground
  pepper to taste

Drain and rinse crabmeat. Make medium white sauce and add onions, nutmeg and chives. Add Sherry and seasonings and stir in crabmeat. Spoon mixture into crepes and roll up. Put seam side down on a lightly buttered pan or cookie sheet which has turned up sides. Place in a 300 degree oven and bake 20 minutes or more. Serve on individual plates garnished with lemon and parsley.

*For a variation of this basic recipe, add curry powder, raisins, dry roasted peanuts to crabmeat mixture before rolling up crepes. Garnish with toasted coconut.*

# SALAD DRESSING

1 recipe blender mayonnaise
¼ tin anchovies
¼ c. wine vinegar
1 t. dry mustard
Chopped chives
Lemon juice (optional)

Decrease oil in making mayonnaise. The mixture should be thinner — just sauce consistency. Remove egg oil mixture from blender. Add anchovies to blender. Add wine vinegar, mustard and puree. Combine with egg oil mixture. Add chives until flecks of green permeate.

# ONION SOUP PARISIENNE

8 large onions
¼ c. butter
¼ c. vegetable oil
1 c. red wine
Pepper to taste
4-10½ oz. cans beef
  bouillon
1½ bouillon cans water
4 slices dried French bread,
  cut in half
8 slices provolone cheese
Paprika
Parsley

Thinly slice onions, cut in half. Saute in butter and oil. Cook down until mushy, at least half an hour. Add beef bouillon, water, pepper and wine. Simmer one hour. Pour into crocks. Top with bread, cover with cheese. Sprinkle with paprika. Broil until cheese melts and begins to turn brown. Garnish with parsley and serve with doily under crock so that it won't slip.

## FILET MIGNON CORDON BLEU

8 filets, well trimmed
8 very thin slices Swiss
  cheese
8 thin slices Canadian bacon
Pepper, freshly ground

Marinade:
2 c. dry red wine
⅓ c. freeze dried chives
½ c. wine vinegar
¼ c. dried onions
1¼ c. sugar
Salt and pepper
2 T. dried parsley

Bearnaise Sauce (see index)

Combine all ingredients. Pour into shallow pan. Marinate steaks 1 hour, turning frequently.

Cut pocket in each steak. Place cheese into pocket next to meat, then Canadian bacon. Pull steak over cheese and bacon. Grind fresh pepper over each steak. Broil to desired doneness. Serve with warm Bearnaise sauce over finished steak, with the remainder in a gravy boat.

## BAKED RICE

3 c. water
4 T. butter, melted
2 T. chopped parsley
2 T. freeze dried chives
½ t. dried tarragon
1 t. mace, scant
3 chicken bouillon cubes
  (dissolved)
Dash ground pepper
1½ c. uncooked rice

In an oven proof 2 quart casserole, place 4 tablespoons butter, parsley, chives, tarragon and mace. Add chicken bouillon to water; add pepper; pour into casserole. Add rice and stir. Cover and bake at 300 degrees 1 hour or until rice has absorbed water and is fluffy. If the mixture isn't yellow enough, add food coloring to it.

## PEANUT BUTTER PIE CHANTILLY

9 inch pie shell, baked
1 recipe vanilla pudding or
  pie filling (see index)
3 T. crunchy peanut butter

Make recipe vanilla pie filling according to directions. Stir in peanut butter and pour into baked shell. Chill.

# COFFEE

**5 ozs. instant coffee**
**5 ozs. Nestle's Quick**
**Brown and white sugar**
**1 oz. Couintreau (or use**
**fresh orange and lemon**
**peel cut as if a twist for a**
**Martini)**
**1 oz. B & B or Grand Marnier**
**3 shakes of cinnamon (or to**
**taste)**
**2 shakes of clove (or to**
**taste)**
**2 shakes of nutmeg (or to**
**taste)**

**Makes 8 cups**

Place in pan or coffee pot the instant coffee and Nestle's Quick and sufficien water for 8 cups of coffee. Add combina tion of white and brown sugars to make the mixture very sweet (a synthetic sweetener may be used to cut calories!). Add remaining ingredients and heat just to below boiling and serve. This entire mixture may be made richer by the addition of more instant coffee and chocolate. Pass Half and Half at the table. It should not require any additional sugar. If you wish this to be more alcoholic, add some vodka.

*Naturally, this dinner is served with hot French rolls or French bread with whipped butter. Have fun!*

WHERE THE PAMPERED PEOPLE DINE

## Rollande et Pierre

COCKTAILS

Filet of Sole Veronique
Belgian Endives Vinaigrette
Steak au Poivre
Lyonnaise Potatoes
Braised Celery Hearts
French Bread

Crepe Suzettes                                              Coffee Royale

*Founded by present owner Mario Loehrer's aunt and uncle, Rollande and Pierre Loehrer, "Rollande et Pierre's Restaurant Francais" enchants you in the cozy and rustic setting of the former world-famous Earl Gresh Wood Parade. Beamed ceilings and a brick fireplace hung with long-handled copper pots greet you, and you're treated to garlic-laced seafoods, game, poultry, beef and numerous other specialties of the house, herb-seasoned vegetables, and flaming desserts served at your table.*

## FILET OF SOLE VERONIQUE

Place filets of fish in a buttered baking dish; add 1 teaspoon lemon juice, ¼ cup dry white wine, salt and pepper to taste. Bake at 375 degrees 12 to 15 minutes. Add sauce and broil until sauce is golden brown and bubbly.

## Veronique Sauce

Melt one tablespoon butter in top of double boiler; blend in one tablespoon flour. Gradually stir in one cup warm cream. Add two egg yolks and one small can seedless grapes without the juice. Add one teaspoon lemon juice. Do not boil or it will separate.

## BELGIAN ENDIVE VINAIGRETTE

¼ c. cider vinegar
Dash salt
½ t. dry mustard
Dash sugar, white pepper
6 oz. salad oil
½ t. chopped parsley
½ t. chopped chives
½ t. chopped capers
1 egg, hard-boiled and
  chopped
Endives cut in half inch
  pieces

Blend all ingredients, mixing well. Pour over endives.

## STEAK AU POIVRE

12 to 14 ounce New York strip steaks, boneless.
Pound the steaks with crushed peppercorns on both sides. Flour the steaks lightly, shake excess off. Saute in clarified butter. When done to your likeness, add one or two ounces Cognac to the pan. Flambe. Remove steaks to platter and pour remaining butter Cognac mixture over the steaks.

## BRAISED CELERY HEARTS

Cut several celery hearts in half lengthwise. Saute in butter until nearly tender. Add one ounce flour and blend well. Cook, stirring constantly, so that celery will not burn. Stir in one cup hot beef stock. Simmer slowly until thickened and smooth. Bring to boil; transfer to lightly greased baking dish. Bake at 350 degrees 30 minutes.

# LYONNAISE POTATOES

quarter onion, sliced thin
large cooked potato,
grated
T. butter

Saute onion in butter until tender. Stir in potatoes and cook like hash browns, until golden on both sides.

# CREPE SUZETTE

1 recipe dessert crepes
(see index)
For one serving:
1 T. sugar
2 T. butter
1 lemon, juiced
Rind of one lemon
1 orange, juiced
Rind of one orange
Cognac
Grand Marnier

Make crepes according to directions. Roll crepes and place seam side down in serving dish.

Place sugar in pan; add butter. Add juices and rinds. Baste crepes with this liquid. De-glaze pan with Cognac and Grand Marnier. Flambe. Pour over crepes.

# COFFEE ROYALE

To each cup of strong coffee, add one teaspoon sugar and ½ ounce Cognac.

Winner of the "Golden Spoon."
One of the top ten restaurants
in Florida according to Florida
Trend Magazine.

## Clearwater, Florida

## Dinner for Four

Strawberry Daiquiri
Shrimp Moutard
Bibb Lettuce with Fresh Mushrooms
Filet Mignon
or
Chopped Sirloin Imperial

Strawberries Jubilee                          Coffee

*Dining in leisurely elegance while looking out across Clearwater Bay through magnificent old oaks---that is the setting at "Siple's Garden Seat," established 55 years ago in Clearwater's infancy. Opened as a tearoom by present owner Dick Siple's grandmother, the popular restaurant has expanded both it boundaries and its menu, serving a variety of exquisitely prepared dishes, each course with its own special touch, and each served to perfection.*

## STRAWBERRY DAIQUIRI

**Juice Mixture:**
**1 pkg. frozen strawberries,**
  **thawed and drained**
**3 T. sugar**
**1 pt. lemon juice**
**1 pt. lime juice**

Combine all ingredients; refrigerate.

**For each individual drink**
  **use the following:**
**2 T. berries**
**1½ ozs. light rum**
**2 ozs. of juice mixture**
**2 T. crushed ice**

Put all ingredients in blender and blend just long enough to puree berries and ice. Serve in 7 or 8 oz. stemmed cocktail glass.

## SHRIMP MOUTARD

Sauce:
4 ozs. Dijon mustard
3 ozs. mayonnaise
2 T. coarsely chopped celery
1 T. finely minced onion
24 shrimp, cooked, peeled
and deveined
Butter

Blend all ingredients together well.

Lightly butter 4 individual baking rame-kins. Place 6 shrimp in each ramekin, and top with equal amounts of sauce. Bake at 400 degree for 8 minutes or until heated through and bubbly.

## BIBB LETTUCE WITH FRESH MUSHROOMS

4 small heads Bibb lettuce
8-10 fresh mushrooms,
  sliced
½ sweet onion, thinly sliced

Greek Style Oil and Vinegar
  Dressing:
3 c. olive oil
1 c. vinegar
1 fresh lime, juiced
¾ t. garlic powder
1 t. oregano
1 t. white pepper
1 t. dry mustard
1½ t. salt
1 t. Accent

Wash lettuce well. Do not break apart. Trim stem end and lightly flatten. Place each head on salad plate; top with sliced mushrooms and onion slices. Pour dress-ing over each.

Blend all ingredients well. Mix 24 hours prior to use. Always shake well before using.

This may be more dressing than you need for 4 people. Refrigerate and have on hand for another day.

421

# FILET MIGNON

## OR

## CHOPPED STEAK IMPERIAL

**4 7-oz. filets or chopped sirloin patties, lightly seasoned with salt and pepper**
**¼ c. butter**
**½ c. chopped onion**
**¼ c. chopped chicken livers**
**¼ c. sliced mushrooms**
**½ c. dry red wine**
**Toasted almonds**

Saute onions in butter until just soft; add mushrooms and chicken livers. Stir in wine. Simmer until reduced by one quarter. Broil meat to desired doneness. Have 4 pieces of aluminum foil (8 x 8 inches) spread out. Put 2 tablespoons sauce in center of each. Place meat on top and divide rest of sauce evenly. Sprinkle toasted almonds on top. Wrap tightly. Put into hot oven 5 minutes to heat through well.

## STRAWBERRIES JUBILEE

**24 large fresh strawberries**
**4 T. butter**
**2 T. brown sugar**
**2 T. sugar**
**1 lime, juiced**
**1 orange, juiced**
**1½ ozs. Grand Marnier**
**1½ ozs. brandy**

Melt butter in skillet or chafing dish; add sugars. As sugars begin to caramelize, add lime and orange juices. Stir rapidly so sugar doesn't burn. Slice fruit directly into pan. Allow fruit to cook down somewhat. Stir in Grand Marnier, then brandy. Ignite. Serve over vanilla ice cream.

# TIKI GARDENS
## "a South Sea Island Paradise"
### 19601 Gulf Blvd. • Indian Shores, Fla. 33535

## TRADER FRANK'S RESTAURANT
## POLYNESIAN DINNER

Cocktail
Tiki Typhoon
Appetizer
Egg Flower Soup
(Soup of the Gods)
Entree
Hula Tail Shrimp — served with
Fried Banana and Steamed Rice
Dessert
Macadamia Nut Sundae Flambe
Beverage
Oriental Tea
Liqueur
Kalua Liqueur

From the Kitchen of Trader Frank's
and the luscious recipes of
Chef Papa Lee and Jo Byars, Trader Frank's Wahine

*A sea shell business begun out of their car trunk, moved to their garage, then to a small shop which burned to the ground in 1963 evolved into Jo and "Trader Frank" Byars' nationally famous "Tiki Gardens" Restaurant on Indian Rocks Beach. A tropical South seas paradise built along 12 1/2 acres of the Intercoastal Waterway, Tiki Gardens is the Suncoast's favorite place to partake of Polynesian cuisine.*

# COCKTAIL

# TIKI TYPHOON

**Mix in gallon jug:**
**½ fifth Gold Rum**
**½ fifth Light Rum**
**10 oz. fresh Orange Juice**
**10 oz. Pineapple Juice**
**10 oz. Passion Fruit Juice**
  **(made from concentrate 3**
  **parts water to 1 part**
  **concentrate)**
**5 oz. Dark Jamaican Rum**
**5 oz. 151 Proof Rum**

**Serves two drinks to each**
  **of a party of eight**

Fill balance of gallon jug with Sweet and Sour. (Make Sweet and Sour from prepared mix following the directions on the package).

Use 26 oz. Brandy Snifters — fill to top with small ice cubes — pour above mixture over ice — garnish with paper parasol, orange slice and cherry on a pick. Now you have the greatest of Polynesian Rum Drinks.

*Now you have the greatest of Polynesian rum drinks!*

# APPETIZER

# EGG FLOWER SOUP

# (Soup of the Gods)

**6 c. chicken stock, fresh**
  **or canned**
**2 t. salt**
**2 T. cornstarch, dissolved**
  **in 4 T. chicken stock (fresh**
  **or canned) or cold water**
**2 eggs lightly beaten**

**Serves 8**

To prepare: Over high heat bring the chicken stock to a boil in a 2 quart saucepan and add the salt. Give the cornstarch mixture a quick stir; add it to the stock, stirring a few seconds until the stock thickens slightly and becomes clear. Slowly pour in the egg and stir once gently. Turn off heat. Taste and add more salt if needed.

# ENTREE

## HULA TAIL SHRIMP

**Shrimp:**
**48 nice size shrimp (6 to each serving)**
**Bacon slices**

Peel raw and butterfly cut shrimp. Flatten out on cutting board and place ¼ piece of sliced, smoked bacon on top of shrimp.

**Batter:**
**2 c. flour**
**2 c. cornstarch**
**1 t. salt**
**1 t. baking powder**
**5¼ c. water**
**1 or 2 drops of yellow food coloring (needed for color only)**
**2 eggs, well beaten**

Mix above dry ingredients, then stir in water and well beaten egg.

Hold shrimp and bacon together and dip in batter and deep fry a golden brown.

**Sauce:**
**5 c. water**
**2 t. sugar**
**2 t. Accent**
**1½ t. salt**
**4 T. cornstarch**
**6 T. tomato catsup**

Put 4 cups of water in pan, add sugar, Accent, salt and tomato catsup. Combine cornstarch and 1 cup water, then blend into the tomato mixture. Cook until it boils so as to blend flavors. Let boil 2 or 3 minutes to cook cornstarch.

**Banana:**
**Peel 8 bananas**
**Brown sugar, pineapple juice**

Deep fry bananas just long enough to heat each banana and brown it. Remove from fryer and roll in brown sugar mixed with pineapple juice.

Serve the above as follows:

Line a 12 inch wooden plate with a large lettuce leaf. Arrange Shrimp, Banana and Steamed White Rice on plate. Pour Tomato Sauce over Shrimp. Garnish with a small Vanda Orchid (real or plastic).

**Serves 8**

*A meal fit for ole King Kamahamaha himself!*

# DESSERT
## MACADAMIA NUT SUNDAE FLAMBE

**A real Hawaiian Treat:**

2 large scoops vanilla ice cream topped with crushed Hawaiian Macadamia Nuts and whipped cream.

Soak a small sugar cube in lemon extract and place on top of whipped cream. Ignite cube and serve.

A favorite at Trader Frank's.

**Serves 1**

*A real Hawaiian treat - a favorite at Trader Frank's.*

# RECIPE CONTRIBUTORS

Mrs. Edward G. Acheson
Mrs. John W. Acheson
Mrs. Justin Albaugh
Mrs. E. J. Alderson
Mrs. Skip Alexander
Mr. Frank Allen
Mrs. Frank Allen
Mrs. Harold B. Allen
Mrs. Mary Wyatt Allen
Mrs. Paul L. Alspaugh
Miss Ruth Anderson
Mrs. Frank B. Andrus
Mrs. Edgar Andruss
Mrs. Arthur Appleyard
Mrs. Leonard Apter
Mr. Wilmot C. Arey
Mrs. Dot Armstrong
Mrs. W. L. Arnold
Mrs. E. Ashby
Aunt Hattie's Restaurant
Mrs. Hastings Palmer Avery

Mrs. Donald Babcock
Mrs. Huston Babcock
Mrs. Robert S. Baer
Dr. Russell C. Bane
Mrs. Russell C. Bane
Mrs. John W. Barger
Mrs. Paul Bartlett
Mrs. Ervin Baumrucker
Mrs. Thomas Bayless
Mrs. Gardner Beckett, Jr.
Mrs. George B. Belting
Mrs. James P. Bennett
Dr. Vance D. Bishop
Mrs. Vance D. Bishop
Mrs. Betty Blair
Mrs. O. D. Bleakley
Mrs. W. Bryan Bolich
Mrs. William Bond
Mrs. Joe Boulware
Mrs. James L. Bradley
Mrs. Stanley R. Brav
Mrs. Wade Brinley
Mrs. Frank Britton
Mrs. J. Mercer Brown
Mrs. W. T. Brown
Mrs. Robert A. Buenzli

Mrs. Louise Burchell
Mrs. Charles W. Burke
Mrs. John T. Burke
Miss Pamela Bush
Mrs. Jane Byers

Mrs. Eloise Cameron
Mrs. Russell S. Cantwell
Mrs. William Caruth
Mrs. Thomas B. Caswell
Mrs. Clyde E. Chapelle
Mrs. Lawrence C. Clark
Mrs. R. E. Clarson, Jr.
Mrs. George Cleveland
Mrs. Craig P. Cochrane
Mrs. Robert W. Cohoe
Mrs. M. Dayton Collner
Mrs. Elizabeth Cooper
Mrs. Benjamin A. Corey
Mr. John D. Cowan
Mrs. A. L. Cowperthwaite
Mrs. James Craig
Mr. Robert Crisp
Miss Myrtle Crooks
Mrs. Charles B. Cunningham

Mrs. John Daniels
Mrs. Lucy W. Decker

Mrs. George Deeb
Mrs. Cecil E. Deighton
Mrs. Jean DeJen
Mrs. William G. DeWitt
Mrs. Allen G. Dillon
Mrs. Charles K. Donegan
Mrs. Charles W. Doyle
Mrs. Thomas Dreier
Mrs. Morgan Driskell
Mrs. Alan B. DuBois
Mrs. Mathon Baldwin Dunn
Mrs. Raymond A. Dunphy
Mrs. Frank Dustan
Mrs. Cecile Z. Dvorak

Mrs. Jane Byer Edwards
Mrs. Paul R. Engberg
Mrs. Richard Engberg
Mrs. Russell C. English

RECIPE CONTRIBUTORS

Mrs. Henry Esteva
Mrs. Bernice Evitt

Mr. Raymond N. Fairfax
Mrs. J. Urben Farley
Mrs. Leone A. Farmer
Mrs. Daniel H. Faust
Mrs. Julian M. Fauvre
Mrs. Robert H. Fayfield
Mrs. John E. Feissner, Jr.
Mrs. Arthur Felsen
Mrs. Kendrick E. Fenderson
Mrs. Dennis R. Fernandez
Mrs. John A. Fields
Mrs. Robert W. Fisher
Mrs. Alvin Flannes
Mr. A. B. Fogarty
Mrs. A. B. Fogarty
Mrs. Franklin J. Fonte
Mrs. Robert A. Francis
Mrs. George V. Frank
Mrs. C. S. Frankle
Mrs. Ralph Frick
Mrs. Lucian J. Fronduti
Dr. F. P. Fudge

Mrs. H. C. Gallagher
Mrs. Polly Gamble
Mrs. W. W. Gay, Sr.
Mrs. Ed Gibson
Mrs. John T. Gibson
Mrs. Laurence Glaser
Mrs. George F. Gramling, Jr.
Mrs. Liza Gray
Mrs. Mafalda Gray
Mrs. Malcolm Gray
Mrs. Harold Grundset
Mrs. Joseph B. Guinane

Mrs. Harold McKinne Hardy
Mrs. William L. Hargrave
Mrs. John D. Harris, Jr.
Mrs. Samuel W. Harris
Mrs. Gerald A. Harty
Mrs. Thomas F. Hatcher
Mrs. N. J. Hendershot
Mrs. James E. Hendry
Mrs. James L. Hennessy
Mrs. Charlotte Hughes Herbert
Mrs. Charles Hicks

Mrs. Dorothy P. Hicks
Mr. Richard Hilburn
Mrs. Arthur R. Hinkley
Mrs. Arthur W. Hodsdon
Mrs. Paul Hoeffer
Mrs. Thomas Hofmann
Mrs. Hurley W. Holland
Mrs. George L. Hollett
Mrs. Edward C. Holmes
Mr. George R. Hoover, Jr.
Mrs. Walter Horne
Mrs. Dean C. Houk
Mrs. Ernest H. Hubbell
Mrs. David A. Huey

Mrs. N. Isserlin

Mrs. Marvin A. Jackson
Miss Billie Japour
Miss Nesrina Japour
Mrs. Theron A. Jernigan
Mrs. E. Ashby Johnson
Mrs. Kenneth R. Johnson
Mr. Rob Johnson
Mrs. Sheena Johnson
Mr. Thomas P. Johnson
Mrs. Wayne Johnson
Mrs. Lowell Johnston
Mrs. Harold T. Joyce
Mrs. Gloria Joye
Mrs. Howard W. Jones

Mrs. Irma Kain
Mrs. Donald Kaiser
Mrs. W. E. Kaitner
Mrs. Takis G. Kapous
Mrs. Al Kazuba
Mrs. B. C. Kehler, Jr.
Mrs. Roland M. Kendall
Mr. Peter Kersker
Mrs. Ernest S. Killgore
Mr. William W. W. Knight
Mrs. John F. Knowlton
Mrs. Walter Koral
Mrs. Alexander Kriloff
Mrs. Thomas Kugeman

Mrs. Harriette Lafean
Mrs. Florine Lajeunesse
Miss Charlotte Lake

Miss Diane H. Lake
Mrs. John B. Lake
Mrs. Eleanor Landes
Ms. Edna Johnson Larson
Mrs. James J. Lawler
Mr. LeRoy Lawson
Mrs. Richard Leavengood
Mrs. Claude V. Lewis
Mrs. Trudi Lidauer
Mrs. Herbert C. Lindelow
Mrs. Raymond M. Long, Jr.
Mrs. Winifred O. Long
Mrs. Vida Lovett
Mrs. William A. Lyons

Maas Brothers
Mr. George P. MacGregor
Mrs. Robert J. Mack
Mrs. Charles W. Mackey
Mrs. Ruth Martin
Mrs. Mike Martinson
Mrs. John M. Matava
Mrs. Ralston Mathis
Mr. Morton D. May
Mrs. Jesse McCaleb
Mrs. James K. McCorkle
Mrs. George McLendon
Mrs. Mary Ellen McManus
Mrs. L. L. McMasters, Sr.
Mr. John A. McNulty
Mrs. John A. McNulty
Mrs. Arthur H. Melin
Mrs. Louis A. Melsheimer
Mrs. J. Harry Miles, Jr.
Ms. Karen Miles
Mrs. Parker E. Miller
Mr. Thomas S. Miller
Mrs. William H. Mills
Mrs. Barbara Montgomery
Mr. Robert Montgomery, Jr.
Mrs. Robert Montgomery, Jr.
Mrs. Margaret P. Moore
Mrs. James W. Moore
Mrs. William T. Moore
Mrs. Howard Moorefield
Mrs. Marion F. Morgan
Mrs. Stephen B. Morrissey
Mrs. Homer Moyer
Mrs. Ralph A. Mullin

Mrs. E. Cary Nalle
Mrs. B. C. Neeld
Mrs. George C. Newman
Mrs. Henry Newman
Mrs. J. Milton Newton
Mrs. Lyle A. Newton
Mr. Maurice Nicholls
Mrs. John H. Nickels
Mrs. Samuel P. Nixon
Mrs. Leon W. Noel

Mrs. Felix Obenshain
Mrs. Merle W. Ogle
Mrs. James F. O'Neill
Mrs. Elizabeth Owens

Miss Margaret E. Page
Mrs. Henry C. Palmer
Mrs. Mike Panayotti
Miss.Beverly J. Pankonie
Louis Pappas Restaurant
Mrs. Sonny Parrish
Mrs. George Pearson
Mrs. Conni Pelley
Mr. Angel P. Perez
Mrs. Betty Perry
Mrs. Laurence A. Peterson
Mrs. Gordon A. Pfeiffer
Mrs. John Phelan
Ms. Susan Philly
Mrs. Walter P. Plumley
Mrs. Clayton Porter
Mrs. Eugenia Porter
Mrs. Nelson Poynter
Mr. Luther C. Pressley
Mrs. Luther C. Pressley
Mrs. Steven E. Puffer
Mrs. Marie Purdsen
Mrs. George S. Purple

Mrs. John P. Rankin
Mrs. Clara Read
Mrs. Henn Rebane
Mrs. Aneita Rehnberg
Miss Florence Reno
Mrs. Arthur Reynolds
Mrs. Lowell DeWight Richardson
Mrs. William M. Rigler
Mrs. G. Forrest Riley

## RECIPE CONTRIBUTORS

Mrs. S. C. Robertson
Mrs. Don E. Robinson
Mrs. Marie D. Robinson
Mrs. Pat Robison
Mrs. Benjamin S. Rogers
Mrs. Joseph H. Rupp
Mrs. Donald Russell
Mrs. Michael P. Russillo
Mrs. Edgar E. Ryan

Mrs. William W. Saitta
Mrs. Stan Salzer
Mrs. John A. Samaha
Mrs. Robert Saron
Mrs. George N. Sarven
Mrs. Elizabeth T. Sauer
Mrs. Richard Sauers
Mrs. John Savage
Mrs. Leon T. Sax
Mrs. Eugene H. Schmitt
Mrs. Liz O'Brien Schuck
Mrs. Marjorie M. Schuck
Mr. Raymond W. Schuster
Mrs. Louis Scian
Mrs. Myron C. Scofield
Mrs. Lee H. Scott
Mrs. Charles Sears
Mrs. Frank L. Seeger
Mrs. Fred C. Shamas
Mrs. Lucille Sharpe
Mrs. Joseph Shepard
Mrs. R. Frederick Shepherd
Ms. Laurie Sheridan
Mrs. Peter Sherman
Mrs. Bea Shineman
Mrs. W. H. Showman
Mrs. Edmund Shubrick
Mrs. Fred H. Simonton
Mrs. Gurney P. Sloan
Mr. Herbert Smith
Mrs. Rachel Lictourneau Smith
Mrs. Raymond B. Smith
Mrs. Irving G. Snyder
Mrs. Robert Speakman
Mrs. L. A. St. Louis
Mrs. George W. Stahlman, Jr.
Mrs. Jack Steeley
Mrs. Andrew Stenger
Miss. Natalee Sterling

Mrs. Willard Ernest Stevens
Mrs. Grace Stewart
Mrs. Wayne Stewart
Mrs. David Stimer
Mrs. J. Roy Stockton
Mrs. Albert P. Story
Mrs. Frank Stowitts
Mrs. Michael C. Swanson

Mrs. Norman C. Thomas
Mrs. R. W. Thomas
Mrs. John Thompson
Mrs. Paul L. Thompson
Mrs. Richard H. Thompson, Jr.
Mrs. Joe Tonelli
Mrs. Leadley D. Trice
Mrs. Clarence H. Tucker
Mrs. C. C. Turnesa

Mrs. Ambrose Updegraff

Mrs. James Valerius
Mrs. Don B. VanBuskirk
Mrs. John L. Volk

Mrs. Richard Wagner
Mrs. John B. Wallace
Mrs. Paul F. Wallace
Mrs. Hester Walther
Mrs. Albert H. Ward, Jr.
Mrs. Rodney Waterman
Mrs. Jack Watson
Mrs. Marjorie Way
Mrs. J. Allen Weaver
Mrs. Paul F. Weber
Ms. Elizabeth Webster
Mrs. Robert Wedding
Mrs. Harman Wheeler
Mr. Edwin Lee White
Mrs. Edwin Lee White
Mrs. C. B. Whitworth
Mrs. Warren Wildrick
Mrs. John Williams, Jr.
Mrs. Douglas Woodruff
Mrs. Robert V. Workman

Mrs. Evelyn A. York

Dr. and Mrs. Vance Bishop _____ Spanish Dinner
Mr. and Mrs. Richard Buckingham __ Beach Party, Family Camping
Mr. and Mrs. Robert A. Buenzli ____ Charity Ball
Mrs. Thomas P. Johnson _____ Charity Ball
Dr. and Mrs. Charles Donegan _____ Stone Crab Dinner
Mr. and Mrs. A. B. Fogarty _____ Stone Crab Dinner
Mrs. Richard Misener _____ Boating Menu
Mr. and Mrs. Evander Preston _____ Chinese Dinner
Mr. and Mrs. Hubert Rutland _____ Rutland Ranch Wild Game Dinner
Mr. and Mrs. George Van Sciver ____ Orange Squeeze
Mrs. Rodney Waterman _____ Christmas Belles Menu
Mr. and Mrs. Charles Wedding _____ Fish Fry

Florida Citrus Commission

**RESTAURANTS:**

The Bath Club
Jay's Ristorante Italiano
Pepins
Peter's Place
Rollands et Pierre
Siples Garden Seat
Trader Frank's Tiki Gardens

# GRACIOUS LIVING TODAY

### Party Spirits

For cocktails before dinner allow two drinks per person and 3 to 4 for a party which will last for several hours. A fifth of liquor contains 25.6 ounces and makes 17 (1½ ounce) drinks. A quart, which contains 32 ounces, will make 21 drinks of the same size.

For a cocktail party, allowing three drinks per person for 24 guests, buy five fifths or four quarts of liquor. For 50 guests buy 9 fifths or 7 quarts.

One rule of thumb for punches calls for 1 quart liquor (rum, vodka, bourbon), 1 quart fruit juice (any one or a mixture), 1 quart ginger ale and 1 quart soda. Combine the liquor and fruit juice, adding the gingerale and soda at serving time.

## HOSTESS SUGGESTIONS

You don't have to use a punchbowl to have punch. Any large mixing bowl, enameled basin, new utility pail, clean aquarium or a scooped-out watermelon can hold a festive punch.

Spray-paint the outside of the punch bowl-to-be with a color — or gold or silver. Spray paint can be removed easily from a glass or porcelain container. Use florists wire to join flowers or fruits and greenery into a wreath. Secure to bowl with tape. Larger pieces of ice, of course, melt more slowly and dilute punch less than cubes. Freeze ahead in large molds or cans.

Arrange fruit or flowers in the bottom of an ice mold in thin layer of water. Freeze until fruit is anchored in place and then fill with more water. Dip quickly into warm water to unmold. Festive ice cubes can be made with cherries, sprigs of mint or orange or lemon twists in each section of an ice cube tray. Boil water before making molds. This way you are assured of clear water without bubbles.

To make tomato roses, peel the tomato with a vegetable peeler. Start at the top of the tomato and peel around to the bottom. Roll into a rose shape. Use the pulp for a sauce.

To make carrot curls, use a potato peeler and cut thin, wide strips of carrot the whole length of the carrot. Fasten with toothpicks, being careful not to break the strip. Drop into salted water and refrigerate overnight. Curls will hold.

To make carrot flowers, use tiny cutters available in housewares departments. Slice crosswise and cut with cutters. Spear on toothpick and add a center which contrasts (such as green pepper). Place a number of the carrot flowers in parsley to decorate a platter or tray.

Cucumber flowers can be made by hollowing out the center and slicing crosswise to make petals. Slices can be scalloped or cut in points for petals. Insert a carrot for the stamen.

Dip lemon slices in parsley for garnishes.

Slip carrot slices (julienne slices) through a black or green olive slice. Peel a cucumber, remove seeds and fill with cheese. Chill and slice crosswise.

# HELPFUL HINTS

**Freezer ideas:**

Cook 6 or 8 portions, freeze half.

Save foil containers from frozen dinners; use for left overs, label.

Save stale bread ends; cut, coat with Parmesan cheese, fry and freeze.

Save stale bread; blend in blender for bread crumbs.

Save bowls by lining with foil; freeze contents. Remove foil-wrapped food; label.

To use, remove contents from foil, return to same bowl to thaw and cook.

If you have over-salted soup, dilute it with water or milk, if the stock is strong enough to stand thinning. If not, cook slices of raw potato in it and throw slices away. They will absorb some of the salt.

If you have put too much salt in vegetables and haven't time to cook more, try disguising it with an unseasoned white sauce.

When you take grease off soup or gravy, and haven't time to chill it to solidify the fat, you might find a bulb baster easier to use than a spoon. When the fat coating is shallow, use paper towels to blot it off.

If your gravy has lumps strain it through a sieve or whip it with a wire whip. You can avoid lumps to start with by shaking the flour and water in a jar before you add them to the gravy. Use a wire whisk for any sauce that you don't want lumpy or crusty.

Cake batters baked in a 9 inch square pan may also be baked in two 8 inch layer pans. Cake batter baked in two 9 inch square pans may be baked in three 8 inch layer pans.

To tell if a custard sauce is done, dip a silver spoon into the mixture. If the custard forms a straight line across the spoon the mixture should be removed from the heat. If the line is wavy the custard has not thickened quite enough.

Many gelatin molds do not have their size stamped on them. You can determine the capacity of a mold by measuring the number of cups it will hold.

To help a pastry shell keep its shape while baking, line it with fitted waxed paper and fill with dried peas or rice. Bake about 5 mnutes or until shell sets; remove paper and dried peas or rice.

Chopped onions have the best flavor if they are browned in shortening before adding to casserole dishes.

To keep cauliflower snowy white, soak for half an hour in cold salt water before cooking.

Get more juice out of lemons; quickly heat them in hot water for several minutes before squeezing; or roll to soften. (Same applies to oranges). Keep lemons fresh longer in a tightly closed jar of water in the refrigerator.

Remove the burnt taste from scorched milk by putting the pan in cold water and adding a pinch of salt to the milk.

To prevent waste of eggs from cracking when they are to be boiled, allow them to stand a few minutes in very warm water before putting them in boiling water.

You can easily prevent vegetables and greens from spoiling in the refrigerator compartment by lining the bottom of the container with paper toweling. This absorbs the excess moisture which accumulates in the bottom of the container.

Place a piece of apple in your brown sugar jar and it will keep the sugar from drying out and lumping. Try the same cure for too-dry cookies.

Bake potatoes in half the usual time. Just let them stand in boiling water for 15 minutes before popping them in a very hot oven.

Don't risk soggy fruit or pumpkin pies. Just brush the sides and bottom crusts with the beaten white of an egg, then sprinkle lightly with flour and add the filling.

A 13½ ounce package of graham crackers usually yields about 3¾ cups crumbs and costs much less than when you buy packaged crumbs.

There's a lot you can do without sugar:

Cook apples in frozen unsweetened apple juice or orange juice concentrate or sweet cider to make applesauce.

Puree naturally sweet fruits such as ripe bananas or prunes and blend into stiffly beaten egg whites or make fruit whips. Little or no sugar will be needed.

Corn syrup can be substituted for sugar in a variety of foods and beverages. Substitute corn syrup for simple syrup (sugar boiled with water) for use in cold drinks and punches. It can take the place of sugar in baked beans, barbecue sauce, dessert sauces and ham glazes. Can be substituted for sugar in making the topping for upside down cakes and sticky buns.

Honey, molasses and cornsyrup can be substituted in many recipes calling for sugar, although you will have to adjust the amount of liquid and sweetness to your taste. In general:

A cup of corn syrup for each cup of sugar — reduce liquid content of recipe by about one fourth

Allow 1 cup of honey for each cup and a fourth of sugar — reduce liquid content by one fourth

## EQUIVALENT MEASURES

3 teaspoons are 1 tablespoon
4 tablespoons are ¼ cup
5 tablespoons and 1 teaspoon are ⅓ cup
16 tablespoons are 1 cup
2 cups are 1 pint
4 cups are 1 quart
4 quarts are 1 gallon
8 quarts are 1 peck
4 pecks are 1 bushel
16 fluid ounces are 1 pint

## CANNED FOODS

| Can Size | Average Servings | Average Cups | Average Net Weight |
|----------|------------------|--------------|--------------------|
| No. 303 | 1 or 2 | 2 | 1 lb. |
| No. 2 | 4 or 5 | 2¼ to 2½ | 20 ounces |
| No. 2½ | 4 or 6 | 3¼ to 3½ | 28 ounces |
| No. 10 | 18 to 25 | 12 to 13 | 6 lbs., 10 ounces |
| 46 ounces | 12 | 5¾ | 1 quart, 14 fl. ounces |

# SUBSTITUTIONS

Buttermilk, 1 cup _____ use 1 or 2 tablespoons vinegar with sweet milk to fill cup (let stand five minutes).

Chocolate, 1 ounce or 1 square _____ use 3 tablespoons cocoa plus 1 tablespoon butter.

Cornstarch, 1 tablespoon _____ use two tablespoons flour.

Eggs, 2 large _____ use 3 small eggs.

Baking powder, 1¼ teaspoons _____ use ½ teaspoon baking soda plus 2 tablespoons vinegar (for 1 cup flour).

Milk, 1 cup _____ use ½ cup evaporated milk plus ½ cup water.

Sour milk, 1 cup _____ use 1⅓ tablespoons vinegar or 1½ tablespoons lemon juice and sweet milk to make 1 cup sour.

For thickening _____ use 1 tablespoon quick-cooking tapioca or 1 tablespoon cornstarch or 1⅓ to 1½ tablespoons flour.

Low-Cal Sour Cream _____ 1 cup cottage cheese and 1 tablespoon lemon juice blended until smooth.

# THE METRIC SYSTEM

The metric system is based on units of 10. It is consistent, logical and easier to work than our system. In the metric system, the multiples of 10 are always designated by the same prefix, regardless of the base unit being used. The most commonly used prefixes are:

Kilo  = 1,000.0
deci  =      0.1
centi =      0.01
milli =      0.001

Thus, a kilogram is 1,000 grams and a centimeter is 1/100th of a meter.

Butter in solidly packed standard eight-ounce cups:

| | | |
|---|---|---|
| 2 cups | = | 400 grams |
| 1 cup | = | 200 grams |
| ½ cup | = | 100 grams |
| ¼ cup | = | 50 grams |

Granulated sugar:

| | | |
|---|---|---|
| 1 cup | = | 190 grams |
| ⅔ cup | = | 125 grams |
| ½ cup | = | 95 grams |
| ¼ cup | = | 50 grams |

Rice:
| | | |
|---|---|---|
| 1 cup | = | 150 grams |

All-purpose Flour:

| | | |
|---|---|---|
| 1 cup | = | 140 grams |
| ⅔ cup | = | 100 grams |
| ½ cup | = | 70 grams |
| ¼ cup | = | 35 grams |

Liquid Measurements:

| | | |
|---|---|---|
| 2 cups | = | 1/2 liter |
| 1 cup | = | 1/4 liter |
| ¾ cup | = | 1/6 liter |
| ⅔ cup | = | 1/7 liter |
| ½ cup | = | 1/8 liter |
| ⅓ cup | = | 1/15 liter |
| ¼ cup | = | 1/16 liter |

## Temperature

When you know:        You can find:        If you substract 32 and
Fahrenheit            Celsius              then multiply by 5/9.

0 degrees Celsius - 32 degrees Fahrenheit

100 degrees Celsius - 212 degrees Fahrenheit

# GALLERY OF WINE AND BRANDY GLASSES

7 OZ. RED WINE

8 OZ. HOLLOW STEM CHAMPAGNE

5 OZ. BRANDY

14 OZ. HOCK RHINE

20 OZ. TULIP CHAMPAGNE

26 OZ. MAGNUM

9 OZ. CABERNET

26 OZ. CABERNET

16 OZ. CLARET

8 OZ. TULIP WINE

12 OZ. ALL PURPOSE WINE

WINE

# WINES

## STORING WINE

e wine in a cool dry place where temperatures are fairly even with no emes. Ideal storage temperature is between 50 and 60 degrees.

e corked wines on their sides. Store Sparkling and White wines in the est racks or bins, (because it is cooler there). Red dinner wines in the t section up. Dessert and Appetizer wines may be stored on top because y are least affected by higher temperatures.

## CHILLING WINE

ite and Rose wines are chilled 1 to 3 hours before serving. Sparkling nes 4 to 6 hours. Red Dinner wines are best at cool room temperature t above 70 degrees). In hot weather you may want to slightly chill a rgundy for instance.

en storing wine in the refrigerator, it is best to use it within 1 to 2 weeks, avoid impairment of flavor. Once chilled however, do not store again at om temperature. Never chill wine below 35 degrees.

## COOKING WITH WINE

ly cook with wine you would serve to your guests.
ine loses its alcoholic content in cooking thus the entire family can enjoy ine flavored dishes. With the alcohol, most of the calories disappear too!

ir up a package of instant vanilla pudding using ¼ cup Sherry for part of e liquid. Add a bit of grated lemon or orange rind.

dd a cup of Claret or Burgundy to your favorite spaghetti sauce or beef ew.

rill fish, lamb or poultry with wine-butter sauce. Combine equal parts utter and Rose or Sauterne, a few drops of lime juice and herbs.

urn canned soups into special soups. Use mushroom, chicken, shrimp or celery soups. Add fresh mushrooms, shrimp or oysters. Flavor with Sherry using 2 tablespoons per cup of soup.

Chicken that is to be barbequed is especially good if marinated in White Dinner wine several hours before cooking.

Wine is an excellent meat tenderizer. Turn economy cuts into juicy tenderness by marinating from 6-8 hours.

Information obtained from California Wine Advisory Board and The Paul Masson Wine Reader

# INDEX

## A

# H

## GOURMET GALLERY
**Museum of Fine Arts**
255 Beach Drive North
Saint Petersburg, Florida 33701

Send me _____ copies of your cook book at $9.95 per copy. Add $1.55 per copy for handling and postage. Enclosed is my check or money order for $_____ Florida residents add 4% sales tax.

**NAME** _____

**STREET** _____

**CITY**_____ **STATE** _____ **ZIP**_____

All proceeds from the sale of this book will be used for the benefit of the Museum of Fine Arts.

MAKE CHECKS PAYABLE TO:

### Gourmet Gallery Cookbook

------------------------------------------------------------

## GOURMET GALLERY
**Museum of Fine Arts**
255 Beach Drive North
Saint Petersburg, Florida 33701

Send me _____ copies of your cook book at $9.95 per copy. Add $1.55 per copy for handling and postage. Enclosed is my check or money order for $_____ Florida residents add 4% sales tax.

**NAME** _____

**STREET**_____

**CITY**_____ **STATE**_____ **ZIP** _____

All proceeds from the sale of this book will be used for the benefit of the Museum of Fine Arts.

MAKE CHECKS PAYABLE TO:

### Gourmet Gallery Cookbook

------------------------------------------------------------

## GOURMET GALLERY
**Museum of Fine Arts**
255 Beach Drive North
Saint Petersburg, Florida 33701

Send me _____ copies of your cook book at $9.95 per copy. Add $1.55 per copy for handling and postage. Enclosed is my check or money order for $_____ Florida residents add 4% sales tax.

**NAME** _____

**STREET**_____

**CITY**_____ **STATE**_____ **ZIP**_____

All proceeds from the sale of this book will be used for the benefit of the Museum of Fine Arts.

MAKE CHECKS PAYABLE TO:

### Gourmet Gallery Cookbook

Re-Order Additional Copies

Names and addresses of bookstores, gift shops, etc. in y
area would be appreciated.

_____

_____

_____

_____

_____

_____

Names and addresses of bookstores, gift shops, etc. in you
area would be appreciated.

_____

_____

_____

_____

_____

_____

Names and addresses of bookstores, gift shops, etc. in your
area would be appreciated.

_____

_____

_____

_____

_____

_____